TEACHING JEWISH CIVILIZATION
A Global Approach to Higher Education

INTERNATIONAL CENTER FOR UNIVERSITY TEACHING OF JEWISH CIVILIZATION (ICUTJC)

Continuing support for ICUTJC has been provided by the Joint Program for Jewish Education (State of Israel, Ministry of Education and Culture—The Jewish Agency for Israel—World Zionist Organization), and the Memorial Foundation for Jewish Culture.

TEACHING JEWISH CIVILIZATION

A Global Approach to Higher Education

Edited by Moshe Davis

NEW YORK UNIVERSITY PRESS
New York and London

NEW YORK UNIVERSITY PRESS
New York and London

Library of Congress Cataloging-in-Publication Data
Teaching Jewish civilization : a global approach to higher education /
edited by Moshe Davis.
p.   cm.
ISBN 0-8147-1866-3. — ISBN 0-8147-1867-1 (pbk.)
1. Judaism—History—Study and teaching (Higher)   2. Jews—
History—Study and teaching (Higher)   3. Jews—Civilization—Study
and teaching (Higher)   I. Davis, Moshe.
BM71.T43   1995
296'.071'1—dc20   95-3207
                         CIP

New York University Press books are printed on acid-free paper,
and their binding materials are chosen for strength and durability.

Manufactured in the United States of America

10   9   8   7   6   5   4   3   2   1

In Tribute to THE FOUNDERS

Ephraim Katzir
Fourth President of the State of
Israel

Philip M. Klutznick
President, Memorial Foundation
for Jewish Culture

Yitzhak Navon
Fifth President of the State of
Israel

Arye L. Dulzin Chairman,
Executive of the World
Zionist Organization and the
Jewish Agency for Israel

Nahum Goldman President,
World Jewish Congress

CONTENTS

INTRODUCTION

Moshe Davis

This volume is intended for all who are involved in the academic world and who are concerned with contemporary civilization, international higher education, and the wide realm of Judaica studies. More specifically, our purpose in this work is to set forth the development of a rather unique institution—the International Center for University Teaching of Jewish Civilization—against the backdrop of university Jewish studies in different parts of the world: its conceptual framework, growth, and achievements, as well as its problems and unfulfilled objectives. Based in Jerusalem, the University Teaching Center is an experiment that may be said to have paved a new path in global higher education.

The first seed for the formation of the ICUTJC was planted in my mind in the spring of 1963. I was invited to come from Jerusalem, where I served as head of the Hebrew University's Institute of Contemporary Jewry, to help inaugurate the B. G. Rudolph Lectureship in Judaic Studies at Syracuse University. For me, that visit was the beginning of a Copernican revolution.

At the founding ceremony, the chancellor at the time, William Pearson Tolley, speaking under the banner of Syracuse University, *Suos Cultores Scientia Coronat*—Knowledge crowns those who seek her—used the occasion to express his views on the cultural and intellectual situation in America. In that context, he underscored the importance of developing the whole field of Jewish studies so that the ideas of Judaism could be integrated organically into higher education for the enhancement of American society generally.

As I delivered my inaugural lecture on "The Jewish People in Metamorphosis" to an overflowing assembly of several hundred young, attentive students, I instinctively felt that the teaching of Judaica could take place in American universities as well as in Jewish institutions. The following morning's experience awakened additional insights. I was scheduled to teach two classes on Judaism in the course on American religions. Several hundred students attended both sessions. The quality of the questions and discussions in both sessions confirmed my feeling that the time had come to attempt to reach the academically trained on advanced levels of knowledge and content, in settings where Judaic content was secondary or missing altogether.

My reflections were deepened as I pursued my responsibilities at the Institute of Contemporary Jewry in Jerusalem. The nature of the subject compelled intensive study of the character of the contemporary Jewish condition worldwide. Unprecedented in content, and characterized by a constant interplay of Jewish and general societal factors, the challenge of modernity confronted the Jewish tradition and the Jewish people in many parts of the world at the same time. The colloquia initiated by the Institute in Latin America, continental Europe, and England enabled me to visit major universities in those regions where the Jewish experience was being taught in diverse disciplines in the humanities and social sciences. Clearly a dominant need was to create interdisciplinary curricula correlating and interacting with scholarship and methodologies across cultures and countries.

These meditations were strengthened by the ongoing discussions emanating from the United Nations on "planetary education." Proposals were put forward by the U.N. Institute for Training and Research (UNITAR) and the U.N. Educational, Scientific and Cultural Organization (UNESCO). "Decentralization" and "coordination" were the key concepts underscored by Secretary General U Thant. Calling for an international network of research and training centers, he emphasized that the desired program should be based on the exchange of interdisciplinary research, careful adaptation for individual locales, and the engagement of leading scholars from countries in different stages of development.

In that climate of world academic thought, varied approaches to international education were introduced on local and national university levels, with such imaginative projects as student programs abroad, joint research undertakings, and exchange faculty appointments. Relating these developments to my own field of teaching about Judaism and the Jews, I pondered a central structural question: Was it feasible to create a coordinating center in Jerusalem that could be involved in the university world in a symbiotic relationship? My thoughts were first crystallized with Ephraim Katzir, the president of Israel at the time, in a seminal conversation on the problems of higher Jewish education in the various diaspora communities. We dared to believe that in an era of accelerated global communication it was possible to form under the aegis of the Israeli presidency a multidisciplinary network of cooperating faculty programs for the advancement of Jewish civilization studies. Thus was born in 1981 the International Center for University Teaching of Jewish Civilization.

The policy proposal on which the ICUTJC was based was distributed privately. It is my notion that in social engineering, while a design is indispensable, the true test is in its realization. If ever the feat of international growth was accomplished by cooperative effort, the sixty-four people who participated in producing this volume and the approximately eight hundred scholars they represent worldwide can serve as case illustration. Their contributions cover a broad range of conceptual, historical, thematic, pedagogic, and administrative areas. We chose to have the individuals speak for themselves, each one elucidating objectives, progress, achievements, and still unfulfilled goals. This decision did not lead to uniformity of style, but it does proclaim a unity of purpose. It is hoped that the description of the ICUTJC's concept and its global development will contribute in some way to the enhancement of higher education.

The book opens with three statements of historical perspective on the basic issues that confront university Jewish civilization studies. One need not hark back to the Renaissance and Reformation, when chairs in Hebrew were incorporated into the curricula of such European universities as the Sorbonne, Padua, and Heidelberg, not to mention the intensive individual studies at the major centers of Christian learning. It is more apposite to the current situation to consider the transformations in the nineteenth-century "Science of Judaism" that prepared the way for the acceptance of Jewish studies in the humanities and social studies in the modern university curriculum. History can be meaningful to the contemporary situation if one fully takes into account the full meaning of *mutatis mutandis*. Nevertheless, the unprecedented and acute variants in the present condition can be seen in global terms.

Within the broad framework of Jewish civilization studies, contributors from several countries view their respective situations critically yet constructively, seeking to glean out of their local reality possibilities for adaptations. As a result of the rapid acceleration of the field, other aspects have come to the fore that will surely have an impact on future developments. For example: In American universities, as Franklin H. Littell forcefully argues in a major statement (manuscript), "Recent Developments in Jewish Studies in America": "The kind of instruction in Jewish studies that belongs in a university should be coordinated with religious studies, with all that approach requires in curricula and professional activities."

Another striking example is in the FSU (Former Soviet Union) and Eastern Europe generally, where the unimaginable has become possible. There the problem is to reintroduce the teaching of Jewish civilization studies in an organizational university structure and methods of teaching that differ completely from what we know in the West. The pioneer efforts of I. Varsat-Warszawski, through the International Committee for the Promotion of Jewish Studies in Eastern Europe, have already succeeded in linking Western scholars to their colleagues in those countries. This ongoing process, concurrent with initiatives of other agencies, is elaborated in the chapters by Mordechai Altshuler and Nehemia Levtzion.

The dynamic quality of Jewish civilization studies on the world scene can also be discerned in their responsiveness to change. In the book's second part, "Reconsiderations," several of the authors propose fundamental shifts in content emphasis, particularly in those areas where the evolutionary process of restructuring has proved to be slow and ineffectual. Others propose the introduction of Jewish studies in general disciplines. All agree that the way to move Jewish studies to a more central position in academe is to raise the quality of course offerings to the level of the best in general studies.

Against the background of this historical, expanding canvas, the ICUTJC emerged in its corner of the world, in Israel, seeking to contribute to contemporary Jewish civilization studies. This volume reviews its primary goals, achievements, difficulties, falterings, and lacunae in the parts entitled "Expanding and Deepening the Field" and "Cooperative Projects." A second purpose is expressed in the section called "The Israel Experience," namely, to enable senior and junior scholars to relate personally to Israel as the place where those involved with Jewish studies can further pursue their scholarly interests. The testimonies of several younger scholars bear out the importance of such a continuing relationship. Because Israel's centrality in Jewish studies is undisputed, we are also concerned with the question of how Israeli universities can serve an ever-widening periphery of universities abroad.

We introduced part VI, "Motivations," in order to redress a common error and thus proclaim an important truth. Institutions of higher learning are not built by scholars alone; academic statesmen, both professional and volunteer, are indispensable initiators and guarantors of their growth. Particularly in our times, when so-called lay volunteers and sponsors are individually of high intellectual caliber, their leadership involvement is essential and instructive. We asked several such visionary partners in different countries three questions: At what point did they understand that the university can serve as an indispensable element in the education of the younger Jewish generation living in an open world with many options? What motivated them to translate this understanding into practical form through their universities? And in what manner has the International Center been of guidance in their effort? Their responses disclose a new strata of unexpected creative human resources including, in some instances, individuals who seek to apply themselves in their adult years to achieve what they missed in their youth. Like Rabbi Akiba of talmudic lore, many such people are coming to the university classroom in their mature years.

In part VII of this volume, ICUTJC's academic chairman, Nehemia Levtzion, imaginatively faces the future. Having assessed the past and determined to strengthen the functioning projects, he has reordered the institution's priorities in two main directions. The first is to integrate Jewish and general studies in the university. To universalize is not necessarily to diminish the integrity of the particular; quite the contrary, the general often fortifies the specific. Toward this end, Levtzion expects that the European continent, both West and East, is the best testing ground to blend particularism, regionalism, and universalism.

His second objective is to tap exciting and optimal new areas of growth. Should not the ICUTJC pursue its mandate and welcome such opportunities as the openings for Hebrew courses in the Department of Oriental Languages of Beijing University; respond to a new awareness of Jewish studies in Japan, Korea, Thailand, Mongolia, and Arab countries; or relate to a fellowship request from a Bible scholar in Nigeria's Obafemi Awolowo University to "broaden her horizon in Jewish and Judaic studies"?

A word about the World Register of universities that offer courses or departments of Jewish studies. This is, to our knowledge, the most complete record available. We have amassed this information in response to a drumming demand for contact with such institutions even in distant places. Admittedly, a straight reading of the listing is as interesting as a telephone book, yet this section, we expect, will soon serve as a standard reference for academic interchange.

As I review this anthology in my mind's eye, gaps and limitations in its composition are evident—all the more reason to expect critical reaction and constructive suggestions from learned circles. I like to think that our mistakes can be rectified. With the advance of the ICUTJC in years and experiences, surely goals and standards will be raised even higher.

It is a pleasure to express my gratitude to the numerous contributors to the volume. Each and every one, I trust, is appropriately recognized in the respective subsections and is listed at the end of the book. Together they constitute a veritable constellation.

There are, however, special stars whose names do not appear in the roster of contributors but without whom this work could not have been accomplished. First among all others is my wife Lottie, who relinquished her professional interests to join me in the two-year exploration of my hypothesis and in the preparation of the *Policy Report*. She has always steadied and strengthened my hand as we traversed the shoals from field study to institutional creation. Shulamit Nardi, assistant to Presidents Shazar, Katzir, Navon, Herzog, and now Weizman, was the guardian advisor of the International Center in the office of the Israeli presidency from the very first discussions to this day. Thomas J. Klutznick, bearer of a noble family tradition, graciously responded to my call for sponsorship and encouraged me to proceed forthwith. Happily, Niko Pfund, editor in chief of New York University Press, caught the spirit of the volume's purpose. His thoughtful and apt counsel governed our preparation of the manuscript for publication.

Although the names of my colleagues Priscilla Fishman and Melvin Fenson appear on the masthead of this volume, the description of their positions in the ICUTJC does not amply state their profound contributions to the making of this book. Priscilla Fishman's editorial talent is particularly evident in the manner in which she succeeded in harmonizing different personal styles and content. Melvin Fenson's veteran newspaper experience was a special gift in bringing distant contributors together in one home. That does not relieve me of final responsibility for all acts of omission and commission. Nehemia Levtzion nurtured the volume within the complex of his many responsibilities. We hope that the work is an augury for a sustained future under his leadership.

For me, it has been a *zechut,* an unusual privilege, to work in the vineyard of higher university Judaic education. Jewish civilization is many-splendored. It is the history and destiny of a singular people which embraces the world. It teaches wisdom and ethics, literature and art. All who probe it, student and scholar, committed and searching, recognize that they have undertaken an endless quest.

I

JEWISH STUDIES IN THE UNIVERSITY

1. THE "SCIENCE OF JUDAISM" AND ITS TRANSFORMATION

Nathan Rotenstreich

The term *Wissenschaft des Judentums* (Science of Judaism) was formulated about 1818, making its earliest appearance in articles, some of which were written by people who, unlike Leopold Zunz, its acknowledged "father," were not later engaged in research.

It is true that Jewish tradition through the ages has been concerned with learning. But it has been a mode of learning that was different from *Wissenschaft des Judentums*. Historically, learning in the Jewish tradition was concerned with what is called in Hebrew *parshanut* (exegesis). Exegesis of texts, and the knowledge of the text, including the awareness of the relationship between exegesis and text, is built into the process of Jewish learning. Acceptance of the normative position of the Scriptures and engagement in interpreting them have been the two interrelated attitudes.

This position changed, however, with the formulation of the *Wissenschaft des Judentums*. Around 1818, we find several articles in which the term was used in order to stress *Wissenschaft* as representing a methodological attitude, and concurrently presenting a detachment from the normative, that is, binding, relation to the subject matter of Judaism. For example, Zunz, perhaps the only person who combined the formulation of the program with research into Judaism and its history—as we know from his studies of liturgy and literature—distinguished between the norm of attachment to Judaism and the scientific study of Judaism's attitudes toward religion, philosophy, history, the legal system, literature, and also concrete existence, that is, what is called in German

Bürgerleben, the life of citizens. All these are now brought within the scope of the Science of Judaism. We find here not only a thematic extension of the notion of Judaism, but also a relationship between the aspiration of the Jews to achieve human rights in the society in which they live—that is, emancipation—and the methodological presentation of Judaism in its broad spectrum.

There are probably several components comprising this approach. The acceptance of the scientific attitude as a norm is basic to it. The scientific attitude is inherently normative, because it affirms the principle of truth; it refers to things as they are, or, as the German adage has it, "Actuality is that which acts."

It is a historical irony that the nineteenth-century Science of Judaism is a subject of historical studies, or of the history of ideas. The present climate of opinion places more stress on the possibility of choice than on naive acceptance of the given. We choose those components of Judaism that are of a binding, normative significance, or, as we say today, have "relevance." We may choose deliberately, because we know the directions or orientations that are considered to be relevant. The difference between exegesis and Scriptures also has normative significance; and therefore we cannot totally disregard the findings of scholarship. However, the aspect of preferential choice becomes central, and expressing preference constitutes the component of guidance interrelated with both decision and adherence to the tradition.

To some extent, those who founded the Science of Judaism incorporated within it the concept of philosophy present in Hegel's system. Obviously, there is a distinction between *Wissenschaft* and philosophy. In the introduction to the *Grundlinien der Philosophie des Rechts,* Hegel says that philosophy appears after what is real comes to an end; philosophy is the "Owl of Minerva," looking at things after they have already ended. To come to an end is, however, not to disappear, but to be incorporated thematically and reflectively in the scope of philosophical thinking. Interestingly, one of those who formulated the program of the Science of Judaism, Eduard Gans, was a student of Hegel, involved in the editing of Hegel's book on the philosophy of history. It was he, it seems to me, who incorporated into the program of the Science of Judaism the metaphor of the Owl of Minerva. In fact, he even went further when he said "it is not only to exist, but also to know. And to some extent, to know replaces, historically and thematically, the position of existence."

These aspects of the program of the Science of Judaism should be considered when we seek to understand the background and the direction of its development in the first part of the nineteenth century. We can discern an apologetic element, both in the program and in its realization in concrete research. The scholars tried to show the creativity of Judaism in the postbiblical period. They tried to show that Jews were engaged in activities other than in the economic sphere, as the stereotype had it. Interestingly, we find among Orthodox Jews in the nineteenth century a critical approach to *Wissenschaft des Judentums,* epitomized by the saying: "They consider science a goal; we consider science a means." According to that formula, the Science of Judaism is self-contained, and was so considered both by those who formulated the program and were engaged in its research, and by those who opposed it.

Thematically speaking, an important focus of the developing Science of Judaism was the postbiblical period of Jewish creativity, an interest that Zunz certainly represents consciously and concretely in his studies. As noted above, the scholars of *Wissenschaft* included within its scope the sociological and demographic aspects of Jewish existence. They tried to present a total profile that would allow for Jewish studies to be incorporated into the curriculum of universities. In this, however, they did not succeed.

Significantly, the Science of Judaism has been superseded by the development of what is now called "Jewish studies." This raises an interesting aspect of terminology. In Hebrew, we now use the plural form *mada'ei hayahadut,* rather than the singular *mad'a hayahadut.* This means that the scientific or scholarly concern with Judaism is being built into a variety of academic disciplines as they have developed in the last fifty or sixty years. This in itself is an indication that the scholarly approach to Judaism has accepted, even taken for granted, the methodological differences between the approaches of various scholarly disciplines, between textual, philological, and historical analyses, as well as differences in periods of Jewish creativity, such as biblical studies versus postbiblical studies, and so on.

One may ask whether we can find in this new stage of Jewish studies a programmatic statement parallel to that of the founders of the Science of Judaism. One such statement is contained in Gershom Scholem's article on the Science of Judaism; his critical stance regarding the nineteenth-century position plus his own attempt to present a new approach were incorporated in his extensive and profound research. He rejected the position that the *Wissenschaft* approach assumed that what was being viewed had necessarily come to its end. Scholem used to quote Steinschneider's statement that he and his colleagues were undertaking an "inventory" of Judaism. He rejected that view, because he began with the assumption that Judaism is ongoing creativity, and that the scientific approach and scholarly findings have to be incorporated into its renaissance. Of course, Scholem distinguished between renascence as a historical process, and scientific investigation that is of a methodological nature and as such could be called "edifying" (in Hegel's term, *erbaulich*). There has to be a difference between edification and the scholarly approach, though the latter may add to the renascence of Judaism.

Developments in Jewish studies have occurred to a very large extent as a result of changes in the scholarly sphere, and also in the world. A very significant change in the scholarly approach has been the incorporation into the academic world of critical studies of the Bible, without accepting biblical criticism as formulated by Wellhausen. If we look into the present-day profile of Bible studies, we find a variety of approaches— of history, comparative religion, philology, and so forth. To a large extent this is due to new linguistic findings such as the Semitic background of the writings of the Bible, as well as to related legal aspects, namely, Hammurabi influences, Assyrian characteristics, and so on.

We can also observe the impact of the day-to-day historical situation—for instance, the significance of archeology in modern Jewish studies, because historical roots in Eretz Israel are conceived as enhanced by archeological findings. A relationship exists between archeological discoveries and the "climate of opinion" that has an impact on scholarship dealing with various aspects and periods of Jewish history. Scholarly interest in modern Hebrew literature has also emerged in recent years, because events gave rise to a literature that had to be studied, employing methods and approaches utilized in the study of literature in general.

Interest in the variety of religious orientations (here Scholem played a most significant role in his emphasis on the impact of Jewish mysticism on various Jewish religious attitudes) is another component in the reformulation of Jewish studies. Again, history interceded, leading to a concern with the creativity of what are called the Oriental Jewish communities, which had not been part of the spectrum of research in previous centuries.

In sum, we may say that the new orientation of the Science of Judaism results from a combination of the impact of reality on Jewish history and the new approaches in scholarly research. Each one of these elements introduces new components of subject matter, as well as of methodological attitude.

In Israel, we find a positive attitude toward the *Wissenschaft des Judentums*; for instance, Zunz's significant book on rabbinic homilies has been translated into Hebrew. Yet the development of Jewish studies has deliberately and consciously changed the horizon of the Science of Judaism. It encompasses new teams of scholars and new approaches, and it addresses itself to a reality that has not come to an end. Jewish studies deals with the continuity of a living Judaism, and as such contains a potential for both new subject matter and new scholarly attitudes.

2. INTEGRATION OF JEWISH STUDIES IN THE HUMANITIES

Ephraim E. Urbach

Both Jewish and non-Jewish scholars involved in Jewish studies must necessarily be aware of the tremendous change that has taken place in the life of this people. An increasing number of Jews live as a nation in their own land. They create in their old-new language, maintain links with the Jewish diaspora as well as with other nations and religions throughout the world, and cope with internal religious and social challenges. They strive to absorb foreign influences while fighting against too great an assimilation of cultures. Perhaps in the last century and at the beginning of the present century, scholars were able to maintain the fiction that there was no connection between the Jews they saw every day and their academic work. Such a fiction is untenable today. It has in fact been untenable ever since Jewish studies became a branch of learning in its own right.

For more than a century, proponents of the *Wissenschaft des Judentums* consistently lamented the fact that it lacked official recognition and status. Abraham Geiger's proposal that a Jewish theological faculty be established alongside Protestant and Catholic faculties gained no response whatsoever. Even Zunz's much more modest request in 1848, that the Ministry of Higher Education in Berlin establish a professorship of Jewish history and literature, was rejected. Seventy years later, due to World War I, nothing came of yet another application to the same

This chapter is adapted from an address given at the dedication of the H. Rosenberg School for Jewish Studies, Tel Aviv University, November 6, 1979.

ministry signed by the two renowned gentile scholars, Noeldeke and Wellhausen. In 1922 Elbogen summed it up: "We shall do well not to count too much on the universities on this subject." Jewish studies were pursued only in the rabbinical and teachers' seminaries of Western Europe during the nineteenth century, and in the United States and Warsaw between World Wars I and II.

In the early days of *Wissenschaft des Judentums* there was an almost total disregard for the original research of Jewish scholars, and needless to say, since much research in Jewish fields was written in Hebrew, important works remained *terra incognita*. Study of the Bible and Jewish history, even when undertaken in the most critical and thorough way, was deemed important by the Christian scholars only insofar as the Old Testament was viewed as a precursor of Christianity; the opinions of Jewish scholars in the field were hardly considered significant.

The renascence of spoken Hebrew and of the Hebrew language as a medium for literary composition, together with the renewed link between the Jewish people and their land, led not by mere chance to the publication in Hebrew of Abraham Cahana's complete and modern Bible commentary, based on all previous works by Jewish writers regardless of their religious inclination. In this context one should also mention the most comprehensive work on the Bible written in Hebrew, the *History of Israel's Faith* by Yehezkel Kaufmann.

Revival of biblical studies in the Hebrew language led to renewed interest in Jewish studies on the part of non-Jewish scholars. The wind of change was first felt in essays and studies written in various European languages and then, increasingly, in essays and periodicals written in Hebrew. For a growing number of scholars in the United States, Germany, Austria, and France, the Hebrew language no longer presented an insuperable problem. Familiarity with the work of Jewish scholars broadened the horizons of non-Jewish students, and aroused their interest in the origins of Judaism as a subject in its own right and not merely as a means of shedding light on other areas of scholarship. Indicative are George Foot Moore's *Judaism in the Time of the Tannaim,* which must surely be considered a pioneering effort, along with the well-known works by Schürer, Bousset, and others.

The change that has taken place in the status of Jewish studies began with the opening of the Institute of Jewish Studies in Jerusalem in 1925, contemporary with the founding of the Hebrew University. The development of the general humanities and social sciences at the university, which attracted scholars in general linguistics and in European or ancient Near Eastern history, contributed directly or indirectly to the field of Jewish studies.

The Institute was not linked to a particular ideological trend, and varied hopes and directions were ascribed to it, from "learning about Judaism in all its guises" to "offering Judaism to the Jewish people as a life-style." In the first decade of its existence, it gathered to it a number of scholars skilled in the best methods of philologic and historic research, who combined love and dedication to every small particular, with the ability and will to tie these details into the broader framework of general phenomenology-based theory. They assumed only the goal of learning to know Judaism in all its forms—where the term "Judaism" encompasses the living entity of the Jewish people.

At first, the Institute was dedicated to pure research and, as the areas of study expanded, a tradition developed of cooperative work, even between scholars with widely differing life-styles and perspectives. A phenomenon well worth noting in this instance is that when literary collaborators employ the scientific method of scholarship, excellent results can be obtained without blurring the individual's religious outlook, since philology and history are no substitutes for theology and individual faith, which require submission and discipline. Nor can theology or religion, or any humanistic attitude, plead that historical or philological research is valueless; any conservative movement that refuses to acknowledge this will, in the long run, not be able to fend off modern trends.

In time, contact with Jewish scholars abroad grew. Some of the Institute's graduates joined research and teaching institutions abroad, and the number of research scholars coming to Jerusalem from the United States multiplied.

In the United States alone, since World War II, the number of chairs of Jewish studies has increased geometrically. There has been a similar development, if on a smaller scale, in England and Europe, and also in Japan, South Africa, and Australia, where it cannot be attributed to a local Jewish factor but to the existence of the State of Israel and the renewed interest in Jewish studies on the part of Christian scholars who teach the Old Testament, the Hebrew language, and the history of the Jewish people.

That we have been able to regard the status of Jewish studies in our own time in a somewhat optimistic light is not attributable solely to developments in the field of scholarship, but chiefly to the dynamic forces, both constructive and destructive, which have shaken our world to its foundations. Two factors finally placed Jewish studies on a par with other disciplines in the humanities: the Zionist movement, with its revival of the creative power of the Hebrew language; and the destruction of European Jewry in its great centers of historical and philological scholarship.

It is important to understand that the history of Jewish studies is full of paradoxes. On the one hand, it followed a general trend toward integration into the nations in which the Jews lived, while on the other, it reflected the essential element of differentiation—the constant striving of Jewish studies to achieve an independent existence although, at the outset, Jewish studies had no Jewish audience to whom its research and articles were appropriate. This dichotomy also found expression in the status of Jewish studies in Jewish society. Despite its secular tendency, it found its place more often within the confines of rabbinical schools, and among their faculties. Non-religious Jewish frameworks dedicated to academic research did not exist. While rabbinical institutions insisted that their teachers be involved in research and in most cases offered as great a degree of freedom of thought as was found in the theological faculties of the universities, these institutions only had the most limited means at their disposal.

Still, for all the difficult conditions and lack of adequate means, one must be amazed at the achievements in research. Reference to writings in related fields was recognized to be fundamental to research in Jewish studies. The need for accuracy and thoroughness in the handling of source materials and the impetus to discover and collect new primary texts and documents were universally accepted. The groundwork was laid for establishing specialized libraries and archives; national organizations were founded uniting those who dealt with Jewish studies and wrote specialized articles, and those involved in larger and more cooperative enterprises. In addition, an informal international group of Jewish studies scholars came into being, developing ties with non-Jewish researchers in Judaica or in related areas such as Near Eastern or classical studies.

Yet a basic difference existed between the humanities scholars and those in Jewish studies. The areas of research of the humanities included national literatures, the various arts and natural sciences, the state—its struggles, wars and ambitions, its cultural and economic life. All this stimulated a continuum of creativity, and even if researchers of the past and its creations wished to disassociate themselves from everyday life and not be swept along in its stream, they unavoidably felt its influence.

A similar stimulus was lacking for Jewish studies during its early development. It was difficult to draw inspiration or challenge from the inner life of the Jewish community; its activities, conflicts, and divisions were of a limited nature, and in the main defensive. In fact, the major service Jewish studies could provide the Jewish community was, with few exceptions, apologetic.

The first steps toward the integration of Jewish studies and the humanities began in Eastern Europe but bore fruit only with the rise of the new nationalistic (Zionist) movement and the renewal and building of Jewish settlements in Israel. Meanwhile, a new generation of young researchers arose, mostly graduates of the traditional yeshivot, who headed to the universities and rabbinical schools in the West. They read the renascent Hebrew literature dealing with contemporary Jewish problems and struggles—for example, the distress of Jews and Judaism, the confrontation between Torah and daily life, the new nationalist vision, the Jewish cultural renaissance, the radical reform of society. These issues began to be reflected in the research into the Jewish past— in the choice of topics and emphases, in the examination of movements heretofore not considered for various reasons. Thus the new Hebrew literature abetted the secular aspect of Jewish studies and furthered the move toward integration into the general society.

SOME PROBLEMS IN JEWISH STUDIES

The picture described thus far basically reflects the Israeli reality until the 1960s. Since then, Israeli society has undergone changes: the secondary school population has increased and there is an insufficient number of secondary school teachers, especially of Judaica. At the same time, Israeli society has become polarized: there has been a distancing from the Jewish heritage, an acceptance of the mass international "culture," and, concomitantly, a radicalization in the religious-traditional camp, with the dismissal of all Western culture. The development of Jewish studies thus assumes new significance.

The Expansion of Knowledge

The status of Jewish studies as a branch of general learning has been strengthened by the abundance of sources that have come to light in this century—from the Cairo Geniza to the archeological excavations in Israel and the Near East, and by a number of ambitious enterprises initiated in different institutions. The Institute of Microfilmed Hebrew Manuscripts of the Jewish National and University Library already holds the vast majority of all known Hebrew manuscripts in the world, including collections of segments of the Geniza manuscripts with every item identified and indexed. The Archive of Jewish History boasts the largest collection in the world of documents and records, either in the original or in photograph, pertaining to the history of the Jewish people throughout all the phases of its wanderings and exiles. No critical and scholarly work in the field of Jewish history, with its vast literature, can be attempted today without recourse to these two enormous enterprises, which preserve evidence of the links in the unbroken chain of Jewish history.

Yet however important these aids to learning may be, in those projects that aim to construct concordances, dictionaries, professional encyclopedias, indices, bibliographies, and paleographies, scholars must be careful not to become so deeply involved with the functioning of their institutions that they forget that all-important figure—the creative personality. Indeed, only scholars of great breadth can infuse their work with creative spirit; only they will know which questions must be asked and how to seek the answers in existing records and documents. Such scholars have the power to reveal new and original vistas in areas thought to be dry and barren, while the most promising material may seem useless and of no significance in the hands of those lacking the necessary intellect and intuitive gifts.

The Creative Personality

What is this creative power, this intuitive capacity for divining the links between different phenomena in a branch of learning whose guidelines are historical and philological? Is it a mere gift, or can it be achieved with diligence and hard work? And, is it requisite that such a talent be well informed about the structure of contemporary life and culture in order to achieve significant insight into the past and its cultural achievements?

There is no doubt that the qualities required by scholars who endow smaller projects with the intuitive achievement of masterpieces are even more essential for scholars who attempt comprehensive works of scholarship. Such works can only be of significance if their authors have the necessary intuition and talent for analyzing the various processes and phenomena with which they are dealing, the qualities that make Graetz's *History of the Jews,* or Yitzhak Baer's *A History of the Jews in Christian Spain,* such great scholarly achievements.

It has thus become increasingly common for scholars to join forces to produce cooperative efforts leading to more comprehensive works. However, not only is each historical period treated by a separate scholar, but often, within individual volumes, different minds can be seen to have left their imprint. This method not only renders impossible the comprehensive view and consistent outlook so essential to narrative composition, but, even worse, the varying approaches of the authors—if indeed they are of sufficient stature to have developed individual approaches—may distort the overall picture. The team approach may be useful in collecting data, publishing documentary material, or providing auxiliary aids, but it fails in the area of creative composition. Such cooperative efforts may lead to works in which the task of summarizing critical episodes is given to scholars whose forte is detailed analysis, but not writing well-constructed or perceptive essays.

These comments reflect an entirely new problem in modern hermeneutics, namely, the "idea of history" and Jewish historiography. Gershom Scholem recognizes two central problems in Jewish historiography. The first is the contradiction between the perception of Judaism as a conceptual system evaluating historical phenomena according to its own standards, and the perception of Judaism as a living body within a developing history. The second problem is the contradiction between the perception of Jewish history as a single compelling dynamic, or as a collection of circumstances of general history. Scholem holds that "from our own awareness and living experience we tend to a unified vision of the history of the Jewish people."

There are two scholars whose individual writings can serve as a guide to peak achievements in Jewish studies, and I do not believe it an exaggeration to maintain that few works in the other branches of the humanities can compete with them. They are Saul Lieberman and Gershom Scholem.

Lieberman, in his work on the Tosefta, composed an exemplary commentary on one of our most basic sources. His work touches on every aspect of Judaica, from questions of language and realia to problems concerning beliefs and opinions. His knowledge is exceptionally expert with regard to all the treasures of literature that pertain to the text with which he deals: parallel sources of the Sages; earlier and later commentaries; all the historical, archeological, epigraphical, or papyrological documentation in Greco-Roman literature of the classical period and later; as well as sources buried in literary works long since forgotten and cast aside, to which no scholar had previously given thought. These manifestations of immense scholarship, as evidenced on almost every page of his magnificent work, must make the student marvel at the vast scope and exquisitely refined exegetic intuition of the author. There is no branch of Judaica, especially where the different aspects of Jewish history are concerned, that can be researched without referring to this large and excellent commentary.

Lieberman also contributes in no small degree to an interpretation of the sources in Roman, Byzantine, and Hellenistic culture and, thereby, to our understanding of the way of life in the entire ancient world. His great contribution was achieved through his unremitting struggle to attain a true understanding of the sources by interpreting each word in the spirit of the great early commentators, and exploiting the most modern research techniques.

Gershom Scholem's approach is very different. He came to Israel from Germany with a rich background of Western scholarship and was completely identified with the movement for the revival of the Hebrew language. His superior intellect led him to realize the need for thorough analytical research, and he therefore looked to Zunz and Steinschneider as his ideals. (Although he may be compared with Steinschneider in the sheer scope of his work, his lucidity of style places him in the ranks of the greatest prose writers. This is equally true whether he is writing in German or in Hebrew, in which he developed a superb scientific style.)

Scholem immediately began to introduce his own great ideas which set new goals for scholarship. He took upon himself the study of those areas of Jewish history that had been neglected by scholars out of aversion. In an effort to assign the messianic movements their rightful place in the scheme of Jewish history, he based his assessment on the role played by these movements in their historical context, rather than on the judgment of later historians. Whereas this branch of Jewish literature had been studied within the history of religion and phenomenology, Scholem, by the strength of his scholarship, brought the mystical and kabbalistic literature (which had such a strong influence on all periods of Jewish history, and whose great authors were central figures and halakhic leaders in Jewish communities) out of its previous state of chaotic neglect into the realm of historic-philological research. Furthermore, in the introductions to his articles, Scholem also shed light on all the periods of Jewish thought, as well as on many phenomena in other religions. It is by virtue of this that he belongs in the front rank of world scholars in the field of religious science.

In singling out these two unique figures, it is not my intention to overlook influential scholars in other branches of Jewish studies who have also discovered new horizons. On the contrary, their work and achievements must also be judged and analyzed, and there can be no greater return for their efforts than our raising a generation of young scholars talented enough to succeed in surpassing them.

The Future Generation

There are signs that we have reached a turning point in academic scholarship, where the humanities have been superseded by the concrete achievements of the exact and natural sciences. This has even stirred in the scientists themselves the fear that the products of their scientific thought may yet prove capable of destroying the very subject of that thought—man and his intellect.

There is, however, still another fear which is unfortunately leading those brought up in the traditions of the natural sciences to try to find redemption from loneliness and alienation in a dream world of uncritical orthodoxy whose main aim seems to be the development of scientific techniques in matters of religion. Here it must be the task of those involved in Jewish studies to demonstrate convincingly that the problems and questions raised in the research of that field are very real ones, and that their methods, if employed properly, can lead to solutions that are very close to the truth. The degree of success achieved in fulfilling this task will depend to no small extent on how many of the superior intellects of our younger generation are attracted to Jewish studies.

The tremendous increase in departments, institutes, and professorships may inevitably lead to lower standards of scholarship in order to meet the increased demand for teaching staff. This can only be avoided if the institutions involved make great efforts to attract talented young people. However, the currently accepted system of appointments and promotions induces many young academics to produce a shower of publications which might better have been left unwritten. Another alarmingly widespread phenomenon is found in the United States, where sociologists, anthropologists, and others with no knowledge of Jewish sources or the scholarly work relating to them persist in lecturing and publishing in the realm of Judaica. These are problems about which we must formulate our own conclusions, not only in general, but in their direct application to Jewish studies.

Contemporary Jewish Studies

We must understand the significance of the period in which we are living, without allowing ourselves the presumption that we can determine the course of future development through efforts of scholarship. The link between historical knowledge and the establishment of new approaches is not a causal or deterministic one. New approaches can only result from an original inspiration or from the initiative of an outstanding talent who is specially equipped for such activity—and even then success depends on the ripeness of the hour and the environment. While historiographical data can prepare us for certain patterns of development, and while it is desirable that the formation of opinions which lead to positive action be based on a full knowledge of the facts, these domains should not be confused. Scholars who presume foreknowledge of future events are generally found to be building castles in the air.

The exaggerated evaluation of scientific research, which leads to its substitution for the very current of life itself and for creative scholarship, has contributed in no small degree to the triumph of those forces that would willingly see history and all study of past events abolished completely, since these latter negate the trends that lead to anarchy and destruction. Historical sources provide evidence that movements which claim to be new are usually not new at all, but merely a reversion to phenomena that have occurred in the past. Historical research and philological criticism, however, aid in developing an active cultural life. A decline in historical research and historical consciousness is usually indicative of a general crisis in the cultural life of society.

What is needed in all the humanities is creative and scholarly work: a sense of responsibility to society, integrity, a mutual respect among scholars and, most of all, the demand for spiritual freedom and intellectual independence. These requirements take on an added dimension when applied to Jewish studies in modern times in general and to the State of Israel in particular, for the ongoing process or normalization that is taking place in our midst gives the humanities an integral role in our contemporary culture.

As Jewish studies concern themselves with events of the more recent past and the present, there is always the fear that we may be treading on ashes that conceal live coals and that we may easily be burned. Yet the truth of the matter is that this same fear will always be with us, even when studying events of the distant past. Indeed, we cannot assert about everything in the past that "what happened, happened."

We speak today from the perspective of a land whose ground has yielded up relics of an early culture that produced a moral and religious code of unquestioned influence on the course of human history. But we must not examine this culture in order to find support for our own attitudes, nor to illustrate any cheap relevance. Rather, the task of viewing Jewish history in the light of the existence of the State of Israel must be pursued with full awareness that the history of this state is bound up with the glory and majesty as well as the terrors of three thousand years of existence. We must undertake the task of surveying the history of the Hebrew language in all of its periods, and study its revival as a living language against that background. We must compare the Jewish Diaspora of the Second Temple period and those who were exiled after its destruction, with the Diaspora and the dark corners of exile in our day, examining the complex problems of fidelity and devotion, treachery and flight, common to both periods. And we must not forget the problems inherent in the process of redemption, including the dangers to the heritage, moral code, and spirit of this nation, that attend its realization.

All these problems and questions must be reassessed in the various realms of scholarship. No evidence must be concealed, omitted, improved upon, or embellished; for the embellishment of the past can only be achieved at the cost of the beauty of the present. The ability of Jewish studies to deal with these problems and questions depends on the talent, initiative, and drive of those involved, as well as on their integrity, honesty, and unbiased approach.

3. REMEMBERING THE ANSWERS: JEWISH STUDIES IN THE CONTEMPORARY UNIVERSITY

David Sidorsky

Courses in Jewish civilization studies have become a recognized curricular feature of universities around the world, as part of a consensus about the expanded scope of the contemporary university, yet there has been little examination of their distinctive character. On the whole—surprising for a community which is continually exercising its penchant for self-analysis—this development has progressed with comparatively little explicit formulation of its purpose or justification.

The distinctiveness of current Jewish civilization studies reflects the current trend of the university toward pluralism, after overcoming the Enlightenment's universalist attitudes toward historical traditions, and after achieving its own form of emancipation from an inherited particularistic culture, whether of religious Christianity or national nativism. This pluralism has legitimated the study of many different cultural traditions and religions within an "internal" frame of reference, often with faculty and students who share the tradition being studied.

Historically, who were the scholars and teachers of Jewish texts? Traditionally, the masters of Jewish scholarship had studied in the religious academies of the community, that is, the yeshivot. These centers of learning rejected any independent intellectual approach that would place the scholar's conclusions at variance with accepted religious views.

With the advent of modernity, European and, later, American theological seminaries made possible the study of traditional texts through the application of virtually all the methodologies of academic inquiry. However, some of the current assumptions of freedom of inquiry in research and scholarship were not completely adopted in the framework of the theological seminary. For example, in addition to scholarly attainment, religious commitment was considered a prerequisite for faculty appointment; and, despite the great latitude of academic freedom in virtually all areas of history and traditional texts, the methods of Higher Criticism were excluded from study of the Pentateuch.

Those who initially moved into university teaching were trained within the culture of the yeshivot but were supportive of full freedom of inquiry being applied to the tradition. They welcomed the empirical verification of historical claims made within sacred or national traditions, the application of comparative critical techniques to texts, and the adoption of the research tools of the social sciences in the investigation of individual or group behavior. Thus, the teaching of Jewish civilization in the university was carried out in ways that were partially continuous with the historical traditions of Jewish learning, by persons identified with aspects or variants of those traditions.

In the expansion of these programs, a series of issues had to be confronted and resolved. Even if the results of that expansion are now taken for granted, it is appropriate to undertake the exercise of "remembering the answers." (As Nathan Glazer reminded us when using this phrase during the campus troubles of the 1960s, it is important to remember the answers that were generated in the course of development of academic freedom within the university.)

Five "answers" seem worth recalling in order to identify some of the issues that are relevant to sustaining and developing the teaching of Jewish civilization in the contemporary university. The issues are as follows:

1. The primacy of disciplinary studies
2. The significance of an interdisciplinary approach
3. The limitations of consciousness-raising
4. The problem of politicization
5. The nature of the relationship between the scholar and the community

THE PRIMACY OF DISCIPLINARY STUDIES

The legitimation of Jewish civilization studies in the postwar period has been, in part, the consequence of scholarly achievement by a small group of pioneering professors in particular disciplinary fields. The expansion of this small faculty base was a factor in the transformation of disciplinary areas of Jewish studies from an external and comparative approach which had often led to distortion or condescension, to a pluralist or internal perspective. Thus, a major intellectual transformation was partly the consequence of the application of the egalitarian hiring principle permitting "discrimination for relevant reasons alone" to faculty appointments in the disciplinary areas related to Jewish civilization studies. Legitimation of Jewish civilization studies by universal standards of inquiry has even made possible an interesting reversal: the teaching by Jewish scholars, from within their frame of reference, of materials like the Church Fathers or the interpretation of the Gospels, which for centuries had been the preserve of Christian university scholars.

The existence of a national university in Israel offering a full curriculum of disciplinary programs in Jewish studies has also provided a functioning model for other universities. In Western universities, the adoption of pluralistic approaches to cultural anthropology, and a relative shift from internal identification with Jewish tradition to Western universalist values in the aftermath of the Holocaust, also played formative roles in disciplines relating to Jewish studies.

Maintenance of universal criteria of scholarly excellence in reasonably defined disciplinary areas has contemporary significance. The critical formula cited above of "discrimination for relevant reasons alone" raises the question of what constitutes a relevant reason. For example, in the context of the replacement of disciplinary areas by "programs of studies" such as Jewish studies, Black studies, women's studies, or gay and lesbian studies, sympathetic identification with the subject matter may be deemed a "relevant reason."

Even the introduction of "religion" as an academic discipline has raised a similar issue, for the offerings would include not only such standard courses as the history or philosophy of religion, but also Catholicism, Judaism, Islam, or Zen Buddhism. A dilemma emerges in the teaching of these subjects. It would be strange to suggest that belief or participation in a particular religion is a ground for exclusion from teaching a course in that religion. On the other hand, there is something disturbing in a university system advocating freedom of inquiry in which, primarily, Christians teach Christianity, Muslims teach Islam, Buddhists teach Buddhism, Jews teach Judaism, and so on. Yet, for a variety of historical and political reasons, where departments of religion include courses in specific institutional religions, it is common for identified members of those religious groups to constitute the faculty. What serves to save this practice from such potential abuses as consciousness-raising and advocacy in lieu of critical inquiry, or informal conversation led by religious partisans or counselors in place of scholarly presentation, is an insistence on the primacy of competence in the disciplines in which research on religion is undertaken.

One must also point to the difficulty of replacing the founding generation of faculty in Jewish studies. The European or American educational system is not able by itself to prepare a generation of younger scholars; continuity depends on recruitment from Israel, or on transfusion from other types of Jewish educational institutions. To a degree, the problem exists in any program in a foreign culture. Even in such entrenched academic disciplines as French, Italian, or German studies, faculty is not trained by the local educational system, but is recruited from persons who have studied abroad. Accordingly, the place of Israel as providing training in the disciplines of Jewish studies is particularly relevant for the question of faculty replacement.

The idea of what constitutes a discipline in the humanities or the social sciences, like the concept of disciplinary standards, is not given or fixed. Contemporary Jewish thought, for example, has been viewed as a part of philosophy, and can also be seen as a form of social commentary, or a type of theology. There would appear to be no substitute for peer judgment regarding the definition of a discipline or of disciplinary scholarship in the legitimation of teaching Jewish civilization in the contemporary university.

THE SIGNIFICANCE OF AN INTERDISCIPLINARY APPROACH

Disciplinary studies have been the curricular center of programs of Jewish studies, but interdisciplinary approaches encircle it from all directions. Interdisciplinary intellectual resources are necessary at the level of advanced studies or research. Moreover, any attempt to interpret the important events or texts of Jewish history, philosophy, or literature at the introductory level of general education requires cutting across academic disciplines.

One of the clearest examples of the unavoidable need of an interdisciplinary approach is the academic rite of passage—the doctoral defense. Virtually all dissertations mandate a committee whose members are not disciplinary peers but faculty who can bring to the subject matter knowledge derived from other disciplinary approaches. A dissertation in medieval Jewish history, for example, may benefit from the comments of historians of other periods and cultures, but requires faculty from other disciplinary areas who possess knowledge of rabbinic sources, philosophical trends, or the contemporaneous languages. The historicity and dating of Joshua's conquest of Jericho involves biblical scholars in both literary analysis and archeological investigation. Again, it is difficult to conceive the ongoing reevaluation of the meaning and significance of kabbalistic texts from the point of view of Jewish history, rabbinic studies, or comparative religion alone.

Indeed, a purely disciplinary paradigm may distort scholarly interpretation. An important example is provided by many studies of "Jewish law" carried out under the rubric of comparative law, based on the analogy that rabbinic law, like the legal system of other nations, represents a process of juridical debate and decision-making, culminating in the rendering of verdicts. For some areas and periods, the analogy holds and the study of *ha-mishpat ha-ivri* vindicates this approach. However, for much material that is popularly and critically examined in comparative legal studies—for example, human rights, women's status, freedom of thought and expression, rights of privacy, and so on—the disciplinary approach lends itself to the illusion that a legal system is understood by the views of its intellectual protagonists in juridical literature. What is overlooked is the absence in Jewish law of an abstract and hypothetical debate, of a mechanism for implementation of "legislative programs" or execution of "judicial verdicts," which would inevitably generate revision, amendment, or reconsideration. The relocation of this subject in an interdisciplinary framework of history, literary exegesis, myth, and philosophy, in addition to comparative law, would serve to rectify misunderstanding.

In the curricular debates that have flared in the universities since the

1960s, the tendency has been to develop introductory courses in the humanities. Courses in "contemporary civilization"—for example, a study of the history of the ideas of social and political thought that have shaped modern culture—are offered in lieu of traditional introductory history or government courses. Courses in "humanities" requiring reading a list of the "canonical" works of Western literature have taken the place of the required survey in English literature. Characteristically, such courses more easily accommodate discussion of varying interpretations than apprenticeship in disciplinary techniques. Such courses have generated debate on a series of issues: whether the traditional canon reflects biases of race, class, gender, and sexual orientation; the place of the classics of non-Western cultures in general education; and the role of dissenting, minority, or counterculture traditions in the shaping of contemporary civilization. The terms of these debates often relate in both supportive and adversarial ways to the position of Jewish studies in the curriculum. In the process, many classics of Jewish civilization have been granted access, on their own terms, to the general curriculum. The Hebrew Scriptures are usually justified as part of the Western canon, while other works may be recognized as aspects of a minority culture within Western civilization.

The challenge that general education sets for the teaching of Jewish civilization in the university is formidable. Unlike many courses in Jewish studies which function in a self-selected, segregated community, these general courses have a wide and diverse constituency. The superficial familiarity with which the faculty or the student body may approach the specific subject matter makes it difficult to provide an adequate interpretation. The burden is on faculty in relevant fields of Jewish studies to transmit the distinctiveness and the significance of the classics of Jewish civilization. The context of general education courses suggests, however, that they are not providing disciplinary training within a specified area, but are interpreting a civilization to a constituency that already possesses a mix of partial interpretation and strong misinterpretation. Despite the unavoidability of interdisciplinary approaches, deeper disciplinary immersion may be the only effective counter to the widespread misunderstanding about the nature of Jewish civilization. Jewish studies programs may provide a model demonstrating that intellectual safeguards can be erected to support interdisciplinary interpretation in ways that avoid the educational abuse implicit in consciousness-raising.

THE LIMITATIONS OF CONSCIOUSNESS-RAISING

The adoption of the interdisciplinary approach in courses in Jewish studies, as opposed to courses in Hebrew or in particular periods of Jewish history, carries with it the risk of bypassing disciplinary competence for the sake of group consciousness-raising. Whatever the anti-intellectual connotations of the term "consciousness-raising" may be, some effort to heighten awareness, to stir or direct interest and emotion, even to transform personality, has always been a valued part of a liberal education. Students attend college for four years not only to acquire information, but also to become aware of and participate in new kinds of experiences in both curricular and extracurricular areas.

It may be difficult to explicitly formulate the criteria distinguishing between a cognitive inquiry including a tacit element of changed awareness, and a propagandistic use of the facade of academic learning for the purpose of changing attitudes; yet it is reasonably easy for students or faculty to discriminate between them in immediate confrontation. Without seeking to develop the criteria, I suggest that there is a provisional test that can be used in programs of Jewish civilization studies.

Courses in Jewish studies are open to a wide range of students and can be taught by persons of diverse religious and ethnic backgrounds. The existence of courses taught by Jewish faculty to Jewish students, to the degree that it occurs, is the undesired consequence of the limits of competence or of interest within faculty and student bodies. A distinctive mark of courses that fall into the negative category of consciousness-raising, however, is their approach to restrictive access. Thus, women's studies courses are often taught by and for those women who accept a set of feminist assumptions or are prepared not to challenge them publicly, just as ethnic studies courses often assume a homogeneous community concerned with exploring a shared ethnic experience. There may well be a need and a value to this kind of sympathetic exploration and group participation. Yet any examination of the distinctive nature of the university as a center of impartial inquiry would recognize the risks of this approach.

Generally speaking, programs in Jewish studies, because of their continuity with the scholarly traditions cited earlier, are free of the abuses that are potentially present in courses organized around a minority group culture. The test case to examine this generalization would be the teaching and researching of Holocaust studies. Students, whether Jewish or not, who register for such courses may be motivated not by the scholarly desire to study the record of the Nazi war against the Jews between 1933 and 1945, but by piety, or solidarity, or a need to become sensitive to this unique phenomenon. In approaching the literature of the Holocaust, from Anne Frank's diary to Nellie Sachs's poetry, there is characteristically a sense of approaching sacred texts that relate to hallowed graves. It would be absurd to insist on a spurious impartiality that makes a hypothetical intellectual case for empathetic understanding of the perpetrators of the Holocaust; objectivity does not require a false symmetry between those who deny or affirm its historicity. The general principles of nonrestrictive access of students and the participation of faculty of differing backgrounds seem particularly appropriate for curricular planning in Holocaust studies.

The development of such studies as instruments of consciousness-raising also brings significant risks of politicization; for example, the loosening of academic norms would permit the use of the classroom as a forum of advocacy against genocide. The transfer from the historical investigation of mass destruction in the Nazi Holocaust to the more up-to-date inquiry into destruction of the human or animal species by nuclear war or environmental negligence may be seen as useful in terms of sensitivity training or politicized advocacy against all forms of genocide. On the other hand, the right of the instructor in a course on the Holocaust to include in his syllabus Israeli acts of "genocide" against the "Palestine people" has already been contested at one American campus. Whatever the flaw might be of not admitting appropriate study of the Holocaust within the university curriculum and, thereby, not fulfilling a moral obligation of our generation, it is less culpable than the trivialization of its study or the politicization of its implications.

THE PROBLEM OF POLITICIZATION

"Politicization" has emerged as a familiar concept in the discussion of currently contested curricular issues. The reference is not to the exclusion of political views that are relevant to the subject matter, but to the introduction of political opinion or advocacy in areas where academic restraint on such expression had traditionally been enjoined. Significantly, criticism of politicization often emerges in curricular areas that appear remote from standard partisan political issues. To a degree, this derives from the epistemological claim, championed by Foucault and many others, that even the most objective knowledge, like physics or mathematics, can be construed inescapably as political support of the status quo. If all knowledge is inherently political, the presentation of an alternative political approach to subject matter is legitimated.

This legitimation has been directed in particular to the "canonical" areas of the humanities curriculum. The decision by members of a distinguished English department to teach Shakespeare by explication of his political attitudes toward race, class, and gender may not seem to affect Jewish civilization studies significantly. Yet a similar strategy that interprets a patriarchal society and its monotheistic theology as a product of a white male chauvinist exploitative culture suggests a reductive and politicized approach to classic Jewish texts. Within programs of Jewish studies, the strong disciplinary traditions that have been mentioned above inhibit the politicized interpretation of Jewish texts. The legitimation of an advocacy approach to teaching probably has more significance in departments of modern Middle Eastern history and politics that are sometimes located within the framework of Jewish studies, where curricula may touch on a relationship to the history of Zionism and of Israel.

On the one hand, because the risk of abusing expression of political opinion and indoctrination has always been present, constraints and conventions for balance have been developed. Certainly, recognized paradigms exist for the objective teaching of courses touching upon contemporary conflicts. On the other hand, during the 1960s there was a partly successful effort to transfer the partisan style of the "Teach-in on Vietnam" to curricular studies of Southeast Asia. Generally, the appropriate scholarly response to politicization in areas of Jewish civilization studies is readily available. In the current political climate, for example, a course on Israel's relationship to the Palestinian Arab community might be the focus of partisan efforts. However, a workshop or courses in human rights, often situated within a school of law, can provide a more congenial advocacy forum. It may be suggested that the presentation and interpretation of the history of the State of Israel in an objective fashion, as part of a curriculum in Jewish studies, can provide an opportunity to illuminate the possibilities of objectivity in areas of contemporary political conflict.

THE RELATIONSHIP BETWEEN THE SCHOLAR AND THE COMMUNITY

Periods of great scholarly or artistic achievement tend to reflect (with some notable historical exceptions) the appearance of a group of scholars or artists, the simultaneous existence of a strongly supportive community of patrons or clients, with both groups sharing values or understandings. The expansion of university studies of Jewish civilization exhibits this pattern of shared values between scholars and public. It is appropriate to provide a retrospective account of the elements which have contributed to the current phenomenon.

The development of Jewish civilization studies has typically been marked by creative tension between the scholar and the community. The latter, representing the communal or public interest, and facilitating the supply of resources for scholarship, bears the responsibilities linked to accountability. Accordingly, its characteristic focus has been on the fairly immediate tangible results that are derivable for the community from the establishment of university programs in Jewish studies. In contrast, the scholar characteristically champions the right of free inquiry, which virtually precludes any commitment to substantive short-term results. The dialectic requires that the sponsoring community, aware of academic resistance to direct and utilitarian projects, continue its support, recognizing that scholarship whose results were externally requisitioned, would not necessarily merit support.

To a small degree this supportive attitude may represent the survival of the tradition rooted in the redemptive religious faith that study of the sacred text is its own reward, benefiting the perpetuation of the human spirit. A secular variant of this faith, holding that a society or community in which Jewish study or scholarship did not continue would be diminished thereby, may retain some measure of resonance, particularly with the contemporary sense of loss of the Jewish tradition.

Generally, Jewish communal motivation has been more pragmatic. There has been an awareness in many Diaspora communities that the presence of Jewish civilization studies within the university represents recognition of Jewish cultural status. The American Jewish community is also aware of the need to develop an appropriate model of the Jewish educator in a society where the communal educational system seems to be failing. A cadre of academic scholars in Jewish studies represents an extraordinary resource for a community in need of educational self-understanding and leadership.

There is also a belief that a university-based program in Jewish civilization studies would provide a second chance for Jewish learning by the next generation. In some instances, it is argued that the knowledge acquired in courses in Jewish sociology or studies in prejudice could be applied to the solution of community problems or for the broad public good. Teachers of Jewish studies who declare their primary allegiance to scholarship with no communal agenda have nonetheless been sympathetic to one or another community goals. More generally, however, the pattern is that of continuing creative tension between the scholar and the community.

It is noteworthy that even as Jewish communities have charged Jewish university scholars with communal responsibility, they have established endowments whose educational purpose is to enable those scholars to pursue their inquiry free of any such demands. At the same time, even in a well-endowed institution, no scholarly group can project future growth except on the basis of the cultivation of community support, through some demonstration of the value of scholarship to the community. This dialectic is recognized by both the community and the scholar; yet the scholar and his scholarship must always remain independent of any community directive.

CONCLUSION

The awareness of a dialectic is a theme shared by all of the issues that have been reviewed in this essay. The tension between disciplinary priorities and interdisciplinary approaches, like the interplay between the *value-neutral* demands of academic impartiality and the appeal to private interest in education, represent a search for balance. Even the rejection of politicization in the academy is compatible with the recognition that some actions of a political nature may be required in defense of the values of the university.

Accordingly, it is perhaps appropriate to conclude with another reminder of the familiar: the recurring need to balance the universal and the particular in Jewish cultural self-expression. A restless and unceasing quest for an ongoing integration of particular Jewish history with universal moral and social ideals has characterized Judaism since the Enlightenment. Before that time, the virtually complete integration of the particular and universal in Jewish life had been predicated on the covenantal tradition as formulated in rabbinic Judaism. In that formulation, the Jewish people, by the sheer act of fulfilling the religious commandments of their tradition, contributed decisively to the preservation and redemption of mankind. Since the loss of that faith, particularity has been tragically eroded, with tragic consequences. Not the least of the virtues of the teaching of Jewish civilization in the Western university is that it is a symbol and a promise for the integration of particularist values, in this case knowledge of the texts and traditions of Jewish culture, and of universal values emerging from rational inquiry, into the significant products of the human mind and spirit.

4. IN COMPARATIVE CONTEXTS

THE UNITED STATES
Alvin H. Rosenfeld

The daunting questions raised by Ephraim Urbach warrant examination within the context of the American university of today and the social and cultural realities of which it is a part. With the growth of Jewish studies, systematic teaching about Judaism and the Jews is now a regular part of the curricular offerings of most leading American colleges and universities. This institutionalization and normalization of Jewish studies means that study of the Jewish experience in all of its ramifications enjoys an intellectual validity and institutional sanction that, for the most part, it did not have previously within the American academy.

For Jewish students, the opportunity to pursue such study within the context of their formal college education tells them that Jewish history—the history that produced them—has inherent interest and is worthy of serious study. The chance to engage in high-level study of Judaism and the Jews, in a setting that fully sanctions such study, is a source of personal enrichment as well as of academic gain.

Non-Jewish students who elect to take courses in Jewish civilization undoubtedly do so for other reasons. Some are serious-minded Christians who believe that acquiring a fuller knowledge of Judaism may enhance their understanding of their own faith commitments; others simply find the Jews an interesting bunch and want to learn more about them in a general sense: Whatever may bring these students to study the Jews, most are bound to benefit from learning about a people and culture that are largely unknown to them, and probably misunderstood. Such learning has a value in itself. In addition, so most of us believe, with learning may come familiarity, understanding, and tolerance.

These reflections naturally point to some of the broader implications of the work of Jewish studies programs and raise questions about their aims and future directions. Inevitably, they also touch on such important and pedagogically sensitive matters as classroom advocacy and strategies of consciousness-raising. In thinking about these issues, it is necessary to recognize that we are living at a time when the American university is in ferment about its aims, and when the purposes of higher education have trouble winning consensus among a diverse range of administrative, faculty, and student bodies. Older ideas about advancing knowledge for its own sake or educating for humane values still obtain, but they are under challenge by ideologies of education that more closely link the functions of teaching and learning to social and political goals. Consciousness-raising and the open advocacy of positions are today a prominent part of what takes place in the American college classroom.

Jewish studies programs have developed within this context of educational ferment and, to some measure, owe their existence to it. "Ethnic studies," "multiculturalism," "advocacy," "diversity," "consciousness-raising," "presentist agendas," "preferential recruitment," "relevance" are not merely fashionable catchwords, but express new forms of ethnic, racial, sexual, religious, and political assertiveness that impact on America's educational institutions today and, if current trends continue, may have even greater impact in the years ahead. Whether they like it or not, the faculty of Jewish studies programs cannot escape these implications as they debate what kinds of programs they wish to develop within their educational settings.

At the very foundation of such programs are a few basic assumptions. One, which is spelled out in persuasive fashion by David Sidorsky, affirms the primacy of competence in the disciplines that comprise Jewish studies. Whatever a scholar's personal religious passions and practices may be, in his or her classroom role nothing must compromise the acknowledged standards of academic accomplishment. Professors of Jewish philosophy or Jewish history, for instance, perform first and foremost as academically trained philosophers or historians and are held to the same standards of professional work as others in their field. Any self-respecting Jewish studies program affirms this most basic of academic principles and makes its faculty appointments accordingly.

Having said as much, one recognizes that most of those who teach in areas of the so-called new humanities—women's studies, African-

American studies, Asian studies, Chicano studies, religious studies, Jewish studies, and so on—are most often internal to the particular areas they teach. Hence the need to look openly and candidly at questions of advocacy.

The question of what is to be expected of Jewish studies does not arise in a social vacuum, but must be addressed within the specific social, cultural, and political circumstances in which we find ourselves today. Similarly, whatever answers we may give are themselves conditioned to some extent by our understanding of these circumstances and their implications for the work we do.

A variety of people may ask this question: the faculty who teach Jewish studies courses, the students who take these courses, college and university administrators who oversee them, alumni and others in the community whose interest and generosity have helped to make Jewish studies possible. For present purposes, we will concentrate on the role of the teaching faculty.

It would be the rare American professor who would answer that Jewish studies programs have been established in the main in order to benefit Jewish society. Rather, they would argue that Jewish civilization has been an integral part of world civilization for millennia and has contributed some of the key terms for the study of major movements within the ancient, medieval, and modern worlds; by right of these facts, Judaism and the Jews warrant serious study within the context of a comprehensive college curriculum. Apart from some such formulation, it is doubtful that the aims of Jewish studies have been consciously spelled out in more explicit terms. Why is that so?

Most faculty who are connected in one way or another to Jewish studies programs probably do not think of themselves as being first and foremost "in" Jewish studies. Having been trained in the established disciplinary fields—anthropology, history, language and literature, philosophy, and so forth—they know that they are primarily anthropologists, historians, philologists, literary scholars and critics, and philosophers. For all of their interest in Jewish materials, such scholars know that Jewish studies are not a discipline but something closer to an area that calls for multidisciplinary or interdisciplinary study. In more recent years, everyone who works seriously in the humanities recognizes the attractiveness and even the necessity of crossing traditional disciplinary boundaries and engaging in interdisciplinary scholarship. Nevertheless, even in an age increasingly dominated by "theory," or a search for cross-disciplinary nexus, historians fundamentally remain historians, and philosophers identify themselves primarily as philosophers. The fact that the first may be a Jewish historian and the second a Jewish philosopher infers a link between them, but does not lessen their primary commitments to their academic disciplines. Nor should it.

The challenge for those of us who work in Jewish studies is to expand consciously and creatively what otherwise is destined to remain merely inferred, namely, the commonality of the scholarly link to Judaica. The link is real enough, but so, too, is the fact that the Jewish historian and the Jewish philosopher speak different disciplinary languages. How often and how well, therefore, are they likely to speak to one another out of the ground of their scholarly interests in Jewish materials? What, if anything, might enable them to transcend the limitations of their academic disciplines and encourage them to do productive work together? For only in thinking and working together can those teaching Jewish studies become more than a loose aggregate of scholarly specialists. What is needed, obviously, is a rationale for Jewish studies that will draw upon, but at the same time be more encompassing than, the specialized interests and talents of the individual faculty members who form the essential core of any Jewish studies program.

Where is such a rationale to be found?

Urbach reminds us that when the Institute for Jewish Studies was established in Jerusalem in 1925, various goals and directions for its work were debated, ranging from the pure intent of "learning about Judaism in all its guises" to an applied program of "offering Judaism to the Jewish people as a life-style." Given the Institute's investment in pure research, it was, not surprisingly, the first of these goals that was adopted as the rationale for the scholarly work it would sponsor. And, needless to say, such a rationale has equal validity for Jewish studies programs today. However, if these programs really intend to pursue knowledge of Judaism in all of its forms and across the millennia of Jewish existence, it is essential that the scholars involved find ways to share common interests.

That is not easy to do, for the tendency in the humanities is for the faculty to become atomized into innumerable separate units. The professional role one plays, and the incentives and rewards for fulfilling it in a demonstrably productive fashion, foster a highly competitive and individualized scholarly enterprise, with all of the gains that can follow upon individual career success but also with all of the disadvantages that inevitably accompany solitary efforts and isolation from one's peers. The challenge for those who work in Jewish studies, as indeed for all who teach in the humanities today, is to maintain the considerable gains that come with disciplinary achievement and individual scholarly success and, at the same time, to begin to work with one's colleagues across the disciplines in a new spirit of collegial scholarly effort.

Because Jewish studies at virtually all American colleges and universities exist not as an autonomous department but as an interdepartmental program, it is probably not common practice for the faculty to ask the kinds of questions that normally are raised about departmentally based teaching, research, and responsibilities. That is understandable, but it is also regrettable. For it is imperative that those teaching Jewish studies be clear about such things as teaching objectives, research goals, and the aims and responsibilities with respect to the community. Otherwise, the program runs the risk of becoming little more than a hodgepodge of ad hoc faculty offerings, with inevitable disadvantages and disappointments for the students.

It would also be desirable for the faculty associated with Jewish studies to deliberate in common about their research and service missions. Can one, in fact, identify such a thing as a "research mission" for Jewish studies that is larger than the sum of its individual parts? Generally what drives research in the humanities is nothing more and nothing less than the focused intellectual passions and interests of individual scholars. Asked to rationalize why one does research, most of us would probably say that we are drawn to read and write about a given subject because it interests us, because it affords us intellectual pleasure, and also because we believe it has inherent importance. There is something noble about such pursuits, for like little else in this busy, overwrought world, they reflect an independence of mind and a commitment to creative effort in a pure sense. These are precious values indeed.

In addition to the motivations of individual interest, however, are there other things that may determine the focus of our research and provide new direction for some of the problems we are drawn to address? Are there issues that a faculty of Jewish studies can engage in collectively, that transcend the limits of individual research initiative? If, indeed, we adopt as a rationale for the work we do the desire to learn about Judaism in all of its forms—"Judaism" used here as a term that encompasses the living entity of the Jewish people—how far toward the fulfillment of such a staggeringly ambitious goal can we expect to move on our own?

By its nature, research in the humanities may be a solitary enterprise, but virtually all scholars in Jewish studies would affirm the wish to discuss ideas about Judaism and the Jews with their closest scholarly peers. Among a broad range of issues that warrant serious reflection today, it makes sense for colleagues to ponder in common the very nature and aims of Jewish studies. The thrust of this question is so enormous and the educational means so underdeveloped that most scholars are apt to retreat from the challenge. In general, the teaching and research missions of universities have not been formulated to solve national, cultural, social, and other human problems, and it would be a mistake to think that they exist for such purposes. At the same time, such problems have a sizable impact on the educational work that universities carry out, and we cannot ignore them or pretend that they make no special demands upon us.

Without doubt, the very existence of Jewish studies already functions as a constructive source of melioration for some of the problems I have alluded to. That is a sizable good in itself, and will continue to yield positive results for the students who come to study with us. A reasonable argument may be made, therefore, that this is sufficient. It may also be argued, however, that at this time when external realities exert a growing impact on the mission of the university, and when various other departments and programs on campus consciously aim to link the work they do to extra-academic agendas of a social and political nature, it may be anomalous for the faculty connected to Jewish studies to lose sight of the broader implications of our own work. While we cannot "solve" the manifold problems besetting the Jews, our educational work is clearly not without social, cultural, and political challenges and opportunities of a compelling kind. The question is, to what extent do we wish consciously and programmatically to reply to these challenges and take advantage of the opportunities before us?

It is probably the case that on most college campuses the faculty members who comprise Jewish studies programs have not asked themselves this question in any direct or serious way. And it is certainly the case that, if the question were to be considered, no ready consensus would emerge. Such a prospect should neither surprise nor disturb us. All that matters at this point is that we agree the question itself is a credible and necessary one and that, as faculty groups, Jewish studies scholars set aside the necessary time to discuss it seriously.

CANADA
Michael Brown

To a considerable degree, Jewish studies programs in Canadian universities have followed the patterns set in other countries, especially the United States. Until well after World War II, where such courses existed at all they tended to serve as the handmaiden of the study of Christianity. In the mid-1960s, increasing acceptance of the legitimacy of Judaism and the growing respectability of ethnic affiliation led to a broadening of the curriculum, which included the study of Jews and Judaism in their own right. Today there are extensive Jewish studies programs in several universities, most notably those located in Toronto (York and the University of Toronto), and Montreal (McGill, Concordia, and l'Université de Montréal), where more than two-thirds of Canadian Jews live. Courses and nascent programs can be found in others of Canada's fifty universities, in a few community colleges, and in the junior colleges of Quebec.

There are, however, some unique aspects of Jewish studies in Canada. An early anomaly of note is the career of Abraham De Sola. Montreal's first rabbi (he was often referred to as "hazzan," in the manner of the Sephardim), De Sola taught Jewish studies at McGill University for many years beginning in 1849, and was awarded an honorary doctorate by that institution, probably the first one bestowed upon a Jew in the English-speaking world.[1] De Sola exemplifies some aspects of nineteenth-century *Wissenschaft,* as outlined by Nathan Rotenstreich. Despite his commitment to "scientific" methodology, there was an apologetic tone to his scholarly endeavors, which were designed, in part, to increase the respectability of Jews and Judaism. Unlike most of his European contemporaries, however, De Sola was staunchly Orthodox in his religious commitments. Moreover, elsewhere in North America and in Europe in those years, such teaching positions were reserved for Christians, often converts from Judaism. McGill was an exception, as was De Sola. Especially for provincial, mid-nineteenth-century Montreal, he was a person of unusually catholic interests and learning. After his death in 1882, Jewish studies at McGill were taught by Christians; and by the early twentieth century that university was pursuing the same discriminatory policies toward Jews followed by most other North American universities.

Of much wider significance are the unusual features of the recent Canadian context for Jewish studies. Until well after World War II, most Canadians regarded their country as a binational, bilingual, bicultural, bireligious federation of French Canadians—who were Roman Catholic, Francophone, and of French origin—and English Canadians, who were Protestant (some were Irish Catholics), English-speaking, and of British origin. Although Jews and Judaism usually fared quite well, they had no recognized, institutionalized place in what was generally regarded as a Christian country. In Quebec for a number of years, they were declared to be Protestants juridically, so that Jewish children could be accommodated in the public schools, which were either Protestant or Catholic. In the university curriculum, Judaism was inevitably studied as the precursor to Christianity.

By the 1960s, Canadians were beginning to look at their country differently. Large numbers of people who were not of British or French origin had immigrated after World War II. French-Canadian nationalists increasingly expressed a desire for autonomy and even "separatism" (independence), thereby threatening the integrity of the country. And the winds of the "new ethnicity" blew northward over the forty-ninth parallel. The result was a revised concept of the nation—Canada as a cultural mosaic, rather than a binational federation—designed to give a measure of autonomy to French Canadians, but to neutralize it by diffusing ethnic rights. Recognition and privileges were granted to the various ethnic groups in the country. The mosaic concept received official sanction and definition in the 1971 policy statement of the federal government on multiculturalism. The "special status of the British and French cultural traditions" was swept away "in favor of ethnic diversity and cultural pluralism, as more authentic reflections of Canadian identity." [2] Theoretically, at least, Jews became one of many legitimately distinct ethnocultural groups in Canada.

There was now validity to ethnic groups seeking to strengthen their own communities in different ways, which included the academic study of their traditions and thought. Moreover, studying ethnic groups became particularly appropriate in the new political context. In an effort to promote the mosaic concept, financing for ethnic studies—including Jewish studies—at the university and lower educational levels was made available by federal, provincial, and local governments. By mid-1993, the federal government, through the Ministry of Multiculturalism, had provided endowments for twenty-six chairs of ethnic studies across the country. In the spring of 1993, the Ministry awarded a shared endowment to York and Concordia universities for Canadian-Jewish studies projects.

It may be noteworthy that especially in the universities, the notion of ethnic studies met with certain reservations. Skeptics voiced fears that scarce funds would be diverted from other areas, that ethnic power might contribute to the Balkanization of society, and that ethnic communities would seek to subvert academic standards and "objectivity" by insisting that ethnic studies be used to reinforce communal identity. On the whole, however, the process of broadening offerings to include the study of Jews and other ethnic groups has proceeded smoothly. Moreover, Jewish studies have maintained an admirable reputation for superior scholarship and academic achievement; faculty members have included a number of world-renowned scholars. This has been the case even though, for the most part, Jewish studies appeal mostly to Jewish students in Canada, where ethnic loyalties continue to be much stronger than in the United States. Thus, Jewish studies in post-World War II Canada serve both as an indicator of the integration of Jews into the general society, and as a means of differentiating Jews from others.

It is not only official multiculturalism that makes the Canadian context unique. Of almost equal consequence is the lack of a strong notion of separation of church and state, coupled with considerable religious diversity. The former two-nations concept of the country gave religion constitutional status, which has been diminished but not abolished by the cultural pluralism model. At least in English Canada, some of the evils of an established church have been avoided by widespread religious diversity. Although all major universities in the country are now provincial institutions, several retain affiliated denominational colleges. Impartiality is maintained not by eliminating religious ties, but by including colleges of several religious groups.

There has never been a Jewish college at any Canadian university, although from time to time discussions about such a possibility have taken place. At three universities, however, programs have emerged that are designed to train personnel for the Jewish community (teacher preparation programs at McGill and York; a social work program at the University of Toronto). Although unabashedly particularistic in their goals, these professional training programs are not seen as problematic in the Canadian context. Their setting in the secular university, moreover, serves to broaden their scope.

The present Canadian university context, then, encourages the interface of the particular and the universal with the aim of strengthening both. It tends to be considerably more nurturing of particularism than is true in the United States. Its goals in this respect are furthered by strong academic connections with Israel through numerous student and faculty exchanges and through the activities of the International Center for the University Teaching of Jewish Civilization. These ties serve as a counterweight to homogenizing pan–North American influences, by providing links to scholars and institutions in Israel and around the world.

NOTES

1. On De Sola, see Michael Brown, *Jew or Juif? Jews, French Canadians, and Anglo-Canadians, 1759–1914* (Philadelphia: Jewish Publication Society, 1987), *passim*; and Gerald Tulchinsky, *Taking Root: The Origins of the Canadian Jewish Community* (Hanover, NH, and London: University Press of New England, 1993), pp. 40–60; and the sources cited in both works.
2. Harold Troper, "Ethnic Studies and the Classroom Discussion of Antisemitism: Personal Reflections," in *Approaches to Antisemitism: Context and Curriculum*, ed. Michael Brown (New York: The American Jewish Committee and the International Center for the University Teaching of Jewish Civilization, 1994).

LATIN AMERICA
Haim Avni and Leonardo Senkman

Development of Jewish studies in Latin American universities lagged far behind other parts of the world. When the universities of Lima, Mexico,

Córdoba, and other colonial centers were created, the predominance of the Catholic Church over their management, and the special character of the church in the Spanish colonies, precluded any academic interest in the spiritual heritage and the history of the Jewish people.

The process of secularization that penetrated the schools of higher education at the turn of the century incorporated a profound detachment from, if not a clear animosity toward, the religious establishment that had dominated national life and learning for so many centuries. Judaism, considered exclusively as a religion (of an extinguished and phantom people) was not deemed to be worthy of academic study. Whenever efforts were made to introduce Jewish studies into the university, as was the case in Mexico in the early 1940s, it was due to the individual initiatives of some Jewish intellectuals and was always limited to the Hebrew language and a small dose of Jewish culture.

By the late 1960s things had changed. In Santiago, Chile, and in São Paulo, Brazil, successful efforts were made to establish centers for Jewish studies in the faculties of humanities of the national universities. At that time, a chair for Hebrew Language in the Department of Ancient Studies of the University of Buenos Aires already existed. Rabbi Fritz Pincus, the spiritual leader of the major community of São Paulo, created a Center of Jewish Studies at the University of São Paulo, which acquired particular importance during the 1970s and 1980s. In Brazil, as well as on a more limited scale, in the Universidad Nacional de Chile, these efforts were supported by the Memorial Foundation for Jewish Culture. The general curriculum of these universities had thus been enriched by an external factor.

After several years, and due to the dedication of several Jewish faculty members in the departments of history and of letters, the Center of Jewish Studies at the University of São Paulo achieved official recognition and was integrated into the Faculty of Humanities. Annually, hundreds of undergraduate students are enrolled in the Center, and some of them proceed to take graduate courses within the graduate studies program of the Center and to choose Jewish themes for their theses.

Jewish studies in Argentine universities did not develop along the lines followed in other countries following World War II. As in other Latin American countries, Argentina rejected the legitimacy of Judaism and did not accept cultural pluralism until the 1970s. Notwithstanding the fact that non-Catholic foreigners were then granted civil and religious equality, the national culture still recognized the immigrant communities solely as religious and ethnic institutions. Judaism, too, was considered exclusively as a religion, and Hebrew was taught solely as the language of the Holy Bible in Universidad de Buenos Aires as late as the 1950s.

Although Buenos Aires has the largest Jewish community in Latin America, the university there did not have a Jewish studies program, but individual courses were introduced in various frameworks. Since the 1960s, for example, a course on the ancient history of the Jewish people was taught within the Oriental Studies Center.

During the 1960s through the mid-1970s Argentina underwent a profound process of secular modernization in which thousands of Jewish intellectuals, academicians, and students participated. The bulk of the Jewish intellectuals were secular, and perceived Judaism only in terms of synagogue affiliation; they separated themselves from the community and its religious culture, in favor of the more attractive challenges of an open society and local politics. Jews comprised a strikingly high percentage of university students relative to their small numbers in the Argentine population. They entered the state university not only to acquire a profession, but in order to become part of the national society. During the 1960s and 1970s Argentine universities were transformed from academic centers into political arenas seeking to mobilize the mass of students for national goals. There was an attempt to delegitimize any area of the humanities and social sciences (including Jewish studies) that was not "politically correct." Within this context of indoctrination, some courses given at Universidad de Buenos Aires on modern Israel and on the Arab-Israel conflict became the focus of a politicized treatment of the history of Israel. At the same time, the military regime that controlled Argentina from 1976 to 1982 drastically limited expenditure on public education, destroyed academic standards, and brutally repressed the left-wing and liberal teachers, sometimes with an evident anti-Semitic bias.

At the same time, the emergence of private institutions of higher learning, such as Universidad de Belgrano and Universidad de El Salvador, attracted a large number of Jewish students whose parents feared the politicization of the national universities. However, few Jews took courses in Jewish studies. Paradoxically, the first initiative to establish a Jewish studies program at the Universidad de Buenos Aires was taken during the last years of the military regime (1980–1981).

With the restoration of democracy, Argentine political leaders and citizens began to accept a revised concept of the nation as a legitimate pluralistic mosaic of ethnic and cultural diversity. This new view of national identity theoretically provides legitimacy to Jews as an ethno-cultural group in contemporary Argentina. In this more optimistic context, Jewish studies and research may be able to expand. Since ethnic loyalties continue to be strong, Jewish studies appeal mostly to Jewish students. In 1982 a non-credit limited program of Jewish studies was set up in the faculty of humanities at Universidad de Buenos Aires, with the academic assistance of The Hebrew University of Jerusalem, which appoints visiting professors annually. In addition, a recently established (1982) private academic institution, Universidad Maimonides, offers Jewish studies; and a "Jewish University" will open faculties of psychology and of humanities.

As in Brazil and Chile, Jewish studies in Argentina have been made possible thanks to academic agreements signed between Israeli universities and the institutions of higher learning, without any community support or sponsorship of local scholars. The absence of such encouragement and the strong academic connections with Israeli universities through faculty exchanges and the activities of the International Center for University Teaching of Jewish Civilization demonstrate the vital role of Israel in this field.

The Argentine Jewish community is aware of the need for Jewish civilization studies within the universities, to provide recognition of its cultural status in the pluralistic national culture, and to meet the needs of the large Jewish student population. At the same time, local and Israeli scholarly groups recognize that no university-based program in Jewish studies can grow without ample demonstration of the value of such scholarship and teaching to the wider values of the community at large.

GREAT BRITAIN
Philip S. Alexander

The chapters by Ephraim Urbach, Nathan Rotenstreich, and David Sidorsky, each in its own way, set out incisively and eloquently some of the major issues facing Jewish studies today. I find myself in broad agreement with what they say, but I feel there is a need for clarification or refinement of a few points.

Urbach seems to me a little too sanguine that the recognition and the standing of Jewish studies in higher education is now assured. This judgment is, in my view, rather premature. The intellectual argument for the entitlement of Jewish studies to a place in the university curriculum has largely been won; the basic case was formulated by the scholars of the *Wissenschaft des Judentums* in the nineteenth century. But the actual acceptance of Jewish studies in institutions of higher learning still remains very patchy. The level of acceptance found in the United States is not replicated elsewhere except, of course, in Israel. I would suggest that it may be a matter of kind, and may point to fundamental differences in educational philosophy. Certainly a very different situation pertains in Britain and, I believe, in Europe as a whole.

I detect a subtly different attitude in the chapters by Rotenstreich and Urbach toward the *Wissenschaft des Judentums* movement that forms the hinterland of the present-day discipline of Jewish studies. Rotenstreich stresses the apologetic concerns of the Science of Judaism both in its program and in its realization in concrete research. This is undeniably true, and has been abundantly documented, but we should not assume that Jewish studies today are somehow more objective and lack hidden agendas. Foucault exaggerates only slightly when he claims that all knowledge (even scientific knowledge) is "political." The solution to this problem is not to deny the existence of bias, but to develop as part of our critical skills a sophisticated awareness of the historical and social pressures under which we all conduct our research, and to bear those pressures in mind when we read each other's work. I am impressed by the continuities between the Science of Judaism and Jewish studies today. At a practical level it is surely not difficult for any of us now, when using the great classics of the *Wissenschaft des Judentums,* to distinguish between their "apologetics" and their "scholarship." In much the same way, no doubt, future generations will distinguish between our "apologetics" and our "scholarship."

This naturally leads me to a final preliminary observation touching on a burning issue that Urbach, Rotenstreich, and Sidorsky skirt, but which I feel needs to be addressed head on. That issue may be starkly formulated in the following question: What part does Jewish studies in higher education play in the survival of Judaism? Urbach asserts *en passant* that the scope of Jewish studies has broadened to such an extent that it constitutes a chapter of its own in the contemporary history of the Jewish people and *in the evolution of their culture* [my emphasis]. Rotenstreich alludes, apparently with approval, to Scholem's view that since Judaism is "an ongoing creativity . . . the scientific approach and scholarly findings have to be incorporated into its renaissance." This view is realistic and simply reflects the ineluctable fact that the object of Jewish studies is a living and developing tradition. But it has some intriguing implications. It decisively refutes the myth that the specialist in Jewish studies works in a Platonic world beyond history; and it implies that non-Jewish scholars working in the field of Jewish studies are contributing to the transmission of Judaism. (That paradox is more apparent than real, since the situation is readily paralleled in other cases where academics become involved in the study of cultures that are not their own.) It involves a return to a broad, almost premodern, definition of Judaism, and a reversal of the trend, powerful since emancipation— in which, paradoxically, many traditionalists connive—to define Judaism in narrow, denominational terms. (Note in this context Rotenstreich's reference to the Science of Judaism as involving "a thematic extension of the notion of Judaism," and Urbach's comment that the stated goal of the Institute for Jewish Studies founded in Jerusalem in 1925, to know "Judaism in all its forms," implies a definition of Judaism that "encompasses the living entity of the Jewish people.")

Rotenstreich stresses the discontinuity between the *Wissenschaft des Judentums* and the traditional study of Judaism. That discontinuity was certainly played up both by Zunz and his collaborators on the one hand, and by the traditionalists on the other. It can, however, be overstated. In fact, the modern academic study of Judaism shadows in an uncanny way the traditional religious study of Judaism. Modernity is often a chimera. That point is, perhaps, somewhat easier to grasp in a place like Oxford, where one is surrounded by constant reminders that the modern university has a premodern, monastic past. The academic study of Judaism is arguably as passionately concerned with the preservation, interpretation, and transmission of Jewish tradition as is the study of Judaism in the most traditionalist yeshivah. This may go some way toward explaining the fact, correctly noted by Urbach, that Orthodox Jewish scholars have found it increasingly comfortable to work in the academic sphere. Jewish studies has emerged as an autonomous field that is strictly speaking neither secular nor religious, but academic—a field in which the religious and the secular share sufficient aims and objectives to allow them to work together constructively.

It now seems broadly agreed what subjects belong to the field, how those subjects interrelate and how they should be studied. Of course, at a philosophical level the definition of Jewish studies remains intensely problematic (as the papers of Urbach, Rotenstreich, and Sidorsky clearly show), but an acknowledgment of this problem should not obscure the consensus that has emerged. Faced with a concrete monograph, a Jewish studies expert will usually have no hesitation in saying whether or not it belongs to his field, however remote its subject matter or its methodology may be from his own scholarly interests. The field is reasonably well articulated, and its principles are generally agreed upon. Adjustments and refinements will doubtless continue to be made, but the greater challenge that now faces Jewish studies is how to achieve its aims and implement its principles in the real world of higher education. For complex historical and political reasons the issues to be addressed differ somewhat from country to country, and depend on the ethos of the educational systems in which Jewish studies is seeking to function.

Jewish studies in Britain has been affected by the profound political and social changes that the country underwent in the 1980s. In that decade, intellectual life was dominated by a political doctrine that came to be known loosely as Thatcherism. A hallmark of this doctrine was its relentless challenge to established ideas and institutions that were seen as bastions of vested interest. Higher education did not escape scrutiny. It would be misleading to suggest that Thatcherism as applied to education was a fully developed, coherent philosophy (in fact it was riddled with unresolved tensions and contradictions), but that policy could be seen as the outworking of a small number of key ideas.

Among those ideas the following deserve to be highlighted:

1. Education should be useful. Utility tended to be defined in rather "hard-nosed" economic terms. The universities and other institutions of tertiary education in Britain are state funded, and they were expected to turn out students with the necessary skills to work in industry and commerce, in the professions and the public services. Education was no longer valued so much as an end in itself (offering self-improvement or self-fulfillment), but as a way of acquiring knowledge and ability or practical or vocational purposes.

2. The educational system should be opened up to market forces. Universities purvey a product (degrees) to consumers or customers (students). One effect of the application of this principle was to give students a greater say over the content of their courses (after all, as "customers" they must be, in the old commercial adage, "always right"), and to curtail the powers of faculty to prescribe the syllabus. Market forces operated not only between the universities and their students, but also between the universities and the governmental agency (the Higher Education Funding Council and its predecessors) that funds tertiary education. Universities had to bid for funds, which were awarded by competition, on the basis of efficiency measured by certain performance indicators.

3. Universities should be required to exercise tight fiscal control over their expenditure, and to eliminate inefficiency and waste. To this end a set of mechanisms was devised that revolutionized university finances. The basic unit of cost was fixed as the cost per annum of training a student taking a given course; that cost varied considerably according to the nature of the course—humanities costing less than science courses. The level of funding for each unit was determined, not by the universities, but by the Higher Education Funding Council. The effect of this mechanism was to make it immediately clear in accounting terms which courses were paying their way, and which were not. The question was simple. Once the cost of an existing course was calculated in terms of staff salaries, accommodation, library resources, and so on, it was easy to work out the number of students that needed to be enrolled for the course to be financially self-supporting. Another fiscal mechanism involved separate funding for teaching and for research. The notion that university teaching was distinctive by its research component was abandoned; research was no longer to be seen as the prerogative or the duty of every university teacher. The limited funds were allocated throughout the system on the basis of competition, and awarded, in theory, only to those with proven research records.

Each of these three principles spells trouble for a subject such as Jewish studies. Within this framework it is difficult to justify a place for Jewish studies in the university curriculum, for it has no obvious "utility." Traditional arguments about the Hebraic factor in Western civilization (however compelling intellectually) cut no ice. Nor are attempts to bring Jewish studies under the umbrella of ethnic studies likely to be successful. There is little stomach for ethnic studies in Britain, and even if there were, the Jewish community in Britain is well integrated into society and is no longer seen as an alien presence. There is a long tradition in Britain (going back to the imperial expansion of the Victorian era) of justifying Oriental studies on the grounds of national interest (trade and foreign policy). That tradition was reaffirmed only a few years ago in the Parker Report, which, at the government's behest, made recommendations regarding the teaching of Oriental studies in the United Kingdom. But a utilitarian case can only be made for languages such as Arabic, Chinese, or Japanese; it cannot be made for Hebrew.

The recognition of Jewish studies as an autonomous discipline in British universities is far from secure. This was illustrated in the Research Assessment Exercise carried out under the auspices of the Higher Education Funding Council. As a result of persistent lobbying by the British Association for Jewish Studies, a Jewish studies advisor was appointed, but he was attached very firmly to the Middle Eastern Studies Panel and as a result was able to comment on only a small portion of Jewish studies in Britain. The field is, for the most part, split up among other disciplines (Oriental studies, religious studies, history, sociology, and so forth), and it is often taught more by fortunate accident than by design. For example, a history department may appoint an expert in modern British history who happens to be interested as well in the history of the Jews in Britain, does some research in this subject, and offers courses in it.

Market forces also create problems for Jewish studies. Experience shows that if students are given a free choice, they will avoid courses with strong linguistic, textual, and philological content, and gravitate toward more general courses that focus on religion, history, or sociology. There are very few students in Britain taking Jewish studies in departments of Middle Eastern or Oriental studies. As a result, the core linguistic and textual subjects are being badly neglected. Jewish studies runs the risk of suffering the fate which befell classics some time ago. Under the pressure of student demand the linguistic element in classics was steadily whittled down, until finally classical civilization courses were substituted in which the primary texts were read only in English translation.

The new funding mechanisms make it clear that Jewish studies, along with other minority subjects, is all too often not paying its way, because it does not attract enough students. It can be seen as a luxury which the financially strapped educational system can ill afford. Jewish studies courses are required to improve their staff-student ratios, and as a result they can be pressured into accepting students who are not able to cope with the academic demands of the course. Once students are admitted, departments feel a moral obligation to see them through, which can lead in subtle ways to a lowering of academic standards.

It is hard to take the pulse of Jewish studies in Britain today; ostensibly it has not fared too badly over the past ten years. When the British Association for Jewish Studies was set up some twelve years ago, it had a membership of about eighty; now it has a membership of around two hundred. Moreover, the number of Jewish studies courses offered throughout the country, and the number of students taking those courses, has greatly increased. However, the expansion has lagged dramatically behind what has been achieved elsewhere in the world (notably in the United States). Only a handful of new posts in Jewish studies have been created, at the Oxford Centre for Postgraduate Hebrew Studies, and at University College, London. The increase in membership of the British Association for Jewish Studies largely reflects the recruitment of scholars in other disciplines who have a collateral interest in Jewish studies. Though the support of these colleagues is most welcome, they cannot fulfill the functions of mainline Jewish scholars. All in all, Jewish studies in Britain rests on shaky foundations.

What is to be done to address the situation?

1. It is important not to give up the intellectual battle for the place of Jewish studies in tertiary education. The arguments should probably be directed primarily at colleagues working in other fields. Ministers of state tend to be moved only by utilitarian considerations; academic colleagues are more likely to take a broader, humanistic view. The indispensability of Jewish studies can be demonstrated in a practical way by engaging in interdisciplinary teaching and research.

2. It is necessary to attract external funding. State funding for Jewish studies has always been small, and is likely to decline. External funding fits in well with the government's policy of encouraging private investment in public services such as health and education. Certain advantages accrue to universities from winning external funding, so they are not averse to the expansion of minority subjects, provided the money comes from outside.

3. The most obvious source of funding for Jewish studies is the Jewish community. That community still needs to be convinced of the value of supporting such studies at the tertiary level. There is a deeply ingrained suspicion of higher education in British society, a feeling that the universities are "ivory towers" with little relevance to the real world. This attitude has rubbed off to some degree on the Jewish community. Jewish studies scholars must be prepared to popularize their subject, and to explain, in ways that relate to the community's concerns, why it deserves support. This must be done, of course, without compromising academic independence and integrity.

4. Finally, it is essential that the various centers of Jewish studies should cooperate. Jewish studies in Britain is badly underresourced, and there is nothing to be gained from competition. Collaboration offers a chance of maximizing scarce resources, and it need not stop at national borders. One can make a compelling case for cooperation among Jewish studies centers, and for growing interchange of university staff and students within the increasingly integrated European community.

In the grand academic scheme of things Jewish studies will always be a minority subject, spread thinly through the educational system. It is imperative, therefore, to globalize it, that is to say, to ensure that the various centers are mutually supportive. Without such networking, the smaller centers run the risk of withering in isolation.

FRANCE
Roland Goetschel

Jewish studies were introduced in France in the 1830s by scholars of German origin—J. Dérenbourg, M. Bréal, and J. Halevy—within such established disciplines as archeology, ancient history, and philology. For example, S. Munk's (1803–1867) research in Hebrew manuscripts within the context of medieval philosophy demonstrated the contribution of the Jews to medieval thinking and to their serving as a bridge between Arab-Islamic philosophy and Christian theology. The studies of Perinne Simon-Nahum showed that the work of medieval Jewish thinkers who dealt with questions of universalism, or of the particular nature of Judaism and its authenticity, were relevant to the preoccupations of mid-nineteenth-century French Jews. Thus the academic study of Judaism was shown to be pertinent both to the Jewish community and to the French people at large.

A second generation of Jewish scholars—James Darmsteter, Theodor Reinach, d'Hartung, and Sylvain Levi—appeared in the 1880s; though they were interested in Judaism, they were more fascinated by Islamic culture and Indian studies. Nonetheless, in 1880, the Société des Etudes Juives emerged from this group. It published its scholarly papers in the *Revue des Etudes Juives,* which is still the main French-language publication dealing with Jewish studies.

After World War II, when Jewish studies burgeoned in the United States and expanded in Western Europe, they expanded in France as well. Prior to 1955, these subjects were taught only in theological schools and in departments of ancient and medieval history, philology, and Semitic languages, offered by the College de France and the Ecole Pratique des Hautes-Etudes (sections 4 and 5) in Paris. The outstanding figure in the field was Georges Vajda, who directed the academic program of the Ecole Pratique des Hautes-Etudes and, until his death in 1981, served as director of research of the Oriental (Arabic and Hebrew) Division of the Institut de Recherches et d'Histoire des Textes. A breakthrough occurred in 1955 with the creation of a chair in postbiblical Jewish literature at the University of Strasbourg. The incumbent was André Neher, who, rather than teaching within the framework of the history of religions, as had been proposed, chose to teach in the department of foreign languages, literatures, and civilizations, thus conferring university status on the teaching of modern Hebrew, Israeli literature, and contemporary Israeli civilization. In 1960, Neher created a program for teachers of Hebrew in Strasbourg, leading to a diploma in higher Hebrew studies and later to the granting of doctorates. This achievement was important in that it introduced Jewish studies in French universities, and made possible the teaching of Hebrew as a living language in secondary schools that recognized it as a subject for the *baccalaureat* (matriculation). At the end of the 1980s, some fifteen hundred pupils were studying modern Hebrew in public high schools, and about three thousand more were students in Jewish frameworks recognized by the state.

The arrival of Jews from North Africa introduced a new dynamism to the teaching of Jewish subjects in the universities. A chair of Hebrew was created in 1958 at the Institut National des Langues Orientales

(INALCO), where elective courses had been taught since 1938. In 1961, another chair of Hebrew was established in Lille. Interest in Hebrew grew after the Six Day War and in the wake of the reform in French higher education (1968). Full Hebrew programs now exist in Paris VIII, Paris II, and Lyon II; and courses are offered in Lille, Nancy, and Aix-Marseille.

Jewish civilization has become a subject for research in the disciplines of the social sciences, ethnography, sociology, and politics. Upon the initiative of the Fondation du Judaism Français, a program in Jewish studies was established in 1982 at the Ecole des Hautes Etudes en Sciences Sociales, which hosts lecturers from the United States and Israel. Research centers at the university level have been established at Paris VIII, Paris-Sorbonne, and elsewhere, and Hebrew courses are now offered in eleven French universities. In addition, several publishing houses produce volumes dealing with Jewish history, society, and thought, as well as translations of traditional texts and of Hebrew and Yiddish literature. Intellectual Jewish life in France is also featured in many symposia; a symposium of francophone Jewish intellectuals, for example, is organized every year by the French section of the World Jewish Congress. The community agencies, especially the Fonds Social Juif Unifié, understand the importance of Jewish studies for the future of French Jewry, and have created the Commission Universitaire du F.S.J.U. to serve as an organ of communication and coordination among the major responsible bodies teaching Jewish studies at the university level.

Although the academic frameworks continue to exist and some have expanded, a decline is currently apparent in the number of courses offered; about 1,000 students were enrolled in Jewish studies courses in 1986/87. Various factors, such as the weakening of the humanities and the social sciences in favor of the pure sciences and economics, have contributed to this decline. One must also take into account the departure for Israel of a number of Jewish students, many of them of high caliber, following their secondary education. Non-Jewish students who would at one time have studied Hebrew are now interested, for pragmatic reasons, in Chinese and Japanese. Nor should one ignore the effect of the French media, which has systematically portrayed a negative image of Israel.

Despite these difficulties, we are certain that teaching and research in

Jewish studies will continue to develop, given the cultural climate in France and the emergence of a cadre of young researchers and lecturers in the field. The creation of the Erasmus program, which has made possible the exchange of students and teachers between France and Italy, raises new hopes. One should also note the establishment by René Shmuel Sirat of the Institut Européen Rashi in Troyes, where the Congress of Jewish Studies, chaired by the late E. E. Urbach, was held in 1990. The essential conditions for further development are the recruitment of qualified teachers and researchers and a high level of training offered students. In this context, further exchanges and joint projects among teachers of Jewish studies in the different European universities are indispensable for the development of a critical mass of scholars that will enable European universities to achieve a position of repute within the field of Jewish studies. This is a realizable objective to which the International Center is particularly well equipped to contribute.

In retrospect, Jewish studies in France has gone through four periods:

1. The laying of the foundation in the nineteenth century, following the model of the German *Wissenschaft des Judentums* with its group of great scholars
2. The period of latency, through the post-World War II years
3. The period of growth beginning with the 1960s
4. The current period of maturation

The young generation of researchers and academics is currently seeking to develop a model for Jewish studies with uniquely French characteristics, that will relate both to the Israeli and the American model. The future will tell whether such an orientation will be realized.

SPAIN
Angel Saenz-Badillos

I have found Nathan Rotenstreich's analysis of the meaning of the *Wissenschaft des Judentums* and its transformation into "Jewish studies," viewed from the perspective of Judaism, very stimulating. However, since the teaching and research of Jewish civilization occurs, in most European universities, in a pluralistic, non-Jewish atmosphere, some observations should be added from the viewpoint of West European academics.

European scholars looked upon the development of the *Wissenschaft des Judentums* in the past century with sympathetic understanding. Before the modern renascence of Jewish culture, they were unable to evaluate the true significance of the contribution of the Jews to European civilization. From their point of view, it was absolutely necessary that the Jewish communities of Europe abandon their particularistic system of teaching and learning, compare their own culture with that of the countries in which they were living, and adopt the same techniques of study employed by Western scholars. Emergence from the isolation of a Jewish framework was required in order to make the cultural legacy of the Jewish people available to the rest of the world and integrate it within the broad panorama of national cultures without losing its uniqueness. We can very well understand the need felt by nineteenth-century Jewish scholars to show the creativity of Judaism in the postbiblical period, and to destroy negative stereotypes of the Jews.

In that sense, Western scholars admire the efforts made by the great masters of the *Wissenschaft des Judentums,* and applaud their results, particularly the research of original texts and materials, preparation of scientific editions of the classical Hebrew authors, and projection of new historical perspectives about the life of the Jews in European countries. They also accept willingly the destruction of the myths and distorted views about the Jews. Thanks to those efforts, the culture of the Jews in the European countries was able to be understood in its true dimensions.

The changes in this century have been still more significant, and they are, undoubtedly, connected with the reality of the State of Israel and its academic institutions. The results are self-evident, and for Western scholars it means that Jewish studies are being undertaken with the same hermeneutical, technical, and scientific methods employed in any other area of the humanities all over the world.

The "confessional" character of Jewish studies is not accepted by European scholars in our days. We do not agree to the idea of projecting into the neutral term "science" a religious or theological category such as the election of Israel, or the divine character of the Torah. We ask ourselves whether the Bible (leaving out its theological aspects) can be studied in the same way by a Jew, a Christian, or an agnostic scholar, or whether Judah Halevi can be understood to the same degree by an Israeli or a Japanese scholar. These are basic questions that determine whether the Science of Judaism is ready in our time to be incorporated into the Western academic world.

The same may be said about viewing the cultural evolution of European Jews as an exclusively internal process, emerging from biblical or rabbinic roots. Efforts to understand the history of the Jewish communities in the light of general history, and to evaluate their cultural, literary, scientific, or philosophical production in the light of the history of Western civilization, are seen to be necessary.

In many European universities, and concretely in Spain, Jewish studies are integrated within Hebrew philology, which may be parallel to English philology, classical philology, or Romance philology. This is something that must not be overlooked, even if scholars in other areas, such as medieval or contemporary history, can offer important studies related to the Jewish history of those periods.

With reference to the field I know better, I would say that the Hebrew language (or any of the Judaic languages) should be studied with the same methods used by modern literary criticism. A critical edition of a Hebrew work should be prepared with the same techniques and principles employed in classical, Romance, or Germanic studies; what is not accepted in those fields (as prescientific or nonscientific) cannot be employed for a Hebrew literary work, notwithstanding traditional usages. Even if Hebrew literature has its own uniqueness that should always be considered, it is necessary to try to understand it within the frame of the cultural background of the countries in which the works were written. In a similar vein, at a literary conference dealing with "La Celestina," for example, one can expect to meet as many English, German, or American scholars as Spaniards. Today, nobody thinks that it is necessary to be a Spaniard in order to become an expert in Spanish medieval literature.

We must avoid any partisanship or confessionalism in teaching Jewish studies, but that does not mean that we need not be enthusiastic in the research of Judaism. Just as a scholar interested in Shakespeare can become personally involved in those works and enjoy the characters and dialogue, research in Judaism does not need to be "cold" or impersonal. Jewish studies can be fascinating to both Jewish and non-Jewish scholars.

POLAND
Nikolai Iwanow

University teaching of Jewish civilization in contemporary Poland is a unique phenomenon, for this country is the largest Jewish cemetery in the world. For centuries Poland was the spiritual and intellectual center of East European Jewry; but the last chapter of Jewish history in this country is drawing to a close. Yet Jews are still present in everyday Polish life, in the Polish national consciousness, traditions, and historic experience. Indeed, some manifestations of anti-Semitism in today's Poland (which several politicians call "platonic anti-Semitism") have been attributed to the spiritual presence of Jews in this country.

During more than four decades the communist totalitarian regime kept the two extreme tendencies within Polish society—anti-Semitism and philo-Semitism—within strict ideologically motivated limits; only at times did it openly initiate organized "outbursts" of anti-Semitic feelings, due to a particular need of its domestic or international policy. The end of communism in Poland permitted an uncontrolled outburst within the general society of real and imaginary attitudes toward the Jews.

At the end of the 1980s, the number of books, newspaper articles, publications, films, theater performances and television discussions about Jews, Jewish culture and tradition, and Israel increased dramatically. This outburst of interest in Jews and Jewishness permeated the entire spectrum of political opinion within Polish society. It also had a great impact on higher education in Poland. Some universities initiated Jewish studies programs, organized lectures on Judaism and the history of Jewish civilization. These initiatives almost never came from the central Polish education authorities, but from local universities. In the case of Wroclaw University, the students themselves asked the authorities to organize a course of lectures in Jewish civilization.

The Mordechai Anielewich Center for Jewish Studies of Warsaw University plays the central role in the university teaching of Jewish civilization in Poland. Organized upon the initiative of Jerzy Tomaszewski, the Center provides lectures and seminars on the history of the Jews of Poland, the history of the State of Israel and the Zionist movement, and language courses in Hebrew and Yiddish.

The chair of Jewish history and culture at Jagellonian University in Cracow is headed by one of the most famous Polish historians and longtime rector of the university, Andrzej Gierowski. Apart from Hebrew language courses, the chair provides lectures and seminars on Polish-Jewish relations in the nineteenth and twentieth centuries, and on Jewish and Jewish-Polish literature.

Some elements of Jewish civilization studies are also present in the framework of ethnic and national minorities studies, in Wroclaw, Gdansk, and Lublin Universities. There are also individual scholars and teachers who, mainly on their own initiative, organize such lectures and courses in Katowice, Lodz, and Poznan, and in the teacher seminars of Cracow, Radom, and Kielce.

Other than in the Mordechai Anielewich center, the university teaching of Jewish civilization in Poland has very little connection with the country's Jewish community, and is organized almost exclusively by Poles and for Poles. Among its unique features one may note the following:

1. There is a growing interest in studying Jewish civilization, which is only partially satisfied because of the lack of qualified specialists in the field.

2. The academic community is open to contacts with Western scholars and institutions, and assistance in the sphere of Jewish civilization teaching and studies is willingly accepted. Such help is regarded as an expression of international scientific cooperation, and its Jewish aspect is to a certain extent suppressed.

3. The study of Jewish civilization is one of the most politicized subjects in the university curriculum. Some students enroll to learn about Jewish history, and find expression for their anti-Semitism. At times, the lectures and seminars are transformed into sharp political discussions that are difficult for a teacher to control and that threaten to turn the process of teaching into a means of spreading anti-Semitic feelings.

4. The painful sensitivity of national feelings is one of the most characteristic elements of the Polish national mentality. Anti-Jewish feelings are sometimes so strangely interwoven into this mentality that a teacher can hardly perceive it. That is why some students, who regard themselves as free of any prejudice against Jews, express solidarity and understanding with the views of open anti-Semites.

5. However, the bulk of the students are philo-Semites and take these

courses in order to express their great sympathy toward the Jewish people. They sincerely would like to understand the essence of the national character of the people who lived on the same land with Poles for more than eight hundred years.

All these aspects of teaching Jewish civilization in Poland create a unique emotional atmosphere of psychological alertness and readiness to absorb new material on the part of the students. This places special responsibility on the teacher and sometimes permits him or her to enter into closer relations with students.

The initial level of the students' preparation is rather low, so that teachers must introduce their course of lectures with preparatory lessons providing basic information about Jews, Israel, and the Jewish religion. With this in mind, thoughts of an interdisciplinary approach to the teaching of Jewish civilization appear to be unrealistic.

The university teaching of Jewish civilization is a new phenomenon in Poland, but it has many enthusiastic supporters, and opponents, as well as those who would like to channel it in an anti-Jewish direction. Thus, the task of disseminating accurate knowledge about the Jews must not remain an internal Polish issue, but become a common task undertaken by the international university community.

RUSSIA
Dmitri Eliashevitch

What are the peculiarities of Jewish studies in contemporary Russia, and what are the problems it has yet to face? First of all, one must note the priority of disciplinary studies in the university framework, and the almost nonexistence of interdisciplinary research. This often results in an unsatisfactory level of scholarship. Changing this approach is one of the most pressing tasks challenging Jewish studies in Russia today.

Another problem is the infiltration of ideology and politics into Jewish studies. Because everything related to the Jews and the Jewish question within the Russian Empire, the USSR, and now the Russian federation, emerges as a political phenomenon, any research in the field of

I want to express my thanks to Yulia Nejitovsky who assisted in preparing this section.

Judaica (or Hebraica) has also taken on political coloration. This has not encouraged scholarship of quality. Moreover, scholars themselves (especially Jewish scholars) frequently inserted into their work political and ideological elements in order to counter the attacks of anti-Semites. This is mostly true for works in Jewish history, sociology, and demography, but it is also apparent in academic research in the fields of biblical studies, Jewish philology and folklore, and even Jewish public health. Unfortunately, we do not have any reason to expect that the political and ideological element will disappear from Jewish studies in Russia as long as the "Jewish question" remains a political issue.

A third peculiarity in the field of Jewish studies in Russia relates to the ties between scholars and the Jewish community. Practically all Jewish scholars, who form the majority in the fields of Hebraica and Judaica, work with scientific and cultural-educational institutions founded or supported by Jewish communities. This fact should be considered to be a positive element. One must note that the long and varied history of teaching Jewish studies included yeshivot (talmudic academies) that taught biblical commentaries; faculties and departments of Hebraica (including Judaica) at the state universities; secular Jewish high schools, such as the Gunzburg courses of Eastern studies and the Petrograd Jewish University. And, lastly, the Orthodox Christian seminaries required their students to learn ancient Hebrew, biblical studies, and Jewish history of the periods of the Scriptures, First and Second Temples. Naturally, all these educational institutions differed in their offerings and approaches.

We will leave an analysis of the yeshivot and the seminaries aside, and focus on the state universities and secular Jewish educational institutions. The main purpose of teaching Jewish studies in the state universities was to prepare specialists in Hebraica (and to a lesser extent, Judaica) for teaching in academic institutions. The approach was purely academic, without any particularist flavor. The Gunzburg courses of Eastern studies and the Petrograd Jewish University saw as their main purpose cultivation of a national intelligentsia and development of a national Jewish culture. The teaching was academic, but to a certain extent partial, based on Jewish spiritual values.

The situation today is similar. Semitics departments of state universities continue to prepare academic specialists in Semitic philology or the history of the Middle East. Hebrew and the study of ancient Hebrew texts are the only well-organized disciplines. Jewish history, modern and contemporary Jewish literature, Jewish philosophy, and other subjects are taught only superficially, and Diaspora Jewish languages are completely absent from the curriculum. The explanation lies chiefly in historical ideological prejudices and in the extremely small number of qualified teachers, mostly of the older generation. Lately, curricular reorganization has started in the Semitics departments of state universities, but it is too early to evaluate practical results.

Since 1989, secular Jewish high schools have been revived. The first was St. Petersburg (formerly Petrograd) Jewish University. It enjoys state accreditation (awarding diplomas of higher education) and includes two departments (history-ethnography and philology), a Beit Midrash (focusing on Jewish texts), the Jewish Diaspora Institute, and the Institute of Jewish Pedagogy. The number of students is close to three hundred.

The activities of Moscow Jewish University are more limited and its student enrollment is smaller than that of its sister institution in St. Petersburg, but it is developing rapidly. It is achieving significant success in the publishing of Hebraica and Judaica scholarship.

The main problem both universities have to face is the absence of a qualified teaching staff. It is almost impossible to find lecturers in such subjects as the historical geography of the Diaspora, the history of European Jews in the Middle Ages and Renaissance, or the ideological movements among Russian Jewry. The "tours" of Israeli and American professors do not solve the problem because the lecturers are very limited in their time and do not understand the level of the students' knowledge.

The absence of modern Hebrew-language textbooks and scholarly literature is acute. In many cases the students have to turn to hundred-year-old monographs and textbooks, which obviously do not correspond with modern scientific views. The popular scholarly literature that is prepared in Russian in Israel often appears to be much too superficial and primitive in a certain way for students who have some experience in Jewish subjects.

The following suggestions focus on ways to solve these problems. First, it is necessary to prepare as quickly as possible a sufficient number of young teachers qualified to lecture on specific Jewish subjects. The occasional seminars held from time to time in Russia by different, mostly Israeli, organizations are insufficient for this purpose. A group of promising young people should be sent for a one-to-three-year program at important Israeli centers of study under the supervision of leading scholars. On returning, the members of this group would be capable of highly qualified and fruitful teaching. It is also important to make more scholarly and didactic literature available in Russian (publishing it mostly in Russia). For this purpose American and Israeli specialists should help their Russian colleagues choose such literature for translation.

Despite the serious problems and difficulties, there are grounds for believing that the scientific knowledge and study of Hebraica and Judaica will develop further in Russia. Of course, a necessary precondition for this is the stability of the political situation. There is hope, in my judgment, for maintaining, expanding, and deepening the teaching of Jewish national culture in Russia.

SOUTH AFRICA
Milton Shain

At a recent inauguration of the Mendel Kaplan Chair of Jewish Civilization at the University of Cape Town, the dean of arts, John Cartwright, noted that questions of "cultural identity, cultural difference, and ethnicity have become probably the most important and most difficult issue in South Africa and the world at large." The Jewish heritage, he maintained, "is one of the main streams of human culture, and the academic study of this heritage under the heading of 'Jewish civilization' not only provides Jews with the means to enrich their own lives through a fuller grasp of the range of their culture, past and present, but also can provide, in the way teaching and research are pursued in the area, a model for the fair minded explanation of cultural difference in a multicultural environment." These comments certainly augur well for Jewish studies at the University of Cape Town.

Acceptance of Jewish studies within the academy has not been without struggle, which imposes a profound responsibility upon the practitioners: engagement has to be unbiased, scientific, objective, and integrated into a wider body of scholarship informed by respected canons of inquiry and investigation. This is as true in Cape Town as it is in New York. Of paramount importance, however, is the integration of Jewish studies into a wider body of scholarship. The ever-present danger of academic ghettoization can only be combatted by scholarly exchange and interchange.

In South Africa at present one notices two intellectual thrusts: on the one hand an Afrocentric push and a call for curriculum "relevance"; on the other, a celebration of diversity and respect for pluralism. Although Jewish studies has a long pedigree at a number of South African universities (a chair of Hebrew was established at the University of Cape Town in 1896), in order to perpetuate its validity in the local context Jewish scholarship needs to relate to both thrusts. At all times "relevance" will be under the spotlight in a new South Africa. Jewish studies must contribute to other fields and its findings have to be integrated into other disciplines. In Cape Town, the Isaac and Jessie Kaplan Center for Jewish Studies and Research pursues such objectives. Visiting scholars are placed in appropriate departments to share expertise with as wide a sector of the academic and student community as is possible.

David Sidorsky's contention that politicized interpretations need to be dealt with in appropriate forums is a valuable observation, with some relevance for South Africa. Certainly at the University of Cape Town, with its high proportion of Jewish and Muslim students, debates surrounding the Israel-Palestinian conflict need to be moved outside of the classroom.

Thus far I have focused my comments on the University of Cape Town. Judaica, in one form or another, is also taught at the University of the Witwatersrand, Natal University, Stellenbosch University (essentially Semitics), and at the University of South Africa (UNISA), a long-distance learning institution. Unfortunately, programs at the University of the Witwatersrand and Natal University have recently been severely curtailed. This is particularly unfortunate since South Africa's well-established Jewish day school network demands trained Jewish studies teachers, rooted in Jewish sources. According to South Africa's most powerful political grouping, the African National Congress, the Jewish day school is under no threat. This is certainly encouraging and ought to ensure the importance of Jewish studies programs at the university level. Ultimately, however, the value of these programs will be judged by students and scholars on their relevance, academic merit, and on the ability of teachers to carry out impartial inquiry.

AUSTRALIA
Louis Waller

The discipline of Jewish studies in Australia's universities is in its early childhood, if not its infancy, even though courses, and even sequences, in subjects that are within the ambit of what is universally regarded as Jewish studies were first introduced into the two oldest nearly fifty years ago. It is only in the past two decades that courses in modern Jewish history and Jewish civilization have been offered in several institutions. Monash University in Melbourne has established the Australian Centre for Jewish Civilisation, committed to both undergraduate and graduate teaching in those areas, as well as in Jewish thought, literature, and language.

The Australian Jewish community was transformed by the immigration of tens of thousands of Holocaust survivors in the aftermath of World War II and by the creation of the State of Israel. What had been characterized in the 1930s as an Anglo-Jewish assimilating community, became one in which East and Central European Jewish experiences were much more prominent.

In those early postwar years, there were some significant developments in university education in what was, tellingly, entitled "Semitic studies." A chair and a department with that title were established in the University of Melbourne in 1945, through the generous gift of Lazarus and Abraham (Hyam) Sicree, two brothers strongly committed to Jewish values. The Melbourne department emphasized the study of biblical Hebrew and Aramaic, biblical archeology and related history, and comparative Semitic philology. Most of its students were drawn from theological colleges, associated with but not part of the secular university. Of those first endeavors in Melbourne, and to a somewhat similar degree in Sydney, Nathan Rotenstreich's observations about the apologetic approach of *Judische Wissenschaft* are apposite. Regrettably few Jewish students were attracted to these departments. After various vicissitudes, the Melbourne department no longer exists. Its Hebrew language and literature courses are offered under the aegis of the department of Classical studies. The University of Sydney's department continues to exist; it offers courses in Jewish and Islamic civilization.

It took the passage of several decades before Semitic studies gave way to Jewish studies and Jewish civilization, seen as disciplines standing alongside Australian studies, or European civilization. The transformation, which these titles signal in a particularly meaningful way, has been the result of changes in the Jewish community and in Australia as a nation. In the late 1970s the Jewish community first expressed its specific interest in Jewish studies and gave its material support through the Joint Committees for Tertiary Jewish Studies in both New South Wales and Victoria, where most of Australia's Jewish population lives. Concurrently, Australia's universities have responded to the economics of tertiary education, where student demand is crucial. Because of the country's self-characterization as a multicultural society recognizing and valuing the distinctive heritages of its many ethnic and national groups, including Australia's Aborigines, a broad range of language studies as well as cross- and multidisciplinary courses in area and civilization studies have been introduced. Universities have encouraged and fittingly acknowledged community support for such courses.

There are clearly shared interests between the Jewish community and the universities—as David Sidorsky has observed about the American situation. The Australian Jewish community sees the university programs providing, in Sidorsky's words, some positive consciousness-raising in young Jewish students. This is of high moment in a community most of whose secondary school graduates go on to universities.

Many of the recently established programs—on modern Jewish history, Holocaust history, and Jewish literature in English translation— have appealed to both Jewish and non-Jewish undergraduates. In a development directly oriented toward the Jewish community, the University of Sydney has and Monash University in Melbourne will offer pre-service and in-service teacher preparation courses in Jewish studies. These serve the immediate interests of the community's day schools and help to relieve them of their very heavy reliance on teachers recruited outside the country.

The future development and sustained existence of Jewish studies in Australian universities will depend largely on the quality of the scholars recruited as faculty, and of the students who are attracted to the programs. The current teachers, most holding subprofessional appointments, are either Australian graduates who have had some overseas training and experience, or a few scholars from overseas who have made their homes in the country. Important publications by some of these have now appeared, especially on Australian Jewish history. Strong connections exist between some Australian and several Israeli universities, with Australian students participating in overseas student programs at the Hebrew University. Monash University has had two senior scholars from Israel as distinguished visitors in its Centre of Jewish Civilisation, and expects this to develop and become an integral element in its academic offerings. The Australian Association of Jewish Studies, which publishes an academic journal, was founded several years ago. All these developments help to bring the very young Australian enterprise into the established scholarly company of the university teaching of Jewish civilization.

II

RECONSIDERATIONS: PROBLEMS AND PARTIAL SOLUTIONS

5. JEWISH STUDIES IN EUROPEAN UNIVERSITIES: ACTUAL AND POTENTIAL

Peter Schäfer

This essay does not propose to enumerate all the appropriate European institutions and summarize their achievements. I will, rather, outline basic features, and point to some problems that seem to me important when we consider the future of Jewish studies in Europe.

I believe I am correct in stating that Jewish studies at European universities emerged from two sources, namely, Christian theology and Semitic languages. Actually the sole and "natural" place for Jewish studies was Christian theology, but with the emancipation of Semitic languages (or "Oriental" studies, in the broader sense which includes both the language and the culture of the different "Oriental" peoples) as an independent field of learning, Jewish studies was integrated within that new framework. Both approaches are still prevalent today. It was only in the post–World War II period that Jewish studies in Europe has evolved as a separate subject, independent of either theology or Oriental studies.

The affiliation of Jewish studies with Christian theology has its own justification (and follows its own guidelines), insofar as Christianity defines itself as the offspring of Judaism and therefore requires Jewish studies in order to understand its own heritage. There can be no doubt, however, that Christian theology never was, and never can be, the proper place for Jewish studies in the true sense of that term. Despite the honorable attempts of scholars of Christian theology to teach Judaism in a historically unbiased way, and to engage in very serious and respectable research in different fields of Jewish studies (for example, in the period that they call, revealingly enough, the "intertestamental period"), it must be emphasized that the field of Jewish studies demands a place of its own within the subjects that constitute the university, that is, the *universitas litterarum*.

The picture is different when we consider Jewish studies as part of Semitic languages or Oriental studies. When I began to survey the various European universities that teach Judaism in one way or another, I was struck by the fact that many such courses are located in departments of Semitic languages or Hebrew, albeit under different titles. In England, Jewish studies at the Universities of Oxford and Cambridge are part of the Oriental Institute; in Manchester, Jewish studies (at least in part) belong to the Department of Middle Eastern Studies. The same holds true for the Université Paris II and VIII, as well as for the Institut National des Langues et Civilisations Orientales in Paris; for the Centre de Recherches et d'Etudes Hebraiques within the Faculté des Langues, Littératures et Civilisations Etrangères at the University of Strasbourg; and for the Istituto di Orientalistica at the Università degli Studi di Torino in Italy. At the Universidad Complutense de Madrid we find the Departamento de Hebreo y Arameo within the Facultad de Filologia. In the Netherlands, the University of Leyden is the host of a *vakgroep* (department) of Hebrew, Aramaic, and Ugaritic languages and cultures; and the Juda Palache Institute at the University of Amsterdam defines itself as a *vakgroep* for Hebrew, Aramaic, Syriac, and Jewish studies— an interesting combination indeed. In Germany, Jewish studies at the University of Freiburg belong to the Oriental Seminar, and at the University of Munich to the Seminar of Semitic Languages.

The advantages and disadvantages of such structures are obvious. Many of these departments are excellent in teaching Hebrew, not only biblical but also medieval and modern. But the danger is that Judaism is thereby restricted to language. It is true that language is the most important tool for studying a culture, but it is equally true that limiting study of a culture to its language runs the risk of making that study sterile. Judaism cannot be limited to Semitic languages, nor can it be defined within the framework of the "Orient" or the Near or Middle East alone. The latter is concerned with an important but nevertheless relatively small segment of Jewish history and leaves out European,

American, and other histories of Judaism. The addition of Jewish studies to Hebrew, Aramaic, and Syriac in Amsterdam shows how difficult it is to incorporate such courses into the confines of Semitic languages and cultures. It is no accident that many of these departments focus on ancient, mainly rabbinic, Jewish literature, and find it difficult to integrate modern Jewish history into their curriculum.

The third possibility, Jewish studies as a subject independent from the organizational and defining structure of either Christian theology or Semitic languages, was the desire of the *Wissenschaft des Judentums* for almost a century. Due to the well-known anti-Semitic attitudes of Germany's universities, this was realized in that country only after World War II, or, to put it more directly, after the Holocaust—after Germany had succeeded in destroying almost all of Jewish life and culture throughout Europe. This is one of the most tragic paradoxes of history. It is the heritage of those of my generation teaching Jewish studies in Germany today—a heritage that determines our scholarly work as well, on whatever remote "corner" of the history of Judaism it may be focused.

Since Jewish studies cannot be separated from the life and culture of the Jews, it is impossible today in Europe, and especially in Germany, to ignore the fate of the Jews in Germany during the Nazi regime. This does not mean that Jewish studies in Germany should deal only with the Holocaust or the history of anti-Semitism. On the contrary, Holocaust studies and the study of anti-Semitism should be situated within *general* history and sociology. Nevertheless, the Holocaust continues to influence our dealings with the history, literature, language, and culture of the Jews.

There are examples of the organization of Jewish studies in Europe as an independent subject (my third model) in England, at the Institute of Jewish Studies in University College, London, and at the Oxford Centre for Postgraduate Hebrew Studies; in Hungary, at the newly founded Institute of Jewish Studies in Budapest; in Sweden, at the University of Lund; and in Germany, at the universities of Cologne, Frankfurt, and Berlin. Some of the institutions previously mentioned should probably be added as well, insofar as the relation of Jewish studies to Semitic languages has become purely formal, and in reality independent institutes of Jewish studies are being developed.

Jewish studies taught as an independent subject, unrestricted by the canon of linguistics or regional studies, let alone by the standards and values of Christian theology, constitutes an important step forward. In this sense, Jewish studies has at its center the Jews *as Jews,* naturally in connection with their respective environments; the emphasis, however, is not upon the environment, but rather upon the Jew, upon the various possibilities of being Jewish in different historical and geographical constellations. This does not mean that Jewish studies determines what constitutes the "Jew" or "Jewishness" within the course of history. On the contrary, it is the purpose of Jewish studies to show the alterations and transformations of Judaism, the relation between a static and a dynamic state or, as Gershom Scholem has put it, between tradition and re-creation. The focal point is the variety and diversity of the Jews and of Judaism, not something else for which the Jews are "also" important.

Such a conception of Jewish studies also has its dangers. The independence or autonomy of which the institutes of Jewish studies in Europe are proud, and rightly so, may lead to an atmosphere of self-sufficiency and sterility that in turn can elevate the study of Judaism to a state of uniqueness and separate it from other disciplines. There is no special method to be employed for Jewish studies in contrast to other areas of teaching and research; the same methods are used as in the study of history, literature, sociology, religion, language, and so forth. The independent status of Jewish studies cannot be an end in itself, but needs to be supplemented by an interdisciplinary approach, through constant contact with, and enrichment by, other disciplines.

There is an additional problem directly related to the "independent" status of Jewish studies. All the institutes of Jewish studies in Europe are relatively small, and despite the fact that some of them are progressing well and even growing, they will never come close to any of the Jewish studies faculties in Israel or the United States. They usually consist of one or two chairs, with an entourage of some teaching and research assistants. How then does such an institute conceive and execute a curriculum that is worthy of its name and fulfills the requirements of its students?

If we define as the object of Jewish studies all aspects and manifestations of Jewish life and culture from the beginning of Jewish history up to the present, it should be more than obvious that such a discipline cannot be taught properly at any one of the very small institutes in Europe, even if there is reason to hope that the future will bring about some expansion of those already in existence, as well as the establishment of new ones. Thus the question remains of how to design a curriculum that conforms to the reality of a small staff but meets the requirements of students who do not wish to be forced into the more or less accidental specialties of their teachers.

1. One possible maximalist answer could be that the question is falsely formulated—that we should not be satisfied with what we have, but that the time has come to argue and fight for the most radical solution: a broadly conceived faculty of Jewish studies in at least one university in Europe that would be comparable to the important centers in Israel and the United States and that could serve as the focus for all the other smaller institutes. At present nobody can say whether such a concept belongs to the realm of pure fantasy or whether it has a chance of being realized, but I would venture to say that this is not utterly outside the realm of the imaginable.

2. A second answer to the question may be called the minimalistic-integrative approach: minimalistic insofar as it is satisfied with only one chair in Jewish studies, integrative insofar as it assembles around the nucleus of this one chair a whole department whose members are not part of the institute of Jewish studies, but rather come from various disciplines, for example, history, literature, religion, languages, and so forth.

This solution, which in the United States is generally called a "program in Jewish studies," would seem to be ideal, at least upon initial examination. It turns the most severe disadvantage of Jewish studies in Europe (the lack of positions and resources) into an advantage—what we cannot get from within, we recruit from outside—and fosters the interdisciplinary approach that can too easily be forgotten in a "self-sufficient" institute of Jewish studies.

However, I am afraid that this solution is not as satisfying as it may first appear. The situation at American universities is quite different from what exists in Europe. In America it may be possible to gather colleagues from different departments under the collective roof of Jewish studies; at European universities this is not possible, because we do not have enough specialists within these departments who can contribute to such a joint enterprise. The reason for this is not only lack of interest, but also the lack of knowledge of Hebrew and of any tradition integrating the study of Jews and Judaism into the scope of the various disciplines. This, in turn, is due to the weak presence of a vibrant Judaism at European universities. The situation may change in the future, but at present I am not very optimistic.

3. Confining ourselves, then, to what exists, what can be the requirements of a curriculum under the conditions outlined above? If I take the curriculum of the Berlin Institute as an example, I can say that there we have stated two things very clearly. First of all, we are convinced that it is absolutely necessary to place the Hebrew language at the center of all our endeavors—not in the sense of Hebrew linguistics (however important this certainly is), but as a tool to enable our students to read not only Jewish sources but also secondary literature in Hebrew. It is impossible today to deal with almost any field of Jewish studies without being able to have access to the vast secondary literature in Hebrew. To quote Lionel Kochan:

> [A danger] is created by what is apparently an increasing tendency to inquire into matters Jewish without a knowledge of Hebrew and/or other "Jewish" languages relevant to a particular context, e.g., Yiddish, Ladino, and Judaeo-Arabic. When the young giant Pantagruel went to study at the University of Paris, he was advised by his father Gargantua that for a knowledge of *les saintes lettres*, familiarity with Hebrew was an indispensable addition to the knowledge of Greek and Latin. This sage counsel has come increasingly to be disregarded. Not only does this mean that the scholar ignorant of Hebrew will be unable to consult secondary works in that language but, even more important, he will lack access to the sources themselves.[1]

It goes without saying that we are far from being able to claim that all of our students achieve this ideal, but this does not allow us to renounce it. It is necessary to make every effort to improve our teaching of Hebrew and to send as many students as possible to study in Israel.

We also believe that one of the focal points to be included in the curriculum of an institute of Jewish studies should be the literature and history of rabbinic Judaism, that is, of the classical or formative period. This period left its imprint on all future developments of Judaism, up until modern times, and our students must have some knowledge of it, regardless of their personal inclinations and future areas of specialization. Again, I do not need to stress how difficult this is in reality. How does one teach rabbinic Judaism to a student who does not want to specialize in Talmud or Midrash? It is almost impossible, and yet I am convinced that we cannot relinquish the task of introducing our students to rabbinic thinking and argumentation, and to the construction of that intellectual world. We therefore require, as the absolute minimum at our institute, that every student take one course in Mishnah and one course in Midrash.

4. All other areas of specialization will build upon these basic requirements and will depend largely on the traditions of the specific country, on local conditions, and, last but not least, on the interest of those who do the teaching and research. If I review which areas of Jewish studies are being taught and researched in Europe, I find many deficiencies, despite all the achievements and considerable progress. What happened to the great talmudic erudition of which Europe was once an important center (although not in the universities, but in the rabbinic seminaries)? It has almost vanished. What happened to the great tradition of Jewish philosophy, especially in the medieval period? It is almost gone. It is true, we still find some important remnants in France, for example, but I do not know of any serious attempt to include Jewish philosophy in the curriculum of any German university.

A considerable deficit has also to be recorded with regard to Jewish history, although the situation here is much better than in other fields. There is a lot of research in local history, most notably in France and Italy, but again there is more to be done in this area. Medieval Jewish history is very seldom part of the curriculum of Jewish studies, and the situation is not much better with regard to modern Jewish history, especially if one considers the new opportunities in Central and Eastern Europe. We have left Jewish history largely to historians who are not trained in Jewish studies, and who lack, or have in a very incomplete way, the most fundamental prerequisite for such an undertaking—the knowledge of Hebrew. This problem has become more acute in the last few years.

Issues of Jews and Judaism are very much in vogue nowadays among medieval and modern historians, a development that is to be welcomed in principle. It does, however, also entail the risk that important subjects will be treated in a rather dilettantish way and, even more serious, that questions and views will be imposed on the field from "outside," without regard for Jewish lines of development. There can be no doubt that the whole field of Jewish history illustrates most graphically the need for an intensified, interdisciplinary approach, and for much closer cooperation between Jewish studies and history.

Finally, another example of what is missing in Jewish studies in Europe is a center that concentrates on modern Hebrew literature. In view of the importance of that literature within the spectrum of contemporary literatures in the different European and Near Eastern countries, and of the increasing interest in it, it is high time for the establishment of at least one chair devoted exclusively to modern Hebrew literature. Again, this is a good example of an area that would profit considerably from an interdisciplinary conception.

5. What can be done under the circumstances to improve the rather poor situation? First, I think that we should exhaust all the instruments already available in Europe. We need a comprehensive inventory of what already exists in the different countries of Europe. For this purpose we can tap the resources of the national associations and, above all, of the European Association of Jewish Studies, which until now has been little more than a tool for the convening of interesting conferences every third year. Furthermore, we must intensify contacts and cooperation among our institutions. This is not a problem of Jewish studies alone, but of all university disciplines in Europe. If we do not do this voluntarily, we will either be forced to do so, or we will be forgotten and become negligible; this is one of the inevitable outcomes of the rapid development of the European Community.

One of the most important means by which to encourage cooperation is the "Erasmus" program, which enables the exchange of teachers and students and the development of common curricula among institutions in different European countries. This is a wonderful opportunity, of which we have not yet taken sufficient advantage in Jewish studies.

Second, we need to intensify our cooperation with Israeli as well as with American universities. It is true that we try to send our students to Israel; for a number of years we have been sending German students to the Hebrew University for one year of study, with the financial assistance of the German Academic Exchange Program. But this is far too little, considering the needs. In addition, we need an exchange program for university teachers. It is not enough that every fourth year we meet in Jerusalem at the Congress of the World Union of Jewish Studies, or that from time to time we are able to invite a colleague to our university for a lecture, or even for a semester. We need an exchange program on a mutual basis, that is, one in which colleagues from Israel or America will teach at our institutions, and we will teach at Israeli or American universities. It is not sufficient merely to write textbooks for us, or to translate Hebrew secondary literature into English. We and our students need personal contact as often as possible with colleagues and students in Israel and America. Close cooperation will create an atmosphere of understanding on our side, and enable our colleagues in Israel and America to learn what we require and how support can be provided.

NOTES

1. "Survival or Renaissance?" *Times Literary Supplement,* April 20–26, 1990.

6. CONTEMPORARY HEBREW LITERATURE ON THE AMERICAN CAMPUS

Yael S. Feldman

The fate of Hebrew in America, which has been the subject of anxiety and self-searching among Hebraists since the 1950s, is still being deliberated by contemporary scholars.[1] While some attribute the difficulties of maintaining Hebrew literacy to the essentially *mono*lingual nature of American culture,[2] others explain its decline by a fundamental change in the status of the language.[3] According to the latter view, the romantic notion of "a sacred language" held by European-born Hebraists such as Isaac Silberschlag and Nahum Glatzer has given way—since the establishment of the State of Israel—to the perception of Hebrew as a modern "foreign language" propagated by the later, mostly American-born, generation.

Whatever the reason, the picture of Hebrew currently prevailing in the American academy is not an encouraging one: while fluency in Hebrew is not rare among the generation trained in the forties and fifties, this is not true for the younger generation. There are few Ph.D. candidates, and positions in Hebrew are slow to be filled. There is, however, a popular demand, sometimes astounding in its proportions, for certain core Jewish topics—Bible, Holocaust, even contemporary Hebrew literature—as long as they are taught in English and texts are read in translation. Classes conducted in Hebrew are much less in demand.

There are some exceptions to this general rule, one of them being

An earlier version of this essay was published in *Shofar*, special issue on Hebrew, 9:3 (Spring 1991): 91–101.

Columbia University, where I taught throughout the 1980s. As in many other areas, New York City is a world unto itself. I have often been asked, in sheer surprise, in both America and Israel: "Do you really teach Hebrew literature *in Hebrew?* To whom?" My colleagues from the Midwest were amazed to hear that courses of Hebrew literature, *in Hebrew,* could draw up to twenty-five students in the lower-level classes, and about a dozen in the higher-level classes.

I am suggesting that we have two different groups of students and two diverging kinds of motivation. On the one hand, there is the all-American campus, in which the study of Hebrew—among other languages—is in decline, often aggravated by the elimination of foreign-language requirements. On such campuses, a student can get to our subject matter only via courses in translation. On the other hand, there is the population graduating from Hebrew day schools and yeshivot, who are fully equipped for the perusal of Hebrew texts, ancient as well as modern. Their linguistic fluency notwithstanding, this latter group raises specific cultural problems that may provide us with some clues regarding the general crisis of Hebrew on the American campus.

Typical yeshivah graduates are mainly concerned with retaining their Hebrew language proficiency; some of them are also interested in extending their familiarity in Hebrew literature. Rarely, however, would any of them undertake graduate studies in Hebrew literature. As a rule, the Hebrew education system does *not* encourage serious engagement in *belles lettres.* In all my years at Columbia, and more recently at New York University, I have not met more than a handful of students with an interest in literary matters. Still, it would be unfair to put the whole blame on Jewish education alone; unfortunately, this attitude toward literature is backed by the all-American university, specifically by what Tzvetan Todorov has called its "crimes against humanities."[4]

According to Todorov's findings, the last two decades saw a decrease of 33 percent in the number of college students graduating in the humanities; 88 percent of all college graduates have never taken a course in "Western Civilization," "American History," or "Foreign Language." So why should we malign the Jewish students? The majority of these students opt for a degree in medicine, law, business administration, or computers. An academic career, not to mention a career in the humanities, is definitely outside their interest. What makes them come to us is something totally different. They are attracted to *Hebrew* literature, not to "literature." For some of them it is *Israeli* literature, without all its historical dowry; for others, just the reverse: they are sharply critical of our "young" literature (from the sixties on), the like of which, they claim, they can also find in American writing.

Put differently, with some exceptions, Jewish students bring to class their problems of ethnic identity. Both their identification and objection to Hebrew literature stem from this source. Generally speaking, they lack any readiness for a critical-objective inquiry. Moreover, very often they transfer to the modern text an attitude of reverence and awe that they have acquired at a yeshivah or Hebrew school, and since the literary text does not properly "respond," they react with indignation and alienation.

It is this problem that challenges us as teachers and scholars: How is the teacher of Hebrew literature—who is generally a product of one of the "isms" of the last half-century (formalism, new criticism, structuralism, postmodernism)—to get through to the American student who often comes to the course for emotional rather than intellectual reasons? How should the teacher cope with the students' total oblivion to the hard questions recently raised about language and literature in general, along with their naive expectations of Hebrew literature in particular?

Questions of this sort arouse heated debates that surface in almost every professional meeting and every panel devoted to the teaching of Hebrew literature. Often enough a debate of this kind revolves around methodological issues; my feeling is, however, that such arguments tend to miss the main issue. I suggest that the major problem is not means and methods, but aims and positions. At the center of our difficulty, as I see it, is a fundamental conflict, both emotional and cognitive, between the position of the average teacher and the position of the average student. For the typical student of the group I am discussing, Hebrew still functions as a "sacred tongue"—if not technically, then emotionally. Hebrew literature is expected to reflect some ideal reality that corresponds to the readers' perception of their own self-identity. It is qualitatively different and therefore not amenable to any comparison. It cannot be studied in a relativistic framework; like the "chosen people," it is *sui generis*. It is a natural continuity of an internal tradition of thousands of years, and not a member in the international club of *belles lettres,* criticism, and theory of literature.

At best, a student of this group would care more about tracing the development leading from the conflicts of the *talush* ("the uprooted") at the beginning of the century to the conflicted protagonists of Israeli fiction, than the line leading, for example, from the European theater of the absurd to the Israeli drama of Nissim Aloni and Hanoch Levin. A class on biblical motifs in medieval and contemporary poetry would be more relevant to them than the classification and elucidation of techniques of deautomatization, of clusters of imagery and arch-metaphors, or of patterns of intertextuality and transfer from *foreign* sources in the very same poetry.[5] Such students regard as secondary or insignificant the question of literary form, of the "literariness" that scholars have been toiling to define since the beginning of this century. They look for reflection not semiotics, values not models, ideals not defamiliarization.

I hope there is no need to clarify that my exemplary pairs of oppositions are themselves an artificial construct, the result of any number of doctrinaire approaches. My sense is, however, that many teachers are not aware that they themselves exacerbate this polarization by taking a no less doctrinaire stance on the other side of the debate. The reason for this, I believe, is the fact that most of the contemporary academic faculty currently teaching Hebrew were trained in twentieth-century pseudo-scientific approaches to literature. As a rule, this apprenticeship has not prepared them for coping with such "irrelevant" questions as "But why is Hebrew literature so 'grim'?"; or "Why is the Israeli literary self-image so negative?" Here one cannot rely on any taxonomies or "grammars" of rhetorical and stylistic structures. The teacher needs to take off her or his scholarly hat and try to step into the students' shoes—or rather into their internal world of turmoil and confusion.

This is more easily said than done. For nothing is as efficient as the "objectivity" of scientific research in providing a defense against the unsettling questions of identity, values, and ideology.[6] One often hears, for example, this argument: "It is not my job to solve the students' identity problems; I teach a college course in literature, not a workshop in ethnicity."[7] What we face here is an unconscious conflict between the desirable (according to certain academic standards) and the available—the ideological matrix not only of our students' expectations, but also of sizable portions of our cultural inheritance.

This is not the place to recapitulate the ramifications of this conflict and its expressions in contemporary Hebrew literature and criticism. I would only like to emphasize that if, a few years ago, it still seemed feasible to establish an edifice of objective-esthetic research that would function as a defense against the pressures of the outside world, and to hope that the defunct *HaSifrut,* the Israeli journal best representing this approach, would be resurrected—today it is clear that such hopes have no basis in reality. That literary journal has not been revived, and Israeli literature at large is bending under the weight of current events.[8] Literary scholarship itself seems to "betray" the scientific-esthetic ideals, and adopts new "cultural" (rather than purely literary) research avenues.[9] In this it echoes several poststructuralist premises and methodologies (e.g., "critique of the canon" or "critique of ideology") that seem to me appropriate in addressing some of the difficulties with which we grapple in teaching Hebrew literature in the American university.

It should come as no surprise that several of the didactic solutions proposed at professional meetings have pointed in similar directions. It was suggested, for example, that the interweaving of noncanonic sources (films, popular or documentary literature) might soften or balance the extreme self-criticism of the canonic literature. These sources may also help clarify how thin the line can be between literary imagination and historical reality: a film documenting the dialogue of some old-time pioneers may demonstrate how life and art overlap in ideological rhetoric. From here it is but a short step to theories of New Historicism and their claim that the narrative and tropological dimensions of historiography question the traditional polarization between literature and history.[10]

Last, but not least, was the suggestion to call students' attention to other literatures that were written under conditions and in sociohistorical contexts similar to those of the Hebrew literature under scrutiny. In some sense, Israeli literature, despite its declared Westernization, still adheres to the Russian tradition of a literature engaged in sociopolitical discourse. But we would be mistaken to limit ourselves to this line of historical continuity. For a most superficial look should suffice to convince us that this tradition is not exclusively Russian, nor even East European. And even though our students may be mostly familiar with contemporary American literature, it is important to direct them to earlier literature of the American pioneering period. Just as valuable is the literature inspired by the two world wars or Vietnam, as well as the literatures of Central Europe or South America that reflect similar realities of a society under internal or external pressures. Thus, for example, the fictional autobiography, one of the most individualistic genres in Western literature, turns out to be quite different not only in Hebrew, but also among Western *women* writers or other nonmainstream groups.[11] In other words, contemporary Hebrew literature calls for literary frames of reference other than the ones automatically used by the average student.

The common denominator underlying the various didactic suggestions enumerated here is the comparative method. In my experience, there is no better way to neutralize positions of defense and resistance than to direct students to a comparative reading. My personal solution for the problems raised above is to plan each course, even when taught in Hebrew, as if it were a course in comparative literature. And if limitations of time do not allow for the inclusion of primary readings from other literatures in class, they are given at least as background reading, to help in framing the discussion. Similarly, secondary sources include readings in English, aimed at relevant issues in other cultures.

With the reality of the American student body in mind, I do not implement a graded program, in which the student progresses annually from lower- to higher-level courses. To the best of my knowledge, only few universities enjoy such a privilege. Most of our students are not majors, so we see them for one or two electives at most. And only rarely do I teach thematic courses. My experience has been that courses defined thematically almost always court the danger of evolving into an ideologically colored query, altogether neglecting the literary-esthetic dimensions of the material. On the other hand, a "generic" definition (the short story, poetic modernism, fictional autobiography) warrants a minimal exploration of the relevant literary concepts (the stylistic, structural, and rhetorical components of the genre), and encourages a comparative reading with the help of appropriate critical sources.

At the same time, I do not approach the genre synchronically. I present the primary sources chronologically, so that every course is also structured as an introduction, a minuscule cultural history of an issue in Hebrew literature. Although the historical section is narrow, it is nevertheless a significant ploy, as it opens the conversation to questions of culture, history, and ideology. It is precisely through these questions that I have been able to reach the students' existential concerns, to cope with them rather than to ignore them.

If this sounds too good to be true, this is indeed the case: my "wonder

formula" is not exempt from drawbacks. For example, the broad historical scope does not allow for an in-depth acquaintance with one or two
authors. To make up for this lacuna, I usually suggest that the term
paper focus on a single author; another option is to return to the
department for another class; and a third one is, of course, to take
courses in translation. But with this we have reached what is for me still
an unresolved issue in the teaching of Hebrew literature in America.

Why "unresolved"? Technically, the answer is quite apparent: How
can one plan a serious comprehensive course when so many core texts
are still unavailable in English, although the situation has much improved in recent years, with the translation of major portions of Israeli
literature, mainly prose and drama?[12] Yet in any of the "generic"
courses that I try to structure I still miss a central link: here Agnon, there
Brenner, U. Z. Greenberg, or Yizhar, and, beyond them, works by
women. Is it conceivable to teach in today's America an introductory
course of any kind without exploring the question of gender difference
(or indifference)?

But this is, I would like to reiterate, only the technical aspect of the
issue. The principle problem is, naturally, the fear lurking between the
lines of Shaked's chapter on "Alexandria of America":[13] If today teachers read the original while students use a translation, what will happen
in the next generation? Already now "commentaries are written on
translated texts . . . and everyone scrutinizes them as if they were the
originals" (p. 143). Aren't we assisting the dangerous process described
by Arnold Band as the transition from "sacred tongue" to "foreign
language"? Don't we offer our students the way of least resistance
instead of encouraging them to cope with original texts?

I assume that it was this kind of reasoning that directed the actions of
the first generation of Hebraists who established the "Hebrew in Hebrew" programs in the American universities. In the name of this reasoning they have also objected to the transition from Hebraica to "Jewish
studies." The fear was that the transfer of emphasis to social and contemporary studies—fields that do not require knowledge of the classical
sources—would be at the expense of the mastery of the language and
the ancient texts required in the study of Judaica.

I do not know if this fear was unfounded. But on the other hand, I
am not sure that the perception of cause and effect underlying this fear

is accurate. In the final analysis, we have to acknowledge regretfully that without some revolutionary changes in academic-level language teaching, we cannot expect college students who begin Hebrew from scratch to reach a level of mastery that will enable them to study literature as literature. Moreover: I suspect that this is not a new phenomenon; I think that the academy has rarely produced its own advanced students in Hebrew and Judaica. Acknowledging this fact should help us realize that classes of literature in translation have another function altogether. They are geared to a different audience and should not constitute a "threat" for the graduates of yeshivot who can read the material in the original. What is this distinct function?

First and foremost, courses of literature in translation can accompany lower-level language classes. This is, in a sense, "seduction," a conscious response to the cultural and literary codes that American students absorb in other areas of their academic studies. It should come as no surprise that popular topics (such as "the Holocaust," "the 'other'," "gender and culture") also draw students who have no specific interest in Judaica, Israel, or Hebrew. This means, naturally, that teachers face a class different not only in its language ability, but in its didactic and social dynamics as well.

My experience with courses of this kind (though mostly on the graduate level) has been very gratifying, in ways I had not originally foreseen. Attracting students with a variety of specialties and ethnocultural backgrounds, these "mixed" classes have often turned into a fascinating exercise in self-reflection. The interaction with "others" usually drives both students and teacher into an overall examination of generally unquestioned presuppositions—us/them, male/female, objective/subjective, self/other. These classes offer a healthy counterbalance to the enclosed, parochial atmosphere that sometimes marks Hebrew courses. At the same time, they also reach out to those who would otherwise never have known about this literature.

This may not be a major breakthrough for Hebrew studies per se, but reaching out, shaking up some rigid perceptions and boundaries are humanistic gains not to be underrated in this day and age. And if Hebrew texts can perform this feat, even in translation—let this be our reward.

NOTES

1. See Zvi Scharfstein, *'Arba'im Shanah be'America* (Tel Aviv: Massada, 1956), p. 187, and more recently, *Hebrew in America: Perspectives and Prospects,* ed. Alan Mintz (Detroit: Wayne State University Press, 1993).
2. Robert Alter, *The Invention of Hebrew Prose: Modern Fiction and the Invention of Realism* (Seattle: University of Washington Press, 1988), p. 73.
3. Avraham (Arnold) Band, "My Road to Hebrew," *HaDoar* 68 (26 May 1989): 15–16; see also his chapter "Hebrew in the American University" in the collection *Hebrew in America* (note 1 above).
4. Tzvetan Todorov, "Crimes against Humanities," *The New Republic* (3 July 1989): 26–30. This essay is just the tip of the iceberg of the raging debate over the canon and the curriculum in the American university that is focused on the humanities.
5. These represent some of the themes I have developed in my courses and research. See my "The Sacred as the Absurd in Israeli Drama," in *Sacred Theatre,* ed. Daniel Gerould, Bettina Knapp, and Jane House (Cincinnati: Hebrew Union College, 1989), pp. 81–97; *Modernism and Cultural Transfer* (Cincinnati: Hebrew Union College, 1986).
6. On this point see my "Poetics and Politics: Israeli Literary Criticism Between East and West," *PAAJR* 52 (1985): 9–35.
7. Ironically, the context of this contention, which I quote from memory, was a paper on the use of Joshua Sobol's play, *The Night of the Twenties,* in a course on Israeli Myth: The Dream and Its Aftermath. I suppose the speaker never asked why a course should be given such a title; furthermore, can this topic be taught from the perspective implied by that statement? And, finally, was Sobol's play really chosen for its esthetic merit? I sincerely doubt this. See Edna Amir-Coffin, "Theatre in a Course on Literature and Cinema," a paper given at the Annual Meeting of the National Association of Professors of Hebrew, Chicago, May 1, 1989. On the ideological aspects of Sobol's play, see my "Zionism—Neurosis or Cure?—The 'Historical' Drama of J. Sobol," *Prooftexts* 7:2 (May 1987): 145–62.
8. I have developed this point in a series of articles and in my study, *Subject to Otherness: Psychology and Ideology in Hebrew Literature* (in preparation); see especially "Poetics and Politics" (note 6 above) and "Zionism on the Literary Couch," in *Vision Confronts Reality,* ed. Ruth Kozodoy et al. (Rutherford, N.J.: Fairleigh Dickinson University/London and Toronto: Associated University Presses, 1989), pp. 310–35.
9. See, for example, Dan Miron, *'Im Lo Tihye Yerushalayim* [If There is No Jerusalem] (Hakibbutz Hame'uchad, 1987); Gershon Shaked, *'Ein Makom 'Aher* [No Other Place] (Hakibbutz Hame'uchad, 1988); and collections of essays by writers Zach, Yehoshua, Oz, and scholars Gertz and Calderon, among others.

10. See Hayden White, *Tropics of Discourse: Essays in Cultural Criticism* (Baltimore: Johns Hopkins University Press, 1978).

11. See my "Ideology and Self-Representation: The Case of Israeli Women Writers," in *Redefining Autobiography in Twentieth Century Women's Fiction,* ed. Janice Morgan and Colette T. Hall (New York: Garland, 1991), pp. 91–101.

12. In poetry there are several translated collections, chief among them T. Carmi's *The Penguin Book of Hebrew Verse* and the new edition, by Harvard University Press, of *The Modern Hebrew Poem Itself* (1989).

13. Gershon Shaked, *'Ein Makom 'Aher* (note 9 above), p. 140 *et passim*. For an English version, see his chapter in *Hebrew in America* (note 1 above).

7. *TANAKH:* A SHARED FIELD

Baruch A. Levine

The study of the Hebrew Bible, known by Christians as the Old Testament, is a shared field of knowledge in universities and other open institutions of higher learning. Historically, the modern field of biblical studies was not pioneered by Jewish scholars, who were, in fact, relatively late in entering it, but rather by innovative Christians. Those Christians had been struggling with questions of religious authority, with the New Testament as well as the Hebrew Scriptures, with church and society, since the Age of Humanism. They understood that in order to sanction Protestantism and all that went with it, they would be required to read the Holy Scriptures differently, so as to refute the claim of the Catholic Church that it had a monopoly on truth, and that its authority was ordained in Scripture. By the end of the eighteenth century, the successors of these early Protestants had reached the point of questioning just about everything about the Hebrew Bible and the New Testament. These were now regarded as products of historical development, synoptic documents with internal differences and even contradictions. Ironically, it was a Jew, Benedict Spinoza (1632–1677), who ultimately exercised considerable impact on modern Christian biblicism. He was, however, vehemently renounced by his contemporary Jewish community, which was hardly ready at the time for what he had to say about the Hebrew Bible.

The contextual investigation of the two testaments by Christian scholars inevitably placed them in distinct relation to each other. The Hebrew Bible was indispensable as the ultimate sanction of the New Testament; the advent of Christ had been prophesied in the *Tanakh*. This meant, for some, that the Hebrew Bible was unimportant for itself; its significance hinged on its fulfillment in Christianity. But there was a more notable consequence of the critical study of the Hebrew Bible by Christians. Christian scholars sought to know the prophets and heroes of the Old Testament as people, and the events of their lives as real; their land as having mountains and rivers, and their society as having problems. In effect, they wanted to identify the *Sitz-im-Leben* of biblical prophecy and law; they searched for the context of the message. In a parallel way, they sought to retrieve the historical Jesus and to comprehend pristine Christianity, to get at the simple meaning of the Gospels and Epistles without the encrustations of traditional commentary. It is this mentality that first stimulated archeological activity in Bible lands, as a phenomenon parallel to the reawakened interest in Greece and Rome by masters of the Renaissance.

In hindsight, and notwithstanding a degree of bias and of distortion that has been offensive to Jewish sensibilities, I regard the massive Protestant endeavor that produced the modern, critical study of the Hebrew Bible as a highly positive development. We must also realize that the modern university itself was pioneered by Christians, in Europe and in the New World. The teaching of the Old Testament in the university was consequently a task for Christian scholars. It was thus that both theory and application, research and teaching, have been largely in Christian hands.

In recent generations, however, both the field of biblical studies and the university as an institution have changed radically. The Western university is now home to an exceedingly large number of Jewish students and instructors in all fields; it is hardly the restrictive institution it once was. Moreover, the study of Judaica has greatly expanded in North American universities, and to a lesser degree in European and other universities; and the Jewish community in modern Israel has established the Hebrew University and other institutions of higher learning wherein the Judaic curriculum, broadly conceived, has a central role. For the first time, the Hebrew Bible is being taught in the general university curriculum as part of the Judaic heritage, not specifically as part of the Christian heritage, or more generally as a feature of Western civilization.

Nonetheless, the manner in which the Hebrew Bible is being taught and investigated in the university as a Judaic subject, largely by Jewish scholars and teachers in Israel and in the Diaspora, has been irreversibly affected by modern methodologies first introduced and developed by Christian scholars. This situation also obtains in most rabbinical seminaries, and in other institutions of higher learning under specifically Jewish sponsorship. The Hebrew Bible is now seen as part of a larger, ancient Near Eastern legacy. Its writings are studied in comparative perspective as historiography, poetry, and narrative, and its commandments as law.

In recent generations, Jewish scholars have become prominent both as the transmitters of earlier, modern methodologies and as exponents of new methods in biblical studies—historicism, comparativism, literary approaches to the Bible, and, of course, archeology. The archeological establishment in Israel, augmented by Jewish and non-Jewish colleagues from abroad, has transformed our appreciation of the material culture of biblical times, and uncovered admittedly scant, but highly informative, written materials. We are now witnessing a cooperative process, whereby Christian and Jewish university scholars with varying degrees of secularization continue to work and teach in the biblical field side by side, with increasing energy and productivity.

In the context of Jewish studies, the shared character of biblical studies in higher education is distinctive, at least in degree. In no other area do we see the same extent of non-Jewish involvement, or the same degree of formative influence from non-Jewish sources. There have been and may now be a few notable students of the history of the Jews after the advent of Christianity who are not themselves Jews, and whose training was not Judaic per se; but for the most part, the field of Jewish history was pioneered by motivated Jews who were recipients of a Western education and trained in modern methods of historical study. These Jewish scholars were not, however, engaging a subject of inquiry introduced by the Western academy—which, in fact, has only recently shown any serious interest in this subject. This same judgment applies to all aspects of postbiblical Jewish literature, such as the rabbinic corpus and Jewish philosophy, as well as the postbiblical development of the Hebrew language. As we draw nearer to the contemporary period, we note, for example, that Israeli literature is being translated from Hebrew into other languages and has captured the interest of the general literary community. The process with respect to most areas of Jewish studies remains centrifugal. It is predominantly Jewish scholars who spin off new knowledge and contribute new writings, which are then appropriated by those of the general academy who are sensitive to the lacunae in their appreciation of other world cultures.

The process with respect to biblical studies is different; it is interactive. Jewish and non-Jewish scholars study the Hebrew Bible in essentially the same ways, although some Jewish scholars utilize the postbiblical exegetical tradition to a greater degree than others, and attach more importance to it. It must be emphasized, however, that to the extent that we view the Hebrew Bible as a document of religious significance, as being meaningful for and functional within religious communities, it inevitably means something different to Christians and to Jews. Israelis, and Jews everywhere who share with Israeli society a common historical consciousness as members of the Jewish people, find a meaning in the Hebrew Bible that is different from its meaning to non-Jews. This is so whether or not their Jewish consciousness is informed primarily by religious belief.

In the evolution of the modern study of the Hebrew Bible by Jewish scholars, problems have arisen with respect to the function and significance of the Hebrew Bible within Judaism, and these problems have not yet been fully resolved. There have also been problems with respect to the place of the Hebrew Bible within the Jewish studies curriculum. To some, Judaism, strictly defined, originated in the post-exilic period, and Jewish history began at that time. And yet, the emergence of modern Israel as a Hebrew-speaking society, and the national rebirth on biblical soil, has made the most ancient phases of the Jews' experience as a people irresistibly relevant, so that slowly but surely it is being acknowledged that Jewish history begins as Israelite history, with Abraham and not with Ezra.

Participation in a shared field of knowledge should not be disabling or limiting in any way. Only those given to the genetic fallacy would contend that the modern study of the Hebrew Bible is less worthy of our attention than the later phases of a Jewish studies curriculum merely because it was, until recently, informed by a Christian agenda. Throughout our history, the interpretation of our canonical books and our understanding of ourselves have been informed by methods of inquiry learned from others; and so it has been in modern biblical studies. Such is the reality of a shared field, and it is this reality that should dictate the character of programs in biblical studies in modern universities, within the context of the Jewish studies curriculum, or as part of Near Eastern studies, programs in religion, literature, and the like.

In the hope that it will be instructive, I will present a series of propositions about the teaching of the Hebrew Bible in the modern university. Notwithstanding differences in the role of biblical studies in Israel and in the Diaspora, the propositions that follow are sufficiently basic as to be relevant to both intellectual environments.

BASIS AND APPROACH

In modern institutions of higher learning, the study of the Hebrew Bible should not, in the first instance, be predicated on any particular religious or theological presuppositions, or on any specific communal affiliation or personal identity. A common approach must be found so as to enable all who wish to study the Hebrew Bible to do so together, regardless of who they are and what they believe. Most needed are shared skills and knowledge, not shared beliefs and doctrines. The doctrinal aspects of biblical study should be addressed in courses on the history of biblical interpretation, and in those dealing with the historic role of the Hebrew Bible wherein it can be shown what the Hebrew Bible meant and said to later generations, and to various communities, up to and including the present.

METHODOLOGY

With the exception of a few chapters written in Aramaic, the Hebrew Bible is written in the Hebrew language. While it is surely acceptable to offer introductory courses in English translation, progressively advanced study of the Hebrew Bible should be based on the Hebrew text, for which there can be no substitute.

Beyond this requirement, the principal methodological caveat in studying the Hebrew Bible is not to overspecialize without a broad base of skills and knowledge. At a time when many different methodologies are receiving a hearing in the marketplace of ideas, it is ill-advised for advocates of one or the other method to train their students solely in their own preferred way. Rather, a broad base of textual skills, and of historical and linguistic competence, is necessary for all who expect to contribute to the advancement of biblical learning, regardless of their eventual focus.

CURRICULUM

It follows from what has been said that the university curriculum in biblical studies must be structured in ways that will assist in accomplishing its scholarly objectives. It is reasonable to propose that the Hebrew Bible can be best understood by those who comprehend the contribution of ancient Near Eastern cultures to its formation; who know the history of the region in which it was formed; who are sensitive to the forms and genres of its literary creativity; and who are conversant with Jewish religion and law, wisdom and prophecy, society and its institutions. Only those who can read the Hebrew text with deep comprehension, who know Hebrew as an ancient Near Eastern language and also know the post-biblical phases of Hebrew to some extent, can possibly derive from its reading a correct understanding of its content. This applies to all students of the Hebrew Bible—Jewish, Christian, and others.

At New York University the doctoral program in Biblical and Ancient Near Eastern Studies is structured around the following required courses and electives:

1. A series of courses in the Hebrew text of the Bible, covering books, themes, genres, and the like. The objective is exegetical, in the first instance, but the content of such courses usually expands to a wider agenda. The text is the point of departure for papers to be written on a variety of related topics. A seminar session of two hours will often proceed from precise philological and exegetical study of the textual unit, to literary and rhetorical considerations, then to historical and other contextual factors, and will conclude with observations about culture and the history of ideas.

2. Two years of Akkadian, one year of Aramaic or Ugaritic (usually both), and a course in Phoenician and Northwest-Semitic epigraphy. Students may elect to study ancient Egyptian, Arabic, and Greek, in addition to the required languages. Given the importance of the Aramaic language, in its many dialects and phases, to other areas of Judaic studies, we are now considering expanding the Aramaic offerings to a two-year sequence.

These requirements reflect the comparative dimension of biblical studies, the sense that the Hebrew Bible and ancient Israelite culture to the degree that we know it were part of something larger. This awareness is still relatively new, and it inevitably clashes with the traditional mind-set which perceives the Hebrew Bible as unique or highly distinctive. We will know that we are doing our job well when a student, learning for the first time that the Moabite stele of the ninth century B.C.E. expresses theological notions we had thought original to Deuteronomy, is prompted to smile with satisfaction, to appreciate the broader context of the biblical world.

3. Seminars in the history of the biblical period and of the ancient Near East, including, as available, courses in biblical archeology. In North America, the field of biblical history is underdeveloped in comparison with its impressive expansion in the Israeli academy. This is an area requiring a greater investment of resources. There are also courses on the Bible as literature, which are acceptable in the fulfillment of requirements.

4. Competence in what is called "academic Hebrew," namely, the Hebrew of modern Israeli scholarship and, indirectly, of premodern Jewish exegesis. Although most students possess such skills when they enter the doctoral program, others do not and are accepted on condition that they will bring their skills up to par. We are currently enhancing our offerings in this area.

We need to emphasize the importance of modern research languages in the biblical curriculum. In North America, insufficient knowledge of European languages remains a stumbling block to scholarly competence, while in Israel it is often a lack of the English language that impedes. Most universities have programs specifically designed to teach foreign languages as research tools.

5. Elective courses in post-biblical Jewish subjects, especially in the Dead Sea literature, the *Targumim,* rabbinic literature, medieval *parshanut,* kabbalah, Hebrew literature of all periods, history, and philosophy are recommended for doctoral students in Bible, who are tested in a general way on some of these areas of study in qualifying or comprehensive examinations before being awarded the Ph.D. degree. The guiding principle is that holders of a Doctorate in Hebrew and Judaic Studies should, at the very least, know who Bialik and Maimonides were, what the Talmud is about, and what happened to the Jewish people since the advent of Christianity.

The elective program suffers from the time constraints placed on doctoral students, and we must rethink the overall question of the duration of doctoral programs in Jewish studies. Three or four years is hardly adequate when so much is being demanded. The situation was less worrisome when most graduate students in Jewish studies came from rabbinic seminaries and yeshivot, where they acquired a general education in Judaica. At the present time, and predictably in the future, more and more of our graduate students will lack such a background and will require more time and study at the university. This problem may not affect Israeli universities to the same degree, but it is becoming acute in North America.

Tanakh as a shared field has an exciting future. The Hebrew Bible is already being studied in universities in Japan, Korea, and China; in parts of Africa and Latin America; in Egypt, and in countries of the former Soviet bloc. In all of these settings, it is not being taught simply as Christian literature or as a feature of Western civilization. The Hebrew Bible is being taught as the creation of an ancient Near Eastern people who inhabited the Land of Israel, were exiled from it, and have returned in modern times to modern Israel, where a vital Hebraic culture defines the life of the society.

8. TEACHING JEWISH HISTORY ON THE AMERICAN CAMPUS

Robert Chazan

Jewish history is being taught today on North American campuses in the widest possible range of settings. Geographically, universities offering courses in Jewish history can be found in every region of the United States and Canada, with a concentration in those areas of densest Jewish population, especially the northeastern and the southwestern United States, and around Montreal and Toronto in Canada. The types of universities involved show a similarly wide range and include both the most prestigious and less prestigious private universities and public universities of all kinds, in addition to Christian and Jewish denominational institutions. The last category deserves special mention, for these schools have considerable numbers of undergraduate and graduate students in Jewish history courses.

Within the universities, Jewish history courses are being offered in many different departments, including history, religion, Near Eastern studies and, in a few cases, departments of Jewish studies. The departmental framework is of significance for both the faculty and students of Jewish history, as approaches to the history of the Jews can vary considerably. For example, the approach to the history of the Jews in a department of religion may contrast with that of a department of history with its tendency toward political or social analysis. Yet differences are by no means automatic, and a religion department may house a historian with strong political and social interests, and a history department may include a historian of religion.

Jewish history courses are currently available at all levels of instruction, ranging from the broadest possible surveys on the undergraduate level, to the most recondite doctoral seminars, though the number of institutions offering instruction at the doctoral level is extremely limited. There are probably no more than a dozen to fifteen institutions of higher learning in North America that are seriously involved in such training.

Who are the students taking courses in Jewish history? What motivates them? It is important to emphasize the essentially impressionistic quality of my observations, and to note that the nature of the student body varies widely from institution to institution. Students enrolled in courses on the history of the Jews are not necessarily committed Jews; indeed, in many instances they are not Jewish at all. My own experience illustrates the varied nature of students of Jewish history. Many of the courses I taught at Ohio State University had considerable enrollments of non-Jewish students; at Queens College of the City University of New York, a radically different environment, there were almost no non-Jewish students in my course.

The motivations of non-Jews to study the history of the Jews are many: a sense that the history of the Jews is interesting and illuminating; a personal encounter with Jews or with Jewishness; the intense emotions aroused by encountering the concentration camps; or the powerful experience of visiting the State of Israel. The history of the Jews may also have profound theological significance. Many universities in North America do not have courses in early Christianity, and Christian pre-theological students may end up deeply involved in Second Commonwealth Jewish history by default. On the advanced level, one only occasionally encounters a non-Jewish student focusing on the history of the Jews.

While non-Jewish students provide an interesting and important component in Jewish history courses, there is little doubt that a considerable majority of the students enrolled in such courses are Jewish. Here again, the motivations vary widely, ranging from casual concern with the Jewish experience, to passionate and committed involvement with Jewish life, and to an intense personal quest. Some students hope to buttress prior convictions about the Jewish experience—convictions which may be religious (in a variety of shadings), or national (again in a variety of shadings).

The divergent course structures make it extremely difficult to formulate generalizations about the range of Jewish history that is taught.

Courses tend to be organized along chronological lines—history of the Jews in antiquity, in the Middle Ages, in the modern period, and in the twentieth century. In academic settings where finer discriminations are possible, the paradigm of centers of Jewish life may be introduced—Jewish life during the Second Commonwealth, the Jews in the medieval Muslim world, medieval Sephardic Jewry, medieval Ashkenazic Jewry, the experience of Emancipation, modern East European Jewry, Zionism and the State of Israel, and American Jewry. More infrequently, courses are organized along topical lines—the history of anti-Semitism, patterns of Jewish self-government, the Jews and the world around them.

The choice of the courses taught is the result of a complex combination of factors that include the particular academic setting, the strength of student interests, and the academic focus of the available faculty. The most popular offerings involve either broad surveys of the Jewish experience, or certain narrowly focused courses such as Second Commonwealth history, because of its religious significance for the development of both rabbinic Judaism and Christianity, and the history of the Holocaust, because of its drama, emotional content, and its religious and moral significance.

It is interesting to note that there is no overwhelming interest in American Jewish history, probably because many students assume that they more or less know the contours of the American Jewish experience through their own lives, and that they would be better served by studying aspects of Jewish history not directly observable. Similarly, there is no overwhelming demand for the history of Zionism and the State of Israel, despite the high level of general interest in the phenomenon of Israel and the Zionist enterprise. In part this may again be the result of the students' assumption that they know the basic story and encounter it regularly in the media.

Turning from the students to the faculty, one may ask the following questions: Who are the people teaching courses in Jewish history? What is the nature of their training? What perspectives do they bring to bear on the subject? Here the lack of broadly based data becomes more significant. Most observers—myself included—derive their impressions from contact with faculty who are most thoroughly trained in Jewish history and most directly involved in research and writing, in addition to teaching. This tends to obscure the considerable number of minimally trained or untrained people who teach Jewish history in a wide variety of academic institutions. The latter group includes historians with training in other fields or, in a smaller number of cases, rabbis who are drafted to teach Jewish history because of an expressed interest within the student body. If such a new course is successful, it may become a permanent part of the curriculum, and the instructor will find a fixed place on the teaching staff. The quality of these courses is wide-ranging. For example, a well-trained instructor in modern European history can offer extremely competent courses in modern Jewish history. In other instances, the level of such courses is essentially interchangeable with high school instruction.

In general, little attention has been devoted to these instructors and courses. This is due partly to the difficulty in identifying them, as well as to a sense of elitism on the part of those with more serious training who fear that recognition of this kind of instruction will adulterate the quality of the field. Problems notwithstanding, this kind of instruction should be examined more seriously, either by a professional organization such as the Association for Jewish Studies, or by an academic body such as the International Center for University Teaching of Jewish Civilization. Rather than turning a blind eye to a sector that functions, albeit with deficiencies, it would be well worth learning more about what is happening in this area and attempting to improve the level of instruction. Summer seminars, aimed specifically at those who have slipped into the teaching of Jewish history through one or another circuitous route, and who are highly motivated toward improving their teaching, would constitute a valuable contribution to the field.

At the larger and better universities and in the major Jewish-sponsored institutions of higher learning, instruction in Jewish history is provided by a cadre of scholars especially trained for the task. These are the people who are actively involved in researching a particular period in the history of the Jews, and who share the fruits of their general knowledge and their more specific investigations with students at both the undergraduate and graduate levels. Most of these people have received their doctoral training at American universities, Jewish-sponsored institutions in North America, or in Israeli universities. Many of those holding doctoral degrees from American universities have also had an exposure to rabbinic education as part of their training, or have spent some time at an Israeli university. In both cases, this segment of their education is generally aimed at securing or enhancing language competence in Hebrew, and/or gaining some knowledge of the classics of Jewish literature, in particular the corpus of rabbinic literature not easily read by the neophyte.

This group of scholars, by virtue of their training and the setting within which they work, find themselves confronted with a new set of issues that bear upon their writing and their teaching. In order to identify properly the innovative elements in the contemporary teaching of Jewish history on the American campus, it will be necessary to consider the traditional patterns of Jewish historical memory, and the new directions introduced into the depiction of the Jewish past by the encounter with modernity.

Yosef Haim Yerushalmi has described briefly but compellingly the traditional patterns of Jewish recollection of the past in his widely read *Zakhor*. He argues convincingly that within this enterprise, the role of the historian was quite limited. Other channels—liturgy and ritual, for example—played a far more significant role in the effort to highlight the nature of the Jewish past. The net result was, according to Yerushalmi, a tradition rich in historical awareness, but rather poor in historians and historical writings.

The onset of modernization and the related emancipation of the Jews in Western Europe introduced significant changes into the writing of Jewish history and, in fact, augmented considerably the importance of that enterprise. At least three major changes took place:

1. Internal shifts in Jewish life necessitated innovative consideration of the Jewish past that would serve, inter alia, to justify some of the alterations seemingly required by the present. Nineteenth-century historical research, for example, aimed at uncovering the dynamism that had characterized earlier Jewish religious history. While this investigation was academic in nature, it was meant, in no small measure, to serve as justification for the development of reforming movements in Judaism. Similarly, the birth and evolution of the Zionist movement late in the nineteenth century placed a different set of historical issues on the agenda and gave rise to new perspectives.

2. The integration of the Jews into European society necessitated a new level of concern with the image of the Jew among non-Jews. This sparked a renewed concern with the Jewish past, to serve as a vehicle for improving that image in society, or at least for combatting some of the canards concerning allegedly antisocial patterns of Jewish behavior.

3. Yet another factor in the new writing of Jewish history was the involvement of Jews in nineteenth-century European intellectual activity. Since there was considerable apprehension on the part of non-Jews regarding the capacity of the Jews to take their place in European society, one of the ways in which Jews might prove themselves worthy of such acceptance was through participation in important social, intellectual, and artistic pursuits. Sharing in the enterprise of writing history would exemplify Jewish capability for full-scale participation in the life of modern society.

Having identified these major stimuli to the new style of Jewish history writing, it should be noted that there is a striking difference between the first two elements and the third. In the first two cases, the motivations for the new historical writing arise essentially from the problematics of Jewish existence and are oriented toward their amelioration; such motivations lead to historical research and writing that is highly tendentious. However, the notion of participation in a major intellectual endeavor on the European scene leads in the direction of a more disinterested scholarship. It will be useful to keep these two divergent tendencies firmly in mind as we now consider those currently writing and teaching on the campuses of North America.

The acceptance of Jewish studies in general, and the study of the Jewish past in particular, on American campuses testifies to the integration of Jews into American society. Never before has the study of the Jewish past been so thoroughly integrated into a broadly humanistic curriculum. The battle over the legitimacy of such study has long been won, although early in my career I met fellow historians who, while quite comfortable with the notion of including Jewish history within the curriculum, were uncomfortable with the notion of specific training for historians of the Jews. They argued that English Jewish history ought properly to be taught by English historians, French Jewish history by French historians, and so on. Today, even that line of thinking seems to have pretty much disappeared. While all would agree that a historian of English Jewry must master the history of England at large, the notion of special training for a historian of English Jewry now seems beyond contention.

The history of the Jews occupies a place in American academic life that is more dignified than anything that the dreamers of the early nineteenth century might have imagined. The leading academic presses in North America are now producing volumes on Jewish studies that once appeared only under the auspices of a Jewish publishing house. These new possibilities represent a remarkable phenomenon and indicate how far the acceptance of Jewish studies in general, and Jewish history in particular, has progressed. This rather full acceptance carries with it a number of significant implications. The first is a marked decline in tendentiousness. The historian of the Jews is encouraged—perhaps even forced—to see himself or herself as the objective observer of a broad scene, rather than as an interested and involved party.

Let me cite a personal example. In the course of preparing a monograph on the Barcelona disputation in 1263, I had occasion to reread with care the prior literature on the event, which affords a striking instance of tendentiousness on both sides—Christian writers favoring the Christian side, and Jewish writers favoring the Jewish side. I eventually wrote up the evolving treatment of the disputation and its sources as an interesting case study in the movement from medieval to modern polemics. A contemporary European student of Jewish history, reviewing the prior treatments of the disputation, had the following to say:

> When the Christian scholar Heinrich Denifle championed the Christian account [of the disputation] as the truth, denouncing Nahmanides (and the Jewish historian Graetz) as a liar, he was well and sufficiently answered by the Jewish scholar Isadore Loeb. But once the battle for the superior truth of the Jewish account was won, Jewish scholars turned their attention to the possible deficiencies of the Jewish account too. Here they have had some just things to say, but have also, in their search for painful objectivity, sometimes succumbed to the pleasures of masochism.

Nothing in my training or academic experiences had prepared me for the tendentious language that I encountered in this passage. Indeed I wondered immediately about the term "Jewish scholars," which was clearly intended to reflect engagement and the championing of a cause. I believe that those involved today in the enterprise of writing and teaching Jewish history on American campuses have largely abandoned the mode of tendentious discourse in both their research and their teaching. They function with the tacit assumption that they are teaching an academic course, and that their responsibility is to present the truth, so far as they can ascertain it. Appeals to purposes of Jewish survival or Jewish identity lie outside the pale of their professional interest.

A second and related implication of the new integration of Jewish history into the academic curriculum is the need to create a neutral stance on the part of the researcher/teacher. In the classroom, the disciplinary professional association, or the university press, it is inappropriate to speak of Jews in the first persons as "we," and of non-Jews in the third person as "they." The significance of that non-Jewish world either as auditor or reader extends far beyond the simple use of pronouns. The teacher or writer must at all times be aware of the variety of perspectives present in the audience. The issue is not one of good manners alone. On a deeper level, real confrontation with non-Jewish audiences leads ineluctably to enhanced sensitivity, to significant wrestling with a multiplicity of perspectives, and to greater insight.

One additional, not yet fully realized, implication of the new setting of Jewish studies must be noted. Fuller integration into the general academic milieu inevitably means the introduction of issues that are highly placed on the broad academic agenda. Examples are simple to note: the women's perspective on the past; concern with the poorer classes in society; sensitivity to the inarticulate masses; the search for alternative sources for illuminating the past; and the development of more perceptive strategies for decoding texts. The bulk of the questions that have loomed large in the new Jewish historiography have emerged out of the problematics of modern Jewish living. I suggest that the agenda of the academy-at-large will increasingly impinge on the issues that will be taught in Jewish studies.

9. JEWISH PHILOSOPHY IN THE ACADEMY

Emil L. Fackenheim

Some years ago when I taught at the University of Toronto, I received an anguished phone call from a Jewish professor at another Canadian university. He and two others felt that their university needed a professor in Judaica, and that the best person to have was a philosopher. So they went to the chairman of their philosophy department, whose reaction was as follows: "Jewish philosophy? There is no such subject!" The petitioners went away hurt and humiliated.

There is a superficial justice in that chairman's reaction. If a university has only one professor of Judaica, a historian may be the best choice although a philosopher is a good second one; but what kind of "philosopher"? Had the Jewish delegation included a philosopher, he might have asked the chairman kindly to define philosophy. And having given one definition after another, only to have the universality of each questioned, the chairman might have ended sheepishly with the tautology that "philosophy is what philosophers are doing." Whereupon his Jewish counterpart might have rejoined, triumphantly, that Jewish philosophy is what Jewish philosophers are doing. The triumph of this hypothetical reply depends, of course, on there being Jewish philosophers doing Jewish philosophy; to employ a useful distinction current in Israel—that there is *filosofiyah yehudit* (Jewish philosophy) in particular, and not just *mahshevet yisrael* (Jewish thought) in general. The latter framework would include, among other genres, midrash, which consists of parables, stories, and the like—perhaps the deepest Jewish thought there has ever been. But it is not philosophy. However, if there is even one "Jewish philosopher" there is Jewish philosophy, and surely there is at least one, namely, Maimonides. And, had that chairman been knowledgeable in the field, he would have conceded that there is, at least, medieval Jewish philosophy.

But is medieval philosophy philosophy? At one time philosophy curricula in non-Catholic institutions would leap straight from the last of the ancients—neo-Platonists, Stoics, Epicureans—to the first of the moderns, on the grounds that philosophy produced in the "dark ages" was itself dark, that is, subject to ecclesiastic authorities and thus ipso facto nonphilosophical.

But that this prejudice has long been abandoned is shown, for example, by the massive, two-volume Scribner's *Selections from Medieval Philosophers,* edited by the distinguished Chicago philosopher Richard McKeon, a work first published in 1929—and the last time I checked, still in print. No one using that text (as I have) can go on holding that there is no medieval philosophy. However, McKeon's anthology is itself shot through with prejudice. It contains selections from no fewer than fifteen medieval philosophers: but not a single one is Jewish, or for that matter Muslim. This was quite characteristic of the time; otherwise critical professors would quite habitually allude to Maimonides for one purpose only—to shed light on Thomas Aquinas when he quotes "Rabbi Moyses."

The situation has improved greatly since then. Presumably the Scribner text is still being used. But there is now also a text such as *Philosophy in the Middle Ages* (Indianapolis: Hackett, 1973). It contains some five hundred pages of Christian philosophy, edited by James Walsh, and about one hundred and fifty pages, respectively, of Muslim and Jewish philosophy, edited by Arthur Hyman. Considering the small number of Jews philosophizing in the Middle Ages, compared to Christians and to a lesser degree also to Muslims, this is no mean Jewish philosophical presence. My 1978 copy of that text was already in its fourth printing.

Medieval philosophy is, of course, a special case. In one way, one may classify it as Aristotelian, neo-Platonic, and so forth; in another, perhaps more profound way, it is classifiable as Muslim, Jewish, and Christian. Modern philosophy, in contrast, comes on the scene as universal, for one need only be human and rational in order to assent to, or dissent from, Descartes' doubt, or Francis Bacon's doctrine of the four idols, or Kant's categorical imperative. Particularity thus appears as ipso facto unphilosophical, and the task of philosophy is to rise above it.

While critical rationality has been the principle of modern philosophy, it cannot be said that it has been applied impartially, either by the modern philosophers themselves or in their treatment in the Academy. Descartes did not extend his doubt to Christianity, and Bacon did not make the Christian faith into yet a fifth idol—he even made a pretense to Christian orthodoxy. As for their critics in the Academy, has anyone ever charged either Descartes or Bacon with a Christian parochialism that is unphilosophical? In contrast, I have read a good many critics assert or imply that, for Spinoza to have the honored place he has in philosophy, he had to transcend his "narrow" or "parochial" Jewish heritage.

Spinoza is a modern philosopher, but hardly a Jewish one. The first modern Jewish philosopher is Moses Mendelssohn, who was highly respected by Kant as a general philosopher. As for Judaism, Kant hoped—presumably for the benefit of Jews themselves, for he was not a nasty man—for its euthanasia. Kant did not, however, wish for the euthanasia of Christianity. Instead, he conducted what may be called a rescue operation on behalf of a Christianity that was liberal in the extreme, by making his Christ into a—perhaps even *the*—teacher of morality. But it never entered his mind to allow a similar operation on behalf of Judaism, say, with the help of Isaiah. Matters did not change much during the next century and a half. Samuel Hirsch's *Religionsphilosophie der Juden* (1842) is a powerful Jewish critique of Hegel from the right, and Moses Hess's *Rom und Jerusalem* (1862) may be viewed, among other things, as a Jewish critique of Hegel from the left. Both works appeared after Hegel's death, and I have reason to believe that had the master been alive, he would have taken both works seriously. But the right-wing Hegel orthodoxy ignored Hirsch, and the Hegelian left took note of Hess only for purposes of vituperation.

To move from the nineteenth to the twentieth century, Hermann Cohen's neo-Kantian philosophy was at one time profoundly influential in the Academy; the same cannot be said for the work in Jewish philosophy which he wrote in old age, his *Religion der Vernunft aus den Quellen des Judentums* (1917). Again, Franz Rosenzweig, who died young, took close note, virtually on his deathbed, of Martin Heidegger's

Sein und Zeit (1927). Heidegger, who lived a long life, ignored Rosenzweig's *Stern der Erlösung* (1921), and most Heideggerians have done likewise.

To move from Germany to France, while Jews never had a better philosophical friend than Jean-Paul Sartre in the darkest period of Jewish history, the philosopher who wrote *Antisemite and Jew* (1946) also wrote that existentialism is either atheist or Christian. For Sartre, Martin Buber and Franz Rosenzweig did not exist.

Until the recent past, then, philosophers have ignored, or all but ignored, Jewish philosophers. They should have given them serious attention. I argue that there is Jewish philosophy whenever a genuine Jewish commitment accompanies an engagement with general philosophy that is philosophically respectable. This definition holds true of all the Jewish thinkers mentioned above, but it holds true superlatively for Hermann Cohen and Franz Rosenzweig. Cohen was a neo-Kantian before he became a Jewish philosopher; and Rosenzweig wrote and published his *Hegel und der Staat* (1920) before he wrote and published *Stern der Erlösung* (1921).

The situation has greatly improved since World War II, at least in part because of the war. Since the Holocaust, the aim of which was to make Jews cease to exist, it has become difficult for the Academy to treat Jewish philosophy as nonexistent. Thus, for example, not only the general but also the Jewish thought of Leo Strauss and Emmanuel Levinas are receiving attention. Again, Cohen's *Religion of Reason* (1972) and Rosenzweig's *Star of Redemption* (1970) are now available in English. In 1986 a truly extraordinary conference about the latter's thought was held in his native city of Kassel, which resulted in the massive two-volume *Der Philosoph Franz Rosenzweig* (Freiburg/Muenchen, 1988).

Still, old stereotypes die hard, and among them is the verdict that whereas philosophy is broad and universal, Judaism, and therefore Jewish philosophy, is narrow and parochial. In consequence, the recent outreach of philosophy toward things Jewish often does not genuinely penetrate the Academy. This may be shown by two examples.

In the case of Martin Buber's thought, one cannot complain of academic inattention. His *I and Thou* has been widely studied in philosophy classes for well over a generation. This very success, however, reveals the problem, for in the process of acceptance his thought has been widely dejudaized. Is there ever a philosophy professor who stresses (let alone explores in depth) that the book's central thesis—an immediate divine-human relation, without need of a mediator—is a Jewish thesis, profoundly at odds with Christianity? A presumably apocryphal story has a Christian theology student listening to a lecture on Buber, liking what he hears, but walking out thinking that this man Buber is a bit weak in Christology!

My second example is the use of the term "Judeo-Christian." Experience has taught me to become suspicious whenever that term is used by a philosopher. The following glaring example is taken from Ninian Smart's *The Philosophy of Religion* (New York, 1970), p. 115:

> Another necessary condition of the acceptability of revelation is a mixture of the ethical and the historical. Still confining our examples to the Judeo-Christian tradition: suppose that tomorrow a new document were turned up in the sands of the Negev, which was seen to be an account of the life of Jesus (or Moses), but by the usual historical criteria was much more reliable than the Gospels (or the Old Testament). Suppose that it showed conclusively that Jesus wantonly murdered one or two people (or that Moses did). Would it be easy to think of Jesus (or Moses) in the way in which orthodox believers do? Would it still be possible to treat this real (not just technical) criminal as *Son of God?* (Emphasis added.)

What Jew ever thought of Moses as the Son of God! The conclusion is clear: any philosopher using "Judeo-Christian" bears the burden of proof that his use of the term is more than tokenism. And is there a Judeo-Christian tradition? This, not without reason, is widely denied.

As regards the stereotype of "philosophical universalism vs. Jewish particularism," the time may be ripe for reflections more radical than the piecemeal criticism offered in this essay, for ours is said to be the "postmodern" age, and one feature of postmodernity is the questioning, or even denial, of the universalism of Western philosophy, beginning with Athens. Any such questioning should not just follow fashion, but must itself be philosophical. It should also move cautiously, and caution might best be served not by traveling directly to far-off Asia or Africa, but by confronting Athens with nearby Jerusalem. Athene remains bound up with Athens, but Jerusalem is ruled by a God who is creator of the world—this is one contrast. With it goes another: whereas Plato addresses Greeks but excludes barbarians, all humanity is included by Isaiah:

Out of Zion shall go forth the law,
And the word of God from Jerusalem
And He shall judge between the nations.
And shall decide for many peoples;
And they shall beat their swords into plowshares
And their spears into pruning-hooks;
Nation shall not lift up sword against nation,
Neither shall they learn war anymore.

Perhaps a new meeting between Plato and Isaiah is a major task of philosophy in the postmodern world. Perhaps its own share in this meeting is a major task of Jewish philosophy.

III

EXPANDING AND DEEPENING THE FIELD

10. ICUTJC: DESIGN AND REALIZATION

Moshe Davis

There is no generally accepted framework of Jewish civilization studies as taught in universities in different parts of the world. Variations accrue under the impact of the environing cultures in all Western countries; similar heterogeneity is apparent in the recent unanticipated growth of such courses in Asia and Africa. Broad cultural differences are further compounded by local historical and institutional factors. Thus definitions, programs, and curricula invariably follow function. Generalizations advanced by representative scholars are often based on purposes and aspirations determined by their own concrete situation.

This salient factor wove through my comparative analysis (1979) of 560 colleges and universities with Jewish civilization departments and/ or accredited courses in interdepartmental programs. The data were set forth in the study and proposal I presented at the behest of the president at the time, Ephraim Katzir, for the development of international cooperation in the burgeoning field of university teaching of Jewish civilization.[1]

The data and recommendations were based on a two-year field study of universities on three continents in eleven countries: in Latin America (Argentina, Brazil, Mexico); the United States and Canada; England and continental Europe. In addition to assembling pertinent documentation, I engaged in consultations with people ranging from university teachers, administrators, and graduate students, to communal leaders. Among other considerations, I sought the following three prerequisites:

1. Universities interested in developing and/or introducing departments for the systematic teaching of Jewish culture;

2. Universities with a relatively large and/or prospective interested student population;
3. Universities that could serve as generating forces to other institutions in a similar cultural ambience.

Several examples suffice to illustrate the varying emphases in different countries.[2] In France at Paris III, where Jewish studies began as a chair in Hebrew languages, the teaching of Jewish history, literature, and philosophy as well as the sociology, anthropology, and psychology of contemporary Jewry was introduced through the curriculum of the Hebrew language section.

On the British scene, it was fascinating to discern how the boundaries of Jewish study programs expanded from their previously limited state of biblical studies, so closely allied to theology, to a ramified program of historical and contemporary subjects. In Canada, at the University of Toronto, Jewish studies constituted, in effect, an interdisciplinary program embracing philosophy, history, medieval studies, and Near Eastern studies; students took courses in these departments as well as within their Judaica specialization.

Within Latin American frameworks, pockets of university courses on Jews and Judaism were sponsored under Jewish communal initiatives and/or support. Slowly but steadily, cooperative programs were developed, essentially Hebrew language chairs, with universities in Rio de Janeiro and São Paulo; while in Buenos Aires, courses in Yiddish were initiated at the Catholic Universidad del Salvador.

In the United States, where the study of Hebrew language and culture has a time-honored history, virtually every conceivable type of program emerged, from the one-person academic "staff," to full-scale departments in institutions with a large student body. Unlike the situation in Latin America and Western Europe where the problem was underdevelopment, in North America it was overly rapid development.

Notwithstanding these structural differences from country to country and the problems that confronted the respective educational systems, when one considered the increase of courses, variegated typological settings, and number of students interested in entering the realm of Jewish scholarship, it was fair to conclude that in sheer quantitative increase an academic revolution had taken place. However, numbers alone did not adequately describe the growth process. Jewish themes were becoming increasingly accepted in such diverse departments as religion, Near Eastern studies, literature, linguistics, history, philosophy, sociology, and political science. In these frameworks, aspects of Jewish civilization were recognized as legitimate dissertation subjects, a development which in itself required special attention. All this led to another feature of the growth process—the emergence of a new generation of scholars in Jewish studies trained in the general university system rather than in exclusively Jewish institutions of higher learning.

The dynamic character of the field inquiry pointed to many novel possibilities, which were fully discussed in the aforementioned *Policy Report*. Central to the specific recommendation was the recognition that we had entered a time when frontiers of learning were expanding immeasurably, when national literatures had cut across boundaries and when world cultures were in ferment. In such an era, with our minds directed to the future, it was not too difficult to envisage how the best national programs, tested on several continents, could become internationalized. The imperative, it seemed to me, was to establish a global intellectual and educational infrastructure for university Jewish civilization studies, which would address itself to such basic problems as developing a faculty and pedagogic literature, and relating Judaica studies within world culture. These issues clearly did not lend themselves to immediate amelioration; rapid solutions could engender a host of new problems. However, we felt they should remain in the foreground of all planning even as some of the urgent questions were to be tackled immediately.

FACULTY

In this area, the principle that governed university appointees, posited by Harvard's Charles William Eliot, was a guiding star: "The good is the enemy of the excellent." In regard to Jewish studies, compromise with lower standards was rationalized on the basis that the needs were greater than available funding for senior scholars. It was the historian Jacob Katz who emphasized that the hasty expansion of Jewish studies programs carries not only a blessing, but a curse as well, particularly when students encounter teachers who cannot compete academically with those in the more established disciplines. The curse becomes especially severe once tenure is granted, for then it affects not one but many generations of students. The problem is how to ensure that those involved in the teaching of Judaica in an accredited university are ranking scholars who can make a contribution to the entire academic community. Great teachers attract superior students. The ultimate test, Sir Isaiah Berlin once remarked, is whether a lecture on Jews and Judaism can interest not only the best graduate students, but also whether any faculty members who may wander in will find personal enrichment.

PEDAGOGIC LITERATURE

Even the finest faculty remains inadequate without an adequate library for student use; scholarly treatises alone are insufficient. In order to provide primary and secondary source literature for variant settings, a long-range translation and adaptation effort is required. Israel is the ideal center for the establishment of a school of translators to create and publish basic books in English, French, Spanish, and Russian—a program which could be of genuine aid not only in international higher educational systems but in the Israeli universities as well. Moreover, in planning regional cooperative enterprises, one cannot overemphasize the importance of an extensive exchange library for the development of a serious department of Jewish civilization studies. Finally, the potential of multimedia teaching should be tapped for all it can offer. Pedagogic exchange can easily include films, videos, and oral history documentation as part of a standard teaching curriculum. In a word: the world of Jewish learning can be brought into any university classroom.

JEWISH CIVILIZATION STUDIES IN RELATION TO WORLD CULTURE

A dramatic new vista of Jewish studies is the ongoing introduction of courses on Judaism and the Jews as factors in world civilization, in settings where there are few or no Jewish students. When Edmund Wilson first proposed the idea for his ideal university, it was considered a novel but impractical suggestion. Wilson urged the incorporation of courses on the literature and history of the Jews for both Gentile and

Jewish students so that Jewish history, thought, and creativity could become "common knowledge."[3]

Our field study revealed that the concept of teaching the entire experience of the Jewish people—their religion, history, thought, and culture—had extended to hitherto closed circles. For example, there was the growing and quite unanticipated phenomenon of such courses taught in Catholic universities. In addition, undoubtedly because of theological, pedagogical, and practical reconsiderations evoked by the existence of the State of Israel, incorporation of Jewish studies became possible even in the Third World. Political realities called for a scholarly response and pointed to the need to bring scholars working in similar specializations, despite their ideological differences, into fruitful working relationships.

Within the parameters of relating Judaism and the Jews to universal history, the higher institutions of learning in Israel could play a crucial role. At the Hebrew University's Institute of Jewish Studies, virtually every department, from archeology up the entire ladder of Jewish history and culture, enjoyed a full faculty. Similar departments rapidly developed at the universities of Tel Aviv, Haifa, Bar-Ilan, and Beersheva. Many yeshivot in Israel also produced a wealth of scholarship. Israeli institutions were clearly an unparalleled source for the training of future scholars in university-level Judaica. They could also play a correlative role on all levels of university education: third-year collegiate training, graduate studies, and exchange and visiting faculty.

With these basic objectives in mind, there were at least two possible approaches for the implementation of the *Policy Report*. The first was to go into the widespread field itself, relying upon existing knowledge and experience, to select institutional models in specific areas, and to work with interested university and communal structures in developing a composite program in Jewish civilization studies. In this manner, immediate experimentation could be undertaken while the process of structural organization was in progress. A second approach was to attempt to create an institution in cooperation with the Israeli universities and directed to the international academic community, which would seek to meet the threefold objectives of faculty building, preparation of pedagogic literature, and incorporation of Jewish civilization studies within the university framework.

The *Policy Report* which was initially planned with President Katzir and his committee, was presented to the fifth president of Israel, Yitzhak Navon, upon his election. He wholeheartedly affirmed the establishment of the International Center for University Teaching of Jewish Civilization under the aegis of the Israeli presidency. We chose to move immediately into the second approach, by creating a series of annual academic workshops in Jerusalem—a direction originally suggested by Seymour Fox, then head of the Hebrew University's School of Education.

Slowly but steadily the workshop programs were built, in consultation with leading figures in world Jewish scholarship. Proceeding from basic areas, for example, Hebrew language and literature, and Jewish history, additional workshops were created in what we termed "breakthrough" disciplines in the university curriculum. The conceptual frameworks for these colloquia, presented by their directors in the chapters that follow, reflect the broad spectrum of Jewish studies taught in the world of academe. In short time, a series of publications and regional cooperative projects emerged. Above all, we were witnesses to the flowering of a new generation of scholars who studied with senior colleagues from different countries and disciplines.

In retrospect, as the original design was being realized and while we were planning for the future, we were in fact stimulating ongoing change. As we evaluated programs together, modifying and initiating fresh ideas, we learned to appreciate the potentialities of an international academic order in Jewish civilization studies.

NOTES

1. Paper submitted to the International Seminar on World Jewry and the State of Israel at the residence of the president of Israel (Jerusalem, December 1979).
2. The full-scale study was published in the *Policy Report, University Teaching of Jewish Civilization* (Jerusalem, 1979); abridged version in Hebrew, English, French, and Spanish, September 1981.
3. Edmund Wilson, *A Piece of My Mind* (New York: Doubleday, 1958), 152–53, also 146–51.

11. CONTEMPORARY JEWISH CIVILIZATION

Gideon Shimoni

It is difficult to arrive at complete agreement among academics regarding a hard and fast definition of "contemporary Jewry." The term refers to a certain time focus, applied to the study of many aspects of Jewish life and culture. "Contemporary" can be consensually understood to connote that part of the past which is covered by the experience of those still living, that is to say, approximately seventy or eighty years. This understanding is compatible with a variety of more specific conceptions to be found among historians, sociologists, and those who identify the term "contemporary" with particular events regarded as turning points in the twentieth century, such as World War I, the Holocaust, or the emergence of the State of Israel. Likewise, it is consonant with the pedagogically oriented view that identifies a "contemporary" approach with the attempt to answer questions of existential importance for the present generation, by methods of the social sciences and by inquiring as far as is relevant into the past.

The number of courses focusing on "contemporary" aspects of Jewish life and culture is expanding at universities throughout the world. In the mid-1980s, Moshe Davis provided a preliminary survey of this development, delineating the variations resulting from the different national settings in which university teaching of contemporary Jewish civilization takes place. The survey showed that wherever Jewish studies was established for the first time, courses in contemporary Jewry also developed, more often than not at a greater pace than ancient or medieval subjects.

In the United States and Canada, where an efflorescence of Jewish studies has taken place in recent years, courses on modern-contemporary Jewish history and the sociology of the Jews tend to concentrate wholly on the American Jewish community rather than on global perspectives. In Latin America and South Africa, regions suffering from a dearth of academic resources in the field of Jewish studies, courses dealing with contemporary Jewry have benefited in recent years by drawing upon the resources of teachers in Israeli universities.

University courses relating to contemporary Jewry are taught in a wide variety of departmental contexts. The Institute of Contemporary Jewry at the Hebrew University is perhaps the only case of a department devoted wholly to teaching about contemporary Jewry. It embraces regional studies (e.g., American Jewry, Latin American Jewry, Soviet Jewry), various academic disciplines (history, demography, sociology, etc.) and specific subjects (e.g., the Holocaust, Zionism).

Another context for such courses is an interdepartmental program. For example, the Jewish Studies Program at Queens College of the City University of New York offers interdepartmental courses in Jewish intellectual and social history, and sociology and folklore of the Jews; a number of these courses include a contemporary focus. Individual courses are also to be found in departments of Jewish studies or religion in many universities and in Jewish-sponsored institutes of higher learning such as Hebrew Union College and the Jewish Theological Seminary. At a number of universities throughout the world, courses relating to contemporary Jewry are offered sporadically within conventional academic disciplines such as history, literature, political science, and sociology.

Recognizing the highly diversified nature of courses in the field, the workshop on contemporary Jewry, first convened in 1982, determined that the overall goal was to enhance the teaching of contemporary Jewish studies in all relevant disciplines, through multidisciplinary exchanges of pedagogic approaches, conceptual frameworks, and bibliographies. It was decided that flexibility was desirable in drawing the line of distinction between the terms "modern" and "contemporary," and that a series of workshop sessions would each be devoted to a different teaching theme.

It was also recommended that priority be given to the publication of selected syllabi as an outgrowth of some of these workshops. These were not to be models of the ideal—this would presume to infringe on the autonomy and individuality of university teachers—but rather examples of what was actually being taught. Such a publication series would expose the work of the workshops to a far wider community of scholars and, hopefully, encourage more teachers in all academic disciplines to undertake courses related to Jewish themes.

The outcome has been a series of annual workshops, each with approximately thirty participants, of whom some twenty were from universities abroad and the remaining ten from Israeli universities. Although the majority were historians, disciplines such as sociology, political science, and literature have also been represented. In 1983 the workshop focused on "Israel: History, Society and Culture," an area widely taught in departments of history, political science, Middle Eastern studies, and sociology. The 1984 session concerned itself with presentation and evaluation of syllabi for courses in contemporary Jewish studies. These were published in 1985 in *Contemporary Jewish Civilization,* a book of selected syllabi, edited by Gideon Shimoni, the workshop director. Succeeding workshops dealt with Jewish emancipation (with papers published as an in-house monograph), the Jews in Muslim countries, and teaching Zionism. The 1988 workshop that dealt with the theme of the Holocaust attracted a particularly large group of participants, reflecting the fact that this is a frequently taught Jewish studies course at universities throughout the world. A collection of selected syllabi dealing solely with this theme was published in 1991 as *The Holocaust in University Teaching,* again edited by Gideon Shimoni and published in England by Pergamon Press.

Both these books contain methodological essays as well as a wide range of syllabi that are presented in a distinctive format. In addition to listing course content and bibliographical readings, they provide the reader with an explanation of the considerations, conceptual frameworks, and objectives that inform each syllabus. At the same time, the autonomy and individuality of each contributor has been respected, allowing for varying degrees of detail in the presentation as well as for differences in course structure, methodology, and prescribed readings. In some cases, the contributors include examples of examination questions and essay topics that further illuminate the scope of the course.

An evaluation session in 1989 recommended a shift of emphasis from consideration of teaching syllabi, to substantive papers on the state of knowledge in the field and conceptual frameworks for teaching. In this vein, a workshop was devoted to "Antisemitism," a subject ubiquitous in courses on Jewish history as well as in other disciplines. A volume drawing on the papers presented, edited by Michael Brown of York University, a member of the workshop's international advisory committee, was published in 1994 in cooperation with the American Jewish Committee, under the title *Approaches to Antisemitism: Contexts and Curriculum.*

Yet another book that was initiated by the International Center and to which many of the workshop participants contributed is *The Modern Jewish Experience,* edited by Jack Wertheimer and prepared in cooperation with The Jewish Theological Seminary of America (New York University Press, 1993). This volume contains essays providing comprehensive guides to readings on a wide range of teaching subjects, many of which belong to the contemporary period.

While the workshop on contemporary Jewry recognizes its accomplishments in the exploration of a variety of themes and the publication of sample syllabi, other related objectives remain as challenges. There is a need for anthologies of source and secondary readings that relate to particular issues in contemporary Jewish civilization on which there are important differences of approach or interpretation among scholars in the field. Such a series, which can be incorporated into modules within a wide variety of courses, would enrich teaching in the field. Another clearly identified need is the production of a textbook for undergraduates, conceptualizing and surveying the entire field of contemporary Jewry. Such an undertaking calls for the pooling of resources from a number of disciplines and the cooperation of a team of subeditors under a unifying initiative.

The continuation of annual workshop sessions remains the main contribution that the International Center can make to the development of the field of contemporary Jewish studies worldwide. New themes of relevance at the close of the century should be explored; an example is "Gender as a Factor in University Teaching of Contemporary Jewish Civilization" which was the theme of the 1994 workshop. It may also be worthwhile to return to some of the topics discussed in past years, with the participation of a new generation of young university teachers.

Experience has shown that expansion in the field is largely the result of initiatives taken by teachers rooted in conventional disciplines. The Center's work can continue to stimulate and assist such teachers in the creation of new course options on Jewish themes relating to the contemporary world.

12. HEBREW LANGUAGE AND LITERATURE

Raphael Nir and Ben-Zion Fischler

Hebrew is the most widely taught subject within the field of Jewish studies in institutions of higher learning outside of Israel. Indeed, the International Center's World Register of university studies in Jewish civilization lists over nine hundred institutions of higher learning throughout the world that offer courses in the Hebrew language. Some have hundreds of students (particularly in the United States and in France); others have fewer than a dozen (e.g., in Romania and in China). Hebrew courses also exist in Arab countries. However, all of them focus for the most part on the classical—mainly biblical—language. Only to a lesser extent do they seek to teach elementary communication skills in the modern Hebrew spoken in Israel.

Thus, when a continuing workshop on the teaching of Hebrew language and literature was inaugurated by the International Center, in cooperation with the Hebrew Language Division, Department of Jewish Education and Culture in the Diaspora (World Zionist Organization), it set as its goal the promotion and enrichment of university teaching of modern Hebrew.

The primary challenge confronting the teaching of Hebrew as a second language is to define the goals and methods of instruction. This was addressed in the summer of 1982 by teachers of Hebrew from the United States, England, France, Holland, and South Africa who met with scholars of modern Hebrew in Jerusalem. They discussed the various aims of language instruction: communicative, cultural, and metalinguistic. In universities, the communicative aim focuses mainly on the reading of texts; oral skills are less emphasized and are introduced as an aid to reading comprehension. The cultural aim enjoys a particular status in the teaching of Hebrew, for the language often serves as a means to become acquainted with Jewish values and Israeli culture. This does not presuppose a necessary connection between the religious faith of the students and the target language. The acquisition of Hebrew is often considered to be a means for learning the Jewish tradition by non-Jewish students, for example, by students of theology. Metalinguistically, the grammar and structure of the language are considered to be a legitimate academic subject in itself. The aim of teaching determines the teacher's approach and the techniques applied in the classroom.

Following this first workshop, a small volume was published, intended for teachers of Hebrew at the university level throughout the world. The articles therein examined some of the linguistic, sociological, and didactic issues related to the teaching of contemporary Hebrew. Subsequent workshops considered another problematic aspect of Hebrew language instruction, namely, creating a syllabus and deciding on methods of instruction beyond the beginner's level, when the students have a limited vocabulary of some two thousand to three thousand words and do not exercise a full command of the language. At this stage, students develop an interest in "authentic" literary texts, but find their progress hampered by a lack of linguistic competence. The study of texts is thus distorted: instead of serving as ends in themselves, they become tools by which the teacher seeks to improve the students' command of the language. The preoccupation with grammar and linguistic structure affects the students' motivation and leads to a high dropout rate at the point of transition from the beginning to the intermediate level of learning Hebrew.

To manage this problem, three working groups were formed, dealing respectively with poetry, narrative literature, and essays. The participants analyzed syllabi and techniques of instruction at the intermediate level, focusing on reading comprehension because of its paramount importance in the context of university requirements. The recommendations of each group were discussed by all the participants, the principal problems in the teaching of intermediate level texts were defined, and ideas were advanced concerning their solution. These subsequently appeared in a book dealing with literary Hebrew on the intermediate level. It presented the theoretical framework for teaching Hebrew texts, focused on specific didactic problems related to the principles of applied linguistics, and listed a wide variety of anthologies of texts in Hebrew, so that teachers might choose those best suited to the individual tastes and particular level of their students. The last part of the book was devoted to the teaching of several literary passages concerned with one central theme—War and Peace. The full text of each passage was printed, together with several detailed suggestions for teaching it at the intermediate level. These guidelines could be adapted by each teacher to the specific needs of his or her classroom.

In succeeding years, the workshop has considered approaches to teaching Hebrew as a second language; the role of grammar in language instruction; computerized teaching; use of television and other audio-visual materials as teaching aids (utilizing the resources available at the Hebrew University); introduction of Hebrew texts from the Bible, midrash, and aggadah into the classroom; and teaching various genres of contemporary Hebrew literature (with the participation of Israeli authors). A third volume dealing with the teaching of Hebrew language and literature at the academic level appeared in 1991. It sought to define the aims, approaches, methods, and techniques of Hebrew instruction, and also included a global survey of universities that offer courses in Hebrew.

The workshop has now established as priority considerations the place of biblical and midrashic texts in the language curriculum, and exploration of methods for the integration of classical Hebrew within the teaching of the modern language. This will encourage the inclusion of modern Hebrew courses within a wider variety of institutions of higher learning.

13. JEWISH POLITICAL STUDIES

Daniel J. Elazar

The modern Jewish quest for community produced by the breakdown of the premodern Jewish order calls for a renewed interest in Jewish political studies. A once flourishing area of import in Jewish tradition, this field has emerged in the past fifteen years to acquire a place in the consciousness of those concerned with Jewish nationhood and community at the highest level and, more immediately, with the life of specific Jewish communities and polities.

Recent Jewish social and historical research has revealed the existence of a continuous thread of political institutions in Jewish life, from the earliest days of the formation of the Israelite tribal confederacy to the present. While investigation of this facet of Jewish life had remained peripheral, subordinate to conventional historical and sociological studies, the changing conditions of Jewish life in the Diaspora, the reestablishment of the State of Israel, and the awakening of Western interest in civilizations outside the Christian European mainstream have given new impetus to research in Jewish political studies.

How do we define "Jewish political studies" as a field, and what are its concerns? Politics itself is concerned with both power and justice, with who gets what, when, and how (in the words of Harold Lasswell), and with the search for the good political order. Jews share these concerns when they function as a corporate body as well as in their individual capacities. Political or public concerns are those involving the community as a whole, the collective interests of people living in the community, activities in society that have a communal bent or character, and the concerns of individuals insofar as they relate to community life and interests. While acknowledgment of some distinction between public and private concerns is crucial, it is equally clear that no sharp division between the two spheres can ever be drawn, even for reasons of convention. Rather, Jewish life can be conceived as revolving around a core of clearly political concerns, for example, the life of the community or the provision of certain public services, surrounded by concentric circles of concern that move out toward the private realm and into a gray area of matters that can be considered "public" for some purposes and "private" for others.

The delineation of Jewish political studies raises certain additional problems by virtue of its Jewish aspect. In the Western world, where the separation between public and private starts from firmly established premises, and the political and the religious aspects of life are separated with equal clarity, public affairs soon resolve themselves into questions of the immediately or essentially political. Within the framework of Jewish civilization, however, the distinctions between public and private, political and religious, are substantially blurred. Moreover, the lack of clearly defined political institutions to help set the formal boundaries of public affairs (at least in the Diaspora) requires examination of Jewish social and communal life with a more careful and penetrating eye. Here, the present state of our knowledge gives us an advantage over preceding generations. Social scientists have discovered in Afro-Asian cultures a blurring of public and private, political and religious, that is similar to what is found in Jewish life; this gives us some new points of comparison.

In sum, intellectual concern for and understanding of political matters deserve to be elevated to a prominent position in the spectrum of Jewish civilization studies. In part, this is simply a matter of recognizing and analyzing the political dimension always present in a tradition devoted to the creation of the good commonwealth here on earth. For, indeed, there is a neglected but extremely significant Jewish contribution to world political ideas and institutions that deserves to be explored and perhaps further developed for our own and future times. The role of Jewish political ideas in the formation of the United States is a case in point. Beyond that, Jewish ideas have played a special role in the development of the federal principle. There is reason to believe that these influences persist and are now being supplemented by institutional ones as well. Furthermore, an understanding of the influence of Jewish political ideas during the epochs of Jewish national independence and communal self-government can be useful in our efforts to meet the problems of public affairs and political organization in Israel and in the modern voluntary communities of the Diaspora.

The first task in the development of Jewish political studies as a field must be the identification of its content and concerns from historical and analytical perspectives. Tentatively, at least, we can start with the following broad questions:

- What are the central matters of concern in Jewish political studies? To what extent are they found universally in the Jewish experience?
- How has Jewish political thought treated the fundamental questions of political life?
- What principles have animated Jewish community organization and government? How have they been developed and applied in various Jewish communities and polities at different periods?
- What conceptions of the good commonwealth have been developed from Jewish sources? What impact have they had? What role can they play today?

In recent years a growing group of scholars around the world has been working together to develop the field of Jewish political studies as a fully articulated element in the Jewish studies constellation. Bar Ilan University offers a concentration in Jewish political studies at the B.A., M.A., and Ph.D. degree levels. An international consortium devoted to the study of Jewish political phenomena was organized in 1970 and within a few years developed into the Center for Jewish Community Studies, now part of the Jerusalem Center for Public Affairs. Since 1969 there have been sessions in Jewish political studies at the World Congress of Jewish Studies and, since 1979, the Association for Jewish Studies has included a Jewish political studies section.

In 1981 the Jerusalem Center for Public Affairs conducted its first summer workshop in Jewish political studies, with the aim of developing a cadre of scholars capable of teaching this field in their respective universities. Two years later, this workshop was institutionalized in cooperation with the International Center for the University Teaching of Jewish Civilization.

The continuing workshop in Jewish political studies has achieved a great deal in the years of its existence. It has attracted over one hundred participants from ten countries on all continents, and it has developed a core of academics who teach and do research in the field. It has considered such topics as leadership, citizenship, and interrelationships; Jewish politics in various countries; integrating Jewish political studies in the political science curriculum; the influence of the Jewish political tradition on the State of Israel; constitutional documents of contemporary Jewish communities; rights and obligations in the Jewish political tradition; liberal democracy and communitarian democracy in the Jewish political tradition; and Israel and world Jewry: contemporary and historical issues. In order to encourage the introduction of such topics into political science courses, a book of selected syllabi, entitled *Jewish Political Studies*, edited by Daniel J. Elazar and Tzipora D. Stein, was published.

The workshop has also generated new courses in Jewish political studies at a number of universities, and its participants have introduced modules into courses in political science, political philosophy, and history. Numerous books and articles that further explore the field and provide basic reading material for students in Jewish political studies courses have emerged from the workshop.

With all of that, we still face serious challenges. While we have achieved a place for Jewish political studies in departments of political science and Jewish studies, we have not yet built that place into the central one that it deserves. The number of political scientists interested in Jewish political studies is growing steadily, but the development of additional scholars and teachers prepared to teach in the field is slow. Moreover, exploration of the materials of Jewish political studies has barely scratched the surface of a vast universe requiring many different methodological skills, for which people have to be trained.

In the future we expect to continue our summer workshops on different themes; to increase the number and range of our participants; through them, to introduce more teaching of the subject in separate courses or integrated into the general political science curriculum; and to publish the results of our work. While there are many institutions and individuals who contribute to the field of Jewish political studies, we see our continuing workshop as the integrating force linking them all.

14. JEWISH HISTORY AND CULTURE: SEPHARDIC AND ORIENTAL STUDIES

Moshe Bar-Asher

When the International Center considered initiating a continuing workshop in Jewish history, it was decided to begin with the history and culture of Sephardic and Oriental Jewries. These groups had largely been ignored in the general burgeoning of Jewish civilization studies. While research institutes and academic courses were being introduced in Israel and France, the two main centers of North African Jewish emigration, there was growing recognition that the unique cultural contributions of these groups called for the expansion of such efforts in wider academic circles.

The workshop was inaugurated in 1983 under the direction of Michel Abitbol. Within the general rubric of Sephardic history and culture, the participants explored such themes as historiography; written, ethnographic, and oral sources; communal organization; and cultural and religious trends. Proceeding from that assessment, the 1986 workshop was devoted to the integration of Sephardic history in the disciplines of social science and literature.

In 1987, the workshop turned to the history and culture of the Jews in Muslim countries, and I took over as director. Israel had become the center for research about North African Jewry because of its numerous scholars and academic centers that produce outstanding documentation on many facets of this Jewish dispersion. It was therefore important to bring researchers from abroad to meet their Israeli colleagues and to spend time in the research centers. An additional goal was to develop a promising generation of young scholars in France, where most students from North Africa and the Middle East seek their graduate education. Scholars working in this field in the universities of France, Spain, Italy, Germany, the United States, Canada, and elsewhere were invited to Jerusalem to participate in joint discussion of their research and teaching. The workshop presentations have been held mostly in French but also in Hebrew and English. About fifty academics have participated, including several Muslim scholars from Morocco.

Workshop sessions are structured as interdisciplinary convocations of historians, scholars of kabbalah and philosophy, researchers of the Hebrew language and literature, and specialists in folklore and folk literature. While the advantages of the disciplinary isolation characterizing many fields of research today are well known, the weaknesses are also evident. But the fact is that all of the participants have found the interdisciplinary approach to be fruitful.

Each year a different broad framework of research is chosen, such as North African Jewry and Spain, North African Jewry and its contacts with other European settlements, and North African Jewry and the Land of Israel. Texts that would be of interest to researchers of different disciplines are selected, with priority given to previously unpublished material. In addition, manuscripts and oral documentation gathered by researchers over many years are shared and discussed.

The emphasis has been on research, in order to expand the store of primary and secondary materials appropriate for university teaching. Indeed, it is our belief that ongoing research and collegial exchange among scholars from a variety of disciplines are indispensable for the enrichment of teaching at the university level. The workshop has undertaken field trips to meet with North African Jews able to provide oral history. The informants were interviewed by seasoned scholars who served as role models for younger colleagues who had not yet had such experience. We have also held guided tours to libraries and research centers, as well as to private collections of relevant documents.

The influence of the workshops is clearly discernible in the research work undertaken subsequently by the participants, and in articles published in academic journals and anthologies, both in Israel and abroad. Some examples: Joseph Chitrit, "The Hebrew-Aramaic Component of Moroccan Judeo-Arabic: A Language of a Muslim Poem written as Jewish," *Massoret* 3/4 (1989); Moshe Bar-Asher, "The Sharh of the Maghreb: Judeo-Arabic Exegesis of the Bible and Other Jewish Literature—Its Nature and Formulation," in *Studies in Jewish Languages, Bible Translations and Spoken Dialects* (Jerusalem, 1988); and Joseph Tedghi, *Jewish Presses in Fez* (Jerusalem, 1994).

The participation of the young researchers from France and Morocco has served to develop close ties between them and many Israeli colleagues, to advance their research, and to integrate them into the international academic world. Four of these young scholars have recently received teaching positions in prestigious universities in France and in Morocco.

15. MODERN HEBREW LITERATURE IN ENGLISH TRANSLATION

Leon I. Yudkin

The teaching of modern Hebrew literature in translation is playing an increasingly prominent role in Jewish civilization courses, partly because of the increased availability of translated material. Contemporary Israeli writers are now widely translated, particularly into English, and primary and secondary source material also exists in translation.

The perspectives and goals of the courses vary, depending on the institutional or departmental framework or the personal predilection of the instructor. Contemporary secular Hebrew literature can be contrasted with traditional medieval Hebrew texts, or with the literary limitations of the early Enlightenment period. Hebrew linguistics can be studied: the syntax was first Europeanized, then nationalized, and the modern language is being used for new purposes and in new ways, extending the previously limited register to a national vernacular. Modern Hebrew literature expresses the culture of the renewed Jewish homeland, and the Jewish situation which occupies the center stage in the unfolding drama being played out in the Middle East is viewed both from the inside and the outside.

Israeli writing reflects on contemporary Jewish issues, ponders the Jewish fate, and becomes a major vehicle for Jewish thought. It is not only a Jewish literature, but a literature of Jews; not only national, ideological, and regional, but existential and personal as well. It has emerged from and responded to specific circumstances affecting the body politic and the individual in a cluster of circumstances that makes for tension and also seeks release.

Modern Hebrew literature is also open to interested inspection and probing from the outside. Through literature, one gains an insight into the national spirit, a somewhat indefinable area that may be regarded as having great significance. Thus, Israeli literature may serve as a barometer of emotional response to the Middle East situation in one of the most articulate centers of free opinion. It provides an inexhaustible mine of information about the place of the Jewish state in the contemporary Middle East, for Israel's writers often deal with national issues on a deeper, more complex, distanced, and multifaceted level than that of journalism (in which they also engage). A necessarily incomplete list would include Amos Oz, A. B. Yehoshua, Yoram Kaniuk, David Grossman, and Anton Shamas, among the writers who relate to the posture of Israel in the Middle East and to the position of individual Israelis in their own society. This natural resource is frequently incorporated in Middle East studies curricula, and in surveys of regional literature seeking to achieve a level of understanding beyond that of journalistic comment or sociological-statistical data.

Another motive for the study of modern Hebrew literature is solely literary. Beyond the framework of Jewish studies, departments of literature or of comparative literature can offer courses or modules including aspects of modern Hebrew writing. Such offerings frequently depend on the initiative of the rare pioneer in the field, as they would not be included automatically within the theory of literature or surveys of major European literatures. In all cases, the works must be recognized as having literary merit in their own right, and must be available in translation.

Emphasis on linguistics provides another motivation for the study of modern Hebrew literature in universities. Literature is the written expression of language, interesting for its development of a variant and perhaps greater vocabulary, a different and perhaps more complex grammar, and a modified syntax. In this regard, modern Hebrew literature may be seen as an ongoing record of the history of that language, and institutions of higher learning whose focus is on Semitic studies or the diachronic study of Hebrew may refer to modern Hebrew literature to highlight specific linguistic issues.

The material taught is as varied as the institutional frameworks. The basic subject is the literature itself, but two factors intervene before it can be studied: the translation, and the presentation—teacher, teaching method, and critical assumptions. Thus the reader/student receives the material through a multiple filter. This filter first selects the material and makes part of it available in translation, presenting it through the medium of the target language, with its specific history, cultural assumptions, and linguistic environment. Then it undergoes the analysis of the teacher/commentator/critic, who sets the scene for the student, provides historical, cultural, and linguistic information, and promotes the material, conditioned by a specific value system (which the reader/student can accept or reject).

Much ink has been spilled over the question of "good" and "bad" translations; the criteria for these standards are by no means fixed. A translation moves not only from one language to another, but from one cultural environment to another; a new associative framework is invoked, some aspects of which may be irrelevant or misleading. The connotations and intonations of the source language may be preserved, transformed, distorted, or lost. And this is quite apart from the question of material that remains totally untranslatable in idiom or associative uniqueness, or may be misunderstood by the translator. The translator engages in an enterprise of cultural transformation and the task is complex. However, a useful distinction may be made between two general approaches to the work of translation.

One approach seeks to obliterate traces of the source and absorb the material imperceptibly into the target language. The second deliberately cultivates traces of the source in order to preserve the flavor of the original, so that the reader is constantly aware of the provenance of the text. The justification of the first approach is readability. The translator argues that had the author been writing in the target language, he or she would have attempted to smooth over the rough edges; the translator stands in for the author, and recreates the material as though it were the original. The justification of the second approach is that it is precisely the original language that is valuable and interesting to the reader. In this view, the function of the translator is to translate the original in a coherent but transparent manner, and to allow the source to peep through at all times. Of course there can be good or bad translations in either approach. For didactic purposes, it is useful to know what the translation seeks in theory, and then see what it achieves in practice.

The transmission of the text may be undertaken by the teacher in the classroom, or through written historical, theoretical, and literary explanation. A translated text in particular demands exposition because it is foreign and strange. An inescapable degree of annotation may be required: explanations of the background circumstances must be provided, and historical and linguistic allusions, disguised polemics, and so forth, may have to be explicated. Apart from the work of exposition, the teacher also engages in criticism and artistic assessment.

A more speculative issue is what motivates the struggle for acquaintance with modern Hebrew literature, when there is more accessible literature available in the reader's own language or drawing on cultures closer to home. Understanding the primary motivation of the student should guide the choice and presentation of the material. One possible motive for curiosity about modern Hebrew literature lies precisely in its distinctive character. Historically and ideologically, it has served defined purposes—linguistic and national revival, confrontation with the tradition, acclimatization to a new environment, definition of ethnic purposes, and struggle for an appropriate esthetic. These are related to a specific Jewish scene at a moment of crisis. For a readership poised in the final decade of the twentieth century, modern Hebrew literature in its path from enlightenment to disillusionment, through nationalism to articulation of Israelism, provides a window into a variety of reflections on a very different world from that inhabited by the reader.

Apparently antithetical to this motivation is the search for a perception of similarity. Readers may discern in modern Hebrew literature a striking relevance for their own situation. The struggle for emancipation and enlightenment, together with its aftermath, has immediate application to the present day, with some adjustment of nomenclature and particular circumstance; even the differences may be illuminating. The struggle for Israeli political independence and the link perceived and created between cultural expression and that struggle have contemporary implications. The place of the individual within the nation, as expressed in modern Hebrew literature, also has meaning for the reader.

Finally, a reader may find a quintessential literary quality in the work itself. Modern Hebrew literature could not have developed and flourished without the linguistic and historical grounding of premodern Hebrew literature. The Bible, rabbinic literature, medieval writings, the drive toward modernization, disillusionment with surrounding societies, and contact with other cultures have all contributed to the development of a sophisticated and interesting modern literature. Israeli literature may see itself as "orphaned," but orphans, too, have had natural parents. The meeting of the past with the present in this literature's most accomplished expressions constitutes a subject of interest and investigation for the reader.

Many options exist for teaching modern Hebrew literature. The material may be read in terms of its history, be presented as a unit, as contemporary—or as timeless, with the historical context irrelevant to the literary value. An English-language course in modern Hebrew literature is composed of translations, plus documentation on the history of the literature, commentaries, and criticism. While Israeli literature in translation is far more available, a wealth of material exists about Moses Mendelssohn and his period, and about Hebrew literature of the nineteenth century—some Mendele (mainly from the Yiddish), some Berdichevsky, Feierberg, Gnessin, Bialik, Tchernichovsky, Brenner, Vogel; there is also a growing corpus of translated works by Agnon. This would provide examples from the earliest phases of this literature through the mid-twentieth century.

Poetry is always a more difficult case than prose, but this difficulty can be mitigated to some degree by the available translations, literal translations, and interlinear commentaries. Although poetry has more to lose in the translation process, it is open to concentrated reading and analysis, which carry their own rewards.

The International Center has provided a unique forum for the interaction of university teachers with modern Hebrew literature in translation. Each year about twenty participants have held intensive discussions, often with the participation of authors or translators. Papers are circulated beforehand to facilitate in-depth discussions, debate, and learning. The topics dealt with in the workshops have included the following: the challenges of teaching Hebrew literature in translation; teaching Agnon in translation; the view of the "other" in Israeli literature; Hebrew literature in the wake of the Holocaust; women writers in modern Hebrew literature; and Israeli literature in the context of world literature. Papers presented at the workshops have been published in the following books: *Modern Hebrew Literature in English Translation, Agnon: Texts and Contexts in English Translation, Israeli Writers Consider the "Outsider,"* and *Hebrew Literature in the Wake of the Holocaust.*

Future workshops will seek to open their discussions to additional university teachers who may be able to incorporate modern Hebrew literature within the framework of courses in comparative literature, contemporary Jewry, and Middle East programs. Toward this end, we contemplate producing a book that will compare various genres of modern Israeli literature with works of a similar type in other languages, for without reference to contemporaneous literature, modern Hebrew writing cannot be fully understood. Writers live in an open world of letters and, inevitably, other approaches to literature are absorbed. Thus, modern Hebrew literature reflects outside influences. It is our purpose to show how these are adapted and then transcended, undergoing a subtle and inevitable transformation, when the writing takes on Hebrew garb.

16. JEWISH CIVILIZATION IN CHRISTIAN ACADEMIC SETTINGS

Betsy Halpern-Amaru

The precursor of the workshop on Jewish civilization in Christian academic settings was a seminar directed by Shemaryahu Talmon, which, during two consecutive summers, dealt with Jewish civilization in the Hellenistic-Roman period, and with Qumran: Between Judaism and Christianity. The papers delivered in those workshops were published as *Jewish Civilization in the Hellenistic-Roman Period,* under the editorship of Talmon, and heightened awareness of the significance of Jewish civilization to Christianity. Prompted by the desire to explore what was being taught about Jews and Judaism in the institutions devoted to the training of Christian clergy and educators, I was asked to undertake a preliminary investigation of the subject. This survey (*The Teaching of Jewish Civilization in Christian Seminaries and Theological Faculties of American Universities: A Preliminary Exploration,* 1991) disclosed that little attention was paid to Jewish civilization in the training of Christian educators and clergy.

Interest in Jewish history and culture was expressed almost entirely in terms of Ancient Israel (Old Testament studies), and in the postbiblical context of the development of Christianity, most frequently framed in the context of apocalyptic and eschatological themes in Pseudepigraphic and Qumran texts. Once the curricular focus moved from background and origins to the emergence of Christianity, this limited concern with Judaism and Jewish texts declined to the point of disappearance. Except for large university settings where divinity or theological school curricula may be supplemented by a graduate program in Judaic studies, there is generally little sense of either a relevant or dynamic continuing Jewish religious culture.

Despite recognition that the agenda of Christian clergy-training institutions necessitates a focus on Christianity, some Christian as well as Jewish educators and scholars believe that too narrow or exclusive a focus belittles the extent to which the development of Christianity was intertwined with Jewish civilization. If only by its silence, this approach fosters a picture of Judaism as an archaic religious tradition whose major function was to prepare the way for Christianity. Moreover, the problem, unfortunately, is not limited to confessional settings. Insofar as the theological faculties and departments of religion of lay institutions are situated within the context of Christian culture, they perpetuate, albeit more subtly, a similar image.

The concern of the International Center with the broader implications of such a characterization of Judaism and Jewish civilization was shared by Father Thomas Stransky of the Tantur Ecumenical Institute, who joined the Center in hosting a select group of Jewish and Christian educators from North America, Europe, and Israel at a consultative session where the broader implications of the survey could be explored. This meeting resulted in the decision to establish, in cooperation with the Tantur Institute, an ongoing workshop devoted to the teaching of Jewish civilization in Christian settings.

Rabbinic Judaism was selected as the topic for the initial gathering because of its place in the history of the relationship between the two religious traditions. During the first century C.E., Judaism and Christianity shared a common history; thereafter they parted ways, each developing its own sacred texts and institutions. Confrontations between the emerging church and the developing rabbinic tradition left their mark particularly on the Christian perception of rabbinic Judaism. Consequently, while the evolving rabbinic heritage not only influenced the early development of Christianity but became central to Judaism, it was a legacy that the Christian tradition little appreciated. The workshop would provide an occasion for Christian and Jewish teachers and scholars to share insights and explore how an understanding of the rabbinic tradition might be incorporated into the training program of Christian educators and clergy.

Fifteen scholars and teachers from Denmark, Estonia, Great Britain, the Netherlands, Italy, Spain, Sweden, the United States, and Israel were invited. They represented a wide range of academic settings—from Catholic and Protestant divinity schools and seminaries to departments of theology in large institutions with no formal religious affiliation; from those concerned with the training of clergy to those mainly involved with the graduate study of religion; from institutions already committed to the development of programs in Jewish civilization to those which offer nothing or, perhaps, a preparatory course in biblical Hebrew. The variety of institutional interests was reflected in the backgrounds of the participants. Several had formally studied rabbinic texts, others had a general understanding of the historical context of rabbinic Judaism, and some came with minimal exposure to Judaism, let alone rabbinics. Given this broad spectrum of backgrounds, the program was organized around lectures and presentations that would provide a common body of information for discussion.

The workshop was convened in July 1992. The first four of the ten-day gatherings were held, together with the Center's other workshops, on the Givat Ram campus; the last four at Tantur, with the intervening two days devoted to a tour of the Galilee and a Shabbat in Safed. These changes of venue were a function of the dual sponsorship and of a wish to give the participants a sense of the environment in which early rabbinic literature developed; they proved to be a great asset. The comfort of the familiar, be it the academic setting of Givat Ram or the Christian retreat setting of Tantur, eased the tensions inevitable in discussions of sensitive topics, such as the charge of spiritual legalism which Christian leaders laid against the rabbinic tradition over the centuries. And incorporating visits to Jewish and Christian sites in Jerusalem and the Galilee went far to convey the extent to which Jews and Christians shared a common physical space in the early centuries of the first millennium. Similarly, the experience of a traditional Shabbat in Safed contributed in no little way to communicating the spiritual tone of the rabbinic tradition as it continues to be expressed today.

The deliberations that followed the lectures and textual study sessions focused on the problems involved in integrating rabbinic material into the programs of the various types of academic settings. In clergy-training institutions, disinterest in, if not an overt bias against, rabbinics was compounded by the problem of a curriculum already overloaded with requirements for ministerial training, the absence of appropriately trained faculty, and inadequate teaching materials. The institutions involved primarily with the graduate study of religion also have problems with staffing and teaching materials; but in those frameworks there is greater interest in the study of Judaism in general and of rabbinics in particular, and the bias against rabbinics is far more subtle, frequently involving the nature of the theological paradigms traditionally used in the formal study of religion in Christian cultural contexts.

These discussions, as well as consideration of more specific curricular issues, stimulated interest in exploring ways by which those involved in the different types of institutional contexts could further common interests and also assist each other in providing for their distinctive needs. The participants recommended continuing the focus on rabbinics, with a particular emphasis on curricular issues and teaching materials.

Critical evaluation of this first workshop made it clear that the project had been successful in its primary goal, namely, to heighten awareness of the significance of Jewish civilization studies in general, and to develop, in particular, an interest in integrating aspects of the study of rabbinic Judaism into the curriculum of the institutions that train the educators and clergy who will be the future leaders of Christian communities in Europe and America.

The continuing workshop, structured around papers presented by participants, will focus on (1) exploring specific topics demonstrating the significance of rabbinic literature to the understanding of Christianity and early Christian texts; (2) development of teaching and critical bibliographical materials; (3) assessment of the current curricular status of the teaching of rabbinic Judaism in the various types of institutional settings; (4) continued exploration of the issues involved in integrating rabbinic material into the curricula both of confessional institutions as well as universities with a Christian cultural frame of reference. Exposure to the study of rabbinic texts, albeit in translation, remains crucial. Hence, textual study sessions, perhaps double-tiered in order to allow for differences in background and interest, will be an ongoing aspect of the workshop program.

17. WESTERN SOCIETIES AND THE HOLY LAND

Yehoshua Ben-Arieh and Yaakov Ariel

In 1987, the International Center decided to build upon the conceptual and methodological approaches of America–Holy Land studies—itself a fairly new field within Jewish studies—and extend academic research to an analysis of the role of the Holy Land in Western societies. A workshop attended by scholars from Israel, the United States, England, France, Germany, and South America undertook to promote research and academic exchange, and to attempt to introduce teaching of this field at the university level.

The participants, who came from a variety of disciplines—history, geography, religion, archeology, literature, and communication—focused on four general areas: diplomatic policy, Christian devotion, cultural expressions, and Jewish involvement in the Holy Land in the nineteenth century. This was a period when the Bible as a spiritual source of Western civilization, and the reawakened interest in the Holy Land, occupied a seminal place in Western minds.

Reports on virtually untapped archival resources revealed political and economic concerns as well as Great Power interests. Investigation of Christian ties to the Land of the Bible referred to both historic Christian traditions as well as to the role of Zion in various modern movements. Similarly, Jewish attachment to the Land of Israel was traced from its roots in three thousand years of history through the central role of Eretz Israel in contemporary Jewish communal life. Finally, the rediscovery of the Holy Land by the Western world in the nineteenth century found expression in the writings of archeologists, historians, biblical scholars, novelists, consuls, missionaries, travelers, and settlers in Palestine.

The scholars examined the relationships between individual Western countries and the Holy Land. Some chose to focus on broad themes: the depiction of the Holy Land in Western art; diaries of nineteenth-century travelers to the Holy Land; the impact and contribution of Western institutions to the shaping and development of the country. In addition to archival materials, diaries, and other written records, nineteenth- and early twentieth-century photographs were used as primary sources that, upon analysis, were shown to reflect the cultural predispositions to the Holy Land of British, French, and American photographers.

One of the workshop's aims—to promote research and academic exchange—has been achieved. *With Eyes toward Zion—III, Western Societies and the Holy Land,* a volume of papers delivered at the workshops, has contributed to the scholarly literature in the field and has sparked the writing of other articles and books. Younger scholars have been recruited from a variety of disciplines to undertake research, and a network has been formed of active participants whose enthusiasm is reflected in their continuing research and publications.

In 1990 the Center decided to begin to focus on "Jerusalem in the Mind of the Western world." The uniqueness of Jerusalem is reflected in the religious, cultural, and historical significance it holds for both Jewish and world civilizations. The many faces of Jerusalem are revealed in creative works of literature and art, in historical records, and in archeological excavations. In addition, Jerusalem holds a special place in the minds of millions of Jews, Muslims, and Christians.

In a university context, topics related to Jerusalem may be integrated into different departments, with departments of religious studies offering the widest range of general courses that lend themselves to such teaching. Two workshops have already been held on Jerusalem in the mind of the Western world, from the late Ottoman period through 1948, with special attention paid to the period of the British Mandate (1918–1948), when Jerusalem, for the first time in almost two millennia, again served as the capital and administrative center of the country and Western ideas were influential in shaping the city's government, architecture, and culture.

Future plans are to invite a group of professors of religious studies who express interest in incorporating material about Jerusalem into their courses to a seminar in Jerusalem, where they will become more intimately acquainted with the city, its history, and its monuments, through lectures and field trips. The participants will be advised that as they learn more about Jerusalem, they are expected to think about integrating the topics dealing with Jerusalem into a course that they teach, and to prepare a detailed syllabus, including proposals for reading.

The concluding sessions of the two-week seminar will be conducted as a workshop, where participants will present their draft syllabi for group discussion. Final versions of the syllabi will be prepared after the participants return to their universities and will then be evaluated by teams of university teachers of Jewish civilization and scholars on Jerusalem. These teams will recommend which syllabi should be further developed, and will provide suggestions for teaching materials. As an ongoing project, the Jerusalem seminar may become an annual event, each time with a new group of university teachers participating.

We anticipate that the first syllabi, with an accompanying sourcebook of primary and secondary material for student use and an instructor's manual that will include methodological suggestions, referrals to research literature, and information about available audio-visual materials, will be ready in 1996, on the 3000th anniversary of King David's establishment of Jerusalem as the capital of the Jewish nation. It is increasingly apparent that Jerusalem as a concept and as a reality is not only of academic interest, but is germane to contemporary religious and geopolitical concerns.

18. JEWISH PHILOSOPHY

Raphael Jospe

Within the expanding framework of university-level Jewish studies, the teaching of Jewish philosophy constitutes a problematic area. Philosophical works written in Greek, Latin, and modern European languages are routinely included in the curricula of philosophy programs. Philosophical works written by Jews, in Hebrew and Arabic, receive little if any attention. A survey of many of the standard college textbooks of Western philosophy provides ready evidence of Christian Eurocentrism. More is at stake than the proper academic recognition of the role of Jewish civilization in the development of the West; the ultimate issue is that the study of Western philosophy is incomplete and flawed without an integral Jewish component.

In the famous thesis of Harry Wolfson of Harvard, all of Western philosophy that followed the Greeks and Romans, whether Jewish, Christian, or Islamic, was "Philonic," in the sense that it was Philo, the Jew of ancient Alexandria, who is the most important Western philosopher after Plato and Aristotle. Greek and Roman philosophy were pagan and independent of revealed scriptural religion; Philo was the revolutionary figure who attempted to bridge the gap, to relate reason and revelation. All Western philosophy, then, whether in Jewish, Christian, or Islamic cultural garb, was Philonic, until Spinoza tore down the structure Philo built and "freed" philosophy from Scripture. In short, in Wolfson's radical theory, it was Philo who built the Western philosophic tradition, and it was Spinoza who broke with that tradition and paved the way for modern philosophy. To teach Western philosophy, then, without its inherent Jewish components, is to pervert it.

We recognize that we are, or can be, a transitional, pioneering generation in turning the present situation about. Thanks to the vast resources
of the Jewish National and University Library in Jerusalem (including its
manuscript collection and its Institute for Microfilmed Hebrew Manuscripts), we have unprecedented access to primary materials, and we are
now also increasingly able to use the previously inaccessible materials in
the libraries of the former USSR and Eastern Europe. The ingathering of
the exiles in Israel, and the expansion of Jewish studies abroad, can
bring together scholars who, in addition to being fluent in Hebrew and/
or in Arabic, are at home in various European languages. We are, then,
at a unique historic juncture. The efforts of our generation—the last to
be taught by the giants of German-Jewish scholarship after World War
II, and the first to experience the rapid expansion of Judaica scholarship
in Israel and abroad since the 1960s, and in Eastern Europe and the
former USSR in the 1990s—will be a critical link in securing the future
of Jewish philosophy in the academy.

Thus, in 1988 a continuing workshop in Jewish philosophy was
initiated under the direction of Emil Fackenheim. Since 1989, Warren
Zev Harvey and Aviezer Ravitzky have served as its co-directors, and
Raphael Jospe as its academic coordinator. One of the first questions to
arise was the challenge of defining "Jewish philosophy." The question
has proved to be both inescapable and unresolvable. Both the terms
"Jewish" and "philosophy" are problematical.

With regard to the term "Jewish," the opposing extreme views would
argue either that Jewish philosophy is formally any philosophy done by
a Jew without any reference to its content, or, conversely, that a philosophy is properly "Jewish" only if it somehow is in accord with the prior
essential standards of Judaism (usually understood in a prephilosophical
religious sense, in terms of biblical revelation and/or talmudic tradition).
In the latter case, "Jewish philosophy" usually really means "philosophy
of Judaism," where Judaism is the subject of the philosophic method of
inquiry. Others try to find a middle ground, arguing for more than the
extreme formalist position, and for less than the extreme essentialist
position. They resort to such criteria as Jewish sources and context,
rather than mere biographical accident or Jewish content, to determine
the "Jewishness" of a philosophy.

The second term, "philosophy," also must be questioned. How narrowly do we wish to apply this term? What is the relation of Jewish

philosophy to other areas of Jewish thought, including the mystical tradition (kabbalah), biblical and talmudic thought, medieval Bible exegesis, Hebrew poetry and literature, modern secular political thought (e.g., Zionist ideology), and so forth?

While the workshop clearly had a mandate to study Jewish philosophy and not other areas of Jewish thought, we faced two obvious problems. First, the demarcations between strictly philosophical and other types of thought are often unclear. Second, the historical fact is that in some cases more purely philosophical and theoretical works exerted less influence on the Jewish community of their day or on subsequent Jewish history and thought than did works which, while including philosophic terminology and doctrines, are not strictly philosophical. Is it our task as Jewish philosophers to restrict ourselves to purely philosophical works that are less important historically and less interesting intellectually, or do we, rather, need to broaden our categories?

These questions are not merely of theoretical philosophical interest. The practical implications of these theoretical considerations are immense, as they affect our curricular choice of material as well as our method of teaching it. They go to the heart of how we conceive Jewish philosophy, and our roles and obligations as teachers. The academic context in which Jewish philosophy is taught also impinges upon the methodology and approach used in the classroom. Given the differing curricular priorities and the divergent student backgrounds and interests in departments of philosophy, religion, Judaica, and the like, the departmental setting may affect the way in which the same material is taught. This is an area in which the differences between universities and students in North America, Europe, and Israel are often most sharply felt. Even in Israeli universities, there is no uniform policy regarding the academic setting of Jewish philosophy.

The problem is exacerbated by the fact that many works of Jewish philosophy require background both in classical, medieval Arabic-Islamic, or modern philosophy, and in nonphilosophical Jewish sources (Bible, Talmud, Midrash, etc.) which were the Jewish philosophers' life-bread. How should this material be taught in the academy? The students' backgrounds and interests and the departmental curricular priorities may force us to emphasize one or another aspect of the material, at the expense of a larger understanding of it and at the expense of what the philosopher's own priorities may well have been.

For example, European students may be thoroughly at home in the modern philosophy that preoccupied many modern Jewish thinkers, yet be unfamiliar with the Jewish sources that were so central in their life and thought. Conversely, Israeli students may find a preoccupation with modern European and Christian thinking to be alien to the culture and experiences that have shaped their lives and their understanding of philosophy. One of the values of the international workshops is the opportunity they afford scholars from different continents, cultures, and educational frameworks to compare their teaching experience and to learn from one another how to deal more effectively with such pedagogic challenges. Thus, invitations are sent to an appropriate balance of senior and junior scholars, those interested in ancient, medieval, modern, and contemporary thought, and colleagues from diverse countries. The workshops have provided the first framework in which participants from the former USSR and Eastern Europe could explore with Western colleagues issues of vital concern to them as scholars and teachers. In addition, younger colleagues, many of whom teach in isolated environments far from important programs in Jewish studies and centers of Jewish population and culture, were able to meet, over several days and in an informal setting, with senior scholars.

Virtually from the outset it was clear that the continuing workshop in Jewish philosophy could not deal exclusively or even primarily with methodological or pedagogic questions by themselves, although the focus must always remain the *teaching* of Jewish philosophy. We have therefore attempted to ensure that each annual workshop will include sessions dealing with the practical issues of teaching. Methodology, however, is widely seen as inseparable from the content of Jewish philosophy, and the sessions, therefore, are never free from "philosophizing." A group of papers that deal with pedagogic issues—such as which Jewish philosophers to include in university courses, in which departments to teach Jewish philosophy, what texts and translations to use, etc.—can be found in *Jewish Studies—Forum of the World Union of Jewish Studies,* vol. 34 (1994).

Although we had originally considered teaching major periods in Jewish philosophy, an increasing consensus has developed that we should focus each year on two major thinkers—one medieval, one modern or contemporary—and use this approach as a "paradigm" for teaching Jewish philosophy. The "paradigm" pattern makes possible a comparison of premodern with modern thinkers and is useful for teaching how similar problems were dealt with in different historical contexts, and for understanding that different issues were of concern to Jewish philosophers of various periods.

The first paradigm paired Moses Maimonides with Emmanuel Levinas, the medieval and twentieth-century Jewish philosophers most often studied in both general philosophical frameworks and Jewish intellectual circles. The second pair was Judah Ha-Levi and Franz Rosenzweig, who was in fact deeply influenced by Ha-Levi and wrote a commentary to his poetry. Each thinker criticized the prevalent philosophy and found in revealed Jewish sources a more significant truth, and in the traditional Jewish way of life a more meaningful existence than that offered by intellectual and spiritual alternatives.

Sa'adiah Ga'on and Moses Mendelssohn, pioneers of Jewish philosophy in the medieval and modern periods, were paired next. Both of them engaged in translating the Bible into the major scientific language of the day (respectively, Arabic and German), and placed the historic truth of the public revelation of the Torah at the core of their philosophy.

The best evidence of the value of this workshop and the need for it is the eagerness of scholars and teachers to join us in Jerusalem each year, in numbers far exceeding our ability to accommodate them. They are willing, too, to prepare serious scholarly papers in order to learn from and with each other about the continuing challenges of teaching Jewish philosophy in the academy.

19. REVIVING JEWISH STUDIES IN EASTERN EUROPE

Mordechai Altshuler

During the seventy-year freeze imposed by the USSR on intellectual freedom, and the resulting genocide practiced against Jewish culture, the teaching of humanities in the former Soviet Union (FSU) and countries of Eastern Europe was grounded in indoctrination and political correctness, with the most severe penalties for deviation. This stood in sharp contrast to the Western concept of teaching the humanities, which favors the presentation of a variety of approaches.

The monolithic FSU framework for presenting humanities and social sciences at the university level continues to this day. True, it was altered somewhat by the relaxation of the Soviet thought-control mechanism in the seventies and the withering of the entire state edifice under Gorbachev in the eighties; but the dictation of a single, "correct" line and the politicization of all disciplines have not yet been fully discarded. Jewish studies were almost totally obliterated, with the possible exception of Bible studies. Ironically, these circumstances served Jewish academic interests well, since any attention paid to the Jewish religion, Zionism, Israel, and Jewish thought inevitably would have been negative.

The limited scope of Hebrew language study during the bleak decades before the Gorbachev thaw was confined exclusively to security and military needs. Still, it is worth noting that Hebrew language instruction for these specific objectives was effective, and graduates of officially sponsored courses attained a high degree of competence in the language.

In the FSU, a small number of scholars, working in institutes rather than universities, pursued advanced research in such fields as medieval

Hebrew literature, Jewish philosophy, and the Dead Sea Scrolls. A firm line divided universities from the institutes that were operating under the auspices of academies of sciences, and there was no trickle-down effect from the isolated research projects of the institutes to universities where students might have enrolled in such courses if they had been offered. Great gaps existed between the rewards and privileges accorded to research scholars in the institutes operated by the academies and those given to university staff. The universities, therefore, could not compete for leading scholars, and the level of talent and teaching was low. As unshaken faith in the old principles wavered, subjects and areas previously considered taboo were legitimated for general study. Sacred cows of the past regimes were demoted—only to be replaced by new ones.

Fortunately, this new breath of liberalism led to the development of a curiosity about Russian history, literature, the history of Orthodox religion, and topics of Jewish interest. Underground *samizdat* literature—illicit, handwritten, or typed copies of taboo novels, texts, and articles of Jewish content—had already achieved wide circulation, beginning in the seventies.

The challenge posed by the revival of Jewish studies in the FSU was first considered by the ICUTJC in a brief consultation in 1989 and a lengthier session in 1990. Since then, annual workshops devoted to Jewish civilization in Eastern Europe have been conducted in the Russian language.

These sessions offered Western scholars access to relics of Jewish cultural survival, and to the nature and shape of a vast Jewish community that had suffered enforced isolation from fellow Jewish communities since the Revolution of 1917. The workshops served as a forum for publicizing newly released FSU archival materials that provided a previously unknown picture of Jewish community life and of a Jewish intelligentsia that had developed in isolation—one that was neither Ashkenazi in origin, nor Yiddish by language preference.

An emotional highpoint of this reintroduction in Jerusalem of former Soviet Jewry to the world Jewish family took place at the end of the 1991 workshop, when a reception for East European participants was held at the President's residence. President Chaim Herzog met and chatted with participants from the FSU and Eastern Europe who had come to Jerusalem from Estonia, Belarus, Birobidzhan, Hungary, Poland, Russia,

Ukraine, and Uzbekistan. At their working sessions, they were joined by scholars from Israel and the Western world.

It soon became apparent that Jewish studies in the FSU could not recover locally without a fallback resource, and that a continuum could be attained only through attendance at training sessions in Israel. In anticipation of this problem, the ICUTJC met with various organizations in the hope of obtaining financial resources to formulate a program for Jewish studies in the FSU.

The workshops have already focused special attention on research possibilities and university teaching of Jewish civilization in the post-communist era. The hope is to penetrate the *terra incognita* of FSU universities and develop a cadre of academics who are capable of leading the renascence of Jewish studies and heading a larger group of scholars in an area that was once the heartland of Jewish scholarly and religious life.

The subjects discussed have included Jewish life in communities outside the pale of settlement, Polish state policy on the "Jewish Question" in the interwar period, twentieth-century emigration from Eastern Europe, the fate of Jewish populations in territories annexed by the USSR between 1939 and 1941, *samizdat* literature, Bukharan Jews in the twentieth century, Caucasian Jews under Soviet rule, Yiddish theater, Jewish religion, and Hebrew and Yiddish literature in the USSR. Also discussed were the problems of teaching Hebrew in the USSR, Palestine and Israel studies in the USSR, creation of a Russian-language bibliography on Jewish topics, the Jewish community in Petrograd before the Revolution, and the role of Jews in Russian parties at the beginning of the twentieth century.

The International Center's workshops on philosophy have attracted a variety of participants: from Poland, Hungary, Russia, and the Ukraine; on teaching modern Hebrew literature in English translation, from the Ukraine; and on teaching Jewish civilization in Christian academic settings, from Estonia. Thus the intellectual input of East European scholars is not limited to parochial concerns in Russian-language sessions, but is extended to contributions in other disciplines as well.

Higher education in the FSU is going through a major transition. Teachers are underpaid, and new posts are unavailable. The resurgence of interest in Jewish studies has inspired a hope that wider demand will create new employment opportunities. At the same time, there are warning signals that this expansion of interest in Jewish studies may involve the lowering of academic standards. Observers fear that the level of teaching might be pseudo-academic, or doctrinaire. Academic researchers may be tempted to abandon their disciplines and find employment as instructors. While large numbers of Jews in the FSU are seeking their roots, many nonacademic organizations, financed from abroad, are meeting this need in the Jewish communities, both among the youth and adults, among the religious and the secular. This is an "occupied field," separate from the Academy.

Here the International Center can play a role. Its adherence to the credo of the university, its wish to preserve a distinction between academic and popular courses in "Judaism," and its ability to train a cadre of people who will meet professional, academic criteria are invaluable. It is vital that training in Jewish studies, at the highest level, be pluralistic rather than doctrinaire. This distinguishes the academic approach from all other learning programs.

20. JEWISH ART

Ziva Amishai-Maisels

Within the last twenty-five years, the study of Jewish art has increased dramatically both in Israel and in the Diaspora. This has been primarily due to the efforts of a few individuals who were dedicated to the promotion of Jewish art through the creation of museums to house it, and to deepening our knowledge of it through research and teaching. Today, there is an ever-growing number of publications, symposia, and trained scholars in the field, and a parallel demand for university-level courses in this subject. Yet, whereas many cities now have Jewish art museums, few universities offer courses in this subject even when they have the staff to do so; most researchers of Jewish art who hold university positions teach other subjects. Under the auspices of the International Center, it was decided in 1989 that the time had come to stimulate the teaching of Jewish art at the university level.

At a consultative meeting, teachers of Jewish art in Israeli universities met to analyze the problematics of teaching the subject. They felt that the main difficulty was to convince universities that Jewish art is a legitimate field of study worth teaching not only in individual courses, but also as part of general courses in art history, archeology, Jewish studies, cultural history, and religion.

One of the problems raised was the difficulty of defining what falls within the purview of Jewish art, from Beit Alpha to Chagall. The lack of a definition has hampered our ability to convince universities that this area is a legitimate field of study, but this dilemma results from the very nature of Jewish art. Since there is no single Jewish style, despite attempts to create one, the art does not *look* different from that of its surrounding environment. Thus it is visually difficult for nonexperts to realize that Jewish art exists, unless they are confronted with Hebrew illuminated manuscripts or with Jewish ritual objects. Art historians therefore conclude that if Jewish art exists, it deals only with the minor arts and has rarely produced anything of sufficient artistic merit to be worth teaching at the university level.

Although art historians may study the influence of ancient synagogues on church architecture, or the relationship of the murals in the third-century Dura Europos synagogue to biblical narrative paintings in early churches, they believe that it was the church which produced the major artworks. Therefore, they say, a course teaching the development of synagogue architecture from antiquity to the present has no relevance for students of art or architectural history, although it might be appropriate in the field of Jewish studies or the history of religions. Ironically, for a course of this kind to be successful in the latter departments, it should be taught by an art or architectural historian, who could deal with and explain the visual data. Yet such a teacher would have to come from an art history department, where the subject is considered irrelevant. Thus, such courses are not taught unless an inspired individual breaks through this circle of reasoning with enough force of personality to convince department heads that the material is important and would attract students.

These difficulties are exacerbated in dealing with modern art. It is hard to convince scholars that anything can be learned about Camille Pissarro and other secular modern artists by studying their Jewish roots. Moreover, the artists themselves insist that they are international, and view their being called "Jewish artists" as parochial and degrading. The academic world thus deduces that one should study Chagall and Soutine in courses on modern art and that nothing will be gained by placing them in a Jewish context. However, in order to understand their art fully, it must be studied both in the broad context of its period and in the narrower aspect of its Jewish content. This duality derives from the fact that Jewish artists adapt the styles and artistic conventions of their times, and that the Jewish element in their art is found in their iconography. There is, however, no awareness that a specific Jewish iconography exists, or even that one must read and understand the Hebrew and Yiddish inscriptions in works of art.

The need to have a knowledge of Hebrew and of Jewish sources has been ignored by art historians and archeologists. Whereas it is obvious that to study Greek art in depth one must learn ancient Greek and read Greek literature and philosophy, at least in translation, this is far from obvious to scholars studying segments of Jewish art. Scholars learn modern research languages or those current in the periods they study, and do not "waste" time on Hebrew and Jewish studies. Rarely do scholars of Dura Europos know Hebrew or Aramaic as well as Latin, and even more rarely do researchers on Chagall know Russian, Hebrew, or Yiddish, languages as important to understanding his work as is a knowledge of French. We must make it clear that a certain cultural and linguistic background is as necessary in studying art of Jewish origin as it is in studying Greek, Japanese, or Islamic art.

Another problem is harder to solve. Universities offer courses in Christian and Islamic art, but not in Jewish art. Courses in Afro-American art and women's art are popular, whether or not the works are of international importance or have a collective style; but universities have not responded favorably to student requests for courses in Jewish art. This is not simply a case of discrimination; rather, to admit the existence of Jewish art or a Jewish way of looking at things may smack of racism in the post-Holocaust world. Moreover, although there is now an awareness that one must take into account Arshile Gorky's Armenian background and iconography, and that one must study Romanian folk art and mythology to understand Constantin Brancusi's art, it is not "politically correct" to suggest that the Jewish background of Mark Rothko or Barnett Newman can help to explain their works. Since few art historians are conversant with either Armenian or Romanian sources, this points to a basic problem that must be addressed. We need to demonstrate that a study of Jewish art within its own parameters will shed new light on the study of the same works in a more universal framework.

The consultative group therefore decided that the time was ripe to develop new tools and arguments to persuade the scholarly community that Jewish art has a vital contribution to make to the study of several disciplines at the university level. Jewish art can be taught in departments of art history and archeology; historians and theologians should be shown that art furnishes them with accessible and highly remarkable documents; and teachers of Jewish literature have to be made aware of parallels with Jewish art. To pursue these aims it was decided to inaugurate a series of workshops on the teaching of Jewish art at the university level.

The first workshop, held in 1991, was attended by twenty scholars from departments of art history, Jewish history, archeology, and Jewish studies, representing seventeen institutions from nine countries. It encouraged scholars from East and West to discuss mutual interests and problems, and to think constructively about teaching Jewish art at the university level. Several important points emerged.

First, we found that university teaching of Jewish art was more widespread than we had thought, and that individual scholars in various countries had been slowly introducing such courses in different contexts. Whereas undergraduate and graduate degrees in Jewish art are granted only at the Hebrew University of Jerusalem, a new graduate program had opened at the Bernard Manekin Institute for Jewish Art in New York. Courses in Jewish art were also being given at the Centre National de la Recherche Scientifique in Paris; at Queens College, Stern College, and at the Jewish Theological Seminary in New York; Seton Hall University in New Jersey; the Rabbinical Seminary in Hungary; the University of Vienna; the Centre for Jewish Studies at the University of Heidelberg; and the Open Jewish University in St. Petersburg. Sections on Jewish art were also offered in courses on general Jewish studies in a number of European universities as well as in the departments of Jewish history and of archeology at the Hebrew University.

It became clear that Catholic institutions were as open to Jewish art as were Jewish ones, and that individual dedication was the key to having courses accepted. Moreover, the initiator could even be a student; one scholar had succeeded in getting her art history teachers at Belgrade University to accept research papers on Jewish art, although no such courses were given there.

The lack of adequately prepared students was raised in two different contexts. Those teaching Jewish art in an art history context complained that their students lacked the requisite knowledge in Jewish studies; while those teaching Jewish art in other contexts complained that their students lacked a knowledge of art—and often of Jewish studies as well. Much class time was thus spent in providing students with the appropriate background. Suggestions for solving this problem included requiring prerequisites, providing readings and tutorials, and limiting the material to be covered in the course. Adequate preparation could be more easily achieved in a program in Jewish art offering several courses, but questions were raised as to how many prerequisites one could require, and whether such a program should be on the undergraduate or graduate level. The severe lack of textbooks and picture collections for student use is also a universal problem in teaching the subject.

These discussions led us to define the different aims in teaching Jewish art. General courses raised Jewish consciousness and created a knowledgeable public who could understand and support Jewish art. Undergraduate studies might inspire future teachers at various levels to incorporate their knowledge of this field into other subjects. Graduate studies in Jewish art aimed to produce scholars and curators. Courses on Jewish art in Eastern Europe and Russia were aimed at rabbinical students, Jewish and non-Jewish curators, and the general public, in order to promote the exhibition, preservation, and restoration of existing works of Jewish art.

The various aims require different approaches to Jewish art. Whereas the formal elements are important in an art history context, with historical and sociological data added to expand an understanding of the work of art, in Jewish history or archeology courses the art work is a document from which one derives historical and sociological data. It was suggested that Jewish art scholars contribute to courses offered by colleagues in other fields, so as to expose them and their students to the benefits such study could provide for their own disciplines.

A summary of the findings of the 1991 workshop appeared in the 1993 issue of *Jewish Studies* published by the World Congress of Jewish Studies. A second workshop, held in 1993, dealt with the curricula, syllabi, and bibliographies currently used in teaching. It was attended by over forty delegates from ten countries, representing twenty institutions. Basic terms and problems in teaching were analyzed, the experiences of teachers in various contexts and countries were explored, and learning aids were discussed. Syllabi and bibliographies will continue to be exchanged through the International Center. It is anticipated that further workshops, and publications that may emerge from them, will enhance the appreciation of this too-often neglected dimension of Jewish creativity and will help Jewish art take its rightful place as an academic discipline on the university level.

IV

COOPERATIVE PROJECTS

21. BINAH: STUDIES IN JEWISH HISTORY AND JEWISH THOUGHT (WITH THE OPEN UNIVERSITY OF ISRAEL)

Joseph Dan and Priscilla Fishman

The revitalization of the Hebrew language and culture in Eretz Israel led to a florescence of scholarly activity at the Hebrew University of Jerusalem and, thereafter, at other institutions of higher learning throughout Israel. Over the years, a sizable corpus of scholarly monographs has appeared in Hebrew, in a wide variety of academic journals, written at first by European-born and trained scholars and later by Israeli scholars as well. However, a basic problem in all scholarship is the restricted access imposed by language, and particularly by a lesser-known language. Because of the linguistic barrier, much of the scholarly material in Hebrew has been largely inaccessible to educated readers in other countries, and certainly to younger students interested in Jewish studies.

The landmark BINAH series was initiated in 1981 to bridge this gap. The idea was developed by Moshe Davis; Joseph Dan, head of the Institute for Jewish Studies of the Hebrew University; and Shulamit Nardi of the Institute of Contemporary Jewry of the Hebrew University, who suggested the name of the series (which means "wisdom" in Hebrew). The goal was to make the products of Israeli research available in English, in a form appropriate for undergraduate use in departments of Jewish studies, religion, history, literature, sociology, cultural anthropology, and philosophy. BINAH was not to be considered a textbook but would present classical and current Hebrew scholarship that appeared in Hebrew journals and *festschrifts* that do not necessarily come to the attention of academics abroad. Articles that develop a specific theme would take precedence over chapters of books.

Everyman's University (now The Open University of Israel), headed first by Abraham Ginsberg, and then by Nehemia Levtzion, agreed to cosponsor this innovative project together with the International Center, and, from 1982 to 1986, a dozen booklets were produced as an experimental edition. Each booklet contained a translated adaptation of a seminal article—some written by giants of earlier generations, others by young scholars exploring new aspects of the rich field of Jewish civilization. The need for an adaptation, rather than a direct translation, reflected the recognition that articles published in Hebrew scholarly journals would have to be somewhat reworked for use by undergraduate students abroad. Thus, the number of bibliographical references to works in Hebrew was decreased; technical terms were explained; and side issues were judiciously deleted in order to focus on the main thrust of the author's exposition.

The first two volumes of BINAH, edited by Joseph Dan, appeared in 1989 in hard-cover and loose-leaf format, and dealt, respectively, with Jewish history and Jewish thought. Both volumes contained an eclectic group of articles. Volume 1, for example, included Yochanan H. Lewy's classical treatment of the writings of Tacitus regarding the Jews; Haim Hillel Ben-Sasson's analysis of the reactions of the Spanish exiles after 1492 who were convinced that this traumatic event heralded the coming of the messiah; Yitzhak Baer's groundbreaking examination of the origins of the Jewish communal organization in the Middle Ages; and Ephraim E. Urbach's understanding of the midrashic material on the death of Joab as an interpretation of political history. Contributions by younger scholars were also included.

The recognition of "Jewish thought" as an academic discipline is recent. Within the past quarter-century the field has expanded from a survey of medieval Jewish philosophy to include a comprehensive overview of Jewish ideas ranging from the Bible through contemporary Zionism and post-Holocaust theology. The articles included in the second volume of BINAH dealing with Jewish thought were chosen not only for their intrinsic value, but also for the scholarly approach of the authors who present ideational concepts within the framework of their historical backgrounds. For example, Victor Aptowitzer's study of the Celestial Temple as it appears in the aggadah brings together material from various periods and traces the development of the idea that there is a Temple in heaven corresponding to the Temple in Jerusalem. Yitzhak Baer's analysis of the socioreligious orientation of *Sefer Hasidim* also refers to the contemporaneous writings of Francis of Assisi and to the superstitions of the Christian population in the region where the book was written. Among the articles by younger Israeli scholars are Warren Zev Harvey's comparison of the views of Maimonides and Spinoza regarding the knowledge of good and evil; and Eliezer Schweid's evaluation of Martin Buber as a philosophical interpreter of the Bible, who urges man not to "go out and read [the Bible] and learn" but, rather, to "go out and learn to listen."

Following the recommendations of teachers of Jewish studies, it was decided to provide a more definite focus for subsequent volumes. Thus, BINAH, volume 3, deals with Jewish intellectual history in the Middle Ages and future volumes will treat such subjects as Hasidism, Maimonides studies, and Jewish thought in early modern Europe. With the more focused approach, each volume can be used as a reader for a specific course, and each will appear in a paperback edition.

Although the original BINAH series was designed for use by English-speaking students, particularly those in American universities, it has also been made available to Russian academics who participate in the International Center's workshops, and who have a good reading knowledge of English. It is anticipated that BINAH will also appear in French and Spanish. In each case, articles appropriate to the curricula in universities abroad will be chosen for inclusion. A recent grant from UNESCO has enabled the center to undertake the translation of selected articles for a French edition.

22. INTERUNIVERSITY FELLOWSHIP PROGRAM (WITH THE OVERSEAS PROGRAM OF THE COUNCIL FOR HIGHER EDUCATION)

Ernest Krausz and Mervin F. Verbit

In 1983, Israel's Council of Higher Education and the Jewish Agency established a joint Committee for University Studies in Israel. Three years later, the International Center was invited to conduct a special academic program designed primarily for students in the United States who were engaged in research in the broad field of Jewish civilization studies at the master's and doctoral level. The educators believed that the students' scholarly development would be greatly enriched by exposure to the vast collection of documentary materials in Israel, and that they would benefit from contacts with prominent Israeli scholars in the various fields in which they wished to specialize.

The Fellowship Program that derived from this agreement rests on two basic principles. (1) The work done in Israel must be an integral part of a student's scholarly development; consequently, students are recruited primarily through nomination by their home universities, and their program of study and research in Israel is designed to meet their individual academic needs. (2) The year of study in Israel also introduces students to the wide-ranging resources available there.

Each student is guided to the academic experts and to resources appropriate to his or her work. Fellows also participate in a seminar organized and conducted by Aviezer Ravitzky, the program's academic advisor in Israel, in which they read and discuss one another's work and hear lectures by some of Israel's leading scholars in Jewish studies. It is a measure of the program's academic value that every year we have been asked to appoint as honorary Fellows qualified students who wish to benefit from the educational advantages of the Interuniversity Fellowship Program but do not need or are not eligible for the stipend because of other grants.

Students at all stages of graduate training, ranging from the first year through dissertation research, have been Fellows. They may work in any university department as long as their studies deal substantially with some aspect of Jewish civilization. The number of Fellows has varied between fifteen and twenty per year. Most have been doctoral candidates; a few were working toward master's degrees. Each year about three of the participants have been on "renewal" grants in order to complete work begun in Israel, and one or two have been honorary Fellows. Many of the students were appointed from American universities that offer a significant graduate program in Jewish studies; they worked within a wide spectrum of disciplines and periods. The subfields represented by Fellows include Bible, rabbinics, medieval and modern philosophy, medieval and modern history, literature, musicology, modern Israel, Sephardic culture, and virtually every other specialization within Jewish civilization.

The institutions in which the Fellows were enrolled include Brandeis, Columbia, Cornell, Emory, Graduate Theological Union, Harvard, Hebrew Union College–Jewish Institute of Religion, Indiana, Jewish Theological Seminary, New York University, Ohio State, Smith, Stanford, UC Berkeley, UCLA, UC Santa Barbara, University of Chicago, University of Pennsylvania, University of Toronto, University of Washington, Wesleyan, Yale, and Yeshiva.

Apart from the purely academic advantages entailed in such a program, these mature students from the best of North American universities are given the opportunity to improve their knowledge of Hebrew, often a *sine qua non* in their studies, and to get firsthand experience of life in Israel.

This program, envisaged to produce an academic elite that would serve universities throughout the world, proved to be an unquestioned success from the very start, attracting some of the brightest students preparing themselves for teaching careers in Jewish civilization studies. A warm and mutually supportive academic environment was created as a result of the close cooperation between the participants' departmental supervisors at the home colleges and universities and their Israeli counterparts. It is hoped that what has worked so successfully in the United States can be expanded to Europe as well.

In 1992, a survey carried out among alumni of the program and their faculty advisors revealed the following:

- Almost all of the Fellows have completed their doctorates and have been appointed to academic positions, or are still working full-time toward their degrees and making appropriate progress. Only four have withdrawn from graduate school, all but one to undertake rabbinical studies.
- Former Fellows are now serving as assistant professors at Gratz College, Haverford College, Jewish Theological Seminary, New York University, Ohio State University, Princeton University, SUNY-Stony Brook, University of Michigan, University of Washington, and Vassar College.
- About two dozen Fellows are actively publishing and reading papers at professional meetings. At the 1992 meeting of the Association for Jewish Studies, nine Interuniversity Fellows read papers, and twelve presented papers at the 1993 A.J.S. meeting.
- Asked what their year in Israel contributed to their development, Fellows most frequently cited the opportunities to work with world-class scholars, to strengthen their ability to do scholarly work in Hebrew, to take highly specialized courses in their fields, and to use the rich resources available in Israel for their research. Other benefits that were mentioned include the opportunities to develop contacts with future colleagues, to understand the Israeli approach to Jewish studies, and to define their own interests more clearly and deeply.

The faculty advisors of the participants have evaluated the academic aspects of the program positively, and have recommended that all graduate students in Jewish civilization studies be given the opportunity of at least one year of study in Israel. This program, initiated under the Council's chairman, Nehemia Levtzion, and carried forward by his successors, Ozer Schild and Ernest Krausz, is now regarded an essential element in the education of future instructors and scholars in the field.

23. A JEWISH CIVILIZATION CURRICULUM (WITH THE JEWISH THEOLOGICAL SEMINARY OF AMERICA)

Gerson D. Cohen

(A proposal to develop a comprehensive curriculum for teaching the history of Jewish civilization was made by Gerson D. Cohen, chancellor of The Jewish Theological Seminary of America. The following chapter [which has been edited] spelled out the project as he saw it, and outlined steps toward its implementation.)

JUDAICA IN THE SPIRIT OF THE HUMANITIES

For the purpose of the university curriculum, Judaica must be treated as humanities, that is, as the cultural depository and record of experience of the Jewish people of every age and of every creative center, as the record of Jewish responses to the past and present, and as the articulation of dreams for the future. In other words, the purpose is the study and appreciation of the total Jewish experience—the languages, literature, political activity, thought, demography, law, art, music, and eschatology of the Jews, to mention but a few of the threads of Jewish civilization.

Since such courses are to be treated as humanities, rather than as vehicles for the orientation of members of the Jewish community, certain conclusions follow.

1. The teaching must reflect not only a sympathy with the culture, but a dispassionate examination of its record as well. The university

teacher may not be an advocate. Hopefully, one of the by-products of knowledge will be identification on the part of many Jewish students with their people, its history and destiny; but that is a by-product and not a consciously sought aim.

2. A fair distribution of time and emphasis must be given to the centers of Jewish demographic concentration and to the areas where they were most creative. This means that the Diaspora, where the great majority of the Jewish people spent the overwhelming portion of Jewish history, requires major emphasis, even in the contemporary period.

The implications of this statement have to be faced squarely. In the first place, the Israeli curriculum may have to be revised to reflect this approach to Jewish humanities, even as Diaspora courses of studies will have to be shaped to reflect it. Jewish history, activity, and creativity in the Diaspora—to the extent that they can be described and analyzed— must be studied even for the period after the rise of the State of Israel, although certainly Israel will occupy a major focus in any study of modern Jewish history.

Special emphasis will have to be given to those turning points in Jewish expression that affected the mentality and internal organization of the Jews—the compilation and translation of Scripture, the redaction and dissemination of the Mishnah, the Babylonian Talmud, the Shulhan Arukh, the migration of the Jews westward in the nineteenth and twenti- eth centuries, the Holocaust, and the State of Israel.

Finally, to treat materials in the spirit of the humanities is to study them historically, sympathetically, and critically. Even Jewish religion must be studied as having a history, which is the story of change. This means that dogmatic presuppositions must be suspended in the course of teaching "sensitive" aspects of the Jewish experience.

Planning a curriculum, which is inevitably a selection, an anthology, of the Jewish experience, is a task of considerable difficulty, particularly if it is to have the cogency of authority (i.e., the acknowledged experts of our day) as well as of substance. Preparing teaching materials is a second major task; and the third step is the retooling of university teachers to identify with the curriculum and to teach its spirit as well as its substance. Only then will they be able to convey the new understand- ing and utilize the new materials willingly and properly.

In a sensitive area like Jewish studies, special mobilization of sympathetic forces is required. In a crucial paper on the formation of curriculum, Joseph Schwab, a veteran of the successful battle to revise science education, pointed to five groups that must be brought together if a curriculum is to have any hope of having a impact: (1) scholars or masters of the materials; (2) psychologists, that is, the authorities on the mentality of the age group to be taught; (3) representatives of the community who will react to the implications of the curriculum; (4) teachers; (5) curriculum writers.

The fact that this joint effort is not carried out consciously and deliberately in most great universities—although, in reality, it exists in many at least in surrogate form—should be no deterrent. Such a complete curriculum has never yet been devised for Jewish studies. Then again, it is only very recently in their history that Jews have begun to take the shaping of their political destiny into their own hands; and now they can begin to move to the cultural arena. However, the process of successful implementation will not be achieved without massive efforts, not least among them overcoming the defensive cynicism on the part of scholars toward pedagogic technique. In addition, Israelis will have to think in terms of the interests of the Jewish people, and Diaspora scholars in terms of the realities of contemporary Jewish trends.

Fortunately, we are not beginning from scratch. Jewish institutions have already achieved much that is of value for the enterprise we propose. The excellent standards of scholarship that obtain in university teaching of Jewish studies were translated from the very high caliber of study, teaching, and research that has been the hallmark of the great seminaries of Breslau, Berlin, Vienna, Cincinnati, and New York—and, in recent years, of the universities in Israel. It remains true that, for all the great scholarship and increased teaching at American universities, the major centers of advanced training, particularly in the requisite linguistic and textual skills, remain the Jewish institutions of higher learning. It is to them that I believe we will continue to look to take the initiative in articulating curricula and preparing materials for use in universities. They will establish the yardstick by which alternative curricula will be measured.

If I now proceed to suggest a tentative plan, it is a proposal that will depend on a cooperative effort. Thanks to the Jewish Publication Society translation of the Bible, we now have a precedent for great Jewish scholarship of all streams of religious thought working together. The scintillating results of the Bible translation give me reason to believe that cooperation can be achieved in other areas as well.

A humanistic education in Judaica will have to prepare materials in the following areas: (1) language: Hebrew and, to a lesser extent, Yiddish; (2) history: political as well as cultural; and (3) thought and religion. Each of these areas is massive and must be divided between ancient and modern periods. I propose that my institution, The Jewish Theological Seminary of America, prepare the material for a survey of Jewish cultural history.

Note: Subsequently, under the aegis of Chancellor Ismar Schorsch, the Jewish Theological Seminary of America, in cooperation with the ICUTJC, prepared two volumes within that master plan: *Medieval Jewish Civilization: A Multi-Disciplinary Curriculum,* edited by Ivan Marcus, appeared in 1988; and *The Modern Jewish Experience,* edited by Jack Wertheimer, was published in 1993. Each was a collective effort on the part of scholars in North America and in Israel who are specialists in particular areas of Jewish civilization.

24. THE AMERICAN JEWISH EXPERIENCE CURRICULUM (WITH HEBREW UNION COLLEGE–JEWISH INSTITUTE OF RELIGION)

Jonathan Sarna

The American Jewish Experience Curriculum project was first conceived at a 1982 colloquium on "Teaching the American Jewish Experience on the College Campus." At that session, Moshe Davis described two central problems faced by instructors who teach American Jewish life and institutions on campuses across the nation: (1) Many who teach the subject specialize in other, often far removed, areas and recognize that they are inadequately prepared; and (2) suitable academic materials dealing with American Jewry's past and present scarcely exist.

The project, jointly sponsored by the International Center for University Teaching of Jewish Civilization, Jerusalem, and the Center for the Study of American Jewish Experience on the campus of Hebrew Union College–Jewish Institute of Religion (HUC-JIR), Cincinnati, was established to deal with these problems. Its first publication, *Jews and the Founding of the Republic* (1985), was described as a "curriculum resource package." In an accompanying "Note to Teachers," the volume's three editors, Jonathan D. Sarna, Benny Kraut, and Samuel K. Joseph, spell out the underlying ideas and methodologies that guided the volume and the project as a whole:

This volume proceeds from a basic belief that the American Jewish experience deserves a place in the school curriculum both as a separate course and integrated into existing courses devoted to American, Jewish, and world history.

Since curricular materials in American Jewish history scarcely exist, and since many libraries possess only the most rudimentary Judaica Americana collections, curriculum resource packages designed for instructors need to be created. *Jews and the Founding of the Republic* represents our initial effort to do just that as part of a larger curriculum project.

The book is divided into six sections, beginning with a short background unit containing an article on colonial American Jewry and a survey overview of some of the topics elaborated upon later in the volume. The next four sections deal with Jews and the coming of the American Revolution, Jews in the Revolution, the impact of the Revolution on American Jews, and the relationship between the new nation and the Jewish community. Section Six, "Biblical Imagery and the Revolution," covers a related theme with which students need to be familiar.

In addition to setting forth the basic facts of American Jewish history, several major themes in the volume may be highlighted in the classroom as a series of five questions:

1. How was the American Jewish experience in the Revolution like and unlike that of other Americans?
2. How did the founding of the Republic affect the subsequent course of Jewish history in America?
3. In what ways does the history of the founding of the Republic demonstrate American exceptionalism with regard to Jews? In what ways was America similar to European countries?
4. How did being Jewish affect one's being an American in the early Republic? How did being an American affect one's being Jewish?
5. How was the American Jewish experience during the Revolution similar to and different from the American Jewish experience today?

The book stresses the importance of viewing the American Jewish experience in its broadest context: as the interrelationship between the narrow history of American Jews and the wider currents of American, Jewish, and world historical developments. Lending significance to the topic in this way avoids many of the dangers traditionally associated with "minority group history." It permits American Jewish history to be viewed as part of the larger mosaic that is the collective Jewish past.

The primary sources that *Jews and the Founding of the Republic* makes available, in some cases for the first time, are extremely valuable for teachers and students alike. The volume's focus, however, is too narrow. Academics have told us that they need a more ambitious text concerning the broad sweep of American Jewish history. Following consultations with leading scholars from major Midwest universities, and with the enthusiastic support of President Alfred Gottschalk of HUC-JIR, the decision was made to create a volume that deals with the totality of American Judaism: the religious experience of America's Jews from the earliest settlers to contemporary times.

Behind this decision lay the recognition that works dealing with other religions in America had multiplied. The volume was to include primary and secondary sources, resource aids, and bibliographies treating all facets of American Judaism as it has evolved. It was envisioned as becoming a standard work on American Judaism that would shape and stimulate a future generation of students, and would fill one of the great remaining lacunae in both Jewish studies and the study of American religions.

Jonathan D. Sarna (then of HUC-JIR and now at Brandeis University) and Benny Kraut (University of Cincinnati), assisted by Alexandra S. Korros (now at Xavier University), undertook to create this volume with the support of a distinguished advisory board of scholars. The editors faced an array of challenges: How should "American Judaism" be defined, periodized, and portrayed? Should the volume's primary emphasis be on history, ideology, or practice? What should be the proper balance between chronological developments and conceptual themes? How much background on Judaism, America, and American religious history needs to be provided? How can the volume serve readers of widely differing backgrounds and preparation, and be kept to a manageable length? To date, seven chapters have been produced in draft, covering the colonial period to the mid-1880s. The editors hope that the entire volume can be ready in draft by 1996.

25. JEWISH STUDIES PROGRAM AT THE UNIVERSIDAD IBEROAMERICANA

Judit Bokser-Liwerant

The development of the Jewish studies program at the Universidad Iberoamericana in Mexico City was the result of a joint effort of several institutions and individuals in Mexico and Israel: the International Center for University Teaching of Jewish Civilization, Jerusalem; academic exchange agreements between Universidad Iberoamericana and the Hebrew University of Jerusalem; and, in particular, the initiative and support of Jaime Constantiner, a leading figure in the Mexican Jewish community. There, prior to the program's inception, the only courses in Jewish studies were a section for Hebrew language in the Center of Foreign Languages at the Universidad Nacional Autónoma de México, the national university. Hebrew was, and still is, offered, like similar foreign language courses, as an auxiliary unit without academic credit; graduates of the Jewish day schools, who comprised the majority of Jewish university students in Mexico City, were not among its student population, for their academic level was more advanced.

The six Jewish day schools in Mexico City have provided an education from kindergarten through pre-university level. Senior educators of these schools, however, were imported from abroad, primarily from Israel. The need to train teachers for these schools, as well as for the extensive educational and cultural frameworks sponsored by the community centers of Mexico City's vibrant Jewish community, became increasingly apparent. That the program had to be at an academic level was dictated by the fact that the community was increasingly composed of university graduates.

Universidad Iberoamericana, a prestigious private college, was chosen as the most appropriate venue for a program in Jewish studies because of its student body, which included a large number of Jewish students, and because it offered the best opportunity for the advancement of Jewish studies on a graduate level. The introduction of such a program in a university with a Catholic and Third World orientation was a challenging task. However, the university administration was sympathetic and agreed to offer courses, initially in its Extension Services Division.

The success of the courses led to the incorporation of a graduate-level university program providing full academic credit. Coordinated by Judit B. Liwerant of the Universidad Nacional Autónoma de México and Haim Avni of The Hebrew University's Institute of Contemporary Jewry, it offers a wide variety of historical and interdisciplinary courses providing a total of forty-eight academic credits. Though the objectives and curriculum are formulated for the program as a whole, each course is conceived as an academic unit in itself. Thus, students may enroll in the program, or take each course separately.

The curriculum encompasses three general areas:

1. *Courses in Bible, Jewish history, and philosophy.* These are broadly conceptual, deal with issues of historical sources and historiography, and trace the development of Jewish thought and its relationship to the evolution of general philosophy. Among the courses are Biblical Values and Modernity; The Heritage of the Medieval Period: Jews between Christian and Muslim Civilizations; The Impact of Spain in Jewish History; Ashkenazi Culture: Yiddish Language and Literature; From Traditional Jewish Thought to Modern Jewish Philosophy.

2. *Courses in the structure of modern and contemporary Jewish society.* Such historic and local themes as the impact of modernity, migration, and the rebuilding of Jewish communities, economic and social stratification, and cultural currents draw upon a variety of disciplines and relate to the cultural milieu in which the students are educated: Latin American Jewry and Other Contemporary Communities: A Comparative Approach; Socio-Demographic Developments in Jewry in the First Generation after the Holocaust; Israel's Social Structure and Political System; Theory and Praxis of Jewish Education; Legal Emancipation and Jewish Migration; Modern Hebrew Literature and Latin American Literature: A Comparative Approach.

3. *Courses and seminars that critically analyze global historical trends and events that define Judaism in the contemporary world.* The following are offered according to the needs and interests of the students: The Society of Nations and the Jewish People: Political and Diplomatic History of the Twentieth Century; Socio-Political Analysis of Zionism, the Jewish National Movement; From Modern Antisemitism to the Holocaust.

Seven compilations of source readings in Jewish studies have been prepared for student use, and the program in its entirety provides specialization at the graduate level, as well as elective options for students in a variety of graduate fields in the humanities and the social sciences.

In addition to preparing senior educators and community leaders, the flexibility of the program's structure and its varied topics and comparative approach have also attracted scholars and university professors from other disciplines. The latter have found within it courses that relate to their own subject matter. This offers them the opportunity to expand and enrich their own courses and introduce elements of Jewish civilization studies into the broader academic framework.

26. WORLD REGISTER OF UNIVERSITY STUDIES IN JEWISH CIVILIZATION (WITH THE BIBLIOGRAPHICAL CENTER OF THE AVRAHAM HARMAN INSTITUTE OF CONTEMPORARY JEWRY)

Sergio DellaPergola and Florinda Goldberg

The World Register of university studies in Jewish civilization records information about undergraduate and graduate courses in universities throughout the world: where they are taught, by whom, in which academic departments, in which disciplines, and with what materials. It also includes a representative collection of syllabi, as taught in a wide variety of fields and in diverse institutional settings. As would be expected, there are enormous variations in the quantity and quality, the content and format, of instruction in Jewish studies. Each country, indeed each university, exercises its own judgment on what to teach and how to integrate Judaic materials into its general curriculum. The World Register constitutes the first systematic collection of such information.

For the purpose of the World Register, Jewish civilization studies has been defined along the most comprehensive lines, because it appears in a variety of disciplines and departments: archeology, art, biblical studies, Talmud, rabbinics, comparative religion, foreign languages, history, Jewish thought, literature, politics, social sciences, and sociology; as well as in interdisciplinary programs such as contemporary Jewry, Holocaust studies, Near Eastern studies, Sephardic studies, Israeli society, and Zionism.

For the past decade, pertinent data were collected in two ways:

through correspondence with universities, seminaries, other institutions, and individuals who were asked for catalogs, syllabi, and other information; and through comprehensive surveys of specific regions, prepared by local academics, mostly through extensive questionnaires sent to institutions in that area.

The following surveys have been published: *The Teaching of Jewish Civilization at European Universities,* by Doris Bensimon (1988); *The Teaching of Jewish Civilization in British and Irish Universities and Other Institutions of Higher Learning,* by Sharman Kadish (1990); *Jewish Civilization Studies in Latin American Universities,* by Haim Avni with Florinda Goldberg (1990); and *Teaching Jewish Civilization in Christian Seminaries and Theological Faculties of American Universities—Preliminary Exploration,* by Betsy Halpern-Amaru (1991). In addition, a global survey of universities that teach Hebrew was included in *Teaching Hebrew Language and Literature at the Academic Level* (1991).

Current information suggests that, in any given semester, courses in Jewish civilization are offered at some 1,250 universities, colleges, and theological seminaries on all continents. The need to classify the courses, and store and retrieve proliferating information about them, led to the decision to computerize the material.

The ICUTJC is presently developing a computerized inventory of university studies in Jewish civilization, in cooperation with the Bibliographical Center of the Avraham Harman Institute of Contemporary Jewry (The Hebrew University of Jerusalem), and with the support of UNESCO. The computerized inventory will be part of the *Aleph* network of The Hebrew University of Jerusalem. This will allow ICUTJC to incorporate information (e.g., computerized catalogs) from institutions throughout the world; and computers connected to that system worldwide will be able to ask for and receive information processed at ICUTJC, including full syllabi. The creation of a computerized database will permit continued updating and will make the information more accessible around the world.

The data will be coded for precise retrieval; a teacher preparing a course on a field in Jewish civilization will be able to call up the collection of selected syllabi on that subject contained in the ICUTJC database. This program will include three kinds of files:

1. Universities and institutions of higher learning that offer any form of studies in Jewish civilization: name and kind of institution; mailing and electronic addresses; departments, programs, and courses totally or partially devoted to Jewish civilization; their administrative frameworks, including academic requisites, credits, and degrees; research projects; faculty members involved in teaching and research.
2. Faculty teaching in the field: name, academic affiliation and position; participation in ICUTJC's activities; list of courses taught; research projects and interests; selected publications.
3. Courses partially or totally devoted to Jewish civilization: full, updated syllabi retrievable by discipline, main and secondary subjects, institution, teacher, country, etc.; course descriptions where syllabi are not available.

The next stage of the project will be the computerization of Jewish civilization themes included in courses of general disciplines.

Many of these materials can already be consulted at the University Resource Library of ICUTJC in Jerusalem. The library serves as a useful source of information for academics who have responsibility at all levels for programs in Jewish civilization; for instructors preparing new courses or revising old ones; for scholars identifying colleagues for possible collaboration; for administrators examining structural options; and for funding resources seeking an assessment of what is available and what lacunae need to be filled. Moreover, any program to further develop university-level Jewish studies worldwide must take account of the diversity of departmental frameworks and of potential students. The surveys already undertaken within the World Register project highlight the wide range of educational systems that reflect the special character of each country and its institutions; at the same time, they identify shared patterns regarding the departmental placement of courses. Thus the World Register provides a valuable resource on a global scale.

27. TEACHING JEWISH LAW IN LAW SCHOOLS (IN ASSOCIATION WITH AN INTERNATIONAL COLLEGIUM)

Yoram Dinstein

In 1986 a project was initiated whose objective was to develop a curriculum in Jewish law that could be offered as a regular (elective) course in law schools, first throughout the English-speaking world, and later in other countries as well. Such a course would be open to anyone interested in it, although the assumption was that, at least initially, its main appeal would be to Jewish students who often constitute a significant segment of the student body.

Law schools in Western countries regularly include in their curricula courses in Roman law or in comparative law. A course in Jewish law (*mishpat ivri*) would reflect the reciprocal relations and influences between the Jewish legal system and the systems of the various polities under whose sovereignty Jews lived at various times and places. Moreover, in the State of Israel *mishpat ivri* holds sway in the area of personal status, and the principles of Jewish law also contribute to court decisions of the emerging legal system, which has historically embraced both religious and civil spheres.

The project began with three consultative meetings of current and prospective teachers of Jewish law in American law schools. The first was at New York University, and the other two were held within the framework of the 1987 and 1988 Annual Conferences of the Association of American Law Schools. These consultations verified the feasibility of the project but indicated that success would be contingent on the preparation in English of a casebook of Jewish law. Each chapter in the casebook would focus on one or two modern cases, derived from the judgments of rabbinical courts, decisions of the state courts in Israel, and, regarding certain issues, from traditional rabbinical responsa. Such case studies would demonstrate to the students that Jewish law is not an abstruse anachronism, but a pulsating legal system. It would also be advantageous, where possible, to draw comparisons between the approach taken by Jewish law in the solution of a legal problem, and that of other modern legal systems with which the students are familiar.

For the purpose of this undertaking, a special type of casebook is required. Owing to the paucity of trained instructors of Jewish law, the casebook must be prepared very thoroughly, include an English glossary of technical terms, and provide detailed explanation of the concepts and institutions characteristic of Jewish law—which are outside the mind-set of the average American law student. The complexity of the undertaking is further affected by three elements:

1. Due to practical considerations, a single casebook must be prepared for use by instructors and students from a variety of backgrounds, and even in different countries. In the nature of things, each instructor has his or her own preferences with regard to theme selection, as well as individual ideological perceptions. It is therefore necessary to produce a casebook that will provide a large measure of flexibility by allowing for choices. In other words, it should encompass materials beyond the span of a regular one-term or even one-year law school course. Some eighteen to twenty chapters are envisaged.

2. Unlike many casebooks, the volume in question must constitute more than a cluster of cases glued together by disjointed editorial notes; each chapter must represent an analysis of the subject assigned to the writer. The leading case(s) should serve as a springboard for an in-depth examination of the principles involved.

3. From a methodological viewpoint, it is imperative not to refer exclusively to Jewish sources, but also to draw comparative analogies to cases from the jurisprudence of the U.S. Supreme Court and from British law, thus highlighting the contemporary relevance of centuries-old issues of contention, and showing that Jewish law is a living legal system.

We decided that each chapter in the casebook should focus on a specific theme. To ensure ideological pluralism and a wider appeal, each chapter would be assigned to a different contributor. After a first draft of several chapters had been produced, a group of instructors in Jewish law would be convened to test the materials in a simulated classroom environment. Contributors to the casebook would present their materials in the form of a class discussion, with their law-instructor peers acting as if they were the students. The ensuing intellectual give-and-take would lead to revision and enhance the quality of the text.

Implementation of these guidelines was begun in 1990–91. Two international colloquia were held in Britain, one in Oxford and the other in London. The dozens of participants included law professors, judges, and rabbis; those present ranged from ultra-Orthodox to Reform and secular Jews. The sessions were a success (so much so, that the Chief Rabbi of France, who attended the London meeting, urged launching a similar project for the teaching of Jewish law in French-speaking countries). As a result of the two colloquia, approximately three-quarters of the chapters of the casebook have already taken shape; nine of them are in final form, subject to editorial changes.

In 1993, a colloquium was convened in New York City. Like its two predecessors, it consisted of five simulated classroom discussions of themes in Jewish law, followed by the exchange of views regarding substance and methodology.

At the present time, the following fourteen chapters of the casebook have either been finished, or are undergoing revision (the list is in alphabetical order of the contributors):

(a) Judge J. Bazak (District Court, Jerusalem), "The Validity of a Testament Made Under Paranoid Delusions"
(b) Prof. D. Bleich (Cardozo Law School), (exact title not yet determined)
(c) Prof. M. Broyde (Emory University Law School), "Child Custody: In Whose Interest, and Based on What Principle?"
(d) Prof. S. Deutsch (Bar-Ilan University Law School), "Business Competition and Predatory Pricing"
(e) Dr. B. Eliash (Tel Aviv University Law School), "Privileged Evidence on Security Grounds"
(f) Prof. A. Enker (Bar-Ilan University Law School), "Self-Defense"
(g) Prof. S. F. Friedell (Rutgers University Law School), "Injuries In-

flicted by a Person's Body: The Standard of Care and Available Defense"
(h) Mr. I. H. Haut (Morris, Duffy), "Causation in Jewish Torts Law"
(i) Prof. A. Kirschenbaum (Tel Aviv University Law School), "Testimony to One's Own Disadvantage in Jewish Law"
(j) Prof. B. Lifschitz (Hebrew University Law School), "Employee and an Independent Contractor—Acquisition and Obligation in Contrast"
(k) Prof. A. Piatelli (University of Salerno), "The Woman in Israel"
(l) Dr. C. Povarsky (Touro Institute of Jewish Law), "Legislative Power in the Jewish Legal System in Antiquity and at Present"
(m) Prof. N. Rakover (Israel Ministry of Justice), "Bailment in Jewish Law—A Case Study"
(n) Prof. E. Shochetman (Hebrew University Law School), "Finality of Judgment"

The list speaks for itself in that it includes contributors from three Israeli law schools, as well as universities from abroad. We are considering a number of candidates to write an additional five chapters.

The future of the project (as envisaged at this juncture) is as follows: a fourth—and final—colloquium of the same nature as the first three will be convened in the United States. Afterwards, we shall need a "harmonization" session. In terms of language, using the same translations into English from the Talmud and from Maimonides throughout the casebook is naturally a matter of editing. But consistency of format must also be considered. Moreover, since it was decided some time ago to allow contributors to write about the subject of their choice (i.e., not to assign chapters in accordance with some master plan), we will also have to determine whether some topics are not conspicuous by their absence.

A lengthy introduction, explaining the structure of Jewish law, tracing its history and shedding light on the complex sources, will then be prepared. While the introduction will appear in print as a prologue, it has to be composed as an epilogue in order to elucidate sections in the casebook that may otherwise prove obscure to the nonspecialist student.

Before publication, and without necessarily waiting for the writing of the introduction, a mimeographed version of the casebook will be circulated informally for use in selected law schools on an experimental basis.

Thus, some feedback from the field will be available before the work is finalized.

Teacher-training workshops will be held, preferably in Jerusalem, once the casebook is ready, and a teachers' manual may evolve from them.

V
THE ISRAEL EXPERIENCE

28. REFLECTIONS ON THE ROLE OF ISRAELI INSTITUTIONS IN JEWISH CIVILIZATION STUDIES

Aviezer Ravitzky

With the establishment of The Hebrew University in Jerusalem [in 1925], a new era began for the "Science of Judaism" [*Wissenschaft des Judentums*]. For the first time it found itself in its entirety within a framework of an institution of higher education and learning—with Jewish life in all its manifestations and developments as its object—to which the Jewish social reality in its ancient homeland gave a territorial-historical continuity and national and cultural stability. . . . New, or almost new, subjects came to the fore. . . . Judaic studies thus replaced the "Science of Judaism."

—Benzion Dinur, "Wissenschaft des Judentums,"
Encyclopaedia Judaica (1972)

The interest of the historian of religion [in Judaism] cannot depend on apologetic, historical, or demographic reasons. . . . Rather it is because of the peculiar position of Judaism within the larger framework of the imagining of Western religion: close, yet distant; similar, yet strange, "occidental," yet "oriental"; commonplace, yet exotic. . . . Judaism is foreign enough for comparison and interpretation to be necessary; it is close enough for comparison and interpretation to be possible.

—Jonathan Z. Smith, *Imagining Religion* (1982)

I

The first and second generation of scholars who established Jewish studies in Israel as a comprehensive field of academic research and

teaching were highly conscious of the innovative character of their enterprise. Some leading figures among them made an explicit attempt to
reflect on the distinction between their scholarly approach and that of
their predecessors; that is, in the words of Benzion Dinur, to explain
how "Judaic studies replaced the Science of Judaism."

The most thoroughgoing analysis of this transformation was made by
Gershom Scholem in his essays "Reflections on the Science of Judaism"
(Hebrew, 1945) and "The Science of Judaism—Then and Now" (Ger-
man, 1959; English translation in *The Messianic Idea in Judaism,* 1971).
One need not agree with Scholem's sharp criticism of the Science of
Judaism to recognize the great importance of his essay for any present
effort to illuminate the self-perceptions and future expectations of the
founders of the Israeli centers of Jewish studies.

Scholem suggested two pragmatic distinctions between the German
school of the Science of Judaism and the emerging new Israeli school of
Jewish studies. First and foremost, the Science of Judaism tended to
reduce Judaism to an idea, a purely spiritual phenomenon. Most of its
scholars attempted "to liquidate, spiritualize, and de-actualize Judaism,"
disregarding most of the vital aspects of the Jewish people as a living
organism. True, Scholem maintained, opposing romantic forces were
also active in the Science of Judaism, yet the dominant spirit of this
school expressed itself in a "certain type of idyll, a peculiar etherealiza-
tion [of Judaism] . . . a breath of the funeral did in fact cling to the
atmosphere of this discipline for a century." As Michael Wyschogrod
humorously relates: A Hebrew poet from Eretz Israel was once introduced to a distinguished figure in the Science of Judaism school. The
scholar looked at him with astonishment and asked, "When did you
live?"

It is interesting to note that, in this particular context (the critique of
the Science of Judaism), Scholem's Zionist motivation was comple-
mented by ideas characteristic of the existentialist revolt against Hegel
and nineteenth-century essentialism. His entire argument is based on
the assumption that "definitions" and "theological formulas" kill their
objects, even if they later give them a decent burial. Judaism as a defin-
able idea and Judaism as a living entity are perceived as almost mutually
exclusive. Therefore, Jewish studies should focus on the dynamic existence rather than on essence alone (my words), and approach Judaism
"as a living organism and not merely as an idea." "The new valuations

of Zionism," Scholem writes, "brought a breath of fresh air into a house that seemed to have been all too carefully set in order by the nineteenth century."

Second, Jewish studies in Israel were called upon to overcome the apologetic tendencies of the authors of the Science of Judaism. The latter, pressed by historical and political needs, used scholarship as a weapon in their battle for human rights, against old and new anti-Semitism, and sometimes even in ideological struggles within the Jewish community. First and foremost, they attempted to portray an enlightened, "purified" picture of Judaism that would please the modern, rationally oriented reader. No longer, said Scholem. Following the Holocaust and the establishment of the State of Israel, "the Jewish people can approach the clarification of all the historical and spiritual issues . . . without any regard for external consideration." Likewise, Judaic studies should be pursued "without any ideological coloring . . . without being bound to any religious (or anti-religious) tendency."

II

What is the current situation in the Israeli academic scene regarding these questions? How would the above programmatic statements look today, when the students-of-students of Benzion Dinur and Gershom Scholem serve as professors of Jewish studies in Israeli universities? This question calls for a dual, perhaps paradoxical, answer.

On the one hand, current developments in Israeli universities confirm the earlier expectations; in fact, they even sharpen them. At the present time, when Jewish studies are taught in an autonomous, dynamic Jewish society and within a Hebrew-speaking environment, it is only natural that scholarly interest would focus on the "living organism" and not on the "idea" alone; that Jewish history would not relate to spirit and text alone but widen its scope to include many other societal and mundane issues. Similarly, one would expect the student of Judaism to be aware of current developments in Jewish life and creativity, and attempt to uncover their roots. No wonder, for instance, that during the last twenty years the writings of Rabbi Abraham Isaac Kook and A. D. Gordon have entered the curriculum of Israeli departments of Jewish thought, and that not long ago the writings of contemporary thinkers such as

Rabbi Joseph Dov Soloveitchik and Emmanuel Levinas have also found their way into the curricula. Parallel developments have taken place in other fields, like the study of Hebrew literature and Hebrew language, not to mention the development of an institute for the study of "contemporary Jewry."

One may, however, approach this question from a very different angle. One can make the claim that the role played today by Jewish studies in the Israeli society manifests a so-called return to the classical role of the Science of Judaism. Many earlier scholars at the Hebrew University envisioned their new approach to the study of Judaism to be a significant expression of the process of "normalization" of the Jewish people in their homeland. Today, however, Jewish studies in Israel are perceived by many as the antithesis of the hypernormalization of the people in their land. The mundane, political revival of the people is not a program or a task, but an existing fact. Therefore, the threat is not that ideas or texts will overshadow reality and the "living organism," but conversely, that the dynamic, demanding reality will eclipse ideas and eliminate texts, that the present will bury the past, and that the spoken language will swallow each of its earlier layers. In the contemporary situation, the emphasis on thought, interpretation, memory, and poetry, and even the attempt to reflect upon the living society, appear to be correctives of the exaggerated trend toward the banal and the normal.

Moreover, in the Israeli reality, the very study of Judaism and Jewish history, even academically, is charged with ideological flavor. It touches sensitive nerve ends of personal identity and collective culture: "Judaism" versus "Israelism," particularity as against universalism, Eastern versus Western orientations, and so forth. One who is vested with the authority to explain what Jewish sources say regarding a specific question deals not only with an academic issue but, in many cases, with an ideological, theological, or even political one. Whether the scholar likes it or not, every disclosure of historical developments or of conflicting classical schools of thought has cultural and social connotations far beyond the world of pure scholarship and research.

My comments regarding the so-called return to the study of Judaism relate only to its external, ideological implications and not to its internal aspirations and methods. On the contrary, the above-mentioned demand for an objective, nonapologetic study of Judaism ("without any ideological coloring") has been widely accepted as a central ethos, in fact as the defining factor, of the academic study of Judaism (as against yeshivah learning or study in any other ideologically oriented institution). Moreover, contemporary Israeli scholars quite often criticize their own teachers for their alleged tendency to portray an overly sophisticated, philosophically oriented image of Jewish religion, and to disregard most mythical and magical aspects of the teachings of the talmudic and midrashic sages, and sometimes even of the Jewish mystics. Similarly, other contemporary scholars point to the nationalist, Zionist-oriented reading of medieval and modern Judaism by their forebears. Admittedly, no one can tell what kind of an ideological bias will be attributed to the present generation of scholars by their successors.

Indeed, recent developments in hermeneutics have made us much more aware of the many problems and ambiguities inherent in such an aspiration to achieve a pure, objective reading of history and text. Needless to say, we lack the meta-criteria needed for making an "objective" judgment among the various competitive claims for objectivity—how much more so when the "object" of our humanistic study is not a fixed, static one, but vibrant, human subjects (not to mention the blurring of the boundaries between reader and text in postmodernism). Nevertheless, these conceptual difficulties should not open the gates to any ideological uses and political abuses of history and texts. Academic discipline is characterized by the subjective effort of the scholar to reach an objective description and evaluation of the sources.

I recall the irony of my late professor, Ephraim Gottlieb, trying to justify his deep immersion in the study of the kabbalah and Jewish mysticism. "I am a believing Jew," he said. "I therefore could not become an objective biblical scholar." Similarly, Gottlieb explained, "I accept the religious authority of the Sages, so I should never pretend to be an academic student of Talmud or midrash. By contrast, however, I do not believe in the teachings of the kabbalah; I therefore could become a good professor of Jewish mysticism."

III

The tensions between idea and life, text and society, scholarship and ideology would appear in a very different garb in the university study of Jewish subjects outside the State of Israel. First, far from the living

Hebrew culture and the autonomous Jewish public space, yet in the midst of other dynamic societies and active cultures, Judaism is relevant to scholars mainly because of its contribution to the shaping of Western civilization and its role in the comparative study of religion and the humanities in general. Second, in the absence of comprehensive departments of Jewish studies in most academic institutions outside Israel, and with the unprecedented growth of Judaica courses in the university curriculum, we are increasingly witnessing an inclination to clothe Judaism in "mystical," "existentialist," "postmodern," or some other attractive contemporary garb.

Let me explain. In the first instance, the unique position of Judaism in the Western tradition makes it central to the comparative study of religions and civilizations. In the words of Jonathan Z. Smith, "Judaism is foreign enough for comparison and interpretation to be necessary; it is close enough for comparison and interpretation to be possible." Stress on the comparative aspect of religion and culture, peculiar to American (and many European) universities, has already been proven to be a powerful catalyst even for the study of Judaism per se. It widens the scope of the field, raises fresh questions, and encourages the student of Judaism to participate in the universal discourse of academe.

On the other hand, a parallel yet opposite process may radically narrow the scope of Jewish studies; that is, it may approach Judaism and define it not in accordance with its own historical or conceptual terms, but in relation to the immediate intellectual demands and spiritual concerns prevalent in many Western universities today, for example, mysticism, existentialism, deconstructionism, and gender issues. In the extreme case, Heiddeger and Sartre (not Aristotle or Kant) would define the parameters for an introductory course on the history of Jewish philosophy. In more moderate cases, Lurianic kabbalah would take precedence over halakhic literature, and contemporary Hebrew poetry would overshadow its classical and medieval antecedents.

Interestingly enough, we can portray this development as the negative image of the German "Science of Judaism": The scholars of that school emphasized the rational manifestations of Jewish tradition; their successors would now underscore the mystical/mythical/magical manifestations of this same tradition. The Science of Judaism tended to view Judaism in light of idealist, Hegelian historiography; contemporary Jewish studies would primarily focus on existentialist approaches. While the former was trying to follow the paradigm of the natural sciences, that is, to "construct" history and texts as hard empirical facts, the latter would now "deconstruct" them and blur the distinction between datum and interpretation, text and reader. Each school thus reveals the spirit (and the bias) of its particular modern or postmodern age.

The second trend undoubtedly expresses an authentic personal inclination of many contemporary scholars; but it is encouraged and accelerated by the institutional situation in most Western universities. With the need of Judaica professors to create and secure a place for their discipline within the general departments of religious studies, history, Near Eastern studies, and so on, it is no wonder that the study of Jewish civilization frequently appears to "adjust" itself to the intellectual and spiritual demands of the surrounding academic world.

How does this compare with the situation of Jewish studies in academic institutions in Israel? In the nature of things, Israeli universities provide independent departments for each of the central areas of Jewish civilization. In the Hebrew University of Jerusalem, for example, there are seven independent departments of Bible, Talmud, Jewish history, Jewish thought, Hebrew language, Hebrew literature, and Yiddish literature (as well as subdepartments in Jewish folklore and Jewish liturgy). All these are subsumed within the Institute of Jewish Studies, which has about seventy tenured professors. Under such conditions, the Jewish studies program finds itself within an encompassing, multidisciplinary academic framework, with the various disciplines enabled to nourish one another. Furthermore, in such an academic framework, internal dialogue and fruitful contact can be developed between "rational" and "mystical-mythical" readings of Judaism, between "constructionism" and "deconstructionism," between the "modern" and the "postmodern," between philologic/historic analysis and intellectual exploration and synthesis.

Of course, under such independent conditions, one must be careful to avoid the danger of isolation of Jewish studies from the universal academic discourse, which is the unique contribution of Western academic institutions. On the other hand, only such conditions permit the development of Jewish studies as a comprehensive, autonomous, academic field of study. And this promises to be the singular contribution of Israeli institutions of higher learning to the academic world at large.

29. ACADEMIC ENRICHMENT IN ISRAEL

DAVID KLATZKER (UNITED STATES)

As a student at Pomona College (of the Claremont Colleges, California), I lobbied for more Jewish studies courses. I have a vivid memory of debating a Protestant professor who candidly declared that "there is no Jewish history of any significance after the days of the Bible." Although the arguments of the Jewish students met with only slight success (and that came mainly as a by-product of the black students' violent demands for "cultural diversity" in the curriculum), I was encouraged by the episode, and resolved to do graduate work in the general area of contemporary Jewish history.

Mainly to improve my Hebrew, I spent 1972–73 as a visiting graduate student at the Hebrew University, where I audited courses with Mordechai Kaplan, Eliezer Schweid, Moshe Davis, and Yehuda Bauer. It was a wonderful year, but I did not then anticipate returning to Israel for further studies. I enrolled in the "dual program" (Rabbi/Ph.D.) of the Reconstructionist Rabbinical College and Temple University in Philadelphia, which attracted me as an experiment in adding social science theory to the classical rabbinical school curriculum. Because of my growing academic interest in integrating Zionist history and American religious history, my advisor, Franklin Littell, urged me to return to the Hebrew University to study for a year with Moshe Davis.

I worked with Moshe Davis in 1976–77, in what he called a bi-institutional arrangement in "correlative training." I became particularly interested in the Southern Baptists in the Holy Land, and my interviews with Israeli Baptists were deposited in the Oral History Archive at the Institute of Contemporary Jewry. I later published my first scholarly

paper on the Baptists' "American" approach to the religion-state problem in Israel. But, like many graduate students, I was looking for a Ph.D.
topic that would "choose me," rather than me it.

Moshe Davis's ambitious reprinting of seventy-two classic works
(*America and the Holy Land,* 1977–78) appeared just in time. I found
the many Holy Land travelogues in the reprint series—a mere fraction
of the total number that were published over the nineteenth and early
twentieth centuries—especially intriguing. Of all the historical records
one could use to examine religious attitudes toward Jews and Zionism,
travel accounts are probably the most colorful and personal. As I delved
deeper into the memoirs written by Americans who visited the Holy
Land, I discovered that they shed light not only on the Jewish-Christian
nexus, but also on other aspects of American religion and popular
culture (e.g., issues of belief and disbelief, millenarianism, and fem-
inism).

With the help of a doctoral dissertation grant from the National
Foundation for Jewish Culture, I did research in Washington, London,
and Jerusalem in 1982. My Temple University thesis was completed in
1987 ("American Christian Travelers to the Holy Land, 1821–1939").
Since then, I have published cognate studies on the "touristification" of
the Holy Land, American Catholic pilgrimage, and the image of Jerusalem in nineteenth-century America, in *Union Seminary Quarterly Review, Catholic Historical Review,* and the *With Eyes Toward Zion* series
edited by M. Davis and Y. Ben-Arieh.

Being a "lone researcher" may sound romantic, but it can be difficult.
Although their number is growing, there are still only a few researchers
in America who share my interests. Conversation, wonderful conversation, has been the chief benefit of the summer workshops of the International Center for University Teaching of Jewish Civilization. In the
seminar room and around the lunch table, I have been privileged to
share ideas with Israeli, European, and American scholars. The participants feel no need to protect their disciplinary turf; I have received
valuable advice from historical geographers, political scientists, and curators of photography.

REINIER MUNK (HOLLAND)

It was during my secondary education that I became seriously interested in Judaism and Jewish studies. After having taken various introductory courses in Jewish history and rabbinic thought at universities in Holland, I went to Jerusalem in 1983 to attend a summer course in Jewish thought at the Rothberg School for Overseas Students of the Hebrew University. It was this course, given by Emil Fackenheim and Jeffrey Macy, that made me decide to specialize in modern and contemporary Jewish philosophy. The decision was confirmed a year later, when I was given the opportunity to study in Jerusalem at the Shalom Hartman Center for Ethics and Religious Pluralism.

After returning to Amsterdam, I took my M.A. degree in Jewish studies under the supervision of Albert van der Heide of Vrije Universiteit, writing a thesis on Rabbi Joseph B. Soloveitchik's concepts of halakhic thought. At the same time, I established contact with Aviezer Ravitzky and Nathan Rotenstreich of the Hebrew University, since I intended to continue with a doctorate on Soloveitchik's thought. It was through their mediation that I was able to work on my doctorate at the Hebrew University during the academic years 1990–91 and 1991–92.

The years in Jerusalem gave me the opportunity to deepen and expand my training in Jewish philosophy in a way that would not have been possible in Amsterdam—to discuss my work with professors in this field, to increase my fluency in Hebrew, and to gain an insight into social, cultural, and political life in Israel. I specifically would like to mention the cordial and artistic contacts with the members of the Opus Singers, an Israeli chamber choir in which I participated during those years. The concerts we performed in Jerusalem and Tel Aviv were cultural highlights which I recall with much pleasure.

After returning to Amsterdam I began teaching Jewish philosophy in the Department of Philosophy at Vrije Universiteit, as well as in various adult education frameworks. At the same time I have continued to write my doctoral thesis, supervised by Albert Van der Heide and Johan Van der Hoeven (VU, Amsterdam) and by Nathan Rotenstreich and Aviezer Ravitzky (HU, Jerusalem).

The International Center contributed extensively to my studies. Participation in its workshop on Jewish philosophy enabled me to meet with distinguished teachers in this field and to gain from their knowledge and experience. As a result of these contacts, I was able to publish several articles.

Participation in the workshop on Jewish philosophy will continue to serve as an important channel for me to exchange approaches and source materials for the teaching of Jewish philosophy. In my opinion, the creation of a global network of scholars engaged in the teaching of Jewish civilization by the International Center constitutes a major contribution to the development of this interdisciplinary academic area.

ILIA RODOV (RUSSIA)

A specific national self-consciousness was probably one of the reasons that I aspired to an academic education. I grew up in the little town of Bobruysk, a typical Jewish "shtetl" situated within the former Jewish Pale in Byelorussia. My father is a specialist in decorative wall painting, and several generations on my mother's side were signboard painters in the provinces. I was born in a house of which half was a studio, so since my childhood I have been familiar with the smell of paint. When the time came to choose my future profession, I decided to go to Leningrad, to begin studying painting seriously. After completing my basic education as a painter, I applied to the Faculty of Art Theory and Art History at the Leningrad Academy of Fine Arts for further study.

My interest in Judaica and Jewish studies was initially conditioned by sociopsychological motivations, among them the aspiration for a more conscious national self-identification. This motivated me to turn to Judaica in my academic studies. As the subject for one of my papers written for the Academy of Art, I chose the book illustrations of Marc Chagall. This was not a preference based on professional knowledge. Russian publications about Chagall were almost nonexistent, and foreign publications were difficult to obtain. It is important to note that official Soviet policy ignored the work of Chagall; therefore, my attempt to have a theme connected to his art approved was also a way for me to protest against academic stagnation and anti-Semitism. At first, my request was not granted.

I turned to a closer investigation of the illustrations, seeking to understand what was "Jewish" about Chagall's work, and I began the analysis of his art without having the originals accessible. I applied to Zezilia Nesselstraus, a scholar in the field of medieval book illumination, and requested her scientific supervision of my work. Nesselstraus was known as a person who would support an initiative even if it went against the established order of the Academy of Fine Arts. For one year, I studied medieval illuminated manuscripts, then returned to Chagall. This occurred during the first attempts to liberalize communist ideology, and my thesis, "The Artistic World of Chagall: The Illustrations of Gogol's *Dead Souls*," was officially accepted.

Coming to the end of my long years of schooling in the renowned educational institutions of the Soviet Union, I felt a lack of knowledge in my particular field of interest, Judaica. This hindered not only my understanding of Jewish art, but also of important cultural phenomena in Russia, the Ukraine, and Byelorussia. The aspiration for a more complete knowledge of Jewish art, and my plans for research on the Jewish-Russian relationship within Russian art, led me to continue my education at the Hebrew University of Jerusalem.

I had learned about the Hebrew University while studying the literature on Chagall's works. At the same time, I had discovered the hundred-year-old tradition of synagogue wall painting in Eastern Europe. Upon my arrival in Jerusalem, I applied for postgraduate training and announced my plans to investigate wall paintings in the synagogues of the former Jewish Pale from the seventeenth century on. During my two years at the Hebrew University, I studied Jewish art, a subject not taught in the former Soviet Union. I also improved my knowledge of modern art, an area that had been closely controlled by the communist regime.

This program proved to be effective. Participating in the seminars and in the lectures given by specialists invited to the university, as well as visiting the Jewish Art Center, the Israel Museum in Jerusalem, and other Israeli museums, brought into relief for me the differences in the teaching and research methods used in the Soviet and the Israeli schools of art history. I am glad to have had the opportunity to experience both scientific traditions.

The knowledge I gained during those two years has helped my research in Jewish art. My work on Shalom Moshkovitz, a folk artist from Safad, was accepted, and I spoke on the subject at the Eleventh World Congress of Jewish Studies in Jerusalem. I also began an intensive collection of materials about East European synagogue wall paintings and made a research trip to Byelorussia and the Ukraine, where I photographed the surviving interiors of old synagogues, and viewed archival materials on the vanished ones. The main part of my work is still to be done.

NAOMI B. SOKOLOFF (UNITED STATES)

I completed my undergraduate training in Spanish literature at Swarthmore College (1975), and my Ph.D. in comparative literature at Princeton University (1980). During my graduate studies I developed an interest in modern Hebrew literature and spent a year (1977–78) at the Hebrew University of Jerusalem to pursue that subject. At that time I studied with Gershon Shaked, who eventually served as one of the readers for my dissertation—a discussion of narrative structures in novels by S. Y. Agnon, John Dos Passos, and Alejo Carpentier. I had already spent several summers in Israel, intent on improving my Hebrew and learning more about the country, but the year at the Hebrew University allowed me to begin to integrate my personal commitment to Israel with my professional plans.

I moved into the field of Hebrew full time with an appointment as an assistant professor at the University of Arizona (1980–83), and later at the University of Washington (1985–present). Between these appointments, a year spent at The Jewish Theological Seminary of America as a faculty fellow provided time to pursue research and to receive additional training in Jewish studies.

My teaching has covered both language and literature; my research has been devoted primarily to the field of modern Hebrew literature. Among my first publications were essays on A. B. Yehoshua, Yehuda Amihai, David Shahar, Dan Pagis, Shulamit Hareven, and other contemporary writers. I have also focused on comparative studies of modern Jewish fiction, and have examined Israeli writing together with American Jewish writing, Yiddish, and French literature. My book, *Imagining the Child in Modern Jewish Fiction* (Johns Hopkins University Press, 1992), examines the representation of children's consciousness and inner life in adult literary texts, discussing works by Sholem Aleichem, H. N. Bialik, Henry Roth, Jerzy Kosinski, Aharon Appelfeld, David Grossman, A. B. Yehoshua, Cynthia Ozick, and Albert Memmi. Another volume, *Gender and Text in Modern Hebrew and Yiddish Literature,* coedited with Anne Lapidus Lerner and Anita Norich (The Jewish Theological Seminary of America, 1992), also adopts a comparative perspective as it examines feminist approaches and gender issues in two major Jewish literatures. My current research involves two book-length projects, one concerning feminist approaches in recent Israeli fiction, and the second considering ways in which Israelis and American Jews have imagined one another in literary texts.

During the early years of my career, the workshop on Modern Hebrew Literature in Translation offered by the International Center provided me an invaluable opportunity to meet colleagues and to spend time in Israel. For someone like me, who began academic pursuits in literary studies other than Hebrew, these occasions proved indispensable in forging closer ties with individuals who teach Hebrew literature in its natural home, Israel. A special attraction of these meetings was the chance to meet Israeli authors in small discussion groups, and to exchange ideas with scholars, not only from the United States but also from Britain and elsewhere.

I find it is crucial to my professional life to visit Israel annually in order to keep up with developments in the field, to find out who is working on what, to purchase books, to pursue research in the library at the Hebrew University, at Genazim in Tel Aviv, and at other archives, and to become acquainted with new colleagues.

JOSEPH TEDGHI (FRANCE)

After receiving my secondary school diploma (*baccalaureat*) at the Israeli and Oriental Normal School, I decided to further my studies in Jewish history and Hebrew language at the National Institute of Oriental Languages and Civilizations (INALCO) in Paris. At the same time, I took a course in Arabic language and civilization at the Sorbonne, for I could not imagine taking Hebrew studies without knowing about the Arab countries surrounding Israel. Moreover, an apprenticeship in the Arabic language seemed to me necessary for learning Hebrew and studying the Semitic world.

At INALCO I specialized in North African Jewish history, writing my thesis on "North African Jews in Israel between 1967 and 1985: Political and Sociological Evolution." I also earned an M.A. degree from the Sorbonne, writing a study of a Jewish-Arabic grammarian from Spain, Yonah Ibn Janah, who wrote the *Kitab al lumna'*.

Since 1987 when I received my Ph.D., my research has focused primarily on the study of Judeo-Arabic and North African Jewish-Arabic civilization. I also am a *maitre de conferences* (assistant professor) at INALCO, where I teach North African Judeo-Arabic language, the commentaries of the responsa rabbis of North Africa as a historical source, and biblical grammar.

My first contact with Israel dates to 1976 when, as a high school student, I was the French representative in the International Youth Bible Competition in Jerusalem. In 1977 and 1978 I participated in a seminar for the training of teachers of Jewish studies in the Diaspora, and, while writing my doctorate, I spent every summer in Jerusalem, doing research in Israeli libraries. Taking advantage of my education in France and Israel, I taught in Hebrew schools in Paris and its suburbs for almost fifteen years.

In 1987 Moshe Bar-Asher of the Hebrew University, who was in Paris for a sabbatical year, invited me to take part in a workshop on Sephardic and North African Jewry, organized by the International Center for University Teaching of Jewish Civilization. Since then I have participated regularly in similar workshops in Jerusalem, and find them extremely valuable because a great number of researchers in related areas are given the opportunity to compare their work. Moreover, the International Center holds parallel workshops on Jewish literature and history which afford an exchange of new ideas and varied orientations, providing the participants with different teaching perspectives and cultural enrichment.

My experience in Israel has also included a postdoctoral year at the Hebrew University which permitted me to undertake research on North African Jews and to finish my book, *The History of Hebrew Printing in Fez, Morocco* (Jerusalem: Ben-Zvi Institute, 1994). I also taught several courses at the Hebrew University: "The History of Judeo-Arabic Literature in North Africa," and "The Study of Judeo-Arabic Texts." Through this double experience of teaching and research, I enjoyed direct contacts with both teachers and students, and gained a better knowledge of the Israeli university system. At various symposia and conferences I exchanged views on research methods with colleagues from Israel and elsewhere, participated in a seminar on Jewish languages organized by Shelomo Morag, and became acquainted with the Language Traditions Project that he directs. I can easily say that the year I spent in Jerusalem in 1992 was a most edifying one for me.

It is increasingly evident that it is not possible to do research or to teach any aspect of Jewish civilization without the help of Israeli universities, research centers, and specialized institutes, the input of the growing number of symposia and conferences, and the stimulation of the articles and reviews published in scholarly journals in Israel. Both Jewish and non-Jewish participants in Israeli conferences and workshops return to their own countries as cultural envoys transmitting new materials and approaches in Jewish studies.

VI
MOTIVATIONS

30. WORLD LEADERSHIP

EPHRAIM KATZIR

It was C. P. Snow, scientist and novelist, who warned us of the alienation developing between the disciples of two diverging modern cultures—the humanist and the scientific. My own experience may be a case in point. Taken out of my laboratory, I found myself as the president of that dynamic country and people called Israel. I was to emerge five years later with, I think, a new perception of the humanist culture, certainly in its relation to my people, its history, and its worldwide contemporary development.

There was a bridge awaiting me when I entered the presidency. It was the President's Circle on Diaspora Jewry, established in the sixties by my predecessor, Zalman Shazar, who was a historian and writer. The Circle's chairman and guiding spirit was Moshe Davis, founder of the innovative Institute of Contemporary Jewry at The Hebrew University of Jerusalem.

The Circle, in a sense, brought the Institute's academic achievement into public life. The subject it dealt with was Jewish life in European and American countries and in areas of distress. It is a many-faceted subject, all too often dealt with in easy generalizations and always involving the problems of the general society in which the Jewish group lives. There were no easy generalizations, no facile conclusions, voiced at the Circle's monthly meetings in the President's Residence. The central talk was always delivered by an authority on the particular field under discussion, while others involved in studying the subject offered their comments and insights in the discussions that followed.

This being Israel, the participants often included distinguished new immigrants who only recently had come from the particular countries and regions being dealt with. We heard "refuseniks" from the Soviet Union, political activists from Latin America, outstanding leaders, academicians, writers from the United States, England, and France. History was alive at the Circle, and to keep the sessions from being abstract and detached, persons involved in the practical problems of each group were also invited to participate. Their personal experiences and conclusions added the flavor and urgency of reality to what might otherwise be simply commentary, no matter how brilliant.

As an experimental scientist and teacher, I began to think in terms of transmitting the Circle's influence further—to other groups concerned with the problems of Diaspora Jewry, or living those problems themselves without sufficient guidance in their perplexity. A university teacher is bound to be particularly concerned with student youth. Having taught in many universities all over the world, I realized that students all too often have very limited knowledge of Jewish civilization.

A proposal made by Moshe Davis, and close to what I had been sensing, was the answer I was looking for. He suggested the establishment of an institution to encourage university teaching of Jewish studies, under the auspices of the Israeli presidency. The concept won my enthusiastic support. So, too, did Davis's thorough examination of the situation. He received leaves-of-absence from his teaching duties at the Hebrew University and circled the world to study the state of university Jewish studies, wherever they did exist. The voluminous, carefully factual report he submitted, reflected a situation where much had to be done almost everywhere.

Some fifteen years later, I can say that much indeed has been done, and I am immensely gratified to have been, along with Philip Klutznick, one of the founding fathers of the International Center for University Teaching of Jewish Civilization.

This is an institution that has made a difference. It has contributed greatly to the remarkable worldwide expansion of Jewish studies, taught now in as many as 1,300 universities. It has consistently expanded the fields of study in which the Jewish component is significant but has often been neglected in the general university curriculum: take as examples, Jewish law, Jewish art, Jewish political studies, Jerusalem in the mind of the Western world, along with more obvious and very important subjects such as Jewish civilization in Eastern Europe and in North Africa,

Hebrew language and literature, philosophy, and contemporary Jewish civilization as a whole.

The Center has contributed to expansion in still another way, playing an important part in introducing Jewish studies into universities in Eastern Europe, the Far East, even Africa.

I have the feeling that out of the small grain of the original concept, great crops are springing up. Vastly significant to my teacherish mind are the summer workshops in Jerusalem attended by faculty members of universities abroad. They serve to reinforce knowledge and understanding, as well as pedagogical approaches, in various aspects of Jewish civilization. Many of these, let us remember, are novel, pioneering subjects in their environments and are still being formulated and shaped.

When I look back on this academic adventure which I undertook with Moshe Davis, I feel that the Center is really going to the heart of the problem as we recognized it. Through international faculty exchanges, publication of papers, syllabi, bibliographies, and books, it is supporting the work of teachers and molding the minds of students. Of no little importance is its preparation of a World Register of university courses in Jewish civilization, and through all its work there emerges the pivotal importance of Israel in the development and dissemination of Jewish studies.

There are other implications of grave significance: acquainting student youth with age-old Jewish moral values, championing peace and nonviolence, the sanctity of human life, and the kinship of the human race. At a time when science can destroy the world, this spiritual legacy can provide tools for the building of a better future for all humanity.

PHILIP M. KLUTZNICK

Since midcentury, the renaissance of Hebrew language and culture in Israel, stimulated by the very existence of Israel as a state, caught the imagination of the world of learning. What the nineteenth-century German-Jewish advocates of *Wissenschaft des Judentums* had in mind but did not achieve—namely, academic study of Jewish history and culture as a recognized component of world civilization—was being advanced under the powerful spur of Israeli scholarship. Students of various faiths and backgrounds, seeking the sources of Judaism, came to Israel for undergraduate and postgraduate study. The works of eminent Israeli scholars were taught at universities in many lands, including Christian denominational schools.

Within American colleges and universities, this development brought forth an outcropping of courses related to Jewish studies, available to the entire student body. A large missing piece in the picture was the focus of many discussions I had in Israel with Moshe Davis, then head of the Institute of Contemporary Jewry at Hebrew University, and Ephraim Katzir, the fourth president of the State of Israel. What, in fact, I asked, was the actual state of the teaching of Jewish civilization in colleges and universities beyond the world of Israel itself? What should such teaching be like? If Jewish subjects were taught as part of a general curriculum, the university campus could become a place for self-discovery by Jewish youth. All this was easy to state, but it was also haunted by an issue that went to the heart of the academic enterprise—namely, the potential tension between university goals of knowledge and scholarship, and Jewish group goals of identification and commitment.

Nahum Goldman, as president of the World Jewish Congress, was of the same mind. Along with Arye Dulzin, chairman of the World Zionist Executive and the Jewish Agency, we managed after much importuning to secure from these two groups support for a major research project entrusted to Moshe Davis. He was to survey the teaching of Jewish civilization in colleges and universities in different parts of the world, including Christian denominational colleges and those with few or no Jewish students. The survey would focus not only on accredited course offerings but on the entire support structure of the academic enterprise— syllabi and textbooks, library resources, research, publications, and faculty.

In an earlier report in 1973 to the Commission on Formal Jewish Studies Program of the Memorial Foundation for Jewish Culture, Davis stated that the sudden and swift expansion of Jewish studies programs was a challenge as well as a blessing, particularly when in some cases the teachers whom students encountered could not compete with those in the established disciplines. The problem was "how to ensure that those involved in the teaching of Judaica are ranking scholars of broad intellect who, though specialized, can make a contribution to the entire academic community." Davis went on to observe that the legitimation of the scientific study and teaching of the Jewish people's experience—their religion, history, thought, and culture—created the need for a new vocation in Jewish life that transcended the seeming contradictions between Jewish commitment and high scholarship. In addition to the modern professions of rabbi, educator, and social worker, there was now "the need to shape the profession of University Jewish Scholar in the image of the university. It must be defined, planned and nurtured for the university setting rather than rely on transplantations from other vocations." Existing Jewish institutions, such as rabbinical schools and teachers' institutes, were not geared either conceptually or structurally to deal with the opportunity for university-based Jewish learning.

The genetic seeds contained in that 1973 statement bloomed eight years later when Yitzhak Navon, then president of Israel, announced the formation of the International Center for the University Teaching of Jewish Civilization; I was the chairman of its Board of Regents. The aim of the Center, under the auspices of the president of Israel and directed by Moshe Davis, was to initiate, stimulate, and coordinate institutional programs without itself becoming a competing academic institution.

Together with my ever-helping wife Ethel, I have established two chairs in the study of Jewish civilization. One is at my alma mater, Creighton University in Omaha, Nebraska (a Jesuit school), where I received my Doctor of Jurisprudence degree. The other is at Northwestern University in Chicago. I am proud to have contributed to the expansion of qualitative university studies in Jewish civilization, and to the founding of the International Center, which has played an important role in that field.

YITZHAK NAVON

When I had the privilege of assuming the presidency of Israel in 1978, I discovered that I was heir to a remarkable survey on worldwide university instruction in Jewish civilization studies. The Policy Report on this subject by Moshe Davis astounded me. Jewish studies were being pursued in places we could never have imagined.

I willingly agreed that the International Center, the product of this report, should function under the aegis of the Israeli presidency, and enthusiastically endorsed the idea of first developing a World Register of universities that teach courses in Jewish civilization. In succession, an annual summer workshop program was inaugurated, followed by a publication program and an interuniversity fellowship program. The University Teaching Center grew from an institution rooted locally in Jerusalem to an international educational enterprise. Its significance grew on me as I came to realize that university-level Jewish civilization studies could contribute to the understanding of the sources of Christianity and Islam, within the diverse academic community.

In 1987, during my visit to Spain as Israel's minister of education and culture, I met a group of Spanish professors engaged in scholarly research on the Hebrew language and culture. A Cultural Agreement signed by the Spanish minister of culture and myself recommended the expansion of Hebrew learning in Spanish universities and stressed the significance of Israel's academic cooperation. It was subsequently personally gratifying to meet professors from Spain attending the annual summer workshops conducted by the International Center.

Academic cooperation and Jewish studies links with Muslim and Arab states preceded the 1992 peace initiative. Contacts have been established with universities in Arab countries. The World Register has information on Hebrew language and Jewish studies courses in seven universities in Morocco, five universities in Egypt, four theological colleges in Lebanon, two universities in Jordan, as well as in Libya and Sudan. Information is currently being gathered on the status of Hebrew and Jewish studies in Syria and Kuwait.

Workshop participants have included Muslim students from Morocco, who supplement their postgraduate studies in France with attendance at the continuing workshops of the International Center in Jerusalem. We have learned that all students specializing in the Arab language in Morocco have the option of selecting Hebrew as an elective, and most of them make this choice. At the University of Jordan in Amman, students have been urging that courses in advanced Hebrew be added to the program of beginners' courses now available. In Egypt, Muslim students are writing graduate theses on Ibn Ezra and Maimonides, as well as on contemporary Israeli novelists.

When further account is taken of the phenomenal expansion of university-level Jewish studies in the former Soviet Union, and other developments such as Hebrew and Jewish civilization courses in universities in China, Korea, and half a dozen African states—many maintaining close ties with the University Teaching Center—we recognize Israel's intrinsic role in world culture.

CHAIM HERZOG

During my two terms as president of the State of Israel, one of my central concerns was international cooperation—the need for joint solutions to the problems facing humanity in this complex century, and in this uneasy Middle East. Closest to home, I endeavored to give special weight to the relationship between Israel and the Jewish communities throughout the world, a bond at the heart of which lies education.

In this context I was gratified to inherit the presidential relationship to the global programs of the International Center for University Teaching of Jewish Civilization. The younger generation has now been enabled to meet Jewish studies on a sophisticated academic level, and thus to find its own relationship to its people's legacy.

For me, a striking example of the expansion of the Jewish academic horizon occurred in 1991 when thirty-eight rectors, presidents, heads of Judaica departments, and junior scholars, representing thirteen European universities, visited the President's Residence during sessions of the International Center's European Regional Development Conference.

Meeting these scholars, including several Christian academics recognized as outstanding leaders in the contemporary field of Judaica, I perceived a graphic illustration of the nonparochial nature of Jewish studies. I recall telling the gathering of the research conducted by my late father, Isaac Halevi Herzog, former Chief Rabbi of Ireland and, later, of Eretz Israel, into the life and work of John Selden. This luminous sixteenth-century British semiticist, a Protestant, successfully combined careers as a lawyer, parliamentarian, and antiquary, producing classic studies of Jewish law, the Jews of England, the Noahide laws, the Jewish laws of marriage and divorce, and the Sanhedrin.

One year later, I was host to a very different kind of gathering of Jewish scholars—a very emotional welcoming back into the fold, after a seventy-year absence, of East European Jewish studies scholars. They were then taking their first tentative steps in rebuilding Jewish learning in all the far-flung, heretofore silent, Jewish communities of the former Soviet Union.

The modicum of Russian I had acquired while serving with the British forces in Berlin was no longer serviceable, so it was through an interpreter that I spoke to each of the thirty pioneers of new Jewish learning, from Estonia to Samarkand to Birobidjhan, and points in between. I asked each scholar to describe his or her particular field of research, and as they spoke I experienced a profoundly moving awareness of the renewal of Jewish life in a region that had been the birthplace of great institutions of Jewish learning and of Zionist movements that changed the face of nineteenth- and twentieth-century Jewish life.

Thus, in both international and intranational frameworks, I have come to appreciate the worldwide ramifications of the task assumed by the University Teaching Center.

Another aspect of the Center's role is to meet the challenge of the revival of the Hebrew language as a living expression of our national identity. This issue is crucial to Israel's cultural development. For Hebrew sustains artists who work with the word as well as those who create from its consciousness. Hebrew has also come to serve as a bond linking the Jewish communities throughout the globe, opening the world of Israeli Jews to their peers in the Diaspora. This is the rich texture of our cultural fabric from which we have woven our independent national experience.

Israel's culture draws from a history of dispersal, rebirth, and constant struggle for peace. And it is still moving along its path of discovery.

31. REGIONAL LEADERSHIP

PHILIP I. AND MURIEL M. BERMAN (UNITED STATES)

In 1983, my wife, Muriel Berman, received a letter asking her to become a member of the Board of the International Center for University Teaching of Jewish Civilization. The academic chairman was Moshe Davis, the convenor was the fifth president of Israel, Yitzhak Navon, and an illustrious group of people and learned scholars served on the Board of Directors. This invitation intrigued Muriel and she accepted. At that time, she was president of the Jewish Publication Society of America, one of the most prestigious organizations of Jewish learning in the United States. As we were going to Israel at that time, she asked me to come along to the meeting and learn about the activities of the International Center.

We remember well the meeting in the President's Residence, where the conversation revolved around the importance of teaching Jewish studies not as an incidental subject but as a core subject in Western universities. We related that upon moving to the Lehigh Valley in Pennsylvania, with its six colleges and a medium-sized Jewish community, we found that the educational institutions were wary of Jewish professors and had a quota, albeit unofficial, for Jewish students. This was slowly changing, but Judaism and the study of Jewish civilization were still considered to be alien to the local world of higher education.

Shortly after our affiliation with the International Center for University Teaching of Jewish Civilization, we received an unexpected phone call from the president of Lafayette College, David Ellis, inviting us to meet with him and Peter Likins, the president of Lehigh University. At that meeting, they informed us that they were interested in establishing a joint appointment in Jewish studies. The plan was to appoint a professor who would teach on both campuses. We both felt a strange set of emotions during the meeting, and our response was, "Yes, we will do whatever is necessary to accomplish this goal. However, we want to think about this being more than one professor and two schools."

Following that meeting, we consulted with a number of people, including Moshe Davis, whose recommendations formed an essential part of our eventual proposal to Lehigh. He emphasized that the position should be seen in terms of the teaching of Judaism as a full civilization, including literature, history, religion, culture, and society. His influence is clearly evident in the language of the original agreement we signed with Lehigh, establishing the Center for Jewish Studies.

We then consulted with members of the Lehigh Valley Jewish community, who urged us to establish a valleywide program to serve all institutions of higher learning. After several weeks of deliberation, we proposed the establishment of a Center for Jewish Studies at Lehigh that would provide Jewish studies courses and programming at each of the Lehigh Valley colleges. Of course, such a program required the coordinated efforts of all six institutions, and more than one professor. At the beginning, the collaboration was carried out within the framework of the consortium known as the Lehigh Valley Association of Independent Colleges.

Shortly after the appointment of a professor of Jewish Studies as the director of the Lehigh Valley Center for Jewish Studies, a public meeting was held where the concept of the Center was presented to the local academic and Jewish communities. The response was enthusiastic; the Jewish community was particularly thrilled at the prospect of courses in Jewish civilization being taught as a permanent part of the curriculum in the local colleges and university.

Within two years, a task force comprised of administrators and faculty proposed a comprehensive program requiring three additional faculty appointments and a regular visiting professor from Israel. Within the next few years, two new faculty members in Jewish studies were appointed, one at Lehigh and one at Lafayette, and eventually we endowed both positions. A visiting scholar from Israel has been in residence every year since 1987. In addition, Muhlenberg College, one of the consortium, has on its own established a permanent position in Jewish studies, which is occupied by a tenured faculty member. All four permanent faculty members received tenure in less than half the time it normally takes, because the institutions found them not only acceptable, but desirable. This is a clear indication of the quality of faculty the Jewish studies program has been successful in attracting.

Since 1989 the Center, now named the Philip and Muriel Berman Center for Jewish Studies, has sponsored three international academic conferences. It has also been publishing a book series, New Perspectives in Jewish Studies, in cooperation with New York University Press. The first three volumes, *New Perspectives on Israeli History: The Early Years of the State; Jewish Fundamentalism in Comparative Perspective: Religion, Ideology, and the Crisis of Modernity;* and *The Other in Jewish Thought and History: Rethinking Jewish Identity and Culture,* have already appeared. A fourth volume is in preparation.

In 1994 the Berman Center, in cooperation with the Philip and Muriel Berman Center for Biblical Archaeology at the Hebrew University, sponsored a two-part conference. The first part, "Archaeology and the Humanities," was held at Lehigh; the second part, "Biblical Archaeology," took place in Jerusalem.

As each year goes by, the Philip and Muriel Berman Center for Jewish Studies is becoming more significant in its own right in the academic world, the local academic community, and the local Jewish community. It has been a great and exhilarating experience in which to participate.

JAIME CONSTANTINER (MEXICO)

I came to an understanding of the central position of the university in Jewish education as the result of a prolonged and gradual process. After many years of devoting myself to Jewish education, I began to realize that our efforts had reached a point beyond which we could not attain many of the goals we were striving for, namely, to guarantee Jewish continuity among the youth, nourished by a renewed process of cultural creativity. My initial worry had been how to guarantee a preuniversity Jewish education that would serve as a foundation for further development. In the specific context of Jewish life in Mexico, the option of assimilation to Latin culture was colored by the special characteristics of the general society and culture that still showed a certain weakness in its capacity to absorb other cultural and ethnic groups. Nonetheless, the weakening of the Hebrew and European cultural and educational tradition among younger generations was extremely worrisome. It was this line of thought that led me to the idea of the university providing an important means for responding to the challenges facing Jewish education.

I recognized the concrete support that Israeli universities could offer to raise the level of Jewish education in Mexico. Because of the high respect and academic recognition that those universities enjoy in the scientific and intellectual environment of Mexico, their presence would redound positively on the value of contemporary Jewish studies, and would benefit the self-esteem of our community and its young people. Fortunately, the Jewish educational system was sufficiently developed in Hebrew to allow us to establish links of cooperation with universities in Israel and carry out experimental academic projects of both a theoretical and a practical scope. I then began to visualize the possibility of extending this fruitful collaboration to other spheres. The natural outcome was to view the university as the proper place to develop Judaic studies. It would permit the systematic academic formation of Jewish educators and, at the same time, allow young Jews to develop their academic vocation in the field.

Various factors contributed to move me from understanding to practice. My initial intention to encourage Jewish cultural life was reinforced when, in the 1970s, I attended a congress on the Holocaust that took place in New York, in which Jewish academics from Israel and the United States participated. I came to the realization that it was necessary to offer our youth the possibility of developing academically in the field of Jewish studies by giving them a free, objective, and ample education that would satisfy both Jewish and universal criteria. This would be possible only in a university framework and with the collaboration of Israeli universities which were so advanced in that field.

The presence of Moshe Davis in Mexico, and his conviction that the university was the proper framework in which to educate new Jewish generations, coincided with my concern. We began to explore what seemed to be utopian expectations and hopes. Everything was an unknown: the potential students, the possibility of carrying out an academic project together, and the existence of a suitable university framework. We began to investigate different academic institutions in which it might be practical to develop Jewish studies, and Iberoamericana University allowed us to promote our plan. This university is relatively small, but it enjoys academic prestige; and, although it is confessional, it had a qualitative academic leadership that was ready and interested in forging ties with universities in Israel.

Collaboration, first with the Institute of Contemporary Jewry of The Hebrew University of Jerusalem, and then with the International Center for University Teaching of Jewish Civilization, was instrumental in helping us to promote our project and guaranteed that we would have the specialized academic personnel to carry out our proposal. We took our first steps by offering some extension courses. The academic seriousness and excellence with which we undertook our work, as well as the favorable reaction on the part of the students, led to the support of Iberoamericana University in the development of a more comprehensive study program.

Seen retrospectively, after more than a decade of close association, I believe that our project has served as a springboard in the development of the cultural and academic life of the community in Mexico.

ISRAEL FINESTEIN, Q.C. (GREAT BRITAIN)

Those of us who see the ethos of Jewish civilization in the traditions of Judaism attach special importance to the ideals and teachings of our inherited faith as well as to the distinctive qualities of Jewishness by which mankind has benefited and through which the universalism of our hopes remains to be fulfilled. Thus, the teaching of Jewish civilization studies at universities is a vital requirement for our times.

I recall the address that Moshe Davis gave at the President's Study Circle on World Jewry, held in Jerusalem, in which he proposed the creation of the International Center, having toured the world and prepared a massive report on the state of Jewish studies in the universities. That address moved everyone deeply, and it was extremely difficult to remain uninvolved in such an exciting venture that had been so well prepared, and for which the argument was immensely strong. This was my first reason for becoming involved.

The case that Moshe Davis presented revealed two aspects of a single phenomenon: the potential for Jewish civilization studies in universities throughout the world, and the paucity of the planning thereof. It seemed extraordinary that so much importance should be attached to Jewish students, the future intellectual leadership of their communities, and that so little was being done. An opportunity was being presented to the Jewish world that could well be missed. Thus, my second reason for becoming involved in the International Center was the sense that an important task waited to be done, that the time for attempting it was ripe, and that the opportunity could well disappear by default unless the need was recognized.

The third reason is the most important, and is interrelated with the first two. Something happened in Jewish life several hundred years ago, when the Jew in the West was becoming Europeanized and the hold of religion was beginning to slacken. The "scientific" explanation of all things seemed to be the new Holy Grail. The walls confining the Jews were ceasing to exist. New chances for public service and advancement, new avenues of intellectual satisfaction, new definitions of the Jews— or, to use the expression of the late Nathan Rotenstreich, a "new version" of the Jew—began to appear. Rotenstreich used that expression to describe both the Jew in the Enlightenment period, and the Jew who ultimately succeeded him and who sought to find his Jewishness in forms of Zionism. The earlier "new" version tended to be a hyphenated Jew posing many risks for the preservation of his or her identity; the danger existed that the noun "Jew" would, in due course, be reduced to nothing other than a generic term bereft of transmissibility.

We are still grappling with the consequences of the events of the last two centuries and with their political, social, economic, and intellectual developments. At the center of all these developments stand gifted men and women who might be able to throw light on the paths to be taken by younger generations. It seemed to me that the ideas enshrined in the International Center could well make a distinct contribution to those who were aware of these problems, who might be somewhat distant from an understanding of their heritage, and who might wish to give an added cultural, and perhaps religious, character to their political Zionism. I felt that the International Center in Jerusalem could well be one of the most significant contributions of Israel in helping to resolve these predicaments, by attaching Jewish students to their heritage so that Jewishness was more than a generic response to anti-Jewish prejudice, more than a matter of politics. These may be high ideals, but so be it.

I might add that it is also important to ensure that those involved in tertiary education throughout the world, as teachers or students, Jewish or otherwise, should have adequate opportunities to understand the Jewish heritage in all its diversity. That, too, carries considerable advantages to the world. The importance of the University Teaching Center increases with time. One notices the significance of it in Europe, including the changing scene in Eastern Europe with the opportunities that are arising there. These are certainly the factors that weigh with me.

RALPH I. GOLDMAN (UNITED STATES)

In my life's span there have been many moments that underscore my belief that to assure group continuity in an open society, Jews must find a variety of frameworks to transmit Jewish learning. The university can serve as one such major arena.

I have long been conscious of the importance of teaching Jewish civilization on a university level. During my youth I attended the Boston Hebrew College, a supplementary educational framework that functioned after general school hours. The founder and dean of the college, Louis Hurwich, sought and obtained accreditation for the college as an academic institution. This was at a time when in Boston, a center for many distinguished universities, there was only one professor, Harry A. Wolfson at Harvard, who taught Jewish history and thought on an academic level. There were, of course, Semitic departments in divinity schools, and Near Eastern civilization departments which offered biblical and Hebrew courses. In the early 1940s, Boston University appointed, on a part-time basis, Dr. Samuel Kurland to teach Jewish history and Hebrew literature. A further development of the field occurred when Brandeis University, established in 1948, offered a program of Jewish studies.

Yet there was a single moment that made me most conscious of the significance of teaching Jewish civilization on the university level. On January 17, 1988, after long negotiations and a fifty-year absence from the Soviet Union, the American Jewish Joint Distribution Committee (JDC, or the "JOINT") was officially received in Moscow by USSR government authorities. They requested that the JDC assume an economic role, as it had in the 1920s when Agrojoint was established to "proletarize" the Jews who were small merchants and not of the "working class." Our response was that this time we would return to the Soviet Union to help restore to the Jews the knowledge of their own civilization, of which they had been deprived for seventy years. I felt then that any vehicle that would make it possible for us to bring Jewish learning to Jews would be welcome, especially on an adult level; at that time—the Gorbachev period when the Communist system still prevailed—teaching Judaism to children was still prohibited.

An opportunity arose when Nehemia Levtzion, then president of The Open University of Israel, was asked by Boris Bim Bad of the newly established Open University of Russia, to develop a joint program of courses, such as management. The JDC then offered to support courses in Judaica, if this would be acceptable to the Open University of Russia. That was the first outreach to the teaching of Jewish civilization on a university level in the USSR.

In 1989, as I was beginning to develop a JDC presence in the Soviet Union, Moshe Davis told me about the workshops that the International Center was conducting each summer for teachers of Jewish civilization in institutions of higher learning, and asked whether I could arrange for some Soviet scholars and researchers to attend them. There were still no formal relations between Israel and the Soviet Union, but I told him that I would look into this matter.

In the course of my visits to the USSR, I had met Evgeny Velikhov, vice-chairman of the Soviet Academy of Science, a distinguished scientist and an important personality in the Gorbachev entourage. I raised the question with Velikhov, who liked the idea, and asked one of his associates, Boris Gontarev, to help me. The rest of the story is now history. In 1989, nineteen participants came from the Soviet Union, and by 1993, forty-nine individuals from thirty-three academic frameworks had attended the workshops of the International Center.

We must now seek many additional academic vehicles to reach the Jewish population in the various republics of the former Soviet Union. Teaching Jewish civilization on a university level is not only important, per se, for the knowledge it conveys, but also for the pride of identity it provides to a population that has long been depressed and declassed because it is Jewish.

NICOLE GOLDMANN (FRANCE)

I first became acquainted with academic Jewish studies during my second year at university in Paris. I come from a traditional Jewish family with a strong Zionist orientation, and as a child I received a basic Jewish education in a French provincial Talmud Torah. That education was in no way able to compete with the deep interest I developed during my secondary-school years in learning Latin, Greek, French literature, and philosophy. Nonetheless, I felt intuitively that there was more to Jewish studies than what I had been exposed to.

When I moved to Paris to study political science, I sought access to Jewish studies at a level of excellence, and discovered a weekly course providing an introduction to Jewish thought. It was taught by Leon Ashkenazi, who was religiously observant and had a master's degree. I remember the conclusion of his first lecture: "The Torah must speak the language of its time. As students in an open world, you should not be orphans of your own Jewish culture. On the contrary, life in the Diaspora means participation in both cultures, the Jewish and the general, on equal terms." The small group of students in this course later served as the core for the creation, upon Rabbi Ashkenazi's initiative, of the Centre universitaire des études juives, which has been instrumental in the development of Jewish studies in French universities and within the Jewish community.

Inspired by my own experience, as a community leader I have always assigned top priority to qualitative Jewish university education, believing that this leads to the permanent involvement of the younger generation of Jews. That is why, since my first meeting with Moshe Davis, I have viewed the International Center as an important means to achieve that goal, serving as a unique bridge and meeting point for those who teach Jewish civilization all over the world.

Regarding the French scene in particular, I believe that the Centre is an important channel for bringing to the attention of the academic community the extraordinary development of the French school of Jewish philosophers and thinkers, such as Emmanuel Levinas, André Neher, and others, as well as the contribution of French academics in such newly developing areas of studies as the Jews of North Africa, and the Holy Land in the mind of the Western world.

As a result of my involvement, and mainly of the splendid achievements of the Centre, France is now firmly "on the map" of Jewish studies. With the permanent support of the Fonds social juif unifié, and the contribution of the Fondation du judaisme français, a large number of young French scholars have received grants to attend annual International Center workshops, where they have the opportunity to meet with their peers from Israel and other countries, and to further their research in Jewish studies. The publication of their work is reinforcing ties between universities in Israel and in France.

MENDEL KAPLAN (SOUTH AFRICA)

In 1979 my family business celebrated its fiftieth anniversary, and the founders of the company and their descendants decided to mark the event by supporting three educational endeavors:

1. A bursary scheme to allow the children of our employees to matriculate and subsequently pursue tertiary studies in an area of their choice. Hundreds of the children of our employees have graduated through this program.
2. A chair for the study of Israel/Egyptian relations at Tel Aviv University, as this was the beginning of the implementation of the Camp David accords. Subsequently, the incumbent of the chair, Shimon Shamir, was appointed Israeli ambassador to Egypt.
3. Establishment of a Centre of Jewish Studies and Research at the University of Cape Town, affiliated informally to Tel Aviv University. The concept, which was developed by Moshe Davis, was to make the study of Jewish civilization accessible to the whole university.

We did not establish a chair with a single incumbent, or become part of the Department of Hebrew which already existed at the University of Cape Town, but developed a threefold objective. (1) We brought visiting lecturers, especially from Israel, to lecture over short periods of time in a variety of fields allied to Jewish civilization, in different university departments such as sociology, comparative literature, and modern history. (2) We wanted to broaden the universe of students who could participate in Jewish studies through enrollment in accredited courses in as many departments as possible. (3) We established an archives and a library that would become the depository of Jewish community records, and a research center for those interested in aspects of the South African Jewish community.

Over the last fourteen years the university has been host to a large number of well-known Jewish academics in a great variety of fields. The research program dealing with the oral history of our community and the systematic collection of its records have proceeded at a steady pace. However, our participation in the university's teaching program has not been as successful as we envisaged at the outset. Accordingly, several years ago the Centre was integrated into a comprehensive Department of Hebrew and Jewish Studies, and its responsibilities were extended to include all the activities of the enlarged department. With this went a decision to establish an additional chair of Jewish Civilization, and appoint a permanent senior lecturer in Judaism. These appointments, together with the existing chair in Hebrew, the ongoing research activities of the Centre, and the provision of visiting lecturers, have created wide choices for the students.

The new structure was developed at a time that other South African universities were closing their Hebrew departments, thus increasing the challenge to provide a comprehensive range of academic offerings in Hebrew, Jewish civilization, and research. A South African graduate of the Centre's Fellowship and Bursary Program, Milton Shain, was recently appointed director of the Centre; and with Ali Dubb as incumbent of the chair of Jewish Civilization and Yehoshua Gitay incumbent of the chair of Hebrew, we have a full staff.

The development of the Kaplan Centre of Jewish Studies and Research has been an interesting and sometimes exhilarating experience, during which time the founding coordinator, Sally Frankental, was responsible for successfully overcoming the growing pains of a very important addition to university campus life. Our current challenge is to widen the range of students who register so that the newly structured Centre can play an active role in the teaching life of the university.

JEROME S. KATZIN (UNITED STATES)

The rapid disappearance of most restrictions against Jews in American society following World War II brought open admission to the universities and the professions as well as frequent successes in finance and business. With this acceptance and participation in the larger society came a greater focus on Jewish philanthropy. The earlier immigrant generations had largely devoted their charitable giving to Jewish causes and institutions; contemporary Jews are, in addition, generous supporters of the arts, medical and social causes, and secular higher education.

Most Jewish students come to a university with a dismaying lack of information and knowledge about Jewish history and writings. There is wide recognition in the Jewish community of the need to provide an adequate university curriculum in Jewish civilization commensurate with the intellectual level of the students' general studies, at a time when their interest in learning is at its height and their future lives and interests are being formed.

The introduction of Jewish studies courses has not emerged from confrontational tactics but is probably attributable to the diminution of faculty anti-Semitism and to their recognition of Jewish civilization as a mature academic field of study in the Western tradition. There is also general agreement that such studies should not be among the growing list of isolated multicultural ethnic fields vying for student attention, but should be viewed in the setting of Western civilization and culture, reflecting Jewish participation in all areas of human learning and conduct. A particular effort is made to enroll both Jewish and non-Jewish students.

Courses in Jewish civilization studies are now given at each of the eight campuses in the University of California system. At the San Diego campus, which was founded a quarter-century ago, courses were first offered in Hebrew language in response to student requests. Subsequently, the literature department began to offer courses in the Hebrew Bible, and, in time, qualified faculty from other disciplines initiated occasional courses. Visiting lecturers and faculty followed. About a dozen years ago the chancellor of the university, meeting with Jewish community leaders, invited the funding of a chair in Jewish studies. The public effort was successful and the UCSD Judaic Studies endowment was established. I was a founder of the endowment and have served as chairman of its Board of Visitors since its inception.

Since its founding, the UCSD Judaic Studies Endowment has grown to more than twice its initial funding. The program now has three named chairs: in Hebrew Bible, Judaic studies, and Jewish civilization. At the time of this writing there are five full-time faculty in Jewish studies and appointments in the departments of literature, history, and anthropology. Other faculty are called on to give related courses and lectures. Visiting-faculty appointments are common for all or part of each year.

A Board of Visitors, appointed by the chancellor from among contributors to the program, meets quarterly to review the program and to assure that the intent of the original founders to establish and maintain a strong curriculum in Jewish civilization studies is being pursued. Further, a broader community support program known as "Friends of the Judaic Studies Program at UCSD" has been organized. It provides lectures and other programs for its members and on occasion for the community at large.

My experience has been a striking example of how Jewish communal efforts can benefit the broad university world.

HERBERT NEUMAN (UNITED STATES)

As I reflect on what motivated me to become active in the International Center for University Teaching of Jewish Civilization, three events come to mind. It is interesting to note that they took place at three different university campuses.

The first incident occurred in the 1980s at Pennsylvania State University, where my wife, Stephanie, had been invited to deliver a paper. I accompanied her on this trip as a traveling companion, but chose to seek out and attend a Hebrew language class that was then being taught by Emanuel Rabinovitch, an Israeli who had developed his own style and system of teaching Hebrew. The enthusiasm in the classroom was infectious; the students, both Jewish and gentile, were not only learning the language but were indeed having a great deal of fun in the process. After class, I met with Rabinovitch and reviewed with him the Jewish studies program at Penn State. I was amazed to learn that *he was* the Jewish studies program. That a large university with a Jewish population of significant number was providing almost nothing in Jewish studies was revealing. Not only was the "program" underfinanced, but Rabinovitch voiced his frustration at not being able to satisfy the demands of his students, who wanted courses in Jewish history, Bible studies, and contemporary Middle East/Israel affairs. The problem was that there was no one to teach these courses, and little money that could be made available to support teaching an additional course.

The second occurrence was more personal in nature. My daughter was enrolled at Cornell University and had come under the tutelage of Stephen Katz, the newly arrived head of Jewish studies. She soon became visibly attracted to the world of Jewish civilization. True, she had been reared in a Jewish home and had attended a supplementary Hebrew high school a number of afternoons per week. But her quest for knowledge was being formed at the university, and her desire to learn about her heritage in an academic sense was being fostered by a well-financed and solid faculty. The result of her "minor" course of studies in Jewish subjects, which included medieval Jewish history, a study of anti-Semitism, researching and writing major papers concerning the Kishinev pogrom, and a study of black-Jewish relations in the late nineteenth century, established a deeper understanding of her roots and tradition.

The contrast between these two experiences is evident—one university providing a strong program in Jewish civilization and thus prompting Jewish identity, and another offering a mere modicum of courses of Jewish content and thus "starving" an interested Jewish population in its quest for learning. The question then arose as to what should be done to strengthen institutions where the demand for courses in Jewish subjects was present but where the program barely existed—if at all.

When I became aware of the International Center for University Teaching of Jewish Civilization, I was immediately struck by the existence of a potential solution to the above dilemma. If a method could be found to provide syllabi and curricula to university teachers who were laboring with the frustration of undercapitalized departments, they might be able to offer a variety of courses without having to spend years in developing them. Obviously, the students would benefit, and programs in Jewish civilization studies would grow by virtue of student demands. Eventually, the university would be stimulated to expand these programs to full departments or subdepartments within larger frameworks. The University Teaching Center could act as a catalyst in initiating this process, and in doing so would not only provide the materials that were so vitally needed, but would also establish a worldwide fellowship of teachers that would enhance the profession.

The third experience dealt with my recent and continuing studies in philosophy at Columbia University. By this time I had already become active in the lay leadership of the International Center—attending meetings both in the United States and Israel. I was presented by Moshe Davis with the notion of helping to establish a workshop that would focus on introducing Jewish philosophy into general programs of philosophy on the university level. This sounded intriguing to me and captured my imagination. The result: the Jewish philosophy workshop has been in operation for the past six years.

RICHARD J. SCHEUER (UNITED STATES)

In 1961, Rabbi Nelson Glueck, president of the Hebrew Union College, asked me to help him with the finishing stages of the building designed by Heinz Rau for the Hebrew Union College campus in Jerusalem. On our frequent trips to Israel, Glueck, a noted archeologist, enjoyed visiting the digs in process. I soon got to know many of the archeologists and became fascinated with the field and with the history of the Land of Israel.

Several years later, I enrolled in New York University's School of Education where Moshe Goshen-Gotstein was offering a course on the Dead Sea Scrolls and one on the Apocrypha. I took both courses and others offered by Cyrus Gordon from Brandeis and by Hayim Tadmor from the Hebrew University in Jerusalem. Trude Weiss-Rosmarin gave a course in modern Jewish philosophy, and Nathan Winter taught four semester-courses in Jewish history. Most of these courses were held in the evening. Some four years later, I found I had earned an M.A. degree—in an adult education framework.

In 1971, Gershon Cohen, the chancellor of the Jewish Theological Seminary, asked Joy Ungerleider to become director of the Jewish Museum. She had brought Yigal Yadin's exhibit on Masada to the museum and hoped to reshape it into a Jewish educational institution. She asked me to join her in this mission and to serve as Board chairman. Buoyed by the academic work at NYU as well as a course in museology taught at the NYU Fine Arts Institute, I accepted and served for seven years

These experiences convinced me of the value, for the nonspecialist, of university-level instruction in Jewish studies, and I was glad to accept, at the suggestion of President Alfred Gottschalk of the Hebrew Union College, an invitation to serve on the Board of Regents of the Interna-

tional Center for University Teaching of Jewish Civilization. The assign-
ment was facilitated by the fact that I had been chairman of the Jerusalem School Committee of the Hebrew Union College Board for many
years, and visited Jerusalem frequently to supervise the creation of four
new Moshe Safdie-designed HUC buildings between 1985 and 1987. It
was not hard to keep in touch with the International Center.

I found Moshe Davis and the colleagues he had assembled a stimulating and impressive group. The program of collecting and distributing
syllabi and bibliographies from leading scholars in each area of Jewish
studies so that teachers in smaller institutions could develop courses
other than those in their primary academic specialties, seemed a very
valuable way of responding to the increasing demand for such teaching
in a variety of disciplines.

It was especially encouraging to see the participation of academics
from the former Soviet Union and Eastern Europe. Putting them in touch
with faculty in Israel and introducing them to the worldwide network of
Jewish scholarship has clearly been most stimulating to these visitors,
whatever their own academic specialties. Their visits give us an extraordinary opportunity to develop an indigenous Jewish leadership in the
many newly independent republics in Eastern Europe and in Asia. The
University Teaching Center is creating communal leaders as well as
teachers of Jewish civilization studies.

VII
THE FUTURE

32. FACING THE FUTURE

Nehemia Levtzion

The initial goal of the International Center for University Teaching of Jewish Civilization was twofold: to help legitimize Jewish studies in the university, and to enhance the quality of such interdisciplinary teaching in a global framework. Now, in the second decade of its existence, ICUTJC turns its attention to the integration of elements of Jewish studies into general disciplines, and the development of regional approaches to the teaching of Jewish civilization.

DEVELOPING MODULES OF JEWISH STUDIES

Many universities do not offer programs in Jewish studies because they lack faculty who have had scholarly training in the field, or because there is an insufficient number of students who would enroll in such a program. However, one may generate interest among teachers in a variety of departments to develop a course, or introduce a single module that touches upon a theme that they are teaching. Such academic exposure frequently awakens the interest of additional students to further explore the field. In an attempt to develop this approach, ICUTJC contemplates convening workshops where specialists in subfields of Jewish studies will work together with teachers in various academic disciplines, to design discrete units that can be introduced into several curricular areas and be adaptable for different linguistic/cultural needs.

Some guidelines toward this end have been provided in a recent book, *The Modern Jewish Experience,* edited by Jack Wertheimer (NYU Press,

1993), which was cosponsored by the International Center for University Teaching of Jewish Civilization and The Jewish Theological Seminary of America. Its aim is "to provide guidance on a range of issues and research pertaining to modern Jewish history, culture, religion, and society."

Examples of themes in the history of the Jews that may be integrated into general courses of European history include, inter alia, the following: the creativity of Jewish civilization and intellectual trends in Europe; the Marranos and other religious minorities (such as the Huguenots); assimilation and self-identity of the Jews and of other ethnic, national, and religious minorities in Europe; the renewal of Jewish life within the context of the reconstruction of European civilization; changes in Jewish and general European leadership; Jewish population movements and demographic trends in Europe; Jewish economic entrepreneurs in an emerging capitalist economy.

EXPANDING GEOGRAPHIC PARAMETERS OF UNIVERSITY TEACHING OF JEWISH STUDIES

The growth of Jewish studies has been most apparent in the United States and, initially, the activities of the International Center reflected this reality through the interchange of Israeli and American scholars, researchers, and teaching approaches. However, new academic programs have been developing in France, England, Germany, and, most recently, in Eastern Europe. ICUTJC is expanding its activities accordingly.

On October 5, 1987, the Parliamentary Assembly of the Council of Europe adopted a resolution, "Recognizing the very considerable and distinctive contribution that Jews and the tradition of Judaism have made to the historical development of Europe in the cultural as well as in other fields . . . Judaism should be—by right—a fundamental element in the construction of Europe." Responding to the move toward the unification of Europe and the growing interest in achieving greater understanding of the Jewish civilization, the International Center conducted a European Regional Development Conference for Jewish Studies in Jerusalem in 1991. At that conference, Peter Schäfer of the Institut für Judaistik, Freie Universität, Berlin, urged the establishment of an exchange program in which colleagues teaching Jewish studies in Israel or America would teach abroad. He added that both faculty and students need frequent personal contact with their peers in Israel and America.

In order to facilitate the development of such exchange programs, the International Center proposes the creation of an affiliated European Center for University Teaching of Jewish Civilization. The European Center would cooperate with the European Association of Jewish Studies and with national associations that emphasize scholarly and research activities.

EASTERN EUROPE

Eastern Europe and the countries of the former Soviet Union (FSU) constitute a geographical area of special concern to the International Center. About one thousand years of Jewish history in Central and Eastern Europe came to an end in the flames of the Holocaust, and in the repression of the Soviet Union. Since the collapse of the communist regimes, however, there has been evidence of growing interest in the teaching of Jewish civilization in universities throughout the FSU and the Baltic states. According to Lajos Vekas, rector of Eötvos University in Budapest, in a talk given at the European Regional Development Conference, the renewal of Jewish studies is viewed by academics there as the "way to preserve ethical integrity and higher universal values among all the cruelty and suffering in the world."

The teaching of Jewish civilization in Eastern Europe is developing within two frameworks: in new institutions like the Jewish universities in Moscow, St. Petersburg, and Kiev, and in projects sponsored by American institutions such as The Jewish Theological Seminary and Touro College; and in the old established state universities. The burgeoning quest for knowledge about things Jewish, after seventy dark years, has created a situation in which scholars in various disciplines have undertaken the teaching of Jewish subject matter, either as a separate course or as part of a more general curriculum. However, these teachers often lack the requisite broad background in Jewish studies.

The International Center seeks to address both teachers and students through an annual workshop in Jerusalem. The process of developing a cadre of instructors in Jewish studies will be accelerated by encouraging individuals who are already showing promise of scholarly ability and interest in the field. Once these individuals are identified, they will be invited to Israel for a period of one month, where they will be assigned Israeli scholars as study companions, introduced to library and archival resources, and learn subject matter and teaching methodology. An initial group has already visited Israel and, in addition to their own study sessions, the young scholars participated in the annual workshops of the International Center where they profited from an invaluable opportunity to meet colleagues, especially from Western countries where Jewish studies have developed significantly.

In view of the interest shown by a variety of Israeli institutions and frameworks in the development of academic Jewish studies in the FSU and the Baltic states, the International Center was asked to chair a forum created and financed by the Joint Distribution Committee (JDC) in Jerusalem, for the purpose of exchanging information, planning courses, preparing teaching materials, and coordinating activities. Among the first fruits of the forum was a seminar held outside Moscow in February 1994. With more than 110 university teachers attending, it was an impressive demonstration of the interest in Jewish studies from Siberia to the southern Ukraine. Representatives of twenty-eight institutions reported about the teaching of Jewish studies in their respective universities.

The academic chairman of the International Center, who presided at the seminar, interviewed university teachers and discussed issues with delegations from Rostov, Kiev, Donetsk, Tbilisi, and Moscow Jewish University. Several follow-up programs are being planned to help develop the new Jewish universities (in St. Petersburg, Moscow, and Kiev), and to promote new programs for Jewish studies in state universities:

1. A coordinating forum in Moscow will meet three times a year with representatives of the Jewish universities, of other Jewish institutions in Moscow (Touro College, JTS/YIVO), The Open University of Israel, Russia's Open University, and the state universities. It is important that delegates from institutions in remote provinces participate in the forum at least once a year.

2. The forum will plan a summer school offering survey courses in Jewish studies. State universities in which Jewish studies are being introduced tend to develop courses with an immediate regional and contemporary emphasis—based on material drawn from local ar-

chives—and students in such courses lack the wider perspective needed to integrate the material into an appropriate historical context. Because state universities, in most cases, do not have the necessary resources to teach general survey courses on Jewish history and culture, such courses will be offered in summer schools for students from different universities. Leading scholars from Israel and other centers of Jewish studies will lecture, and group tutorials will be led by Russian-speaking instructors who have attended ICUTJC annual workshops in Jerusalem.

3. One of the major problems reported by university teachers of Jewish studies in Eastern Europe is the shortage of textbooks and resource materials in Russian. The forum will seek to identify the lacunae and to encourage the frameworks involved in publication of Jewish educational materials to meet these needs. To make available in Russian books on Jewish studies, as well as some books in Hebrew and in English, a Central Academic Library of Jewish Studies in Moscow will be created. A circulation service will mail books upon request to teachers and students in universities throughout the FSU.

4. The integration of Jewish themes into general courses has proven to be the best way to introduce the teaching of Jewish civilization where a strong academic basis in the field is lacking. In Moscow Jewish University, for example, the best teachers apply their training in general disciplines to related Jewish topics. ICUTJC had suggested adoption of this strategy after the 1993 workshop in Jerusalem. Following the visit to Moscow and discussions with the seminar participants, we are convinced that we should aim at a more comprehensive program to encourage the integration of Jewish themes into general courses.

This approach was followed in the 1994 workshop in Jerusalem. The invitees were asked to prepare papers on integrating topics of their choice into courses already taught in Russian universities. The majority of the participants in the Jerusalem workshop came from Moscow. A continuation of this workshop will be held in Moscow, where detailed modules, including syllabi and teaching materials, will be prepared to help integrate Jewish topics into general courses. The workshop in Moscow will be a joint venture of the International Center, the JDC, and several foundations, as well as Moscow Jewish University and Moscow State University. A series of seminars for university teachers from all over the FSU will be organized where members of the continuing workshop will demonstrate how to use the modules they have prepared.

THE ASIA-PACIFIC RIM

Recognizing the "global village" in which we live at the close of the twentieth century, the International Center has turned its attention to the Asia-Pacific Rim, which has been described as a "sleeping giant." Unlike the Judeo-Christian West, or even the Islamic world, in most Asian countries Jews have no historic presence and no cultural resonance. There has been nothing in the local cultures or, by extension, in the local idiom, that has enabled people or governments in these countries to challenge widely held vicious stereotypes about Jews and the Jewish state. The void in the cultural consciousness of this extremely important part of the world is deeply disturbing, and the International Center seeks to fill this vacuum.

Japan

In consultations with ICUTJC about teaching Jewish civilization in Japan, Hiroshi Ichikawa of the Faculty of Letters at the University of Tokyo (who has studied in Israel and speaks fluent Hebrew) explains that Jewish studies are regarded as a subfield within history or philosophy. However, with the development of a trend toward interdisciplinary studies, such as comparative cultures, international relations, and area studies, there are growing possibilities for the development of Jewish civilization studies in Japan, although to date there is no such department or faculty at any university. According to a preliminary survey, courses in Jewish studies are taught in twenty-nine universities and colleges and in two theological seminaries. The Japan Association of Jewish Studies, established in 1960, now has sixty-five members.

South Korea

South Korea, with its increasing interest in Christianity in general and Protestantism in particular, also displays a growing search for knowledge about Judaism, Israel, and Bible studies. The Koreans identify with the State of Israel, seeing it as a role model: a small democratic country surrounded by hostile neighbors, standing steadfast against them.

Hebrew and Jewish studies are taught in Kon-Kuk University. Five theological universities teach biblical Hebrew, and several universities have expressed interest in establishing Jewish studies departments. The chairman of Kon-Kuk University at Seoul, Seung Yune Yoo (who also studied in Israel and speaks Hebrew), has led two delegations from his university to Jerusalem, and junior faculty members from this university attend Center workshops.

China

China and Israel are two of the most ancient nations, their civilizations going back over four thousand years; they developed along parallel lines without any direct communication. The Jewish experience in China has had two dimensions: the old communities centered on Kaifeng, which became assimilated into Chinese Han or Muslim societies; and the modern Jewish communities of Shanghai. The Chinese served as hosts to these Jewish communities, and the latter made their own modest contribution to the rich Chinese civilization.

Study of these Jewish communities should be undertaken within the wider Jewish cultural and historical context, and an understanding of contemporary Jewish culture would be an organic extension of such an undertaking. Mutual interest in the history, culture, and society of China and Israel will help develop friendship and understanding based on the integrity of authentic knowledge. At present, hundreds of students study Chinese language, history, culture, and society at the Hebrew University of Jerusalem, and at the same time, teaching and research of Jewish subjects in Chinese universities is expanding.

The Center for Jewish Cultural Studies, established in 1991 in the School of Foreign Studies at Nanjing University, has developed a unique program of teaching, research, and publications on Jewish literature and culture. The commitment of its director, Xu Xin, and the support of the university authorities are assets that may serve as the foundation for a comprehensive project of university teaching of Jewish culture and literature. The Jewish Studies Center at the Shanghai Academy of Social Sciences, directed by Pan Guang, has shown interest in Jewish history in general, and in the history of the Jewish communities of Shanghai in particular. Similar interest has recently been manifest at Fudan University and at the East China Normal University. Cooperation among these three institutions is bearing fruit and ought to be encouraged by inaugurating a comprehensive project for university teaching of Jewish studies that would aim to (1) develop curricula and syllabi for courses at the undergraduate and graduate levels; (2) create modules for the integration of Jewish themes into general courses; (3) prepare textbooks and readers that would serve the courses and modules; (4) train future scholars and teachers who would be able to teach these courses at the university level; and (5) provide enrichment to those who teach general courses about Jewish themes and topics.

These aims can be achieved through the following means:

1. Workshops for Chinese scholars who are teaching Jewish literature and culture and for university teachers of relevant general courses, who will be joined by scholars from Israel and other parts of the world. The workshops will discuss subject matter and methodological problems related to the teaching of Jewish literature and culture in Chinese universities.
2. Teams of Chinese scholars, with advisors from other countries, to develop teaching materials dealing with Jewish literature and culture. The texts will include translated sources and analytical essays.
3. Modules for the integration of Jewish themes into general courses at universities in the different provinces, in order to introduce more Chinese students to Jewish literature and culture.
4. The opportunity for Chinese scholars who teach courses on Jewish culture and literature to visit Israel. Participation in the annual workshops of the International Center will enable them to become acquainted with colleagues who teach in different cultural contexts. They will also have the opportunity to meet Israeli scholars in their field and to use the libraries and archives. A special program can be developed for graduate students in Chinese universities who concentrate on the study of Jewish literature and culture.

OTHER REGIONS

In addition to the regional development programs which are already in different stages of planning and implementation, the following regions should also be considered for future development: Latin America, with its several large Jewish communities; Africa, where Christians feel at home with the tribal and patriarchal society of the Old Testament; and, with eyes to the future, Muslim countries (like Egypt, Morocco, Turkey, and the Muslim republics of the former Soviet Union) that are genuinely concerned with the contribution of Jews to their cultural heritage.

THE UNIVERSAL THRUST OF JEWISH CIVILIZATION STUDIES AND ISRAEL'S CENTRALITY THEREIN

The field of Jewish studies has its roots in the living, developing culture of the Jews. However, it has increasingly moved from a self-centered posture to an outer-oriented approach, as the Western world has openly acknowledged the long contribution of Jewish thought to Western civilization and to the history of ideas. At the same time, the continuing expansion of Jewish studies in parts of the world that lack a historical Jewish presence brings to the field teachers and students of many faiths and disciplines. Their new perspectives contribute to an understanding of the universal aspects of Jewish civilization.

The International Center's workshops have attracted scholars from six continents. Through the process of mutual academic enrichment we have come to appreciate the great strides made in this interdisciplinary field of study, even as we have become aware of the unmet needs of such a global expansion. Rather than having each university seek to meet these needs independently, it is clear that a regional framework of institutions sharing a common cultural background can provide systematic academic support in the form of exchanges of visiting faculty, teaching materials, and even students. ICUTJC seeks to initiate projects that will coordinate the resources and experience of such frameworks.

There are several centers of Jewish studies in different parts of the world—foremost among them in the United States—each with its own unique contribution to teaching and research. However, when we evaluate what is happening on a global scale, we realize that Israel occupies the central place in these developments. In Jerusalem alone, over three hundred courses in Jewish studies are taught at the Hebrew University; these are augmented by courses given in four additional universities. The wealth of specialized research and teaching and the extensive libraries and archives in Israel are unmatched in any single geographical area.

As Jewish studies continue to expand in countries around the world, professors, researchers, and students come to Israel in increasing numbers to make use of the available human and documentary resources, making it the hub of an international academic network—and providing a sterling paradigm of a global approach to higher education.

VIII

WORLD REGISTER OF UNIVERSITY STUDIES IN JEWISH CIVILIZATION

33. WORLD REGISTER

The following list includes institutions of higher learning in which Jewish civilization is taught or researched, ranging from full departments and programs to single courses totally or partially devoted to Jewish subjects. A list of sources for the information is provided.

Institutions are listed according to continents and in alphabetical order within each continent, country, or state. The entry includes: (1) name of institution; (2) faculties, colleges, departments, programs, centers, and fields in which Jewish civilization courses take place; indentations indicate subordinations of the different entries; interdisciplinary programs are followed by a list of the participating departments; (3) address of the main institution or the relevant department. The notation "research only" ("Thèses de doctorat" in France) means that no formal teaching is offered.

A significant percentage of the institutions listed have confirmed or corrected our original information (covering 1986–1993). We are grateful for their interest and cooperation. We shall be pleased to receive further corrections and additions.

Every effort has been made to identify all institutions of higher learning that offer courses in Jewish civilization studies. If such an institution does not appear on this list, we would appreciate receiving the pertinent information and will include it in the global data base that we are constantly updating.

Prepared by Florinda Goldberg

SOURCES OF INFORMATION

Holdings of the International Center for University Teaching of Jewish Civilization, Jerusalem (Catalogs, correspondence with individuals and institutions, etc.)

Avni, Haim (ed.). *Estudios Judaicos en Universidades Latinoamericanas.* Jerusalem: Centro de Estudios Universitarios de Cultura Judía, 1985.

Avni, Haim, with Florinda Goldberg. *Jewish Civilization Studies in Latin American Universities.* Jerusalem: International Center for University Teaching of Jewish Civilization, 1989 [also in Spanish.]

Bar-Asher, Moshe (ed.). *European Regional Development Conference for Jewish Civilization Studies.* Jerusalem: International Center for University Teaching of Jewish Civilization, 1992.

Bensimon, Doris. *L'enseignement des disciplines juives dans les universités européennes.* Jerusalem: Centre international d'étude de la civilisation juive dans les universités, and comité français pour l'enseignement universitaire de civilisation juive, 1988 [also in English.]

Berlin, Charles (ed.) *Jewish Studies Courses at American and Canadian Universities—A Catalog.* Cambridge, Mass.: Association of Jewish Studies, 1992.

Catalogue des Doctorats Hebraica-Judaica. Paris: Centre de documentation et de recherche, etudes hébraïques et juives, modernes et contemporaines, and Fichier central des thèses, Université de Paris X-Nanterre, 1993.

Cohen, Erik H., and Laurence Sigal (eds.). *Etudes juives et hébraïques dans l'enseignement supérieur et dans la recherche.* Paris: Comité de coordination pour l'education Juive, 1988.

Cohen, Michael (ed.). *Studies in Jewish Civilization at Tertiary Level in the Asia-Pacific Region—A Pilot Survey.* Asia Pacific Jewish Associaton and International Center for University Teaching of Jewish Civilization, 1989. [Internal circulation only.]

Halpern-Amaru, Betsy. *Teaching Jewish Civilization in Christian Seminaries and Theological Faculties of American Universities—Preliminary Exploration.* Jerusalem: International Center for University Teaching of Jewish Civilization, 1991.

Kadish, Sharman. *The Teaching of Jewish Civilization in British and Irish Universities and Other Institutions of Higher Learning.* Jerusalem: International Center for University Teaching of Jewish Civilization, 1990.

Lenowitz, Harris. "Hebrew Study Programs at U.S. Institutions of Higher Education: Materials Towards an Assessment." *Shofar,* vol. 9, no. 3, Spring 1991, pp. 21–49.

Lenowitz, Harris. Computerized Inventory of Hebrew Language Teaching in American Universitites. 1989. [Working copy.]

Nir, Raphael, with Abigail Neubach (eds.). *Teaching Hebrew Language and*

Literature at the Academic Level. Jerusalem: International Center for University Teaching of Jewish Civilization, 1992.

Robinson, Ira (ed.). *Survey of Courses in Jewish Civilization at Canadian Post-secondary Institutions.* International Center for University Teaching of Jewish Civilization, 1989. [Internal circulation only.]

Verbit, Mervin F. *World Register of University Studies of Jewish Civilization — Inventory of Holdings Number 1.* New York: Markus Wiener, 1985.

The World of Learning 1993. London: Europa Publications Limited, 1992.

NORTH AMERICA

Canada

Alberta

Athabasca University
Dept. of Humanities
Box 10000, Athabasca, T0G 2R0

Canadian Union College
Dept. of Religion
Box 430, College Heights

Edmonton Baptist Seminary
Dept. of Bible
Dept. of Old Testament
Dept. of New Testament
Dept. of Religion
11525 23rd Ave.,
Edmonton, T6J 4T3

North American Baptist College
(associated with the University of Alberta)
Dept. of Bible
Dept. of Old Testament
Dept. of English
Dept. of History
11525 23rd Ave.,
Edmonton, T6J 4T3

University of Alberta
Faculty of Arts
Dept. of Religious Studies
11045 Saskatchewan Dr.,
Edmonton, T6G 2E1

University of Calgary
Faculty of Humanities
Dept. of History
Dept. of Political Science
Dept. of Religious Studies
2500 University Drive NW,
Calgary, T2N 1N4

University of Lethbridge
Religious Studies Program
4401 University Dr.,
Lethbridge, T1K 3M4

British Columbia

Trinity Western University
Faculty of Arts & Religions
Dept. of Hebrew
Dept. of Religious Studies
7600 Glover Rd.,
Langley, V3A 6H4

University of British Columbia
Faculty of Arts
Dept. of Religious Studies
Vancouver, BC V6T 1Z1

Vancouver School of Theology
*(associated with the Univ. of
. British Columbia)*
Biblical Division
6000 Iona Dr.,
Vancouver, V6T 1L4

Manitoba

Brandon University
Dept. of Religion
Brandon, R7A 6A9

Providence College and Seminary
Dept. of Biblical Studies
Dept. of Theological Studies
Jewish-Christian Studies
Otterburne, R0A 1G0

University of Manitoba
Faculty of Arts
Dept. of Religion
Faculty of Graduate Studies
Dept. of Religion
Winnipeg, R3T 2N2

Winnipeg Bible College
Div. of Biblical & Theological
    Studies
Otterburne, R0A 1G0

New Brunswick

Atlantic Baptist College
Dept. of Hebrew
Box 1004, Moncton, E1C 8P4

Mount Allison University
Dept. of Religious Studies
Sackville, E0A 3C0

Université de Moncton
Dépt. de Sciences Religieuses
Moncton, E1A 3E9

University of New Brunswick
Dept. of History
Fredericton Campus, College Hill
POB 4400
New Brunswick E3B 5A3

Newfoundland

Memorial University of
    Newfoundland
Dept. of Religious Studies
St. John's, A1C 5S7

Nova Scotia

Acadia University
Dept. of Religious Studies
Wolfville, B0P 1X0

Atlantic School of Theology
Dept. of Old Testament
Halifax

Dalhousie University
Dept. of Comparative Religion
Halifax, B3H 3J5

Mount St. Vincent University
Dept. of Religious Studies
166 Bedford Highway,
Halifax, B3M 2J6

St. Francis Xavier University
Dept. of Theology
Antigonish, B2G 2W5

St. Mary's University
Religious Studies Dept.
Halifax, B3H 3C3

University of King's College
*(affiliated with Dalhousie
    University)*
Dept of Classics
Dept of Comparative Religion
Halifax, B3H 2A1

Ontario

Carleton University
Dept. of Religion
1125 Colonel By Drive,
Ottawa K1S 5B6

Collège Dominicain de
    Philosophie et de Théologie
Dépt. de Théologie
96 Empress Ave.,
Ottawa, K1R 7G3

Lakehead University
Faculty of Arts & Sciences
Interdisciplinary Program in
    Religious Studies
Thunder Bay, P7B 5E1

Laurentian University—Université
    Laurentienne
Faculty of Arts & Sciences
Joint Dept. of Religious Studies
Ramsey Lake Rd.,
Sudbury, P3E 2C6

McMaster University
Dept. of Religious Studies
McMaster Divinity College
Dept. of Old Testament
Dept. of New Testament
1280 Main St. W.,
Hamilton, L8S 4K1

Ontario Theological Seminary
Dept. of Old Testament
25 Ballyconnor Court,
Willowdale, M2M 4B3

Queen's University
Faculty of Arts
Dept. of Hebrew Language &
    Literature
Dept. of History
Dept. of Religion
Kingston, K7L 3N6

Toronto School of Theology
*(federation of 7 theological
    colleges)*
Dept. of Bible
Dept. of Theology
47 Queen's Park Cres. E.,
Toronto, M5S 2C3

Université St. Paul—St. Paul
    University
*(associated with the University of
    Ottawa)*
Faculty of Theology
223 Main St., Ottawa, K1S 1C4

University of Ottawa
School of Graduate Studies &
    Research
Dept. of Religious Sciences

Dept. of Modern Languages &
Literatures
550 Cumberland St.,
Ottawa, K1N 6N5

University of Toronto
Faculty of Arts & Sciences
Dept. of Classics
Dept. of French
Dept. of German
Dept. of History
Dept. of Liberal Studies
Dept. of Near Eastern Studies
Dept. of Philosophy
Dept. of Religious Studies
Dept. of Sociology
Toronto, M5S 1A1

University of Waterloo
Dept. of Religious Studies
Dept. of English
Waterloo, N2L 3G1

University of Western Ontario
Dept. of Hebrew
Dept. of History
Dept. of Religious Studies
London, N6A 3K7

University of Windsor
Dept. of Religious Studies
Windsor, N9B 3P4

Wilfrid Laurier University
Faculty of Arts & Sciences
Dept. of Religion & Culture
Faculty of Graduate Studies
Dept. of Religion & Culture
Waterloo, N2L 3C5

York University
Centre for Jewish Studies
Program in Canadian Jewish
Studies *(with Concordia
University)*
Program in Jewish Studies
Program in Hebrew Language &
Literature
Program in Jewish Teacher
Education
Faculty of Arts
Faculty of Education
Faculty of Fine Arts
Atkinson College
Glendon College
4700 Keele St.,
North York, M3J 1P3

Prince Edward Island

University of Prince Edward
Island
Dept. of Religious Studies
Charlottetown, C1A 4P3

Quebec

Bishop's University
Dept. of Religion
Lennoxville, J1M 1Z7

Concordia University—Université
Concordia
Chair of Canadian Jewish Studies
(with York University)
Faculty of Arts & Sciences
Dept. of English
Dept. of Modern Languages

Dept. of Religion
Dept. of Theology
1455 de Maisonneuve Blvd. W.,
Montreal, H3G 1M8

Dawson College
Faculty of Arts
Dept. of Hebrew
Dept. of Israel Studies
Dept. of Jewish Studies
350 Selby St.,
Montreal, H32 1W7

McGill University
Faculty of Arts
Dept. of History
Dept. of Jewish Studies
Dept. of Philosophy
Dept. of Religious Studies
Faculty of Graduate Studies &
   Research
Dept. of Jewish Studies
Montreal, H3A 2T6

Université Laval
Faculté de Théologie
Cité Universitaire,
Quebec, G1K 7P4

Université de Montréal
Dépt. d'Etudes Bibliques
Dépt. d'Etudes Juives
Dépt. d'Histoire
Dépt. de Réligion
Dépt. de Sociologie
Montreal, H3C 3J7

Vanier College Cégep
Jewish Studies Programme

821 Av. Ste. Croix,
St. Laurent, H4L 3X9

Saskatchewan

Saskatoon Theological Union
(consortium)
College of Emmanuel & St. Chad
Dept. of Biblical Studies
1337 College Dr.,
Saskatoon, S7N 0W6

Lutheran Theological Seminary
Biblical Studies
114 Seminary Cres.,
Saskatoon, S7N 0X3

St. Andrew's College
Dept. of Biblical Studies
1121 College Dr.,
Saskatoon, S7N 0W3

University of Regina
Faculty of Arts
Dept. of History
Religious Studies Program
Regina, S4S 0A2

University of Saskatchewan
College of Arts & Sciences
Dept. of Classics
Dept. of Religious Studies
Saskatoon, S7N 0W0

Mexico

Universidad Iberoamericana
Dirección General de Posgrado e
   Investigación

Programa de Especialización en
Estudios Judaicos
Paseo de La Reforma 880, Lomas
de Santa Fe, México 01210 DF

Universidad Nacional Autónoma
de México
Centro de Enseñanza de Lenguas
Extranjeras
Facultad de Derecho
Ciudad Universitaria, Delegación
Coyoacán, México 04510 DF

Escuela Nacional de Estudios
Profesionales Acatlán
Av. Alcantores y San Juan
Totoltepec, México DF

United States of America

Alabama

Athens State College
Dept. of Religion & Philosophy
Athens, AL 35611

Birmingham Southern College
Division for Humanities
Dept. of Hebrew
Dept. of Religion
900 Arkadelphia Rd.,
Birmingham, AL 35254

Faulkner University
Alabama Christian College of Arts
& Sciences
Dept. of Foreign Languages
5245 Atlanta Highway,
Montgomery, AL 36193

Huntingdon College
Dept. of Religion & Philosophy
1500 E. Fairview Ave.,
Montgomery, AL 36194-6201

International Bible College
Dept. of Bible
POB IBC, 3625 Helton Dr.,
Florence, AL 35630

Oakwood College
Dept. of Religion & Theology
Huntsville, AL 35896

Samford University
Beeson Divinity School
Dept. of Biblical Languages
Dept. of Religion
800 Lakeshore Drive,
Birmingham, AL 35229

Southeastern Bible College
Dept. of Languages
3001 Highway 280 S.,
Birmingham, AL 35205

Southern Christian University
1200 Taylor Road, POB 240240,
Montgomery, AL 36124-0240

Spring Hill College
Dept. of Theology
4000 Dauphin St.,
Mobile, AL 36608

Stillman College
Division of Humanities
Dept. of Religion & Philosophy
POB 1430,
Tuscaloosa, AL 35403-9990

University of Alabama
College of Arts & Sciences
Critical Languages Program
Dept. of Religious Studies
Aaron Aronov Chair of Judaic
   Studies
Box 870264,
Tuscaloosa, AL 35487-0264

University of Mobile
School of Religion
POB 13220, College Parkway,
Mobile, AL 36663-0220

Arizona

Arizona College of the Bible
Hebrew Program
2045 W. Northern Ave.,
Phoenix, AZ 85021

Arizona State University
Dept. of English
Dept. of History
Dept. of Religious Studies
Albert Plotkin Professorship of
   Jewish Studies
Tempe, AZ 85287

Phoenix College
Dept. of Hebrew
1202 West Thomas Rd.,
Phoenix, AZ 85013

Southwestern College
Division of General Education
Communication Department
2625 E. Cactus Rd.,
Phoenix, AZ 85032

University of Arizona
Committee on Judaic Studies
Interdisciplinary Program of
   Judaic Studies
Dept. of History
Dept. of Near Eastern Studies
Dept. of Religious Studies
Dept. of Political Science
Tucson, AZ 85721

Arkansas

Arkansas Baptist College
Dept. of Religion
1600 Bishop St.,
Little Rock, AK 72707-6099

Central Baptist College
Dept. of Bible
1501 College Ave., CBC Station,
Conway, AK 72032

Harding University
College of Bible & Religion
School of Biblical Studies
Biblical Languages Division
Historical Division
Searcy, AK 72143

John Brown University
Division of Biblical Studies
Siloam Spring, AK 72761

Ouachita Baptist University
Division of Religion & Philosophy
410 Ouachita St.,
Arkadelphia, AK 71923

University of Arkansas—Little
   Rock

College of Arts, Humanities &
Social Sciences
Dept. of Foreign Languages
2801 S. University,
Little Rock, AK 72204

California

Ambassador College
Dept. of Hebrew
300 W. Green St.,
Pasadena, CA 91129

American Baptist Seminary of the
West
Hebrew Program
2515 Hillegass Ave., Berkeley, CA

Antelope Valley College
Language Arts Division
Dept. of Foreign Languages
3041 W. Avenue K,
Lancaster, CA 93536

Bethany Bible College
Division of Biblical Studies
Division of Philosophy
800 Bethany Dr.,
Santa Cruz, CA 95066

Biola University
Talbot School of Theology
Division of Biblical Studies
13800 Biola Ave.,
La Mirada, CA 90639

California Baptist College
Division of Religion
Dept. of Biblical Studies
8432 Magnolia Ave.,
Riverside, CA 92504-3297

California Lutheran University
Dept. of Religion
60 W. Olsen Rd.,
Thousand Oaks, CA 91360-2787

California State University—
Chico
Center for International Studies
Dept. of Middle Eastern Studies
Dept. of Hebrew Language
Dept. of Religious Studies
101 Salem St., Chico, CA 95929

California State University—
Fresno
School of Arts & Humanities
Dept. of Linguistics
Dept. of Philosophy
School of Social Sciences
Dept. of Geography
Dept. of History
5241 N. Maple,
Fresno, CA 93740-0048

California State University—
Fullerton
School of Humanities & Social
Sciences
Dept. of Anthropology
Dept. of English & Comparative
Literature
Dept. of Foreign Languages—
Hebrew
Dept. of History
Dept. of Religious Studies
Fullerton, CA 92634-4080

California State University—
International Programs

Judaic Program *(with the Hebrew University of Jerusalem)*
400 Golden Shore,
Long Beach, CA 90802-4275

California State University—Long Beach
Dept. of Comparative Literature & Classics
Dept. of Religious Studies
Dept. of Sociology
1250 Bellflower Blvd.,
Long Beach, CA 90840

California State University—Los Angeles
Dept. of English
Dept. of Religious Studies
5151 State University Drive,
Los Angeles, CA 90032

California State University—Northridge
School of Humanities
Dept. of English
Dept. of Geography
Dept. of Foreign Languages & Literatures
Dept. of History
Dept. of Judaic Studies
Dept. of Religious Studies
18111 Nordhoff St.,
Northridge, CA 91330

California State University—Sacramento
School of Arts & Sciences
Dept. of Anthropology
Dept. of Humanities
6000 J St., Sacramento, CA 95819

Chapman University
Dept. of English
Dept. of Religion
333 N. Glassell St.,
Orange, CA 92666

Christian College—Irvine
Division of Religion
Dept. of Biblical Languages
1530 Concordia St.,
Irvine, CA 92175

Church Divinity School of the Pacific
(member of the Graduate Theological Union)
Dept. of Old Testament
2451 Ridge Rd.,
Berkeley, CA 94709-1211

Claremont Graduate School
Religion Program
150 E. Tenth St.,
Claremont, CA 91711-6160

Claremont McKenna College
(Claremont College System)
Dept. of History
Dept. of Religion
Claremont, CA 91711

Coastline Community College
Hebrew Program
11460 Warner Ave.,
Fountain Valley, CA 92708-2597

College of the Siskiyous
Hebrew Program
800 College Ave.,
Weed, CA 96064

Dominican School of Philosophy
& Theology
Dept. of Biblical Studies
2401 Ridge Rd.,
Berkeley, CA 94709

Foothill College
Language Arts Division
Main Campus,
12345 El Monte Rd.,
Los Altos Hills, CA 94022-4579

Franciscan School of Theology
*(Member of the Graduate
Theological Union)*
Dept. of Old Testament Studies &
Semitic Languages
1712 Euclid Ave.,
Berkeley, CA 94709

Fresno Pacific College
Division of Biblical & Religious
Studies
1717 S. Chestnut Ave.,
Fresno, CA 93702-4798

Fuller Theological Seminary
Division of Biblical Studies
Dept. of Old Testament
135 N. Oakland Ave.,
Pasadena, CA 91182

Golden Gate Baptist Theological
Seminary
Dept. of Old Testament
Strawberry Points,
Mill Valley, CA 94941-3197

Graduate Theological Union
*(member seminaries: American
Baptist Seminary of the West;*
*The Church Divinity School of
the Pacific; Dominican School
of Philosophy & Theology;
Franciscan School of Theology;
Jesuit School of Theology at
Berkeley; Pacific Lutheran
Theological Seminary; Pacific
School of Religion; San
Francisco Theological
Seminary; Starr King School for
the Ministry)*
Center for Jewish Studies
Jewish Studies
Comparative Studies
2400 Ridge Rd.,
Berkeley, CA 94709

Grossmont College
Division of Humanities & Social
Sciences
Dept. of Hebrew Language
El Cajon, CA 92020

Hebrew Union College—Jewish
Institute of Religion
Jerome H. Lonchheim School of
Judaic Studies
School of Jewish Community
Service
3007 University Ave.,
Los Angeles, CA 90007-3796

Irvine Valley College
School of Arts & Languages
Dept. of Foreign Languages
5500 Irvine Center Dr.,
Irvine, CA 92720

Life Bible College
Dept. of Biblical Languages

1100 Glendale Blvd.,
Los Angeles, CA 90026

Loma Linda University
School of Religion
Dept. of Biblical Studies
Loma Linda, CA 92350

Long Beach City College
Dept. of Foreign Languages
4901 E. Carson St.,
Long Beach, CA 90808

Los Angeles City College
Dept. of Hebrew
855 N. Vermont Ave.,
Los Angeles, CA 90029

Los Angeles Valley College
Dept. of Jewish Studies
5800 Fulton Ave.,
Van Nuys, CA 91401-4096

Loyola Marymount University
Dept. of Religious Education
Dept. of Theology
Loyola Blvd. at W. 80th St.,
Los Angeles, CA 90045

Mennonite Brethren Biblical
　Seminary
Division of Biblical Studies
Dept. of Old Testament
4824 E. Butler at Chestnut,
Fresno, CA 93727-5097

Moorpark College
Dept. of Hebrew
7075 Campus Rd.,
Moorpark, CA 93021

Occidental College
Dept. of Religious Studies
1600 Campus Road,
Los Angeles, CA 90041

Pacific Christian College
General Studies Division
2500 E. Nutwood Ave.,
Fullerton, CA 92631

Pacific Lutheran Seminary
*(member of the Graduate
　Theological Union)*
Dept. of Semitic Languages
Dept. of Biblical Studies
2770 Marin Ave.,
Berkeley, CA 94708-1597

Pacific School of Religion
*(member of the Graduate
　Theological Union)*
Dept. of Biblical Studies/Hebrew
　Scriptures
1798 Scenic Ave.,
Berkeley, CA 94709-1323

Pacific Union College
Dept. of Religion
Angwin, CA 94508-9707

Palomar College
Dept. of English
Dept. of Judaic Studies
1140 West Mission Rd.,
San Marcos, CA 92069

Pasadena City College
Dept. of English & Foreign
　Languages
Dept. of Hebrew

1570 E. Colorado Blvd.,
Pasadena, CA 91106-2003

Patten College
Division of Biblical & Theological
Studies
Bernstein Chair of Judaica Studies
2433 Coolidge Ave.,
Oakland, CA 94601

Pepperdine University
Humanities Division
Dept. of Foreign Languages
Dept. of Religion
24255 Pacific Coast Highway,
Malibu, CA 90263

Pitzer College
(Claremont College System)
Dept. of Classics
Dept. of Foreign Languages
Dept. of History
1050 N. Mills Ave.,
Claremont, CA 91711-6110

Point Loma Nazarene College
Dept. of Philosophy & Religion
1900 Lomaland Dr.,
San Diego, CA 92106-2899

Pomona College
(Claremont College System)
Dept. of Politics
Dept. of Modern Languages &
Literature
550 College Ave.,
Claremont, CA 91711-6303

Saddleback Community College
Dept. of Hebrew

18000 Marguerite Parkway,
Mission Viejo, CA 92692

San Diego City College
Dept. of Foreign Languages
1313 Twelfth Ave.,
San Diego, CA 92101

San Diego Mesa College
Dept. of Hebrew
7250 Mesa College Dr.,
San Diego, CA 92111

San Diego State University
College of Arts & Sciences
Dept. of Classical & Oriental
Languages & Literatures
Dept. of Comparative Literature
Dept. of History
Dept. of Humanities
Program in Judaic Studies
Lipinsky Institute Distinguished
Visiting Israeli Professorship
Abraham Nasatir Professorship in
Modern Jewish History
Dept. of Religious Studies
5300 Campanile Drive,
San Diego, CA 92182-0763

San Francisco City College
Dept. of Hebrew Language
33 Gough St.,
San Francisco, CA 94103

San Francisco State University
Dept. of History
Dept. of Philosophy
1600 Holloway Ave.,
San Francisco, CA 94132

San Francisco Theological
 Seminary
Dept. of Biblical Studies
2 Kensington Rd.,
San Anselmo, CA 94960

San Jose Bible College
Dept. of Old Testament
790 S. 12th St., POB 1090,
San Jose, CA 95108

San Jose State University
College of Humanities & Arts
Dept. of Foreign Languages
Middle East Studies Program
Religious Studies Program
Program in Jewish Studies
1 Washington Square,
San Jose, CA 95192-0097

Santa Clara University
College of Arts & Sciences
Dept. of Biblical Hebrew
Dept. of Classics
Dept. of English
Dept. of Religious Studies
Santa Clara, CA 95053

Santa Monica College
Dept. of Foreign Languages
1900 Pico Blvd.,
Santa Monica, CA 90405-1628

School of Theology at Claremont
Dept. of Biblical Studies
Dept. of Religion & Society
Dept. of Religious Education
Dept. of World Religions &
 Ecumenics

1325 N. College Ave.,
Claremont, CA 91711-3199

Scripps College
(Claremont College System)
Dept. of Classics
Dept. of Foreign Languages
1030 Columbia Ave.,
Claremont, CA 91711-3948

Simpson College
Biblical Studies Division
801 Silver Ave.,
San Francisco, CA 94134

Skyline College
Dept. of Hebrew
3300 College Drive,
San Bruno, CA 94066

Southern California College
Division of Religion
Biblical Studies Department
55 Fair Drive,
Costa Mesa, CA 92626

Stanford University
School of Humanities & Sciences
Dept. of Foreign Languages
Dept. of Jewish Studies
Aaron Roland Lecturer in Jewish
 Studies
Daniel E. Koshland Chair in
 Jewish History & Culture
Larry I. & Eva Chernov Lokey
 Chair in Jewish Studies
Reinhard Family Curator of
 Judaica & Hebraica Collections
Dept. of Religious Studies
Stanford, CA 94305-3005

University of California—
Berkeley
College of Letters & Sciences
Dept. of History
Dept. of Near Eastern Studies
Dept. of Hebrew Language &
Literature
Class of 1937 Chair in Hebrew &
Comparative Literature
Koret Chair in Jewish History
Taubman Chair of Talmudic
Culture
Dept. of Philosophy
Dept. of Semitics
Berkeley, CA 94720

University of California—Davis
Dept. of History
Dept. of Religious Studies
Jewish Studies Program
Davis, CA 95616-0853

University of California—Irvine
School of Humanities
Dept. of Classics
Dept. of History
Teller Family Chair in Jewish
History
Irvine, CA 92717

University of California—Los
Angeles
College of Letters & Sciences
Dept. of Ancient Near East
Dept. of Comparative Religions
Dept. of German
Dept. of Hebrew
Dept. of History
Dept. of Jewish Studies

1939 Club Chair in Holocaust
Studies
Dept. of Near Eastern Languages
& Cultures
Dept. of Semitics
Dept. of Yiddish
Los Angeles, CA 90024

University of California—
Riverside
College of Humanities & Social
Sciences
Dept. of Sociology
Program of Religious Studies
Riverside, CA 92521-0419

University of California—San
Diego
Arts & Humanities
Cultural Traditions Program
Dept. of Anthropology
Dept. of History
Dept. of Literature
Dept. of Sociology
Judaic Studies Program
La Jolla, CA 92093

University of California—Santa
Barbara
College of Letters & Sciences
Dept. of Germanic Languages &
Literatures
Dept. of History
Dept. of Philosophy
Dept. of Religious Studies
Dept. of Semitic Languages
Santa Barbara, CA 93106

University of California—Santa
Cruz

College of Humanities
Dept. of Hebrew
Dept. of History
Dept. of Literature
Dept. of Modern Society & Social
  Thought
Cowell College, 1156 High St.,
Santa Cruz, CA 95064

University of Judaism
(West Coast campus of the J.T.S.)
Jewish Studies Program
15600 Mullholland Drive,
Los Angeles, CA 90024

University of Redlands
Dept. of Religion
1200 E. Colton Ave.,
Redlands, CA 92373-0999

University of San Francisco
College of Arts & Sciences
Dept. of Theology & Religious
  Studies
Melvin M. Swig Judaic Studies
  Program
Mae & Benjamin Swig Chair in
  Judaic Studies
2130 Fulton St.,
San Francisco, CA 94117-1080

University of Southern California
College of Arts, Letters & Science
Dept. of Religion
Program of Judaic Studies *(with
  H.U.C.-J.I.R.)*
University Park Campus,
Los Angeles, CA 90089

Graduate School
Dept. of Religion

3501 Trousdale Parkway,
Los Angeles, CA 90089-0355

West Los Angeles College
Hebrew Program
4800 Freshman Dr.,
Culver City, CA 90230

Westminster Theological Seminary
Dept. of Biblical Studies
1725 Bear Valley Parkway,
Escondido, CA 92027-4128

Westmont College
Dept. of Religious Studies
Hebrew Program
955 La Paz Road,
Santa Barbara, CA 93108

Yeshiva University of Los Angeles
Program in Jewish Studies
9760 W. Pico Blvd.,
Los Angeles, CA 90035

Colorado

Colorado College
Dept. of Religion
14 E. Cache La Poudre,
Colorado Springs, CO 80903

Colorado Christian College
Dept. of Biblical Studies
Dept. of Foreign Languages
180 S. Garrison St.,
Lakewood, CO 80226

Colorado State University
Dept. of History
Fort Collins, CO 80523

Denver Conservative Baptist
Seminary
Dept. of Old Testament
POB 10000, 3401 S. University
Blvd., Englewood, CO 80210

The Iliff School of Theology
Div. of Biblical & Historical
Interpretation
Dept. of Biblical Languages
Dept. of Biblical Exegesis
Hebrew Program *(with University
of Denver)*
2201 S. University Blvd.,
Denver, CO 80210

Mesa State College
School of Humanities & Fine Arts
Dept. of Languages & Literatures
POB 2647,
Grand Junction, CO 81502

University of Colorado—Boulder
Dept. of Anthropology
Dept. of History
Dept. of Political Science
Dept. of Religious Studies
Boulder, CO 80302

University of Denver
College of Arts & Sciences
Center for Judaic Studies
Program in Judaic Studies
Eva and Emil Hecht Chair in
Judaic Studies
Dept. of Foreign Languages
Dept. of History
Dept. of Philosophy
Dept. of Religious Studies
Dept. of Sociology

Graduate School
Center for Judaic Studies
Dept. of Religious Studies
2199 S. University Blvd.,
Denver, CO 80208

Connecticut

Central Connecticut State
University
College of Arts & Sciences
Dept. of Modern Languages
POB 2008,
New Britain, CT 06050

Connecticut College
Dept. of Religious Studies
Elie Wiesel Chair of Judaic Studies
New London, CT 06320

Trinity College
Dept. of Classics
Dept. of European Civilization
Dept. of Modern Languages
Dept. of Religion
Hartford, CT 06106

University of Bridgeport
College of Arts & Humanities
Bridgeport, CT 06601

University of Connecticut
College of Liberal Arts & Sciences
Dept. of Modern & Classical
Languages
Hebrew Program
Hebrew Civilization Department
Center for Jewish Studies &
Contemporary Jewish Life
Storrs, CT 06269-5144

University of Hartford
College of Arts & Sciences
Dept. of English
Dept. of History
Maurice Greenberg Center of
Judaic Studies
Maurice Greenberg Professorship
of Judaic Studies
Stephen Joel Trachtenberg School
(with Hebrew University)
200 Bloomfield Ave.,
West Hartford, CT 06117-0395

Wesleyan University
Dept. of German Language &
Literature
Dept. of Philosophy
Dept. of Religion
Hebrew Program
Wesleyan Program in Israel
Middletown, CT 06457

Yale University
Dept. of English
Dept. of History
Dept. of Literature
Dept. of Near Eastern Languages
& Civilizations
Dept. of Religious Studies
Program of Judaic Studies
Robert F. & Patricia Ross Weiss
Assistant Professorship of
Religious Studies in Hebrew
Bible
Frederick P. Rose Chair in Jewish
History
Jacob & Hilda Blaustein Chair in
Hebrew Language & Literature

Lucy Moses Chair in Modern
Jewish History
Mark Taper Chair in History of
Judaism
Yale Station,
New Haven, CT 06520

Graduate School
Dept. of Biblical Languages
Divinity School
POB 1303A, Yale Station,
New Haven, CT 06520

Summer Language Institute
POB 2145, 53 Wall St., Yale
Station, New Haven, CT 06520

Delaware

University of Delaware
College of Arts & Sciences
Jewish Studies Program
Newark, DE 19716

District of Columbia

The American University
College of Arts & Sciences
Program of Jewish Studies
Dept. of Language & Foreign
Studies
Dept. of Philosophy & Religion
4400 Massachusetts Ave. NW,
Washington, DC 20016-8012

The Catholic University of
America
School of Religious Studies
Dept. of Religion & Religious
Education

Dept. of Biblical Studies
Graduate Studies in Arts &
  Sciences
Dept. of Semitic & Egyptian
  Languages & Literature
620 Michigan Ave. NE,
Washington, DC 20064

Gallaudet College
College of Arts & Sciences
Dept. of Foreign Languages &
  Literatures
Germanic & Classical Languages
800 Florida Ave. NE,
Washington, DC 20002

George Washington University
Columbian College of Arts &
  Sciences
Dept. of Classics
Dept. of History
Dept. of Political Science
Dept. of Religion
Washington, DC 20052

Georgetown University
Dept. of Government
Dept. of History
Dept. of Theology
School of Linguistics
Hebrew Program
37th & O Sts. NW,
Washington, DC 20057

Howard University
School of Divinity
2400 Sixth St. NW,
Washington, DC 20059

St. Paul's College
3015 Fourth St. NE,
Washington, DC 20017-1199

Trinity College
Dept. of Theology
Washington, DC 20017

Wesley Theological Seminary
Field of Biblical Interpretation
4500 Massachusetts Ave. NW,
Washington, DC 20016

Florida

Bethune-Cookman College
Dept. of Religion & Philosophy
640 Second Ave.,
Daytona Beach, FL 32015

Brevard Community College
Hebrew Program
151a Clearlake Rd.,
Cocoa, FL 32922

Broward Community College
Dept. of Modern Foreign
  Languages
A. Hugh Adams Central Campus,
  3501 SW Davie Rd.,
Fort Lauderdale, FL 33314

Clearwater Christian College
Div. of Biblical Studies
3400 Gulf to Bay Blvd.,
Clearwater, FL 34619

Daytona Beach Community
  College
Dept. of Foreign Languages

Daytona Beach Campus,
1200 Volusia Ave.,
Daytona Beach, FL 32144

Florida Beacon Bible College
Dept. of Biblical Languages
6900 142nd Ave. N.,
Largo, FL 34641

Florida College
Dept. of Biblical Languages
Temple Terrace, FL 33617-5578

Florida International University
College of Arts & Sciences
Dept. of Hebrew
Dept. of History
Dept. of Political Science
Dept. of Religion
Institute of Judaic Studies
University Park, Tamiami Trail,
Miami, FL 33199

Florida State University
College of Arts & Sciences
Dept. of Classics
Tallahassee, FL 32306-4031

Hobe Sound Bible College
Dept. of Languages
POB 1065,
Hobe Sound, FL 33475

Jacksonville University
Dept. of Religion
Jacksonville, FL 32211

Luther Rice Seminary
Bible College
1050 Hendricks Ave.,
Jacksonville, FL 32207

Miami Christian College
Biblical Languages Program
2300 NW 135th St.,
Miami, FL 33167

Miami-Dade Community College
Dept. of Hebrew Language
Dept. of Religion
North Campus,
11380 NW 27th Ave.,
Miami, FL 33167-3495

Palm Beach Atlantic College
Hebrew Program
POB 24708,
West Palm Beach, FL 33416-4708

Pensacola Junior College
Dept. of Foreign Languages
Pensacola Campus, 1000 College
    Blvd., Pensacola, FL 32504

Rollins College
Dept. of Philosophy & Religion
Winter Park, FL 32789-4499

St. Vincent de Paul Seminary
Dept. of Scripture
10701 S. Military Trail,
Boynton Beach, FL 33436-4811

Southeastern College of the
    Assemblies of God
Dept. of Languages
1000 Longfellow Blvd.,
Lakeland, FL 33801

Spurgeon Baptist Bible College
Dept. of Biblical Languages
4440 Spurgeon Dr.,
Mulberry, FL 33860

University of Central Florida
College of Arts & Sciences
Jewish Studies Program
Dept. of English
Dept. of Foreign Languages
Dept. of History
Dept. of Humanities
Dept. of Literature
Dept. of Philosophy & Religion
Dept. of Political Science
Dept. of Sociology &
  Anthropology
Orlando, FL 32816

University of Florida
College of Liberal Arts & Sciences
Center for Jewish Studies
Samuel M. Melton Legislative
  Professorship in Jewish History
Asian & African Languages &
  Literatures
Dept. of Anthropology
Dept. of English
Dept. of History
Dept. of Political Science
Dept. of Religion
Gainesville, FL 32611

University of Miami
College of Arts & Sciences
Dept. of English
Dept. of Foreign Languages &
  Literatures
Dept. of Hebrew
Dept. of History
Dept. of Judaic Studies
Dept. of Musicology
Dept. of Politics & Public Affairs

Dept. of Religious Studies
Dept. of Sociology
Dept. of Yiddish
POB 248106, University Station,
Coral Gables, FL 33124

University of South Florida
College of Arts & Sciences
Dept. of Religious Studies
4202 Fowler Ave.,
Tampa, FL 33620-5550

University of Tampa
Dept. of Religion
401 W. Kennedy Blvd.,
Tampa, FL 33606

Georgia

Berry College
Dept. of Religion
Mt. Berry Station,
Mt. Berry, GA 30149

Columbia Theological Seminary
Dept. of Old Testament
    Languages, Literatures &
    Exegesis
POB 520, 701 College Dr.,
Decatur, GA 30031-0520

Covenant College
Dept. of Foreign Languages
Lookout Mountain, GA 30750

Emory University
Chandler School of Theology

Dept. of Biblical Studies
Dept. of History
Dept. of Near Eastern & Judaic
 Languages & Literatures
Jay & Leslie Cohen Chair of
 Judaic Studies
Dept. of Religion
Dorot Professorship of Modern
 Jewish & Holocaust Studies
Dept. of Old Testament Studies
Dept. of New Testament Studies
Dept. of Yiddish
1655 North Decatur Rd.,
Atlanta, GA 30322

Georgia State University
College of Arts & Sciences
Dept. of Foreign Languages
Hebrew Program
University Plaza,
Atlanta, GA 30303-3085

Interdenominational Theological
 Center
Dept. of Biblical Studies &
 Languages
671 Beckwith St. SW,
Atlanta, GA 30314

La Grange College
Div. of Humanities & Fine Arts
Dept. of Religion
Hebrew Studies
601 Broad St.,
La Grange, GA 30240-2999

Mercer University
Cecil B. Day College of Arts &
 Sciences

Dept. of Foreign Languages
3001 Mercer University Dr.,
Atlanta, GA 30341

North Georgia College
Dept. of Modern Languages
Dahlonega, GA 30597

Toccoa Falls College
General Biblical Studies
Toccoa Falls, GA 30598

University of Georgia
Franklin College of Arts &
 Sciences
Dept. of Religion
Dept. of Semitic
Dept. of Social Sciences
Div. of Languages & Literatures
Dept. of Hebrew
Graduate School
Dept. of Religion
Athens, GA 30602

Hawaii

Chaminade University
College of Arts & Sciences
Dept. of Religious Studies
3140 Waialae Ave.,
Honolulu, HI 96816

University of Hawaii
Dept. of Philosophy
Dept. of Religion
2444 Dole St.,
Honolulu, HI 96822

Idaho

Northwest Nazarene College
Div. of Fine Arts
Dept. of English
Dept. of Foreign Languages
Hebrew Program
Dept. of Religion
Nampa, ID 83651

Illinois

Augustana College
Dept. of Religion
639 38th St.,
Rock Island, IL 61201

Barat College
Dept. of Religious Studies
700 East Westleigh Rd.,
Lake Forest, IL 60045

Bethany Theological Seminary
Dept. of Biblical Studies
Butterfield & Meyers Rds.,
Oak Brook, IL 60521

Bradley University
College of Liberal Arts & Sciences
Dept. of English & Foreign
  Languages
Dept. of Philosophy & Religious
  Studies
Peoria, IL 61625

Catholic Theological Union
Dept. of Biblical Literatures &
  Languages
5401 S. Cornell Ave.,
Chicago, IL 60615-5698

Chicago Theological Seminary
Center for Jewish-Christian
  Studies
Dept. of Old Testament
5757 S. University Ave.,
Chicago, IL 60637

College of Lake County
Dept. of History
19351 W. Washington St.,
Grayslake, IL 60030

Concordia College
Dept. of Modern & Classical
  Languages
7400 Augusta St.,
River Forest, IL 60305-1499

De Paul University
College of Liberal Arts & Sciences
Dept. of Religious Studies
Jewish Studies Program *(with
  Spertus Institute)*
Lincoln Park Campus, 2323 N.
  Seminary Ave,
Chicago, IL 60614-3298
Loop Campus, 25 E. Jackson
  Blvd., Chicago, IL 60604

Garrett-Evangelical Theological
  Seminary
Dept. of Old Testament
Hebrew Program
2121 Sheridan Rd.,
Evanston, IL 60201

Harold Washington College
(Formerly Loop College)
Dept. of Continuing Education
30 E. Lake St., Chicago, IL 60601

Hebrew Theological College
7135 N. Carpenter Rd.,
Skokie, IL 60077

Lake Forest College
Dept. of Religion
555 N. Sheridan Rd.,
Lake Forest, IL 60045-2399

Lincoln Christian College
Dept. of Bible & Theology
Lincoln, IL 62656

Lincoln Christian Seminary
Bible & Theology Div.
Field of Old Testament
100 Campus View Dr.,
Lincoln, IL 62656

Loyola University Chicago
College of Arts & Sciences
Graduate School
Dept. of Theology
6525 N. Sheridan Rd.,
Chicago, IL 60626-5385

Lutheran School of Theology
*(Member of the Association of
    Chicago Theological Schools)*
Div. of Biblical Studies
Dept. of Biblical Languages
Dept. of Old Testament
1100 E. 55th St.,
Chicago, IL 60615

Malcolm X College
Hebrew Program
1900 W. Van Buren St.,
Chicago, IL 60612-3197

McCormick Theological Seminary
Biblical Field

5555 S. Woodlawn Ave.,
Chicago, IL 60637

Moody Bible Institute
Dept. of Bible
820 N. La Salle Dr.,
Chicago, IL 60610

Mundelein College
Dept. of Humanities
Dept. of Religious Studies
Jewish Studies Program *(with
    Spertus Institute)*
6363 N. Sheridan Rd.,
Chicago, IL 60660

Mundelein Seminary
Dept. of Bible
Chicago, IL 60060-1174

North Park Theological Seminary
Biblical Field
3225 W. Foster Ave.,
Chicago, IL 60625

Northern Baptist Theological
    Seminary
Dept. of Biblical History &
    Thought
660 E. Butterfield Rd.,
Lombard, IL 60148-5698

Northern Illinois University
College of Liberal Arts & Sciences
Dept. of English
Dept. of Foreign Languages &
    Literatures
DeKalb, IL 60115-2857

Northwestern University
Dept. of African & Asian
    Languages

Dept. of Comparative Literature
& Theory
Dept. of European Thought &
Cultures
Dept. of History
Dept. of History & Literature of
Religions
Philip M. & Ethel Klutznick Chair
in Jewish Civilization
Dept. of Slavic Languages &
Literatures
Evanston, IL 60208

Oakton Community College
Hebrew Program
1600 E. Golf Rd.,
Des Plaines, IL 60016-1268

Olivet Nazarene University
Dept. of Biblical Literature
Kankakee, IL 60901

Principia College
Dept. of Religion & Philosophy
Elsah, IL 62028-9799

Seabury-Western Theological
Seminary
Dept. of Old Testament & Biblical
Languages
2122 Sheridan Rd.,
Evanston, IL 60201

Southern Illinois University
Dept. of English
Carbondale, IL 62901

Spertus Institute of Jewish Studies
Academic Programs in Jewish
Studies
Professional Programs in Jewish
Studies

Susman Program in Jewish
Communal Studies
Continuing Education Program
618 S. Michigan Ave.,
Chicago, IL 60605

Trinity Evangelical Divinity
School
Dept. of Old Testament & Semitic
Studies
2065 Hal Day Rd.,
Deerfield, IL 60015

Truman College
Dept. of Foreign Languages
1145 W. Wilson Ave.,
Chicago, IL 60640

University of Chicago
Div. of Humanities
Dept. of Arabic & Islam
Dept. of Hebrew
Dept. of Germanic Languages &
Literatures
Dept. of Languages & Linguistics
Dept. of Medieval Jewish Studies
Dept. of Religion & the
Humanities
Dept. of Near Eastern Languages
& Civilizations
Nathan Cummings Chair in
Jewish Studies
Ludwig Rosenberger Chair in
Jewish History & Civilization
School of Divinity
Dept. of Bible
5801 Ellis Ave.,
Chicago, IL 60637

University of Illinois—Chicago
Circle

College of Liberal Arts & Sciences
Dept. of English
Dept. of Hebraic & Judaic Studies
  (with Spertus Institute)
Box 4348,
Chicago, IL 60680

University of Illinois—Urbana-
  Champaign
Dept. of Humanities
Dept. of Linguistics
Hebrew Program
Dept. of Religious Studies
Hebrew Language Program
707 S. Mathews,
Urbana/Champaign, IL 61801

Graduate School
Dept. of Linguistics
801 S. Wright St.,
Urbana, IL 61820

Wheaton College
College of Arts & Sciences
Dept. of Archaeology
Dept. of Bible & Theology
Dept. of Foreign Languages
Dept. of Religious Studies
  Graduate School
Dept. of Theological Studies
501 E. College,
Wheaton, IL 60187-5593

Indiana

Anderson University
Dept. of Bible & Religion
Dept. of History
School of Theology

Biblical Division
Anderson, IN 46012

Associated Mennonite Biblical
  Seminary
Dept. of Biblical Studies
Eckhart, IN 46517

Bethel College
Division of Graduate Studies
Dept. of Biblical Studies
Dept. of Social Sciences
Division of Languages &
  Literatures
Hebrew Studies
Division of Social Sciences
1001 W. McKinley Ave.,
Michawaka, IN 46545

Butler University
College of Liberal Arts & Sciences
Dept. of Philosophy & Religious
  Studies
4600 Sunset Ave.,
Indianapolis, IN 46208

Christian Theological Seminary
School of Graduate Studies
Hebrew Program
6600 N. Clinton St.,
Fort Wayne, IN 64825

Earlham College
Dept. of Religion
Richmond, IN 47374

Fort Wayne Bible College
Division of Biblical Studies
1025 W. Rudisill Blvd.,
Fort Wayne, IN 46807

Grace Theological Seminary
Dept. of Old Testament
    Languages & Literatures
200 Seminary Dr.,
Winona Lake, IN 46590

Huntington College
Division of Humanities & the
    Bible
Dept. of Foreign Languages
2303 College Ave.,
Huntington, IN 46750

Indiana State University
Dept. of English
Dept. of Humanities
Terre Haute, IN 47809

Indiana University
College of Arts & Sciences
Robert A. & Sandra S. Borns
    Jewish Studies Program
Borns Visiting Professorship in
    Jewish Studies
Dept. of Anthropology
Dept. of Comparative Literature
Dept. of English
Dept. of History
Dept. of Folklore
Dept. of Near Eastern Languages
    & Cultures
Dept. of Philosophy
Dept. of Political Science
Dept. of Religious Studies
Graduate School
Institute for Biblical & Literary
    Studies
Dept. of Near Eastern Languages
    & Cultures
Bloomington, IN 47405-2401

Indiana University—Indianapolis
School of Liberal Arts
Dept. of Foreign Languages
Indianapolis, IN 46202

Indiana University—Southeast
Dept. of English
Dept. of Religious Studies
4201 Grant Line Rd.,
New Albany, IN 47150

Martin Center College
Dept. of Religious Studies
2171 Avondale Pl.,
Indianapolis, IN 46218

Purdue University
School of Liberal Arts
Interdisciplinary Program in
    Jewish Studies
Dept. of English
Dept. of Foreign Languages &
    Literatures
Dept. of History
Dept. of Philosophy
Dept. of Political Science
Dept. of Sociology
West Lafayette, IN 47907-1350

St. Mary's College
Dept. of English
Dept. of Religious Studies
Notre Dame, IN 46556

St. Meinrad School of Theology
School of Theology
Dept. of Biblical & Historical
    Studies
St. Meinrad, IN 47577

Summit Christian College
Division of Biblical Studies

1025 W. Rudisill Blvd.,
Fort Wayne, IN 46807

Taylor University
Dept. of Biblical Studies, Christian
Education, & Philosophy
500 W. Reade Ave.,
Upland, IN 46989-1001

University of Indianapolis
Dept. of Religion
1400 E. Hanna Ave.,
Indianapolis, IN 46227

University of Notre Dame
College of Arts & Sciences
Dept. of Classical & Oriental
Languages & Literatures
Dept. of Government &
International Studies
Dept. of History
Dept. of Theology
Abrams Professorship of Jewish
Studies
Graduate School
Dept. of Theology
Specialization in Christianity &
Judaism in Antiquity
Notre Dame, IN 46556

Valparaiso University
Dept. of Foreign Languages &
Literatures
Hebrew Program
Dept. of Theology & Islam
Valparaiso, IN 46383-9978

Iowa

Cornell College
College of Humanities

Dept. of Religion
600 First St. W.,
Mt. Vernon, IA 52314

Dordt College
Hebrew Program
Sioux Center, IA 51250

Drake University
Dept. of Religion & Philosophy
Dept. of Biblical Studies
2507 University Ave.,
Des Moines, IA 50311

Faith Baptist Bible College
Division of General Studies
Dept. of Languages
Dept. of Bible
100 NW Fourth St.,
Ankeny, IA 50021

Grinnell College
Dept. of Religious Studies
POB 805,
Grinnell, IA 50112-0807

Luther College
Dept. of Religion & Philosophy
Dept. of Classical Languages
Dept. of Religion
Decorah, IA 52101

Morningside College
Dept. of Religious Studies
1501 Morningside Ave.,
Sioux City, IA 51106

University of Iowa
College of Liberal Arts
Dept. of Asian Languages &
Literatures

School of Religion
Iowa City, IA 52242

Vennard College
Division of General Studies
Dept. of Languages & Literatures
University Park, IA 52595

Kansas

Benedictine College
Dept. of Classics
Dept. of Religious Studies
Atchison, KS 66002-1499

Central Baptist Theological
  Seminary
Dept. of Biblical Studies
Seminary Heights, 31 St. &
  Minnesota,
Kansas City, KS 66102

Kansas State University
College of Arts & Sciences
American Ethnic Studies
Dept. of English
Dept. of History
Manhattan, KS 66506-1005

Kansas Wesleyan University
Division of Humanities
Dept. of Religion & Philosophy
Salina, KS 67401

Manhattan Christian College
General & Supportive Studies
Hebrew Program
1415 Anderson,
Manhattan, KS 66502

University of Kansas
College of Arts & Sciences
Dept. of English
Dept. of Linguistics
Hebrew Program
Dept. of Religious Studies
Lawrence, KS 66045

Wichita State University
Fairmount College of Liberal Arts
  & Sciences
Dept. of English
Dept. of History
Dept. of Religion
Wichita, KS 67260-0005

Kentucky

Asbury College
Dept. of Foreign Languages
Ancient Languages
201 N. Lexington Ave.,
Wilmore, KY 40390

Asbury Theological Seminary
Division of Biblical Studies
Dept. of English Bible
Dept. of Old Testament
Hebrew Program
204 N. Lexington Ave.,
Wilmore, KY 40390-1199

Bellarmine College
Dept. of Theology
2001 Newburg Rd.,
Louisville, KY 40205

Berea College
Dept. of General Studies

Dept. of Hebrew
Dept. of Religion
Berea, KY 40404

Cumberland College
Dept. of Religion, Philosophy &
  Biblical Languages
Chair of Old Testament &
  Biblical Hebrew
7989 College Station Dr.,
Williamsburg, KY 40769-1331

Kentucky Christian College
Dept. of Biblical Studies
617 N. Carol Malone Blvd.,
Grayson, KY 41143-1199

Kentucky Wesleyan College
Dept. of Religion & Philosophy
3000 Frederica St.,
Owensboro, KY 42301

Lexington Theological Seminary
College of Bible
Dept. of Old Testament
631 S. Limestone,
Lexington, KY 40508

Lindsey Wilson College
Dept. of Philosophy & Religion
Columbia, KY 42728

Louisville Presbyterian
  Theological Seminary
Dept. of Biblical Studies
1044 Alta Vista Rd.,
Louisville, KY 40205-1798

Southern Baptist Theological
  Seminary
School of Theology

Dept. of Old Testament
2825 Lexington Rd.,
Louisville, KY 40280

University of Kentucky
College of Arts & Sciences
Dept. of Classical Languages &
  Literatures
Dept. of English
Dept. of History
Dept. of Russian & Eastern
  Studies
Lexington, KY 40506

University of Louisville
College of Arts & Sciences
Dept. of History
Dept. of Humanities
S. Third St., Louisville, KY 40292

Western Kentucky University
College of Arts, Humanities &
  Social Sciences
Dept. of Philosophy & Religious
  Studies
Dept. of Modern Languages &
  Intercultural Studies
Bowling Green, KY 42101

Louisiana

Louisiana College
Dept. of Religion & Philosophy
Biblical Languages
1140 College Dr.,
Louisiana College, LA 71359

Louisiana State University
College of Arts & Sciences

Dept. of Foreign Languages &
Literatures
Dept. of Philosophy & Religion
Graduate School
Hebrew Program
Baton Rouge, LA 70803

Loyola University
College of Arts & Sciences
Dept. of Religious Studies
6363 St. Charles Ave.,
New Orleans, LA 70118-0195

New Orleans Baptist Theological
Seminary
Division of Biblical Studies
3939 Gentilly Blvd.,
New Orleans, LA 70126

Tulane University
College of Arts & Sciences
Colloquia Program
Dept. of Classical Languages
Dept. of English
Dept. of History
Dept. of Music
Dept. of Political Science
Program of Judeo-Christian
Studies
6823 St. Charles Ave.,
New Orleans, LA 70118

Newcomb College
Program with Hebrew University
1229 Broadway,
New Orleans, LA 70118

University of New Orleans
Dept. of English
Dept. of History
New Orleans, LA 70122

Maine

Bangor Theological Seminary
Dept. of Old Testament
300 Union St., Bangor, ME 04401

Bates College
Dept. of Languages
Lewiston, ME 04240

Bowdoin College
Dept. of English
Dept. of History
Dept. of Religion
Brunswick, ME 04011

Colby College
Dept. of Religious Studies
Dept. of Classics
Dept. of English
Dept. of Government
Dept. of History
Dept. of Sociology &
Anthropology
Samuel & Esther Lipman
Memorial Lecture in Judaica
Waterville, ME 04901

University of Maine
Dept. of Philosophy
Orono, ME 04469

Maryland

Baltimore Hebrew University
Peggy Meyerhoff Pearlstone
School of Graduate Studies
Dept. of Hebrew Languages &
Literatures

5800 Park Heights Ave.,
Baltimore, MD 21215

Capital Bible Seminary
Dept. of English Bible Exposition
Dept. of Old Testament Literature
& Exegesis
Dept. of Systematic Theology
6511 Princess Garden Parkway,
Lanham, MD 20706-3599

Community College of Baltimore
Hebrew Program *(with Baltimore
Hebrew University)*
Harbor Campus,
600 E. Lambard St.,
Baltimore, MD 21202

Goucher College
Dept. of Philosophy & Religion
Baltimore, MD 21204

Johns Hopkins University
School of Arts & Sciences
Dept. of Anthropology
Dept. of Near Eastern Studies
3400 N. Charles St.,
Baltimore, MD 21218-2690

Loyola College
Dept. of Theology
4501 N. Charles St.,
Baltimore, MD 21210

Montgomery College
Hebrew Program
900 Hungerford Dr.,
Rockville, MD 20850

Towson State University
College of Liberal Arts
Dept. of History

Dept. of Modern Languages
Hebrew Program
Dept. of Philosophy
Towson, Baltimore, MD 21204

University of Baltimore
Yale Gordon College of Liberal
Arts
Dept. of History
1420 N. Charles St.,
Baltimore, MD 21201

University of Maryland
College of Arts & Humanities
Dept. of Architecture
Dept. of Comparative Literature
Dept. of German
Dept. of Hebrew & East Asian
Languages & Literatures
Dept. of History
Jewish Studies Program
Meyerhoff Center for Jewish
Studies
Harvey Meyerhoff Professorship
of Jewish History
Louis L. Kaplan Professorship of
Jewish History
Robert Smith Chair in Hebrew
Literature
College Park, MD 20742

University of Maryland—
Baltimore County
College of Arts & Sciences
Dept. of Ancient Studies
Program of Judaic Studies
Program of Religious Studies
5401 Wilkens Ave.,
Baltimore, MD 21228-5398

Washington Theological Union
Dept. of Sacred Scripture
9001 New Hampshire Ave.,
Silver Springs, MD 20903-3189

Massachusetts

American International College
Dept. of English
1000 State St.,
Springfield, MA 01109-3189

Amherst College
Concentration in Judaic Studies
Dept. of English
Dept. of History
Dept. of Religion
Amherst, MA 01002

Andover Newton Theological
  Seminary
Division of Biblical Studies
Dept. of Old Testament
210 Herrick Rd.,
Newton Center, MA 02159

Atlantic Union College
Dept. of Theology
POB 1000,
South Lancaster, MA 01561

Berkshire Community College
Dept. of Yiddish
1350 West St.,
Pittsfield, MA 01201

Boston College
Dept. of Theology
Chestnut Hill, MA 02167

Boston University
College of Liberal Arts

Center for Judaic Studies
Judaic Studies Concentration
Dept. of Geography
Dept. of International Relations
Dept. of Modern Foreign
  Languages & Literatures
Hebrew Program
Dept. of Religion
School of Theology
Area of Biblical & Historical
  Studies
725 Commonwealth Ave.,
Boston, MA 02215

Graduate School
705 Commonwealth Ave.,
Boston, MA 02215

Brandeis University
College of Arts & Sciences, &
  Graduate School of Arts &
  Sciences
Dept. of American Studies
Dept. of Comparative Literature
Dept. of European Cultural
  Studies
Dept. of Oriental Studies
Dept. of Philosophy
Dept. of Politics
Dept. of Sociology
Dept. of English & American
  Literature
Dept. of Germanic Languages &
  Literature
Dept. of History
Dept. of Near Eastern & Judaic
  Studies
Program in Islamic & Near
  Eastern Studies

Program in Judaic Studies
Hebrew Language Program
Yiddish Language & Literature
Philip W. Lown Chair in Jewish
  Philosophy
Jacob D. Berg Chair in Yiddish
  Culture
Dora B. Golding Chair in Biblical
  Studies
Rose B. & Joseph H. Cohen Chair
  in Judaic Studies
Helen & Irving Schneider Chair in
  American Jewish Studies
Richard Koret Chair in Modern
  Jewish History
Myra & Robert Kraft & Jacob
  Hiatt Chair in Christian Studies
Samuel Lane Chair in Jewish
  Religious History & Social
  Ethics
Klutznick Chair in Contemporary
  Jewish Studies
Walter Stern Hilborn Chair in
  Judaic Studies
Jennie & Mayer Weisman Chair
  in Judaic Studies
Joseph H. & Belle R. Braun Chair
  in American Jewish History
Joseph H. & Belle R. Braun Chair
  in Modern Hebrew Literature
Medieval Studies Program
Peace & Conflict Studies Program
Philip W. Lown School of Near
  Eastern & Judaic Studies
The Hornstein Program in Jewish
  Communal Service
Cohen Center for Modern Jewish
  Studies

Program in Non-Western &
  Comparative Studies
Waltham, MA 02254-9110

Clark University
Classics Program
Dept. of Foreign Languages &
  Literatures
Dept. of Government &
  International Relations
Dept. of History
Dept. of Sociology
Jewish Studies Program
950 Main St.,
Worcester, MA 01610-1477

College of the Holy Cross
Dept. of Religious Studies
Kraft-Hiatt Chair in Judaic
  Studies
Worcester, MA 01610

Emerson College
Dept. of History
Dept. of Philosophy & Religion
100 Beacon St.,
Boston, MA 02116

Episcopal Divinity School
Dept. of Biblical Studies
99 Brattle St.,
Cambridge, MA 02138

Gordon College
Division of Humanities
Dept. of Bible & Theological
  Studies
Dept. of Biblical Studies &
  Exegesis
Dept. of English

Dept. of Literature & Theology
Wenham, MA 01984

Gordon-Comwell Theological
Seminary
Division of Biblical Studies
Dept. of Old Testament
Dept. of Oriental Languages
South Hamilton, MA 01902

Hampshire College
Dept. of Social Science
Amherst, MA 01002

Harvard University & Radcliffe
College
College of Arts & Sciences
Center for Jewish Studies
Hancock Professorship of Hebrew
& Other Oriental Languages
Nathan Littauer Professorship of
Jewish History & Philosophy
Lee M. Friedman Bibliographer in
Judaica
Gerard Weinstock Visiting
Professorship of Jewish Studies
Jacob Safra Professorship of
Jewish History & Sephardic
Civilization
Harry Starr Professorship of
Classical & Modern Jewish &
Hebrew Literature
Albert A. List Professorship of
Jewish Studies
Dorot Professorship of the
Archaeology of Israel
Harry Austryn Wolfson
Professorship of Jewish Studies
Caroline Zelaznik Gruss & Joseph

S. Gruss Professorship in
Talmudic Civil Law
Littauer Hebraica Technical &
Research Services Librarian
Professorship of Yiddish
Literature
Dept. of Aramaic
Dept. of Comparative Literature
Dept. of English
Dept. of Foreign Cultures
Dept. of General Education
Dept. of Government
Dept. of History
Dept. of Literature and Arts
Dept. of Moral Reasoning
Dept. of Near Eastern Languages
& Civilizations
Hebrew Program
Dept. of History
Dept. of Comparative Literature
Dept. of Government
Cambridge, MA 02138

Harvard Divinity School
Dept. of Near Eastern Languages
45 Francis Ave.,
Cambridge, MA 02138

Hebrew College
B.A. Program in Hebrew
Literature
B.A. & M.A. Program in Jewish
Education
M.A. Program in Jewish Studies
Akiba Scholars Program
Kerem Summer Institute
Jewish Family Educators Training
Program

Jewish Early Childhood Education
Program
Jewish Music Institute & Program
43 Hawes St.,
Brookline, MA 02146

Hellenic College—Holy Cross
Greek Orthodox School of
Theology
School of Theology
Dept. of Biblical Studies & Old
Testament
50 Goddard Ave.,
Brookline, MA 02146

Lesley College
Dept. of History
29 Everett St.,
Cambridge, MA 02138-2790

Merrimack College
Dept. of Religious Studies
315 Turnpike St.,
North Andover, MA 01845

Mount Holyoke College
Dept. of History
Dept. of Religion
Program of Judaic Studies
Irene Kaplan Leiwant
Professorship of Jewish Studies
South Hadley, MA 01075

Saint John's Seminary College
College of Liberal Arts
Dept. of Ancient & Modern
Languages
197 Foster St.,
Brighton, MA 02135

Simmons College
Dept. of Comparative Literature

Dept. of English
Dept. of Political Science
Hebraic Studies Program *(with
Hebrew College)*
300 The Fenway,
Boston, MA 02115-5898

Smith College
Jewish Studies Program
Professorship in Jewish Studies
Dept. of Government
Dept. of History
Dept. of Religion & Biblical
Literature
Dept. of Sociology
Northampton, MA 01063

Stonehill College
Dept. of Religious Studies
North Easton, MA 02357

Tufts University
College of Liberal Arts
Dept. of English
Hebrew Language Studies
Judaic Studies Program
Dept. of Religion
Medford, MA 02155

University of Lowell
Dept. of English
Dept. of Western Cultural
Heritage
1 University Ave.,
Lowell, MA 01854

University of Massachusetts—
Amherst
College of Arts & Sciences
Dept. of Anthropology

Dept. of English
Dept. of Hebrew
Dept. of History
Dept. of Judaic & Near Eastern
  Studies
Dept. of Music
Dept. of Yiddish
Amherst, MA 01003

University of Massachusetts—
  Boston
Dept. of History
Dept. of Study of Religion
Harbor Campus,
Boston, MA 02125

Wellesley College
Dept. of History
Dept. of Religion
Sophia Moses Robinson
  Professorship of Jewish Studies
  & History
Dept. of Spanish
Dept. of Writing
Wellesley, MA 02181

Wheaton College
Dept. of German
Dept. of Religion
Norton, MA 02766

Williams College
Dept. of English
Dept. of Religion
Williamstown, MA 01267

Michigan

Alma College
Dept. of English

Dept. of Foreign Languages
Dept. of Religious Studies
Alma, MI 48801-1599

Andrews University
College of Arts & Sciences
Dept. of Art History
Dept. of English
Dept. of Old Testament Studies
  Biblical Languages
Dept. of Religion
Seventh-Day Adventist
  Theological Seminary
Dept. of Old Testament Studies
Berrien Springs, MI 49104-1500

Calvin Theological Seminary
Dept. of Old Testament
3233 Burton St. S.E.,
Grand Rapids, MI 49546

Concordia College
Division of Languages &
  Literatures
Dept. of Biblical & Classical
  Languages
4090 Geddes Rd.,
Ann Arbor, MI 48105

Grace Bible College
Division of Biblical Studies
1011 Aldon St. SW, POB 910,
Wyoming, MI 49509

Grand Rapids Baptist College
Division of Bible, Religion &
  Ministries
Dept. of Ancient Languages
1001 E. Beltline NE,
Grand Rapids, MI 49505

Grand Rapids Baptist Seminary
Dept. of Biblical Studies
1001 E. Beltline NE,
Grand Rapids, MI 49505

Hillsdale College
Dept. of Philosophy & Religion
Hillsdale, MI 49242-1298

Hope College
Dept. of Religion
POB 9000,
Holland, MI 49423-9000

Michigan Christian College
Dept. of Biblical Studies
800 W. Avon Rd.,
Rochester, MI 48063

Michigan State University
College of Arts & Letters
Jewish Studies Program
Center for Integrative Studies
James Madison College
East Lansing, MI 48824-1044

Oakland University
Dept. of Religious Studies
Rochester, MI 48309

Sacred Heart Major Seminary
Dept. of Sacred Scripture
Dept. of Biblical Languages
2701 Chicago Blvd.,
Detroit, MI 48206

Saint Mary's College
Hebrew Program
Orchard Lake, MI 48033

Spring Arbor College
Dept. of Religion
Spring Arbor, MI 49283

University of Detroit Mercy
College of Liberal Arts
Distinguished Professorship of
  Jewish Studies
Dept. of Religious Studies
4001 W. McNichols, POB 19900,
Detroit, MI 48219-0900

University of Michigan
College of Literature, Sciences &
  the Arts
Jean & Samuel Frankel Center for
  Judaic Studies
David W. Belin Lecture in
  American Jewish Affairs
David W. Belin Professorship of
  Rabbinic Literature
William Haber Professorship of
  Modern Jewish History
Louis & Helen Padnos Visiting
  Professors of Judaic Studies
Preston R. Tisch Professorship of
  Judaic Studies
Dept. of English Language &
  Literature
Dept. of History
Dept. of Near Eastern Studies
Ancient & Biblical Studies
General Near East
Hebrew Studies
Dept. of Political Science
Dept. of Religion
Dept. of Social Work
Dept. of Sociology
Graduate School
Ann Arbor, MI 48109-1003

Wayne State University
College of Liberal Arts

Dept. of Near Eastern & Asian
Studies
Hebrew Program
Detroit, MI 48202

William Tyndall College
Dept. of Languages
35700 W. Twelve Mile Rd.,
Farmington Hills, MI 48018

Minnesota

Bethany Lutheran College
Division of Humanities
Mankato, MN 56001

Bethel Theological Seminary
Dept. of Hebrew & Old
Testament
3949 Bethel Drive,
St. Paul, MN 55112

Carleton College
Dept. of Judaic Studies
Dept. of Religion
1 N. College St.,
Northfield, MN 55057

Concordia College
Dept. of Classics
Dept. of Religion
901 South Eighth St.,
Moorehead, MN 56560

Concordia College—Hamline &
Marshall
Dept. of Archaeology
Division of Religion
Dept. of Biblical Languages

275 North Syndicate,
St. Paul, MN 55104-5494

Gustavus Adolphus College
Dept. of Religion
800 W. College Ave.,
St. Peter, MN 56082-1498

Hamline University
Dept. of Religion
St. Paul, MN 55104

Luther Northwestern Seminary
Dept. of Old Testament
2481 Como Ave.,
St. Paul, MN 55108

Macalester College
Dept. of History
Dept. of Religious Studies
1600 Grand Ave.,
St. Paul, MN 55105

North Central Bible College
Dept. of Bible-Related Studies
Dept. of Biblical Languages
Dept. of History
Dept. of Old Testament Studies
Dept. of Theology
910 Eliot Ave. S.,
Minneapolis, MN 55404

St. John's University
Dept. of History
School of Theology
Scriptural Studies Department
Collegeville, MN 56321-7222

St. Paul Seminary
School of Divinity

Dept. of Sacred Scripture
2260 Summit Ave.
St. Paul, MN 55105-1039

United Theological Seminary
Christian Heritage
Dept. of Biblical Interpretation
Dept. of Old Testament Theology
3000 5th St. NW,
New Brighton, MN 55112

University of Minnesota
College of Liberal Arts
Dept. of Ancient Near Eastern
   Studies
Dept. of Art & Archaeology
Dept. of Hebrew
Dept. of History
Dept. of Jewish Studies
Dept. of Philosophy
Graduate School
College of Liberal Arts
Dept. of Classical & Near Eastern
   Studies
Jewish Studies Program
77 Pleasant St. SE,
Minneapolis, MN 55455

University of St. Thomas
Center for Jewish-Christian
   Learning
Dept. of Foreign Languages
Dept. of History
Dept. of Sociology
Dept. of Theology
Graduate Divnity School
2115 Summit Ave., SOD,
St. Paul, MN 55105-1096

Mississippi

Belhaven College
Dept. of Biblical Studies
1500 Peachtree St.,
Jackson, MS 39202

Reformed Theological Seminary
Dept. of Old Testament Studies
5422 Clinton Blvd.,
Jackson, MS 39209

Wesley Biblical Seminary
Division of Biblical Studies
5980 Floral Drive,
Jackson, MS 39206

William Carey College
College of Arts & Sciences
Dept. of Religion
Hattiesburg, MS 39401-9913

Missouri

Aquinas Institute of Theology
Biblical Studies
Dept. of Language Studies
3642 Lindell Blvd.,
St. Louis, MO 63108-3396

Assemblies of God Theological
   Seminary
Dept. of Bible & Theology
Hebrew Language & Exegesis
1445 Boonsville Ave.,
Springfield, MO 65802

Calvary Bible College
Division of Biblical Education

Bible Languages Program
15800 Calvary Rd.,
Kansas City, MO 64147-1341

Central Bible College
Division of Biblical Education
Dept. of Biblical Languages
300 N. Grant Ave.,
Springfield, MO 65803

Central Christian College of Bible
Dept. of General Studies
POB 70,
Moberly, MO 65270

Conception Seminary College
Division of History & Humanities
Division of Philosophy
Division of Religion
Division of Social & Behavioral
  Sciences
Conception, MO 64433

Concordia Seminary (Misssouri
  Synod)
Dept. of Exegetical Theology
Hebrew Program
St. Louis, MO 63105

Covenant Theological Seminary
Dept. of Old Testament
12330 Conway Rd.,
St. Louis, MO 63141

Eden Theological Seminary
Dept. of Scriptural Studies
475 E. Lockwood Ave.,
Webster Groves, MO 63119-3192

Evangelical College
Dept. of Biblical Studies &
  Philosophy

Dept. of Language Studies
1111 N. Glenstone,
Springfield, MO 65802

Hannibal–La Grance College
Division of Christian Studies
Dept. of Biblical Languages
2800 Palmyra Rd.,
Hannibal, MO 63401

Kenrick Seminary
Glennon-Kenrick School of
  Theology
Dept. of Scriptural Studies
5200 Glennon Dr.,
St. Louis, MO 63119

Midwest Baptist Theological
  Seminary
Biblical Field
Dept. of Old Testament
  Interpretation & Hebrew
5001 N. Oak St. Trfway.,
Kansas City, MO 64118

Nazarene Theological Seminary
Jewish Chautauqua Society
  Scholar Program
1700 E. Meyer Blvd.,
Kansas City, MO 64131

Northeast Missouri State
  University
Division of Languages &
  Literatures
Kirksville, MO 63501

St. Louis Christian College
Dept. of Biblical Languages
1360 Grandview Dr.,
Florissant, MO 63033

St. Louis Community College
Hebrew Program
Florissant Valley Campus,
3400 Pershall Rd.,
St. Louis, MO 63135
Forest Park Campus,
5600 Oakland Ave.,
St. Louis, MO 63110
Meramec Campus,
11333 Big Bend Blvd.,
Kirkwood, MO 63122

St. Louis University
College of Arts & Sciences
Dept. of Philosophy
Dept. of Theological Studies
221 N. Grand Blvd.,
St. Louis, MO 63103

Saint Paul School of Theology
Dept. of Hebrew Bible
5123 Truman Rd.,
Kansas City, MO 64127-2499

Southwest Baptist University
Redford School of Theology
Dept. of Bible
Bolivar, MO 65613

Southwest Missouri State
    University
College of Arts & Letters
Dept. of Foreign Languages
Graduate School
Dept. of Foreign Languages
901 S. National,
Springfield, MO 65804-0094

University of Missouri—
    Columbia

College of Arts & Sciences
Dept. of German, Russian &
    Asian Studies
Dept. of Religious Studies
Columbia, MO 65211

University of Missouri—Kansas
    City
College of Arts & Sciences
Dept. of English
Dept. of Foreign Languages
Dept. of History
Dept. of Philosophy
4825 Troost Ave.,
Kansas City, MO 64110-2499

University of Missouri—St. Louis
College of Arts & Sciences
Dept. of English
Dept. of History
Dept. of Modern Foreign
    Languages
Dept. of Philosophy
8001 Natural Bridge Rd.,
St. Louis, MO 63121-4499

Washington University
College of Arts & Sciences
Program in Jewish & Near
    Eastern Studies
Gloria M. Goldstein Chair in
    Jewish History & Thought
Dept. of Anthropology
Dept. of Asian & Near Eastern
    Studies
Dept. of Classics
Dept. of History
Dept. of Philosophy
St. Louis, MO 63130-4899

Webster University
Dept. of Literature & Language
Dept. of Religion
470 E. Lockwood Ave.,
St. Louis, MO 63119

Westminster College
Dept. of Religion
501 Westminster Ave.,
Fulton, MO 65251-1299

William Jewell College
Dept. of Religion
500 College Hill,
Liberty, MO 64068-9988

Montana

University of Montana
College of Arts & Sciences
Dept. of Religious Studies
Missoula, MT 59812-1608

Nebraska

College of St. Mary
Dept. of Theology
Omaha, NE 68124

Concordia College
Hebrew Program
800 N. Columbia Ave.,
Seward, NE 68434

Creighton University
College of Arts & Sciences
Dept. of Classics
Dept. of History

Philip M. & Esther Klutznick
   Chair in Jewish Civilization
Dept. of Theology
Omaha, NE 68103

Nebraska Christian College
Dept. of Biblical Studies &
   Languages
1800 Syracuse Ave.,
Norfolk, NE 68701

Nebraska Wesleyan College
Division of Humanities
Dept. of Religion
Biblical Studies
5000 St. Paul Ave.,
Lincoln, NE 68504

Platte Valley Bible College
Dept. of Languages
305 E. 18th St.,
Scottsfield, NE 69363-1227

University of Nebraska—Lincoln
Norman & Bernice Harris Center
   for Judaic Studies
Dept. of Classics
Dept. of English
Dept. of Geology
Dept. of History
Dept. of Modern Language &
   Literature
Dept. of Philosophy
Dept. of Political Science
Dept. of Sociology
Hymen Rosenberg Endowed
   Chair of European History &
   Judaic Studies
POB 880346,
Lincoln, NE 68588-0346

Nevada

University of Nevada—Reno
College of Arts & Sciences
Dept. of Foreign Languages &
 Literatures
Reno, NV 89557

New Hampshire

Dartmouth College
College of Arts & Sciences
Dept. of Asian Studies
Dept. of Hebrew Studies
Dept. of History
Dept. of Religion
Hanover, NH 03755

New Jersey

Caldwell College
Dept. of Religious Studies
Ryerson Ave., Caldwell, NJ 07006

Drew University
College of Liberal Arts
Dept. of Religion
Program in Jewish Studies
Julian Wallerstein Professorship in
 Jewish Studies
Theological School
Biblical Studies, Old Testament &
 Israel
Theological & Religious Studies
Madison, NJ 07940-4060

Glassboro State College
Dept. of Foreign Languages &
 Literatures
Glassboro, NJ 08028

Kean College of New Jersey
School of Liberal Arts
Dept. of English
Dept. of Foreign Languages
Dept. of History
Dept. of Religion
Dept. of Sociology
Judaic Studies Program
Movies Ave., Union, NJ 07083

Monmouth Seminary
Dept. of Foreign Languages
W. Long Branch, NJ 07764-1898

New Brunswick Theological
 Seminary
Dept. of Biblical Studies
17 Seminary Place,
New Brunswick, NJ 08901

Northeastern Bible College
Division of Biblical Education
Essex Falls, NJ 07021

Princeton Theological Seminary
Dept. of Biblical Studies
Princeton, NJ 08542

Princeton University
Dept. of Comparative Literature
Dept. of Hebrew
Dept. of Near Eastern Studies
Khedouri A. Zilkha Professorship
 of Jewish Civilization in the
 Near East
Dept. of Religion
Princeton, NJ 08544

Rutgers University—Camden
 Campus
College of Arts & Sciences

Dept. of English
Dept. of History
Dept. of Religion
311 N. Fifth St.,
Camden, NJ 08102

Rutgers University—New
    Brunswick Campus
College of Arts & Sciences
Dept. of Comparative Literature
Dept. of English
Dept. of Hebraic Studies
Dept. of History
Dept. of Philosophy
Dept. of Political Science
Dept. of Religion
Dept. of Yiddish
2 Richardson St., POB 2101,
New Brunswick, NJ 08903

Rutgers University—Newark
    Campus
College of Arts & Sciences
Dept. of English
Dept. of Hebraic Studies
249 University Ave.,
Newark, NJ 07102

Saint Peter's College—Main
    Campus
Dept. of Theology
2641 Kennedy Blvd.,
Jersey City, NJ 07306

Seton Hall University
College of Arts & Sciences
Dept. of Philosophy
Dept. of Religious Studies
Theological Immaculate
    Conception Seminary

Dept. of Biblical Studies
Graduate Dept. of Judeo-Christian
    Studies
400 South Orange Blvd.,
South Orange, NJ 07079

Trenton State College
College of Arts & Sciences
Dept. of English
Dept. of History
Dept. of Religion
Hilwood Lakes, CN 4700,
Trenton, NJ 08650–4700

Upsala College
Dept. of Religion
East Orange, NJ 07019

William Paterson College of New
    Jersey
Dept. of Languages & Cultures
300 Pompton Rd.,
Wayne, NJ 07470

New Mexico

Eastern New Mexico University
College of Arts & Sciences
Dept. of Hebrew
Dept. of Religion
Portales, NM 88130

New Mexico Highlands University
School of Literature & Fine Arts
Dept. of Languages & Literatures
School of International Affairs
Las Vegas, NM 87701

New Mexico State University
College of Arts & Sciences

Dept. of History
Box 3H, Las Cruces, NM 88003

University of New Mexico
College of Arts & Sciences
Dept. of English
Dept. of History
Dept. of Religious Studies
2701 Campus Blvd. NE,
Albuquerque, NM 87131

New York

The Academy for Jewish Religion
Rabbinical Program
15 W. 86th St.,
New York, NY 10024

Adelphi University
College of Arts & Sciences
Dept. of English
Dept. of Religious Studies
Garden City, NY 11530

Alfred University
College of Liberal Arts & Sciences
Dept. of Religion
Alfred, NY 14802

Alliance Theological Seminary
Dept. of Old Testament
122 S. Highland Ave.,
Nyack, NY 10960-4121

Bard College
Dept. of History
Dept. of Religion
Division of Languages &
  Literatures
Annandale-on-Hudson, NY
  12504

Broome Community College
Dept. of Foreign Languages
POB 1017,
Binghamton, NY 13902

Canisius College
Dept. of Religious Studies
2001 Main St.,
Buffalo, NY 14208

Christ the King Seminary
Graduate School of Theology
Dept. of Sacred Scripture
711 Know Rd., POB 607,
East Aurora, NY 14052-0607

City University of New York:

CUNY—Baruch College
School of Liberal Arts & Sciences
Dept. of English
Dept. of Germanic, Hebraic &
  Oriental Languages
Dept. of History
Dept. of Literature in Translation
Dept. of Religion & Culture
Dept. of Yiddish
17 Lexington Ave.,
New York, NY 10010

CUNY—Brooklyn College
College of Arts & Sciences
Dept. of Anthropology &
  Archaeology
Dept. of Art
Dept. of Classics
Dept. of Comparative Literature
Dept. of Education
Dept. of Hebrew & Judaic Studies
Dept. of History

Dept. of Music
Dept. of Modern Languages &
Literatures
Dept. of Political Science
Dept. of Sociology
Dept. of Theater
Dept. of Yiddish
Division of Graduate Studies
Dept. of Judaic Studies
2900 Bedford Ave. & Ave. H,
Brooklyn, NY 11210-2889

CUNY—City College
Division of Humanities
Dept. of Classical Languages &
Hebrew
Dept. of English
Dept. of Jewish Studies
Dept. of History
Convent Ave. at 138th St.,
New York, NY 10031

CUNY—Graduate School &
University Center
Dept. of German
Dept. of History
Institute for Sephardic Studies
33 W. 42nd St.,
New York, NY 10036

CUNY—Hunter College
Dept. of Classical & Oriental
Languages
Division of Hebrew
Jewish Social Studies Program
Dept. of History
Dept. of Literature
Dept. of Political Science
Dept. of Sociology

695 Park Ave.,
New York, NY 10021

CUNY—Herbert H. Lehman
College
Dept. of Classical Languages
Division of Hebraic & Judaic
Studies
Bedford Park Blvd. W.,
Bronx, NY 10468-1589

CUNY—Queens College
Center for Jewish Studies
Harold Proshansky Professorship
of Jewish Studies
Dept. of English
Dept. of Classical & Oriental
Languages
Dept. of History
Dept. of Jewish Social Studies
Dept. of Music
Dept. of Philosophy
Dept. of Religious Studies
Dept. of Romance Languages
Dept. of Sociology
Dept. of Yiddish
65–30 Kissena Blvd.,
Flushing, NY 11367-1597

CUNY—York College
Dept. of Behavioral Science
Dept. of Education
Dept. of English
Dept. of Foreign Languages
Dept. of History
Dept. of Humanities
Dept. of Political Science
Dept. of Yiddish
Jamaica, NY 11451

CUNY—Bronx Community
College
Dept. of English
Dept. of History
University Avenue & W. 181st St.,
Bronx, NY 10453

CUNY—Kingsborough
Community College
Dept. of English
Dept. of Foreign Languages
Dept. of History
Dept. of Literature
Dept. of Yiddish
2001 Oriental Blvd.,
Brooklyn, NY 11235

CUNY—Queensborough
Community College
College of Liberal Arts & Sciences
Dept. of English
Dept. of Foreign Languages
Dept. of History
Dept. of Interdisciplinary Studies
Dept. of Religion
222–05 56 Ave.,
Bayside, NY 11364-1497

Colgate Rochester Divinity School
Division of Biblical Studies
Dept. of Old Testament
110 S. Goodman St.,
Rochester, NY 14620-2592

Colgate University
Dept. of Philosophy & Religion
Humanities Division
Jewish Studies Program
Hebrew Language

13 Oak Drive,
Hamilton, NY 13346-1398

College of Mount Saint Vincent
Dept. of Religious Studies
263rd St. & Riverdale Ave.,
Riverdale, NY 10471

College of New Rochelle
Dept. of English
Dept. of Religious Studies
New Rochelle, NY 10805

Columbia University
Barnard College
Columbia College
Graduate College
Dept. of Aramaic
Dept. of Archaeology
Dept. of Art History
Dept. of English
Dept. of History
Dept. of Linguistics
Dept. of Middle Eastern
Languages & Literatures
Nathan J. Miller Professorship of
Jewish History
Salo Wittmayer Baron
Professorship of Jewish
History, Culture & Society
Leonard Kay Professorship of
Hebrew & Comparative
Literature
Russell & Bettina Knapp
Professorship of American
Jewish History
Dept. of Philosophy
Dept. of Religion & Oriental
Studies

Dept. of Yiddish
Atran Professorship of Yiddish
   Language, Literature & Culture
University Seminars
3009 Broadway,
New York, NY 10027-6598

Concordia College
Division of History, Languages &
   Religion
Bronxville, NY 10708

Cornell University
College of Arts & Sciences
Dept. of Classics
Dept. of Comparative Literature
Dept. of German Studies
Dept. of History
Dept. of Near Eastern Studies
Program of Jewish Studies
Ithaca, NY 14853-2502

Graduate School
Dept. of Near Eastern Studies
Sage Graduate Center,
Ithaca, NY 14853-6201

Elmira College
Dept. of Philosophy
Park Place, Elmira, NY 14901

Fordham University
Dept. of Anthropology
Dept. of Art History
Dept. of Economics
Dept. of English & Comparative
   Literature
Dept. of Languages
Dept. of History
Dept. of Literature

Dept. of Middle Eastern Studies
Dept. of Philosophy
Dept. of Political Science
Dept. of Religion
Division of Theology
Rose Hill Campus, Fordham Rd.,
Bronx, NY 10458

Division of Humanities—Lincoln
   Center
Middle East Studies Program
   (departments listed above)
Lincoln Center, 113 W. 60 St.,
New York, NY 10023-7475

General Theological Seminary
Biblical Department
175 Ninth Ave.,
New York, NY 10011

Hamilton College
Dept. of Religion
Chair in Jewish Studies
Clinton, NY 13323

Hebrew Union College—Jewish
   Institute of Religion
Dept. of Hebrew Language
1 W. 4th St.,
New York, NY 10012-1186

Hilbert College
Dept. of English
Dept. of Religious Studies
Hamburg, NY 14076

Hobart and William Smith
   Colleges
Dept. of Religious Studies
Geneva, NY 14456-3397

Hofstra University
College of Liberal Arts & Sciences
Dept. of Comparative Literature
Dept. of English
Dept. of History
Dept. of Jewish Studies
Dept. of Literature in Translation
Hempstead, Long Island,
 NY 11550

Houghton College
College of Liberal Arts & Sciences
Dept. of Bible
Dept. of Hebrew
Division of Languages &
 Literatures
Houghton, NY 14744

Institute of Traditional Judaism
261 E. Lincoln Ave.,
Mt. Vernon, NY 10552

Iona College
Dept. of Religion
715 North Avenue,
New Rochelle, NY 10801

Ithaca College
School of Humanities & Sciences
Dept. of Modern Languages &
 Literatures
Dept. of Philosophy & Religion
Ithaca, NY 14850

Jewish Theological Seminary of
 America
Dept. of Bible
Dept. of Hebrew Language
Dept. of History
Dept. of Jewish Education

Dept. of Jewish Literature
Dept. of Philosophy
Dept. of Talmud
Program in Arts & Jewish
 Material Culture
Program in Ancient Judaism
Program in Liturgy
Program in Medieval Judaism
Program in Modern Jewish
 Studies
3080 Broadway,
New York, NY 10027-4649

King's College
Dept. of Religion & Philosophy
Biblical Languages
Briarcliff Manor, NY 10510

Le Moyne College
Dept. of Hebrew
Dept. of Religious Studies
Syracuse, NY 13214-1399

Long Island University—Brooklyn
 Campus
College of Liberal Arts & Sciences
Dept. of History
Dept. of Sociology
University Plaza,
Brooklyn, NY 11201-5372

Long Island University—C.W.
 Post Campus
College of Liberal Arts & Sciences
Dept. of English
Dept. of Foreign Languages
Dept. of History
Dept. of Religious Philosophy
Brookville, Long Island,
 NY 11548

Manhattan College
Dept. of Religious Studies
Manhattan College Parkway,
Riverdale, NY 10471

Marist College
Jewish Studies Program
290 North Rd.,
Poughkeepsie, NY 12601-1387

Marymount Manhattan College
Dept. of English
Dept. of History
Dept. of Religious Studies
221 E. 71st St.,
New York, NY 10021

Mercy College—Dobbs Ferry
Dept. of English
Dept. of Religion
555 Broadway,
Dobbs Ferry, NY 10522

Mohawk Valley Community
    College
Dept. of Humanities
Foreign Languages
Utica, NY 13502

Molloy College
Dept. of Theology
1000 Hempstead Ave.,
Rockville Centre, NY 11570

Nassau Community College
Dept. of English
Dept. of Foreign Languages
Dept. of History
Garden City, NY 11530-6793

New School for Social Research
Dept. of Philosophy

66 W. 12th St.,
New York, NY 10011

New York Institute of Technology
Dept. of English
Dept. of Social Studies
Old Westbury, NY 11568-0170

New York Theological Seminary
Dept. of Biblical Studies
Biblical Languages
5 W. 29th St.,
New York, NY 10001

New York University
Faculty of Arts & Sciences
Dept. of Anthropology
Dept. of History
Dept. of Liberal Studies
Dept. of Near Eastern Languages
    & Literatures
Dept. of Performance Studies
Dept. of Politics
Dept. of Religious Studies
Washington Square,
New York, NY 10012

Skirball Dept. of Hebrew &
    Judaic Studies
Abraham I. Katsh Professorship of
    Hebrew Education & Culture
Ethel & Irvin A. Edelman
    Professorship in Hebrew &
    Judaic Studies
Scheuer Professorship of Hebrew
    & Judaic Studies
Skirball Professorship of Jewish
    Thought
Skirball Professorship of Modern
    Jewish History

51 Washington Square S.,
New York, NY 10012

Niagara University
College of Arts & Sciences
Dept. of History
Dept. of Political Science
Dept. of Religious Studies
Dept. of Sociology
Niagara Falls, NY 14109

Nyack College
Dept. of Bible
Dept. of Theology
Nyack, NY 10960

Pace University
College of Arts & Sciences
Dept. of English
Dept. of Hebrew
Dept. of History
Dept. of Religious Studies
Pace Plaza, New York, NY 10038

Rockland Community College
Dept. of Foreign Languages
Dept. of Jewish Studies
145 College Rd.,
Suffern, NY 10901

Russell Sage College
Dept. of English
Dept. of Values & Consequences
45 Ferry St., Troy, NY 12180

Saint Francis College
Dept. of Religious Studies
180 Remson St.,
Brooklyn Heights, NY 11201

Saint John's University—New
York

College of Liberal Arts & Sciences
Hebrew Program
Grand Central & Utopia
    Parkways, Jamaica, NY 11439

Saint Lawrence University
Dept. of Hebrew
Dept. of History
Dept. of Religious Studies &
    Classical Languages
Canton, NY 13617

Saint Vladimir's Orthodox
    Seminary
Dept. of Biblical Studies
474 Scarsdale Rd.,
Crestwood, NY 10707-1699

Sarah Lawrence College
Dept. of History
Bronxville, NY 10708

Seminary of the Immaculate
    Conception
Master of Divinity Program
M.A. in Theology Program
440 West Neck Rd.,
Huntington, NY 11743

Siena College
Dept. of Religious Studies
Institute for Jewish-Christian
    Studies
515 Loudon Rd.,
Loudonville, NY 12211-1462

State University of New York:

SUNY—Albany
College of Arts & Sciences
Dept. of English

Dept. of History
Dept. of Judaic & Near Eastern
    Studies
Dept. of Spanish
1400 Washington Ave.,
Albany, NY 12222

SUNY—Binghamton
College of Arts & Sciences
Dept. of Classical & Near Eastern
    Studies
Dept. of English
Dept. of History
Dept. of Judaic Studies
Dept. of Political Science
Dept. of Yiddish
Binghamton, NY 13901

SUNY—Cortland
College of Arts & Sciences
Dept. of English
Dept. of History
Dept. of Interdisciplinary Studies
Cortland, NY 13045

SUNY—Stony Brook
College of Arts & Sciences
Dept. of Comparative Literature
Program of Judaic Studies
Dept. of English
Dept. of Political Science
Dept. of Religious Studies
Stony Brook, NY 11794-3355

SUNY College—Brockport
Jewish Studies Program
Dept. of English
Dept. of Foreign Languages &
    Literatures
Dept. of History

Dept. of Political Science
Dept. of Psychology
Brockport, NY 14420

SUNY College—Buffalo
Dept. of Foreign Languages
Hebrew Program
1300 Elmwood Ave.,
Buffalo, NY 14222-1095

SUNY College—New Paltz
Dept. of English
Dept. of Foreign Languages
Dept. of History
Dept. of Political Science
Dept. of Yiddish
New Paltz, NY 12561

SUNY College—Old Westbury
Dept. of Comparative Humanities
Old Westbury, NY 11568

SUNY College—Oneonta
Dept. of English
Dept. of Foreign Languages
Dept. of History
Dept. of International Studies
Dept. of Political Science
Oneonta, NY 13820-1361

SUNY College—Purchase
Dept. of Anthropology
Dept. of History
Dept. of Languages & Cultures
Dept. of Literature
735 Anderson Hill Rd.,
Purchase, NY 10577

Stern College
245 Lexington Ave.
New York, NY 10016-4699

Syracuse University
College of Arts & Sciences
Jewish Studies Program
Dept. of Anthropology
Dept. of Art Media Studies
Dept. of English & Textual
  Studies
Dept. of Fine Arts
Dept. of Foreign Languages &
  Literatures
Dept. of History
Dept. of Philosophy
Dept. of Political Science
Dept. of Public Affairs
Dept. of Religion
B.G. Rudolph Chair in Judaic
  Studies
Dept. of Sociology
Syracuse, NY 13244

Touro College
Dept. of Judaic Studies
27-33 W. 23rd St.,
New York, NY 10010-4202

Jacob D. Fuchberger Law Center
Institute of Jewish Law
300 Nassau Rd.,
Huntington, NY 11743

Touro Women's College
160 Lexington Ave.,
New York, NY 10016

Union College
Dept. of English
Dept. of History
Dept. of Modern Languages &
  Literatures

Dept. of Political Science
Schenectady, NY 12308

Union Theological Seminary
Biblical Field
Dept. of Old Testament
3061 Broadway,
New York, NY 10027

University of Rochester
College of Arts & Sciences
Dept. of Hebrew
Dept. of Rarely Taught Languages
Dept. of Religion & Classics
Dept. of Women's Studies
Wilson Blvd.,
Rochester, NY 14267

Vassar College
Dept. of Religion
Poughkeepsie, NY 12601

Wells College
Dept. of Religion
Dept. of Religious Studies &
  Human Values
Aurora, NY 13026

Yeshiva University
Bernard Revel Graduate School
Graduate Institute of Jewish
  Education & Administration
Harry Fischel School for Higher
  Jewish Studies
Isaac Breuer College of Hebraic
  Studies
James Striar School of General
  Jewish Studies
Mazer School of Talmudic Studies

Yeshiva College
500 W. 185 St.,
New York, NY 10033-3299

North Carolina

Appalachian State University
Dept. of Philosophy & Religion
Boone, NC 28608

Belmont Abbey College
Dept. of Modern & Classical
  Languages & Literatures
Belmont, NC 28012

Davidson College
Dept. of Religion
Davidson, NC 28036

Duke University
Faculty of Arts & Sciences
Dept. of English
Dept. of Hebrew
Smart Family Professorship in
  Judaic Studies
Lerner Professorship of Judaic
  Studies
Dept. of History
Dept. of Political Science
Dept. of Religion
Dept. of Yiddish
Divinity School
Dept. of Biblical Studies
Durham, NC 27706

Elon College
Dept. of Religion
Elon, NC 27244

Greensboro College
Dept. of Religion
815 W. Market St.,
Greensboro, NC 27401-1875

John Wesley College
Division of Biblical Studies/
  Theology
Dept. of Biblical Languages
2314 N. Centennial St.,
High Point, NC 27260

Mars Hill College
Division of Humanities
Dept. of Religion & Philosophy
Mars Hill, NC 28754

Southeastern Baptist Theological
  Seminary
Dept. of Biblical Studies
POB 1889,
Wake Forest, NC 27587-1889

University of North Carolina—
  Asheville
Dept. of Classics
1 University Heights,
Asheville, NC 28804-3299

University of North Carolina—
  Chapel Hill
College of Arts & Sciences
Dept. of Classics
Dept. of English
Dept. of Political Science
Dept. of Religious Studies
Chapel Hill, NC 27599

University of North Carolina—
  Charlotte

College of Arts & Sciences
Dept. of Foreign Languages
Dept. of Religious Studies
Charlotte, NC 28223

University of North Carolina at
Greensboro
College of Arts & Sciences
Dept. of Religious Studies
Greensboro, NC 27412-5001

University of North Carolina—
North Carolina State University
College of Humanities & Social
Sciences
Dept. of Hebrew Language &
Literature
Dept. of Religion
NCSU POB 7505,
Raleigh, NC 27695

Wake Forest University
Dept. of English
Dept. of Hebrew
Dept. of Politics
Dept. of Religion
7305 Reynolds Station, Box 7205,
Winston-Salem, NC 27109

North Dakota

North Dakota State University
Faculty of Humanities & Social
Sciences
Dept. of Hebrew
Dept. of Religion
Cardinal Muench Seminary
Fargo, ND 58105

Ohio

Antioch College
Dept. of Philosophy
Yellow Springs, OH 45387

Ashland Theological Seminary
Dept. of Biblical Studies
910 Center St.,
Ashland, OH 44805-4099

Athenaeum of Ohio/Mount St.
Mary's Seminary
Seminary Division
Dept. of Language Studies
6616 Beechmont Ave.,
Cincinnati, OH 45230

Baldwin-Wallace College
Dept. of Religion
275 Eastland Rd.,
Berea, OH 44017-2088

Bowling Green State University
College of Arts & Sciences
Dept. of English
Dept. of History
Bowling Green, OH 43403

Capital University
College of Arts & Sciences
Dept. of Religion
East Main St.,
Columbus, OH 43209

Case Western Reserve University
Faculty of Arts & Sciences
Dept. of Religion
Abba Hillel Silver Chair in Jewish
Studies

10900 Euclid Ave.,
Cleveland, OH 44106-7112

Cedarville College
Dept. of Biblical Education
Box 601, Cincinnati, OH 45314

Cincinnati Bible College &
Seminary
Division of Biblical Studies
2700 Glenway Ave., POB 04320,
Cincinnati, OH 45204-3200

Cincinnati Bible Seminary
Biblical Studies Field
2700 Glenway Ave.,
Cincinnati, OH 45204-3200

Cleveland College of Jewish
Studies
Cleveland Fellows Program
Hebrew Studies Program
Jewish Communal Service
Program
Judaic Studies Program
Dept. of Hebrew Language
26500 Shaker Blvd.,
Cleveland, OH 44122-7197

Cleveland State University
College of Arts & Sciences
Dept. of English
Dept. of Religious Studies
Euclid Ave. & E. 24th St.,
Cleveland, OH 44115

College of Wooster
Dept. of Religious Studies
Wooster, OH 44691

Cuyahoga Community College
Dept. of Hebrew

700 Carnegie Ave.,
Cleveland, OH 44115

Denison University
Dept. of English
Dept. of Religion
Granville, OH 43023-0603

Hebrew Union College—Jewish
Institute of Religion
Dept. of Bible & Ancient Near
East Studies
Dept. of Hebrew, Cognate &
Oriental Languages
Dept. of Hebrew Literature
Dept. of History
Dept. of Jewish Studies in the
Greco-Roman Period *(with the
Univ. of Cincinnati)*
Dept. of Linguistics
Dept. of Liturgy
Dept. of Modern Hebrew
Literature
Dept. of Music
Dept. of Philosophy & Theology
Dept. of Practical Rabbinics
Dept. of Rabbinics
School of Graduate Studies
3101 Clifton Ave.,
Cincinnati, OH 45220-2488

Hiram College
Dept. of Religious Studies
Hiram, OH 44234

John Carroll University
College of Arts & Sciences
Dept. of Classical & Modern
Languages
Dept. of Religious Studies

20700 N. Park Blvd.,
University Heights, OH 44118

Kent State University
College of Arts & Sciences
Dept. of German
Dept. of Classical Studies
Dept. of History
Kent, OH 44242

Kenyon College
Dept. of Classics
Dept. of Interdisciplinary Courses
Dept. of Religion
Gambier, OH 43022-9623

Lourdes College
Dept. of Religious Studies
Sylvania, OH 43560

Marietta College
Dept. of Religion
Marietta, OH 45750

Methodist Theological School in
   Ohio
Biblical Studies
3081 Columbus Pike,
Delaware, OH 43015

Miami University
College of Arts & Sciences
Dept. of Classics
Dept. of Religion
Oxford, OH 45056

Mount Vernon Nazarene College
Division of Religion & Philosophy
Biblical Languages
800 Martinsburg Rd.,
Mount Vernon, OH 43050-9987

Oberlin College
College of Arts & Sciences
Dept. of History
Dept. of Religion
Judaic & Near Eastern Studies
   Program
Oberlin, OH 44074

Ohio State University
College of Humanities
Dept. of History
Dept. of Judaic Studies
Samuel & Esther Melton Chair of
   Jewish History
Hebrew Language Program
Dept. of Near Eastern & Hellenic
   Languages & Literatures
Dept. of Philosophy
Dept. of Sociology
Dept. of Yiddish
Melton Center for Jewish Studies
230 W. 17th Ave.,
Columbus, OH 43210-1311

Ohio University
College of Arts & Sciences
Dept. of English
Dept. of History
Athens, OH 45701

Payne Theological Seminary
Dept. of Bible
POB 474, Wilberforce, OH 45384

Pontifical College Josephinum
College of Liberal Arts & Sciences
Dept. of Foreign Languages
7625 N. High St.,
Columbus, OH 43235

Temple Baptist College
Dept. of Biblical Education
Dept. of Biblical Languages
65 Kenn Rd.,
Cincinnati, OH 45240

Trinity Lutheran Seminary
Dept. of Biblical Studies
2199 E. Main St.
Columbus, OH 43209

United Theological Seminary
Dept. of Biblical Studies
1810 Harvard Blvd.
Dayton, OH 45406

University of Cincinnati
McMicken College of Arts &
 Sciences
Dept. of Judaic Studies
Cincinnati, OH 45221-0169

University of Dayton
College of Arts & Sciences
Dept. of Philosophy
Dept. of Religious Studies
300 College Park,
Dayton, OH 45469-0001

University of Toledo
College of Arts & Sciences
Dept. of English
Dept. of History
Dept. of Philosophy
Toledo, OH 43606-3390

Ursuline College
Dept. of Jewish Studies *(with
 Cleveland College of Jewish
 Studies)*

2550 Lander Rd.,
Pepper Pike, OH 44124

Winebrenner Theological
 Seminary
Dept. of Biblical Studies
701 E. Melrose, POB 478,
Findlay, OH 45839

Wittenberg University
Dept. of Religion
N. Wittenberg Ave.,
Springfield, OH 45501

Wright State University
College of Liberal Arts
Dept. of History
Dept. of Religion
Colonel Glenn Highway,
Dayton, OH 45435

Xavier University
College of Arts & Sciences
Dept. of English
Dept. of Theology
3800 Victory Parkway,
Cincinnati, OH 45207-4442

Oklahoma

Oklahoma City University
Wimberly School of Religion &
 Church Vocations
2501 N. Blackwelder,
Oklahoma City, OK 73106

Oklahoma State University
College of Arts & Sciences
Dept. of Religious Studies
Stillwater, OK 74078

Oral Roberts University
School of Theology & Missions
Dept. of Biblical Literature
Modern Hebrew Program
Graduate School of Theology
Area I—Biblical Literature
7777 S. Lewis Ave.,
Tulsa, OK 74171

Phillips University
Hebrew Program
Enid, OK 73702

Southern Nazarene University
Dept. of Biblical Languages
Dept. of Religion
6729 NW 39th Expressway,
Bethany, OK 73008

University of Oklahoma
College of Arts & Sciences
Dept. of Classical Studies
Dept. of Hebrew
660 Parrington Oval,
Norman, OK 73019

University of Tulsa
Faculty of Arts & Sciences
Dept. of Hebrew
Dept. of Religion
600 S. College Ave.,
Tulsa, OK 74104

Oregon

Columbia Christian College
Division of Bible & Religion
9101 E. Burnside,
Portland, OR 97216-1515

Concordia College
Dept. of Religion
Dept. of Classical Languages
2811 NE Holman,
Portland, OR 97211-6099

Eugene Bible College
Dept. of Biblical Education
2155 Bailey Hill Rd.,
Eugene, OR 97405

Lewis and Clark College
Dept. of History
Dept. of Religious Studies
Portland, OR 97219

Mount Angel Seminary
Dept. of Sacred Scripture
St. Benedict, OR 97373

Multnomah College & Biblical
Seminary
Dept. of Bible
8435 NE Glisan St.,
Portland, OR 97220-5898

Northwest Christian College
Dept. of Languages
828 E. 11th Ave.,
Eugene, OR 97401-9983

Portland State University
College of Liberal Arts & Sciences
Dept. of English Literature
Dept. of Geography & History
Dept. of Middle Eastern Studies
Dept. of Political Sciences
International Studies Program
POB 751,
Portland, OR 97207-0751

Reed College
Dept. of Religion
Moe & Izetta Tonkon
    Professorship in Judaic Studies
3203 SE Woodstock Blvd.,
Portland, OR 97202-8199

University of Oregon
College of Arts & Sciences
Dept. of Anthropology
Dept. of Classics
Dept. of English
Dept. of Religious Studies
Eugene, OR 97403

Western Evangelical Seminary
Graduate School of Theology
Dept. of Biblical Studies
POB 23939,
Portland, OR 97281-3939

Western Seminary
Dept. of Biblical Literature
Old Testament Languages &
    Literatures
5511 SE Hawthorne Blvd.,
Portland, OR 97215

Willamette University
Dept. of Religion
900 State St., Salem, OR 97301

Pennsylvania

Academy of the New Church
Division of Religion & Sacred
    Languages
Bryn Athyn, PA 19009

Albright College
Dept. of Modern Foreign
    Languages & Literatures
Reading, PA 19612-5234

Allegheny College
Dept. of History
Dept. of Modern Languages
Dept. of Religious Studies
North Main, Meadville, PA 16335

Allentown College of St. Francis
    de Sales
Center Valley, PA 18034
*(in cooperation with the Berman
    Center, Lehigh University)*

Baptist Bible Seminary
Dept. of Old Testament
POB 800,
Clarks Summit, PA 18411

Biblical Theological Seminary
Dept. of Old Testament
200 N. Main St.,
Hatfield, PA 19440

Bryn Mawr College
Dept. of Classical & Near Eastern
    Archaeology
Dept. of History of Religion
Dept. of Philosophy
Dept. of Religion
Bryn Mawr, PA 19010-2899

Bucknell University
College of Arts & Sciences
Dept. of English
Dept. of Religion

Hebrew Program
Lewisburg, PA 17387

Carnegie-Mellon University
College of Humanities & Social
  Sciences
Interdisciplinary Program
Dept. of History
5000 Forbes Ave.,
Pittsburgh, PA 15213-3890

Cedar Crest College
Allentown, PA 18104-6196
*(in cooperation with the Berman
  Center, Lehigh University)*

Chatham College
Dept. of Religion
Woodland Rd.,
Pittsburgh, PA 15232

Community College of Allegheny
  County
Division of Humanities
Dept. of Foreign Languages
Pittsburgh, PA

Community College of
  Philadelphia
Dept. of Hebrew
1700 Spring Garden St.,
Philadelphia, PA 19130

Dickinson College
Dept. of Classical Studies
Dept. of History
Dept. of Religion
Jewish Studies Program
Carlisle, PA 17013-2896

Drexel University
Dept. of Sociology &
  Anthropology
32nd & Chestnut Sts.,
Philadelphia, PA 19104

Duquesne University
Core Courses Program
Dept. of Classics
Dept. of Theology
600 Forbes Ave.,
Pittsburgh, PA 15282

Eastern Baptist Theological
  Seminary
Dept. of Biblical Studies
6 Lancaster Ave.,
Wynnewood, PA 19096

Eastern College
Dept. of Religion
St. Davids, PA 19087

Evangelical School of Theology
Division of Biblical Studies
Dept. of Old Testament
121 S. College St.,
Myerstown, PA 17067

Franklin & Marshall College
Dept. of English
Dept. of History
Dept. of Religious Studies
POB 3003,
Lancaster, PA 17601-3003

Gratz College
Undergraduate & Graduate
  Programs in Jewish Studies

Graduate Program in Jewish
Liberal Studies
Graduate Program in Jewish
Education
Graduate Program in Jewish
Music
Joint Graduate Program in Jewish
Education *(with the
Reconstructionist Rabbinical
College)*
Joint Graduate Program in
Jewish Communal Service *(with
the University of Pennsylvania)*
Joint Graduate Program in Judaic
Librarianship *(with Drexel
University)*
Old York Rd. & Melrose Ave.,
Melrose Park, PA 19126

Gwynedd-Mercy College
Dept. of Religious Studies
Gwynedd Valley, PA 19437

Haverford College
General Program
Dept. of Religion
Haverford, PA 19041

King's College
Dept. of Theology
Wilkes-Barre, PA 18711-0801

Lafayette College
Dept. of English
Dept. of Languages
Dept. of History
Dept. of Religion
Jewish Studies Program *(in
cooperation with the Berman
Center, Lehigh University)*

Philip & Muriel Berman
Professorship of Jewish Studies
Easton, PA 18042

La Salle University
Dept. of Religion
20th St. & Olney Ave.,
Philadelphia, PA 19141

Lehigh University
College of Arts & Sciences
Dept. of Modern Languages &
Literatures
Dept. of Religion
Philip & Muriel Berman Chair of
Jewish Civilization
Philip & Muriel Berman Chair of
Jewish Studies
Dept. of Philosophy
Dept. of Urban Studies
Philip & Muriel Berman Center
for Jewish Studies
9 W. Packer Ave.,
Bethlehem, PA 18015-3082

Lutheran Theological Seminary
Division of Biblical Studies
Gettysburg, PA 17325

Lutheran Theological Seminary at
Philadelphia
Biblical Area
Dept. of Old Testament
7301 Germantown Ave.,
Philadelphia, PA 19119-1794

Lycoming College
Dept. of Foreign Languages &
Literatures
Biblical Languages
Williamsport, PA 17701

Mary Immaculate Seminary
Biblical Department
Northampton, PA 18067

Marywood College
Dept. of Religious Studies
Dept. of Religious Education
2300 Adams Ave.,
Scranton, PA 18509

Messiah College
Dept. of Bible
Dept. of Cross-Cultural Studies
Dept. of Hebrew
Dept. of Integrated Studies
Grantham, PA 17027

Millersville University of
  Pennsylvania
Dept. of English
Dept. of History
Millersville, PA 17551

Moravian College
*(in cooperation with the Berman
  Center, Lehigh University)*
Dept. of Classical Languages
Dept. of Religion & Philosophy
Bethlehem, PA 18018

Moravian Theological Seminary
Dept. of Biblical Old Testament
60 W. Locus St.,
Bethlehem, PA 18018

Muhlenberg College
Dept. of Foreign Languages &
  Literatures
Dept. of Religion & Jewish
  Studies *(in cooperation with the
  Berman Center, Lehigh
  University)*
24th & Chew Sts.,
Allentown, PA 18104-5586

Northeastern Church Junior
  College
Biblical Studies Division
1860 Montgomery Ave.,
Villanova, PA 19085

Pennsylvania State University
College of the Liberal Arts
Dept. of Anthropology
Dept. of Comparative Literature
Hebrew Language Program
Jewish Studies Program
Endowed Chair in Jewish Studies
Mitrani Professorship of Jewish
  Life & Literature
103 Weaver,
University Park, PA 16802-5500

Philadelphia College of the Bible
Division of General Education
Dept. of Missions
Jewish Missions Program
Langhorne Manor,
Langhorne, PA 19047

Pittsburgh Theological Seminary
Studies in Bible
Studies in Biblical Languages
616 N. Highland Ave.,
Pittsburgh, PA 15206-2596

Reconstructionist Rabbinical
  College
Rabbinical Seminary Program
2308 North Broad St.,
Philadelphia, PA 19132

Reformed Episcopal Seminary
Dept. of Old Testament & New
   Testament Languages &
   Literatures
4225 Chestnut St.,
Philadelphia, PA 19104

Reformed Presbyterian
   Theological Seminary
Dept. of Biblical Studies
7418 Penn Ave.,
Pittsburgh, PA 15208

Rosemont College
Dept. of History
Dept. of Religious Studies
Rosemont, PA 19010

Saint Joseph's University
Dept. of Theology
5600 City Ave.,
Philadelphia, PA 19131-1395

Saint Vincent College
Dept. of Religious Studies
Latrobe, PA 15650-2690

Saint Vincent Seminary
School of Theology
Scripture Area
Latrobe, PA 15650-2690

Seton Hill College
The National Catholic Center for
   Holocaust Education
Greensburg, PA 15601

Slippery Rock University
College of Arts & Sciences
Dept. of History
Slippery Rock, PA 16057

Swarthmore College
Dept. of History
Dept. of Political Science
Dept. of Religion
500 College Ave.,
Swarthmore, PA 19081

Temple University
College of Arts & Sciences
Dept. of Hebrew & Near Eastern
   Languages
Dept. of History
Dept. of Political Science
Dept. of Religion
Jewish Studies Minor
Broad St. & Montgomery Ave.,
Philadelphia, PA 19122

United Wesleyan College
Division of Bible & Theology
141 E. Cedar St.,
Allentown, PA 18103

University of Pennsylvania
School of Arts & Sciences
Jewish Studies Program:
Dept. of Asian & Middle Eastern
   Studies
A.M. Ellis Chair in Hebrew &
   Semitic Languages &
   Literatures
Dept. of English
Dept. of Folklore & Folklife
Dept. of Germanic Languages &
   Literature
Dept. of History
Joseph Meyerhoff Professorship of
   Modern Jewish History
Dept. of Political Science

Dept. of Religious Studies
Moritz & Josephine Berg
　Professorship for Teaching
　Religious Studies
Dept. of Sociology
Law Schools
Caroline Zelaznik Gruss &
　Joseph S. Gruss Chair in
　Talmudic Civil Law
Penn Language Center
Hebrew Program
University Museum
James B. Pritchard Professorship
　of Biblical Archaeology
Philadelphia, PA 19104-6305

Center for Judaic Studies
(Merger of Annenberg Institute
　with School of Arts & Sciences)
420 Walnut St.,
Philadelphia, PA 19106

University of Pittsburgh
College of Arts & Sciences
Dept. of Religious Studies
Jewish Studies Program
4200 Fifth Ave.,
Pittsburgh, PA 15260-0001

University of Scranton
College of Arts & Sciences
Dept. of English
Dept. of Theology & Religious
　Studies
Scranton, PA 18510-4699

Valley Forge Christian College
Graduate Education Division
Language Program

Charleston Rd.,
Phoenixville, PA 19460

Villanova University
College of Arts & Sciences
Dept. of History
Dept. of Library Science
Dept. of Religious Studies
Villanova, PA 19085

West Chester University
College of Arts & Sciences
Dept. of English
Dept. of Foreign Languages
Dept. of History
Dept. of Philosophy
West Chester, PA 19383

Westminster Theological Seminary
Field of Biblical Studies
Dept. of Old Testament
POB 27009,
Philadelphia, PA 19118

York College
Dept. of Foreign Languages
York, PA 17403-3426

Rhode Island

Brown University
Dept. of Classics
Dept. of English
Dept. of Religion
Judaic Studies Program
Samuel Ungerleider Jr. Chair in
　Judaic Studies
Dorot Assistant Professorships of
　Judaic Studies

79 Waterman St., Box 1826,
Providence, RI 02912

Providence College
Dept. of Religious Studies
Providence, RI 02918

University of Rhode Island
College of Arts & Sciences
Dept. of English
Dept. of Hebrew
Dept. of History
Dept. of Political Science
Kingston, RI 02881

South Carolina

Bob Jones University
College of Arts & Sciences
Foreign Languages & Literatures
    Division
1700 Wade Hampton Blvd.,
Greenville, SC 29614

Claflin College
Dept. of Religion & Philosophy
Orangeburg, SC 29115

College of Charleston
Jewish Studies Program
Charleston, SC 29424-0001

Columbia Bible College
Dept. of Biblical Languages
POB 3122, Columbia, SC 29230

Columbia Biblical Seminary
Dept. of Biblical Languages
POB 3122, Columbia, SC 29230

Lutheran Theological Southern
    Seminary
Dept. of Biblical Studies
4201 N. Main St.,
Columbia, SC 29203

Presbyterian College
Dept. of Hebrew & Greek
Dept. of Religion
Clinton, SC 29325

University of South Carolina
College of Humanities
Dept. of Foreign Languages &
    Literatures
Dept. of Religious Studies
Columbia, SC 29208

South Dakota

North American Baptist Seminary
Biblical Studies
1321 W. 22nd St.,
Sioux Falls, SD 57105-1599

Tennessee

American Baptist College
Division of Biblical & Theological
    Studies
1800 White Creek Pike,
Nashville, TN 37207

Carson-Newman College
Humanities Division
Dept. of Foreign Languages
1646 Russell Ave.,
Jefferson City, TN 37760

David Lipscomb University
Dept. of Bible
Dept. of Hebrew
Nashville, TN 37204-3951

Emmanuel School of Religion
Dept. of Old Testament
1 Walker Dr.,
Johnson City, TN 37601-9438

Freed-Hardeman College
Dept. of Bible
Henderson, TN 38340

Harding Graduate School of
  Religion
Biblical Division
Old Testament Area
1000 Cherry Rd.,
Memphis, TN 38117

Lambuth College
College of Humanities
Dept. of Religion
Lambuth Blvd.,
Jackson, TN 38301

Memphis State University
Bornblum Chair of Excellence in
  Judaic Studies
Bornblum Professorship in Jewish
  Studies
Memphis, TN 38152

Memphis Theological Seminary
Biblical Studies Division
168 E. Parkway S.,
Memphis, TN 38104

Mid-America Baptist Theological
  Seminary

Dept. of Old Testament &
  Hebrew
1255 Poplar Ave.,
Memphis, TN 38104

Milligan College
Area of Humane Learning
Dept. of Foreign Languages
Milligan College, TN 37682

Southern College of Seventh-Day
  Adventists
Dept. of Religion
Biblical Studies
Biblical Languages
POB 370,
Collegedale, TN 37315-0370

University of the South
College of Arts & Sciences
School of Theology
Dept. of Religion
Dept. of Old Testament
Sewanee, TN 37375-4001

University of Tennessee—
  Knoxville
College of Liberal Arts
Dept. of Asian Studies
Dept. of Religious Studies
Judaic Studies Program
Knoxville, TN 37996-0450

Vanderbilt University
College of Arts & Sciences
Dept. of Fine Arts
Dept. of History
Dept. of Religious Studies
Nashville, TN 37240

Divinity School
113 D.S. Quad,
Nashville, TN 37240

Graduate School
Dept. of Religion
West End Ave.,
Nashville, TN 37240-2701

Texas

Abilene Christian University
College of Biblical Studies
Dept. of Bible & Ministry
ACU Station Box 6000,
Abilene, TX 79699-6000

Graduate School
College of Biblical Studies
Dept. of Bible
ACU Station Box 8108,
Abilene, TX 79699-6000

Arlington Baptist College
Dept. of Bible & Theology
3001 W. Division,
Abilene, TX 76012

Baylor University
College of Arts & Sciences
Dept. of Religion
Dept. of Hebrew
POB 97824, Waco, TX 76798

Concordia Lutheran College
Hebrew Program
Austin, TX 78705

Criswell College
Dept. of General Studies
Dept. of Hebrew

Dept. of Old Testament
Dept. of Theological & Historical
  Studies
4010 Gaston Ave.,
Dallas, TX 75246

Dallas Christian College
Hebrew Program
2700 Christian Parkway,
Dallas, TX 75234-7299

Dallas Theological Seminary
Division of Biblical Studies
Dept. of Old Testament Studies
3909 Swiss Ave.
Dallas, TX 75204

Episcopal Theological Seminary of
  the Southwest
Biblical Studies
606 Rathervue Place, POB 2247,
Austin, TX 78768-2247

Hardin-Simmons University
School of Theology
Dept. of Biblical Studies
Abilene, TX 79698

Howard Payne University
School of Christianity
Dept. of Biblical Languages
Brownwood, TX 76801

Lubbock Christian University
College of Liberal Arts & Sciences
Dept. of Biblical Studies
5601 19th St.,
Lubbock, TX 79407-2099

Oblate School of Theology
Dept. of Scriptural Studies

285 Oblate Dr.,
San Antonio, TX 78216-6693

Rice University
Faculty of Humanities
Dept. of History
Dept. of Religious Studies
Anna Smith Fine Chair in Judaic
  Studies
POB 1892, Houston, TX 77251

St. Mary's University
School of Humanities
Dept. of Theology
One Camino Santa Maria,
San Antonio, TX 78228

San Antonio College
Dept. of Foreign Languages
1300 San Pedro Ave.,
San Antonio, TX 78284

Southern Methodist University
Perkins School of Theology
Division I: The Biblical Witness
Dallas, TX 75275

Southwestern Adventist College
Dept. of Religion
Keene, TX 76059

Southwestern Baptist Theological
  Seminary
School of Theology
Dept. of Old Testament
POB 22000,
2001 W. Seminary Dr.,
Fort Worth, TX 76122

Southwestern Christian College
College of Arts & Sciences

Division of Bible & Related
  Subjects
POB 10, Terrell, TX 75160

Texarkana College
Hebrew Program
2500 N. Robinson Rd.,
Texarkana, TX 75501

Texas Christian University
Brite Divinity School
Dept. of Old Testament
Add Ran College of Arts &
  Sciences
Dept. of English
Dept. of Religious Studies
2800 University Drive,
Fort Worth, TX 76129

Texas Lutheran College
College of Humanities
Dept. of Classical Languages
Seguin, TX 78155

Trinity University
Dept. of English
Dept. of Foreign Languages
Dept. of Religion
715 Stadium Drive,
San Antonio, TX 78212

University of Houston
Dept. of Hebrew
Houston, TX 77024-2162

University of St. Thomas
Dept. of Theology
3812 Montrose Blvd.,
Houston, TX 77006

University of Texas—Austin
College of Liberal Arts & Sciences

Dept. of English
Dept. of Middle Eastern Studies
Dept. of Oriental & African
 Languages & Literature
Jewish Studies Program
Gale Chair in Judaic Studies
Dept. of Slavic Languages
Austin, TX 78712-1157

University of Texas—San Antonio
College of Fine Arts &
 Humanities
Division of English, Classics, &
 Philosophy
Dept. of Hebrew
San Antonio, TX 78285

Wayland Baptist University
Division of Religion
Plainview, TX 79072-6998

Utah

Brigham Young University
College of Family, Home & Social
 Sciences
Dept. of Anthropology
Dept. of History
College of Humanities
Dept. of Asian & Near Eastern
 Languages
Dept. of English
College of Religious Education
Dept. of Ancient Scripture
Dept. of Church History &
 Doctrine & World Religions
Jerusalem Center for Near Eastern
 Studies
Provo, UT 84602-4446

University of Utah
Faculty of Humanities
Dept. of Anthropology
Dept. of Comparative Literature
Dept. of Hebrew
Dept. of Philosophy
Dept. of Political Science
Middle East Language Center
Salt Lake City, UT 84112

Vermont

Community College of Vermont
Dept. of Foreign Languages
POB 120, Waterbury, VT 05672

Middlebury College
Dept. of Classics
Dept. of Religion
Middlebury, VT 05753

St. Michael's College
Dept. of History
Dept. of Religious Studies
Winooski Park,
Colchester, VT 05439

University of Vermont
College of Arts & Sciences
Dept. of German & Russian
Dept. of Religion
Burlington, VT 05405-0160

Virginia

Averett College
Dept. of Religion
Hebrew Program
Danville, VA 24541

College of William and Mary in
  Virginia
Dept. of Classical Studies
Dept. of Religion
Judaic Studies Program
Nathan & Sophia Gumenick
  Professorship of Judaic Studies
POB 8795,
Williamsburg, VA 23187-8795

Eastern Mennonite College
Dept. of Biblical Studies
Harrisonburg, VA 22801

George Mason University
College of Arts & Sciences
Dept. of Foreign Languages &
  Literatures
Fairfax, VA 22030-4444

Hampden-Sydney College
Dept. of Religion
Hampden-Sydney, VA 23943

Liberty University
School of Religion
Dept. of Biblical Studies
Dept. of Hebrew
3765 Candlers Mountain Rd.,
  POB 20000,
Lynchburg, VA 24506-8001

Mary Washington College
Dept. of Religion
Fredricksburg, VA 22401-5358

Radford University
Dept. of Religion
East Norwood St.,
Radford, VA 24142

Regent University
(formerly CBN University)
School of Divinity
Dept. of Old Testament
1000 Centerville Turnpike,
Virginia Beach, VA 23464-9800

Sweet Briar College
Dept. of Religion
Sweet Briar, VA 24595

Tidewater Community College
Hebrew Program
Portsmouth Campus, State Route
  135, Portsmouth, VA 23703

Union Theological Seminary in
  Virginia
Dept. of Old Testament
3401 Brook Rd.,
Richmond, VA 23227

University of Richmond
Faculty of Humanities
Dept. of English
Dept. of Religion
Richmond, VA 23173

University of Virginia
College of Arts & Sciences
Dept. of Religious Studies
Program in Christianity &
  Judaism in Antiquity
Edgar M. Bronfman Professorship
  of Modern Judaic Studies
Graduate Studies in Religion
Charlottesville, VA 22903-3196

Virginia Commonwealth
  University

College of Humanities & Sciences
Center for Judaic Studies
915 West Franklin St.,
Richmond, VA 23284

Virginia Theological Seminary
Dept. of Old Testament
    Languages & Literatures
Alexandria, VA 22304

Washington

Lutheran Bible Institute
Division of Biblical Studies
Issaquah, WA 98027

Northwest College Assembly of
    God
Division of Religion & Ministerial
    Studies
POB 579,
Kirkland, WA 98083-0579

Pacific Lutheran University
Dept. of Anthropology
Dept. of Religion
Tacoma, WA 98447-0003

Puget Sound Christian College
Division of Biblical Studies
Biblical Research
410 Fourth Ave. N.,
Edmonds, WA 98020-3171

Seattle University
College of Arts & Sciences
Dept. of English
Dept. of Theology & Religious
    Studies
Institute for Theological Studies
Seattle, WA 98122

University of Puget Sound
Dept. of Religion
1500 North Warner,
Tacoma, WA 98416-0460

University of Washington
College of Arts & Sciences
Dept. of English
Dept. of Near Eastern Languages
    & Civilizations
Jewish Studies Program
The H.M. Jackson Scholar of
    International Studies
Samuel & Althea Stroum Chair in
    Jewish Studies
Dept. of Religion
1400 Northeast Campus Parkway,
Seattle, WA 98195

Walla Walla College
School of Theology
Dept. of Religion
204 S. College Ave.,
College Place, WA 99324-1198

Western Reformed Seminary
Dept. of Old Testament
5 South G St.,
Tacoma, WA 98405

West Virginia

Bethany College
Dept. of Religious Studies
Bethany, WV 26032

Ohio Valley College
Division of Bible & Religion
Parkersburg, WV 26101

West Virginia University
Eberly College of Arts & Sciences
Dept. of English
Dept. of Religious Studies
POB 6286,
Morgantown, WV 26506-6286

Wheeling Jesuit College
Dept. of History
Dept. of Theology & Religious
   Studies
Wheeling, WV 26003

Wisconsin

Beloit College
Division of Arts & Humanities
Jewish Studies Program (in
   formation):
Dept. of Modern Languages &
   Literatures
Dept. of English
Dept. of Philosophy
Dept. of Religion
700 College St., Beloit, WI 53511

Cardinal Strich College
Dept. of Religious Studies
6801 N. Yates Rd.,
Milwaukee, WI 53217

Carroll College
Dept. of Religion
100 North East Ave.,
Waukesha, WI 53186

Concordia College—Wisconsin
Division of Theology & Social
   Sciences
Pastoral Ministry Program

Theological Languages
12800 N. Lake Shore Drive,
Moquon, WI 53092

Edgewood College
Dept. of Foreign Languages
Dept. of Religious Studies
Swarsensky Chair of Jewish
   Studies
855 Woodrow St.,
Madison, WI 53711

Immanuel Lutheran College
Dept. of Foreign & Classical
   Languages
Eau Claire, WI 54701

Lawrence University
Dept. of Religious Studies
Appleton, WI 54912

Marquette University
College of Arts & Sciences
Dept. of Theology
Milwaukee, WI 53233

Mount Mary College
Dept. of Theology & Religious
   Education
2900 N. Menomonee River
   Parkway,
Milwaukee, WI 53222

Nashota House Seminary
Dept. of Biblical Languages
2777 Mission Rd.,
Nashota, WI 53058-9793

Northwestern College
Dept. of Greek & Hebrew
Dept. of Religion

1300 Western Ave.,
Watertown, WI 53094

Sacred Heart School of Theology
Dept. of Scripture Studies
Dept. of Systematic Studies
7335 South Hwy. 100, POB 429,
Hales Corners, WI 53130-0429

University of Wisconsin—
   Madison
College of Letters & Sciences
Center for Jewish Studies
Weinstein Chair in Jewish Studies
1220 Linden Dr.,
Madison, WI 53706-1538

University of Wisconsin—
   Milwaukee
College of Letters & Sciences
Dept. of English
Dept. of Hebrew Studies
Dept. of History
Dept. of Political Science
Milwaukee, WI 53201

University of Wisconsin—
   Superior
Dept. of History
1800 Grand Ave.,
Superior, WI 54880-2898

CENTRAL AND SOUTH AMERICA

Argentina

Universidad de Belgrano
Centro de Estudios de Medio
   Oriente
José Hernández 1820,
1426 Buenos Aires

Universidad Nacional de Buenos
   Aires
Cátedra Martin Buber
Viamonte 430/444,
1053 Buenos Aires

Instituto de Historia Antigua
   Oriental
25 de Mayo 217, 3o.,
1002 Buenos Aires

Universidad Nacional de Cuyo
Centro Universitario, Parque Gral.
   San Martín, 5500 Mendoza

Universidad Nacional de La Plata
Cátedra Libre de Estudios
   Judaicos
Avda. 7, No. 776, 1900 La Plata

Universidad Nacional de Luján
(Research only)
Casilla de Correo 221,
6700 Luján

Universidad Nacional de Rosario
Depto. de Lenguas Modernas
Córdoba 1814, 2000 Rosario

Universidad Nacional del Sur
Avda. Colón 80,
8000 Bahía Blanca

Universidad Nacional de
   Tucumán
Instituto de Literatura Española

Ayacucho 491,
4000 San Miguel de Tucumán

Universidad del Salvador
Escuela de Estudios Orientales
Rodríguez Peña 640,
1020 Buenos Aires

Brazil

Faculdade de Teologia Nossa
 Senhora da Assunçao
Av. Nazaré 993,
04263-100 Ipiranga, SP

Pontifícia Universidade Católica
R. Marqués de S. Vicente 225,
22453 Rio de Janeiro RJ

Pontifícia Universidade Católica
Depto. de Linguística
R. Monte Alegre 984, Perdizes,
05014 Sao Paulo SP

Universidade do Estado de Rio de
 Janeiro
Instituto de Letras
Depto. de Português-Hebraico
Programa de Estudos Judaicos
R. Sao Francisco Xavier 524,
Maracana, 20550-013 RJ

Universidade Estadual de
 Campinas (UNICAMP)
Caixa Postal 6063, Campinas,
 13081 SP

Universidade Federal de Rio de
 Janeiro
Faculdade de Letras
Depto. de Línguas Orientais e
 Eslavas

Av. Brig. Trompowski s/n,
21941 Rio de Janeiro RJ

Universidade do Rio Grande do
 Sul
Instituto de Filosofia e Ciências
 Humanas
Avda. Paulo Gama 110,
90040 Porto Alegre RS

Universidade de Sao Paulo
Faculdade de Filosofia, Letras e
 Ciências Humanas
Depto. de Línguas Orientais
Centro de Estudos Judaicos
Depto. de Historia
Faculdade de Direito
Rua do Lago 117, Caixa Postal
 8105, 05508-900 Sao Paulo SP

Chile

Pontificia Universidad Católica
Ismael Valdés 368, Casilla 114,
 Santiago

Universidad Católica de
 Valparaíso
Instituto de Ciencias Religiosas
Casilla 4059, Valparaíso

Universidad de Chile
Facultad de Filosofía y
 Humanidades
Avda. Bernardo O'Higgins 1058,
 Santiago

Centro de Estudios de Cultura
 Judaica
Casilla 13583, Correo 21,
 Santiago

Universidad Metropolitana de
  Ciencias de la Educación
Casilla 147, C. Central, Santiago

Colombia

Pontificia Universidad Javeriana
Carrera 7, 40-76, AA 56710,
  Bogotá

Dominican Republic

Universidad Interamericana
Apdo. Postal 20687,
Santo Domingo

Ecuador

Pontificia Universidad Católica
Avda. 12 de Octubre 1076,
Apdo. 17-012184, Quito

Panama

Universidad de Panamá
Depto. de Filosofía
Estafeta Universitaria, Panamá

Peru

Universidad Femenina del Sagrado
  Corazón
Avda. Los Frutales s/n,
  Urbanización Santa Sofía,
La Molina, Apdo. 3604, Lima

Uruguay

Universidad de la República
Facultad de Humanidades y
  Ciencias
Cátedra de Estudios Judaicos
Avda. 18 de Julio 1968,
Montevideo

Venezuela

Universidad Católica Andrés Bello
Urbanización Montalbán,
La Vega, Apdo. 29068,
Caracas 1021

Universidad Central de Venezuela
Ciudad Universitaria, Los
  Chaguaramos, ZP 104,
Caracas 1051

EUROPE
(including all former USSR countries)

Austria

Karl-Franzens Universität Graz
Institut für Alttestamentliche
  Bibelwissenschaft
Parkstrasse 1/II, A 8010 Graz

Leopold-Franzens Universität
  Innsbruck
Alttestamentliches Institut
Karl-Rahner-Platz 3, 6020
  Innsbruck

Institute for Languages &
  Cultures of the Ancient Near
  East
Universitätsdirektion,
6020 Innsbruck

Universität Salzburg
Katolisch-Theologische Fakultät
Institut für Alttestamentliche
  Bibelwissenschaften
Universitätsplatz 1, 5020 Salzburg

Geisteswissenschaftliche Fakultät
Alte Geschichte und
  Altertumskunde
Mühlbacherhofweg 6,
5020 Salzburg

Universität Wien
Institut für Judaistik
Ferstelgasse 6/12, 1090 Wien

Evangelisch-Theologischen
  Fakultät
Institut für Alttestamentliche
  Wissenschaft und Biblische
  Archäologie
Rooseveltplatz 10/16, 1090 Wien

Katolisch-Theologische Fakultät
Institut für Alttestamentliche
  Bibelwissenschaft
Schottenring 21, 1010 Wien

Belarus

Grodno State University
Faculty of Humanities
Chair of Theory & History of
  World Cultures

Dept. of Philosophy
Ozheshko 22, 230023 Grodno

Belgium

Faculté Universitaire de Théologie
  Protestante de Bruxelles
R. des Bollandistes 40,
1040 Bruxelles

Faculteit voor Vergelijkende
  Godsdienstwetenshappen
(Faculty for Comparative Study of
  Religions)
Dept. of World Religions
Bist 164,
2610 Wibrijk-Antwerpen

Institutum Judaicum
Inter-University Center of Judaic
  Studies
Dreve de Nivelles 95,
1150 Bruxelles

Katholieke Universiteit Leuven
Erasmushuis Faculteit Letteren
Blijde Inkomsstraat 21, PB 33,
3000 Leuven

Faculteit voov Godgeleerdheid
Sint-Michielsstraat 6,
3000 Leuven

Universitaire Fakulteiten Sint-
  Ignatius te Antwerpen
Prinstraat 13, 2000 Antwerpen

Université Catholique de Louvain
Faculté de Théologie et de Droit
  Canonique

Grand-Place 45,
1348 Louvain-La-Neuve

Université de Liège
Section of History & Oriental
   Literatures
Place du 20-Août 32, 4000 Liège

Université Libre de Bruxelles
Faculté de Philosophie et Lettres
Institut des Langues et
   Civilisations Orientales
Institut d'Etude des Religions et de
   la Laïcité
Av. F.D. Roosevelt 50,
1050 Bruxelles

Institut d'Etudes du Judaïsme
   (Martin Buber)
Av. F.D. Roosevelt 17,
1050 Bruxelles

Universiteit te Gent
Seminar of Semitic Studies
Sint-Pietersplein 6, 9000 Gent

Bulgaria

Sofia University
Theological Faculty
Sveta Nedelyan Sq. 19, 1000 Sofia

Veliko Turnovo University "Sveti
   Kiril i Metodyi"
Teodosyi Turnovsky St. 2,
5000 Veliko Turnovo

Czech Republic

Univerzita Karlova (Charles
   University)

Faculty of Theology
Wuchterlova 5, 16000 Prague 6

Faculty of Philosophy
Department Near Eastern Studies
Celetna 20, Stave Mesto,
11000 Prague

Denmark

Århus Universitet
Faculty of Divinity
Dept. of History of Religions
Ndr. Ringgade, 8000 Århus C

Kobenhavns Universitet
Faculty of Arts
Institute of History of Religion
Dept. of Sociology of Religion
Njalsgade 80, 2300 Copenhagen S

Faculty of Theology
Kobmagergade 44-46,
1150 Copenhagen K

Estonia

Academy of Sciences (*research
   only*)
Institute of Estonian Languages
Department of Finno-Ugric
   Languages
Roosikrantsi 6, 0100 Tallin

Estonian Institute of the
   Humanities
Sakala 3, Tallinn

Tartu University
Faculty of Theology
Ülikooli 18, 202400 Tartu

Finland

Åbo Akademi University
Institutionem for Exegetik
Biskopsgatan 16, 20500 Åbo

Religionshistoria
Biskopsgatan 10, 20500 Åbo

Helsingfors Universitet
Faculty of Humanities
Department of Asian & African
    Studies
Meritullinkatu 1, POB 13,
00014 Helsinki

Faculty of Theology
POB 36, 00014 Helsinki

University of Turku
Institute of Teacher Training
Koskenniemenkatu 4,
20500 Turku

France

Ecole des Hautes Etudes en
    Sciences Sociales
Histoire et Civilisations
Centre de Recherches Historiques
Cycle d'Etudes Juives
Thèses de doctorat:
    Anthropologie; Histoire;
    Sociologie
54, Boul. Raspail, 75006 Paris

Ecole Pratique des Hautes Etudes
Section V—Sciences Religieuses
45-47, r. des Ecoles, 75005 Paris

Faculté de Théologie Reformée
33, ave. Jules Ferry,
13100 Aix-en-Provence

Institut Catholique de l'Ouest
Faculté de Théologie
3, place André Leroy, BP 808,
49008 Angers Cedex 1

Institut Catholique de Paris
UER de Théologie et de Sciences
    Religieuses
Section d'études juives
21, r. d'Assas,
75270 Paris Cedex 6

Institut Catholique de Toulouse
Faculté de Théologie
31, r. de la Fonderie,
31608 Toulouse Cedex

Institut d'Etudes Politiques
Thèses de doctorat: Science
    politique; Histoire
27, r. St. Guillaume,
75341 Paris Cedex 7

Institut Inter-Universitaire
    d'Etudes et de Culture Juives
(Universités d'Aix-Marseille I, II,
    III, d'Avignon, Nice et Toulon)
Diplôme Interuniversitaire
    d'Etudes Juives
58, blvd. Charles Livon,
13007 Marseille

Institut National de Langues et
    Civilizations Orientales
(I.N.A.L.C.O.)
Dépt. Proche et Moyen Orient,
    Afrique du Nord

Section d'études hébraïques
2, r. de Lille, 75343 Paris Cedex 7

Ecole des Hautes Etudes du
  Judaïsme
Thèses de doctorat: Histoire
Centre de Clichy, 104 quai de
  Clichy, 92110 Clichy

Institut Protestant de Théologie—
  Faculté Libre de Théologie
  Protestante
Hébreu biblique et Ancien
  Testament
13, r. Louis Perrier,
  34000 Montpellier

Institut Protestant de Theologie—
  Faculté Libre de Théologie
  Protestante
Dépt. biblique
83, boul. Arago, 75014 Paris

Institut Universitaire Pratique
  d'Information
Programme d'Etudes Juives
48 bis, Quai de la Marne,
  75019 Paris

Université d'Aix-Marseille I
  (Université de Provence)
Faculté des Lettres
Thèses de doctorat: Histoire
29, ave. Robert Schumann,
  13621 Aix-en-Provence

Université d'Aix-en-Marseille II
Faculté des Sciences Economiques
14, r. Puvis de Chavannes,
  Marseille

Nouvelle Faculté des Sciences
  Economiques
14, ave. Jules Ferry,
  Aix-en-Provence

Université d'Aix-Marseille III
Faculté de Droit
Thèses de doctorat: Science
  politique
3, ave. Robert Schumann,
  Aix-en-Provence

Université d'Avignon et des Pays
  du Vaucluse
Faculté des Lettres
5, r. Violette,
  84010 Avignon Cedex

Université de Bordeaux III (Michel
  de Montaigne)
Thèses de doctorat: Etudes
  nordaméricaines;
Littérature française; Etudes
  arabo-islamiques
Espl. Michel-Montaigne, Domaine
  Universitaire,
  33405 Talence Cedex

Université de Caën
Thèses de doctorat: Philosophie;
  Science politique
Esplanade de la Paix,
  14032 Caën Cedex

Université Catholique de Lille
Faculté de Théologie
60, blvd. Vauban, B.P. 109,
  59016 Lille Cedex

Université de Clermond-Ferrand I
Thèses de doctorat: Science
  politique

49, boul. Gergovia, BP 32,
63001 Clermont-Ferrand Cedex

Université de Clermond-Ferrand II
Thèses de doctorat: Histoire
34, ave. Carnot, BP 185,
63006 Clermont-Ferrand Cedex

Université de Dijon
Thèses de doctorat: Etudes
   ibériques
Campus universitaire de
   Montmuzard, BP 138,
21004 Dijon Cedex

Université de Franche-Comté
30, r. Mégevand,
25030 Besançon Cedex

Université de Grenoble III
   (Université Stendhal)
Thèses de doctorat: Littérature
   française; Etudes littéraires
BP 25, 38040 Grenoble Cedex 9

Université de Lille I
Thèses de doctorat: Sociologie
Cité scientifique,
59655 Villeneuve d'Ascq Cedex

Université de Lille II
Thèses de doctorat: Droit
42, r. Paul Duez, 59800 Lille

Université de Lille III (Charles de
   Gaulle)
Département d'Etudes du Moyen
   Orient
Langue et littérature hébraïques
Thèses de doctorat: Etudes
   nordaméricaines; Etudes
   germaniques; Histoire

BP 149,
59653, Villeneuve d'Asq Cedex

Université Lumière de Lyon II
Thèses de doctorat: Littérature
   française; Histoire;
   Linguistique; Musicologie
86, r. Pasteur,
69365 Lyon Cedex 7

Université de Lyon III (Jean
   Moulin)
Faculté des Langues
Département d'Hébreu
Thèses de doctorat: Histoire;
   Philosophie;
Droit internationnel
74, r. Pasteur, BP 0638,
69239 Lyon Cedex 2

Université de Metz
Faculté des Lettres et Sciences
   Humaines
Thèses de doctorat: Etudes
   germaniques; Géographie
Ile du Saulcy,
57045 Metz Cedex 1

Université Montpellier I
Thèses de doctorat: Droit; Science
   politique
5, boul. Henri IV, BP 1017,
34006 Montpellier Cedex

Université Montpellier III (Paul
   Valéry)
Faculté d'Histoire
Faculté des Langues et
   Civilisations Etrangères
Thèses de doctorat: Etudes
   ibériques; Littérature comparée

Route de Mende, BP 5043,
34032 Montpellier Cedex

Université de Nancy II
Département de Langues
  Etrangères
Institut d'Hébreu
Thèses de doctorat: Philologie;
  Exégèse médiévale;
Lexicographie biblique; Massorah
3, place Godefrei-de-Bouillon,
BP 3397, 54015 Nancy

Université de Nantes
Thèses de doctorat: Droit
1, quai de Tourville, BP 1026,
44035 Nantes Cedex 1

Université de Nice
Faculté des Lettres
Thèses de doctorat: Littérature
  comparée; Histoire; Ethnologie
28, parc Valrose,
06034 Nice Cedex

Université de Paris I (Panthéon-
  Sorbonne)
Département d'Etudes Juives
Thèses de doctorat: Histoire;
  Philosophie; Archaeologie;
  Esthétique; Science politique;
  Cinéma; Histoire de l'art; Droit
12, place du Panthéon,
75231 Paris Cedex 5

Université de Paris II
Thèses de doctorat: Droit; Science
  politique

12, place du Panthéon,
75231 Paris Cedex 5

Université de Paris III—Sorbonne
  Nouvelle
Département de Inde-Orient et
  Afrique du Nord
Section des Etudes Hébraïques
Thèses de doctorat: Etudes
  sémitiques; Espagnol; Etudes
  anglaises; Etudes orientales;
  Théâtre; Linguistique; Histoire
13, r. de Santeuil,
75005 Paris Cedex 5

Université de Paris IV—Sorbonne
Centre d'Etudes Juives
Thèses de doctorat: Littérature
  française; Histoire; Histoire des
  religions; Etudes grecques;
  Etudes ibériques; Musicologie;
  Etudes portugaises; Etudes
  nordaméricaines; Science
  politique
1, r. Victor Cousin,
75230 Paris Cedex 5

Université de Paris V
Thèses de doctorat: Sciences de
  l'éducation; Linguistique;
  Sociologie; Sciences humaines
1, r. Victor Cousin,
75230 Paris Cedex 5

Université de Paris VII
Centre d'Etudes Judéo-Américains
Centre d'Etudes Yiddish
Centre d'études germaniques

Centre d'études anglosaxons
Thèses de doctorat: Etudes
   littéraires; Ethnologie; Etudes
   anglaises; Histoire; Sociologie
2, place Jussieu,
75221 Paris Cedex 5

Université de Paris VIII (Vincennes
   à St. Denis)
Département d'Hébreu
Thèses de doctorat: Sociologie;
   Etudes germaniques; Histoire;
   Linguistique; Sciences de
   l'éducation; Géographie; Droit
2, r. de la Liberté,
93526 St. Denis Cedex 2

Université de Paris X (Paris-
   Nanterre)
DEUG d'Histoire
DEUG de Philosophie
Unités libres de Langues,
   Civilisations et Cultures
Thèses de doctorat: Littérature
   française; Histoire; Sciences de
   la éducation; Cinéma; Science
   politique; Droit civil;
   Sociologie
200, ave. de la République,
92001 Nanterre Cedex

Université de Paris XI
Thèses de doctorat: Droit; Science
   politique
15, r. Georges Clémenceau,
91405 Orsay Cedex

Université de Paris XII (Paris-Val
   de Marne)

Département de Lettres Divers
Thèses de doctorat: Histoire;
   Science politique
61, ave. Général De Gaulle,
94010 Créteil Cedex

Université de Pau et des Pays de
   l'Adour
Faculté des Lettres
68, r. Montpensier, BP 576,
64000 Pau

Université de Picardie
R. Solomon Mahlangu,
80025 Amiens

Université de Reims
Thèses de doctorat: Histoire;
   Droit
23, r. Boulard, 51096 Reims

Université de Rennes I
Thèses de doctorat: Science
   politique
2, r. du Thabor, BP 1134,
35014 Rennes Cedex

Université de Rennes II (Haute
   Bretagne)
Département de Littérature
   Française
Département de Relations
   Internationales
6, ave. Gaston Berger,
35043 Rennes Cedex

Université de Rouen
Thèses de doctorat: Linguistique;
   Etudes latinoaméricaines

1, r. Lavoisier,
76281 Mont-St-Aignan Cedex

Université de Strasbourg II
(Sciences Humaines)
Faculté de Langues, Littératures et
Civilisations Etrangères
Institut d'Etudes Hébraïques et
Juives
Faculté de Théologie Protestante
Thèses de doctorat: Littérature
française; Philosophie; Sciences
religieuses; Archaeologie;
Histoire; Sociologie
22, r. René Descartes,
67084 Strasbourg Cedex

Université de Toulouse I
Thèses de doctorat: Droit; Science
politique
Place Anatole France,
31042 Toulouse Cedex

Université de Toulouse II (Le
Mirail)
Centre Interdisciplinaire de
Recherche et d'Etudes Juives
(C.I.R.E.J.)
Département de Langues
Etrangères
Thèses de doctorat: Littérature
française; Histoire; Cinéma
5, allée A. Machado,
31058 Toulouse Cedex

Université de Tours (François
Rabelais)
Institut d'Etudes Germaniques
Section d'hébreu et d'études juives
Thèses de doctorat: Musicologie

3, r. des Tanneurs,
37041 Tours Cedex

Georgia

Georgian Academy of Sciences
George Tsereteli Institute of
Oriental Studies
(research only)
Institute of Asia and Africa
Hebrew Language
Acad. G. Tsereteli str. 3,
380062 Tbilisi

Sulkhan Saba Orebeliani State
Pedagogical Institute
Hebrew Language
Chavchavadze Ave. 32,
380079 Tbilisi

Tbilisi State University
Faculty of Oriental Studies
Dept. of Hebrew & Aramaic
Philology
Chavchavadze Ave. 1,
380028 Tbilisi

Germany

Augustana Hochschule
Waldstrasse 11, Postfach 20,
91561 Neuendettelsau

Christian-Albrechts Universität zu
Kiel
Theologische Fakultät
Olshausenstrasse 40, 24098 Kiel

Eberhard-Karls-Universität
Tübingen

Evangelisch-Theologische Fakultät
Institutum Judaicum
Biblische Archäologie
Altes Testament
Institut für antikes Judentum und
hellenistische
Religionsgeschichte
Katholisch-Theologisches Seminar
Abteilung Altes Testament
Liebermeisterstrasse 12,
72076 Tübingen 1

Ernst-Moritz-Arndt Universität
Greifswald
Theologische Fakultät
Gustav Dalman Institut
Domstrasse 11, 17487 Greifswald

Freie Universität Berlin
Fachbereich Philosophie und
Sozialwissenchaften II
Institut für Judaistik
Schwendenerstrasse 27,
1000 Berlin 37

Georg-August-Universität zu
Göttingen
Faculty of Theology
Der Praesident Wilhem Platz 1,
3400 Göttingen

Hochschule für Jüdische Studien
Friedrichstrasse 9,
69117 Heidelberg

Humboldt Universität zu Berlin
Vorderasiatisches Institut
Hebraistik/Israelwissenchaften
Unter den Linden 9-11,
1086 Berlin

Faculty of Theology
Burgstrasse 25, 1086 Berlin

Johann-Wolfgang-Goethe
Universität Frankfurt
Fachbereich Evangelische
Theologie
Religionswissenchaft/
Religionsphilosophie
Biblische Theologie
Martin-Buber-
Stiftungsgastprofessur
Hausener Weg 120, Postfach
111932, 60489 Frankfurt

Johannes-Gutenberg Universität
Mainz
Fachbereich Evangelische
Theologie
Seminar für Religions- und
Missionswissenschaft und
Judaistik
Fachbereich Katholische
Theologie
Seminar für Biblische
Wissenschaften
Akademisches Auslandsamt,
55099 Mainz

Justus-Liebig-Universität Giessen
Institute of Oriental Studies
Otto Behaguelstrasse 10,
6300 Giessen

Faculty of Evangelical & Catholic
Theology
Karl-Glöcknerstrasse 21H,
35394 Giessen

Katholische Universität Eichstätt
Faculty of Theology

Biblische Theologie
Pater-Philipp-Jeningen-Platz 6,
85072 Eichstätt

Kirchlichen Hochschule Berlin
Institut Kirche und Judentum
Leuchtenburgstrasse 39-41,
1000 Berlin 37

Ludwig-Maximilians-Universität
  München
Institut für Semitistik
Veterinärstrasse 1,
80539 München

Martin-Luther-Universität Halle-
  Wittenberg
Department of Ancient Art &
  History
Theologische Fakultät
Institut für Bibelwissenschaften
Universitätsplatz 9-9, Postfach,
4010 Halle/Saale

Philipps-Universität Marburg
Fachbereich Evangelische
  Theologie
Hebrew Studies
Lahntor 3, 35032 Marburg

Rheinische Friedrich-Wilhelms-
  Universität Bonn
Katholische Fakultät
Regina-Pacis-Weg 1, 5300 Bonn 1

Evangelisch-Theologische Fakultät
Am Hof 1, 53113 Bonn

Ruhr Universität
Evangelische Fakultät
Universitätstrasse 150,
4630 Bochum

Technische Universität Berlin
Institut für Geschichtwissenschaft
Ernst Reuter Platz 7,
1000 Berlin 10

Universität Augsburg
Faculty of Catholic Theology
Universitätstrasse 10,
8900 Augsburg

Universität Duisburg
  Gesamthochschule
Faculty of Evangelical Theology
Lotharstrasse 65, 4100 Duisburg

Universität Hamburg
Fachbereich Evangelische
  Theologie
Sedanstrasse 19, 20146 Hamburg

Institut für die Geschichte der
  Deutschen Juden
Rothenbaumchaussee 7,
20148 Hamburg

Universität zu Köln
Philosophische Fakultät
Martin-Buber-Institut für
  Judaistik
Kerpenerstrasse 4, 50923 Köln

Universität Leipzig
Theologische Fakultät
Institut für Alttestamentliche
  Wissenchaften
Forschungstelle Judentum
Judaistisches Institut
Emil-Fuchs-Strasse 1,
O-7010 Leipzig

Fachbereich Orientalistik/
Afrikanistik
Augustusplatz 9, O-7010 Leipzig

Universität Potsdam
Fachbereich Geschichte
Schwerpunkt Deutsch-Jüdische
Geschichte
Am Neuen Palais 10,
14415 Potsdam

Moshe Mendelssohn Zentrum
Europäisch-Jüdische Studïen
Postfach 601553, 14415 Potsdam

University of Saarland
Institute of Evangelical Theology
Im Stadtwald, 6600 Saarbrücken

Universität Trier
Sprach-und
Litteraturwissenschaften
Fachbereich Jiddistik
Universitätsring 15, Postfach
3825, 54286 Trier

Westfälisch Wilhelms-Universität
Münster
Evangelisch-Theologische Fakultät
Institutum Judaicum
Delitzschianum
Wilmergasse 1-4, 4400 Münster

Greece

Aristoteleio Panepistimio
Thessalonikis
Department of History
Jewish Studies Program
University Campus,
54006 Thessaloniki

Athinisin Ethnikon Kai
Kapodistriakon Panepistimion
(National & Capodistrian
University of Athens)
Odos Panepistimiou 30, Athens

Hungary

Jewish Theological Seminary of
Hungary
Joszef Körút 27, 1085 Budapest

Loránd Eötvös University
Department of Assiriology &
Hebrew Studies
Center of Jewish Studies
POB 107, 1364 Budapest

Theological Academy
Department of New Testament
Eötvös Lorand u. 7,
1053 Budapest

Iceland

Háskóli Islands
Faculty of Theology
Department of Biblical Studies
Sudurgata, 101 Reykjavik

Ireland

University College Dublin
Department of Near Eastern
Languages
Belfield, Dublin 4

University of Dublin
Department of Theology
Trinity College, Dublin 2

Italy

Istituto Universitario Orientale
Dipartimento di Studi Asiatici
Hebrew Studies Program
Piazza San Domenico Maggiore
12, 80134 Napoli

Pontificia Università Gregoriana
Interfaculty Programme of Judaic
Studies
Piazza della Pilotta 4,
00187 Roma

Pontificia Università Lateranense
Facoltà di Teologia
Piazza S. Giovani in Laterano 4,
00120 Città del Vaticano

Pontificia Università S. Tomasso
d'Aquino—Angelicum
Facoltà di Teologia
Facoltà di Filosofia
Largo Angelicum 1, 00184 Roma

Pontificia Università Urbaniana
Facoltà di Teologia
Sezione Lingue
Via Urbano VIII 16,
00120 Città del Vaticano

Pontificio Ateneo Antonianum
Cattedra di Teologia della Croce
Facoltà di Teologia
Istituto Francescano di Spiritualità
Istituto di Studi Ecumenici S.
Bernardino
Istituto Superiore di Scienze
Religiose "Redemptor
Hominis"

Studium Biblicum Franciscanum
Via Merulana 124, 00185 Roma

Pontificio Ateneo San Anselmo
Facultà di Teologia
Pontificio Istituto Liturgico
Piazza Cavalieri di Malta 5,
00153 Roma

Pontificio Istituto Biblico
Facoltà Biblica
Facoltà Orientalistica
Via della Pilotta 25, 00187 Roma

Università Catolica del Sacro
Cuore
Largo A. Gemelli 1,
20123 Milano

Università degli Studi di Bologna
Faculty of Arts & Philosophy
Via Zamboni 33, 40126 Bologna

Università degli Studi di Firenze
Facoltà di Lettere e Filosofia
Dipartimento di Linguistica
Piazza Brunelleschi 4,
50121 Firenze

Università degli Studi di Genova
Faculty of Arts
Via Balbi 4/III, 16126 Genova

Università degli Studi di Milano
Facoltà de Lettere e Filosofia
Via Festa del Perdono 7,
20122 Milano

Università degli Studi di Pavia
Corso Strada Nuova 65,
27100 Pavia

Università degli Studi di Perugia
Faculty of Philosophy
Piazza dell'Università,
06100 Perugia

Università degli Studi di Pisa
Department of Ancient History
Via Galvani 1, 56100 Pisa

Università degli Studi di Roma—
La Sapienza
Facoltà di Lettere
Filologia Semitica
Piazza Aldo Moro, 00185 Roma

Università degli Studi di Torino
Faculty of Arts
Institute of Oriental Studies
Via S. Ottavio 20, 10124 Torino

Università degli Studi di Venezia
Department of Euro-Asiatic
Studies
Palazzo Cappello, S. Polo 2035,
30125 Venezia

Università di Calabria
Faculty of Arts
87036 Arcavacata di Rende,
Cosenza

Università di Napoli
Faculty of Arts & Philosophy
Corso Umberto I, 80138 Napoli

Università Pontificia Salesiana
Facoltà di Teologia
Istituto Superiore di Scienze
Religiose Sacra Scrittura
Piazza dell'Ateneo Salesiano 1,
00139 Roma

Università Pontificia Salesiana—
Sezione di Torino
Istituto Internazionale Don Bosco
Via S. Caboto 27, 10129 Torino

Latvia

University of Riga
Theological Faculty
Bulvar Rainisa, 19, 226098 Riga

Lithuania

Jewish State Museum of Lithuania
(research only)
Pamenkalnio 12, Vilnius 2001

Vilnius University
Faculty of History
C. & F. Hollander Center for
Judaic Studies
Universiteto 3, 2734 Vilnius

Malta

The Royal University of Malta
Faculty or Arts
Dept. of Holy Scripture &
Hebrew
Msida

Moldova

Moldavian Academy of Sciences
Department of Jewish History &
Culture *(research only)*
Bul. Stefan cel Mare 1,
277001 Kishinev

The Netherlands

Katholieke Theologische
    Universiteit te Utrecht
Heidelberglaan 2,
3584 CS Utrecht

Katholieke Universiteit Nijmegen
Faculty of Theology
Faculty of Arts
Dept. of History
Dept. of Art History &
    Archaeology
Erasmusplein 1, POB 9103,
6500 HD Nijmegen

Rijksuniversiteit te Groningen
Faculty of Theology
Broerstraat 5, POB 72,
9700 AB Groningen

Rijksuniversiteit te Leiden
Faculteit der Lettern
Dept. of Hebrew, Aramaic &
    Ugaritic Languages & Cultures
Matthias de Vrieshof 4, Postbus
    9515, 2300 RA Leiden

Rijksuniversiteit te Utrecht
Heidelberglaan 2,
3808 TC Utrecht

Theologische Universiteit van de
    Gereformeerde Kerken in
    Nederland
Division of Biblical Studies
Koornmarkt 1 en Oudestraat 6,
    Postbus 5021,
8260 GA Kampen

Universiteit van Amsterdam
Faculty of Theology
Oude Turfmarkt 147,
1012 GC Amsterdam

Juda Palache Institute
Vakgroep Hebreeuws, Aramees,
    Syrisch en Joodse Studien
c/o Universiteitsbibliotheek, Singel
    425, 1012 WP Amsterdam

Norway

Misjionshogkolen (School of
    Mission & Theology—MHS)
Section of Theology
Misjonsveien 34, 4024 Stavanger

Möre og Romsdal
    Distrikshogskule (Regional
    College of Möre and Romsdal)
Department of Biblical Studies
POB 188, 6101 Volda

Teologiske Menighetsfakultet I
    Oslo (Free Faculty of Theology
    of Oslo)
Collegium Judaicum
Gydas Vei 4, 0363 Oslo 3

Universitetet i Bergen
Institutt for Religionsvitenskap
Sydnesplass 9, 5007 Bergen

Universitetet i Oslo
Det Historisk-Filosofiske Fakultet
School for Cultural & Social
    Studies
Dept. of History of Religions
POB 1010 Blindern, 0315 Oslo

Department of History of Ideas
POB 1056 Blindern, 0315 Oslo

Department of East European &
Oriental Studies
P.O.B. 1030, Blindern, 0315 Oslo

Universitetet i Trondheim
College of Arts & Sciences
Department of Religious Sciences

Norges Laererhogskole (Teachers
Training School)
University Center,
7055 Dragvoll, Trondheim

Poland

Gdańsk University
Faculty of Languages & History
Department of History
ul. Bazyñskiego 1A,
80–952 Gdañsk

Highest Pedagogical School
Krakow

Jagiellonian University
Research Center on Jewish
History & Culture in Poland
Chair of Jewish History &
Culture
ul. Batorego 12, 31–135 Kraków

Maria Curie Sklodowska
University
Dept. of English
20-031 Lublin

Nicholas Kopernick University
Gagarina, 11, 87-100 Toruñ

University of Lódz
Department of Drama & Theater
Chair of Theory of Literature,
Theater and Film
ul. Narutowicza 65, 90-131 Lódz

Warsaw University
Department of Hebrew
ul. Tlomackie 3/5,
00-090 Warsaw

Historical Institute
Mordechai Anielevich Center for
the Study & Teaching of
History & Culture of Jews in
Poland
ul. Krakowskie Przedmiescie 26/
28, 00-325 Warszaw

Wroclaw University
Chair for the History of Polish
Churches and National
Movements
Szewska 49, 51-000 Wroclaw

Portugal

Universidade Católica Portuguesa
Faculdade de Teologia
Faculdade de Ciências Humanas
Palma de Cima, 1600 Lisboa

Universidade de Coímbra
Faculdade de Letras
Paço das Escolas, 3000 Coímbra

Universidade de Lisboa
Faculdade de Letras
Depto. de História

Alameda da Universidade,
1600 Lisboa

Universidade Nova de Lisboa
Institute of African Studies
Avda. Berna 24, 1000 Lisboa

Romania

Babes-Bolyai University
Faculty of History & Philosophy
Dr. Moshe Carmilly Institute for
   Judaistic & Jewish History
str. Universitatii 7-9,
3400 Cluj-Napoca

Russia

Academy of Sciences
Jewish Research Center
Institute of Sociology *(research
   only)*
Krzhyzhanovskogo 24/35,
117259 Moscow

Institute of Oriental Studies
Dept. of Languages
Rozhdestvenke 12,
103031 Moscow

Association for Israeli Studies
(Research only)
Rozhdesvenka 12,
1037543 Moscow

Bashkir State University
Courses in Jewish History &
   Traditions
ul. Frunze 32, 450074 Ufa

Jewish University in Moscow
Dept. of Religion & Philosophy
Dept. of History
Dept. of Philology
Dept. of Sociology & Pedagogics
9, Mokhovaya st.,
103009 Moscow

Moscow Institute of Electronics
Department of Philosophy
Vernadsky pr. 78,
117454 Moscow

Moscow M. V. Lomonosov State
   University
Institute of Afro-Asian Studies
Department of Arabic & Hebrew
   Philology
Department of Hebrew Literature
   & Language
Center for Jewish Studies
Mokhovaya 18, 103009 Moscow

Moscow State Institute of Foreign
   Relations
Faculty for Foreign Relations
Chair for Middle Eastern
   Languages
Chair for State Law
Vernadsky pr., 76,
117454 Moscow

Petersburg Jewish University
Faculty of Philosophy
Faculty of History & Ethnography
POB 610, 196247 St. Petersburg

Rostov Pedagogic Institute
History Department
Bolshaya Sadovaya 33,
344082 Rostov-on-Don

Rostov State University
(Research only)
Bolshaya Sadovaya 105,
Rostov-on-Don

Russian Research & Educational
Center "Holocaust"
Bulatnikovskyproezd 14-4-77,
113403 Moscow

Russian State University for the
Humanities
Program in Jewish Studies *(co-
sponsored by JTS & YIVO,
New York)*
Nikolskaya 15, 113642 Moscow

St. Petersburg Academy of
Sciences
Institute of Ethnography *(research
only)*
Universitetskaya nab. 7,
St. Petersburg

Institute of Oriental Studies—St.
Petersburg Branch
Dvortzovaya nab. 18,
St. Petersburg

St. Petersburg Institute of Culture
Dvortzovaya nab. 2/4,
191011 St. Petersburg

St. Petersburg State University
Universitetskaya nab. 11,
199164 St. Petersburg

Samara State University
(Interfaculty) Chair of the World
Art Culture
ul. Akademika Pavlova 1,
443011 Samara

Tomsk State University
Faculty of International Relations
Lenina pr. 36, 634010 Tomsk

Volgograd State University
(research only)
2-ya Prodolnaya 30,
400062 Volgograd

Slovak Republic

Comenius University
Faculty of Philosophy
Department of Comparative
Literature
Inst. Semitic Studies
Safárikovo 6, 81806 Bratislava

Evangelical Theological Faculty
Palisády 46, 81106 Bratislava

Spain

Universidad de Barcelona
Departamento de Filologia
Semítica
Gran Vía de las Corts Catalanes
585, 08007 Barcelona

Universidad de Castilla-La
Mancha
Cultura Hispano-Judía y Sefaradí
(cursos de verano)
Museo Sefardí, Sinagoga del
Tránsito,
C. Samuel Leví s/n, 45002 Toledo

Universidad Complutense de
Madrid
Facultad de Filología

Departamento de Estudios
Hebreos y Arameos
Ciudad Universitaria,
Madrid 28040

Universidad de Extremadura
Facultad de Filosofía
Avda. de Elvas s/n, Badajoz

Facultad de Filosofía
Plaza de los Caldereros 2, Cáceres

Universidad de Granada
Facultad de Filosofía y Letras
Depto. de Estudios Semíticos
Ph.D. Program: Estudios
Superiores de Cultura Hebrea
18071 Granada

Facultad de Teología
Campus Universitario Cartuja,
Apdo. 2002, 18080 Granada

Universidad de Navarra
Facultad de Teología
Depto. de Sagrada Escritura
Facultad de Historia
Ciudad Universitaria, Apdo. 170,
31080 Pamplona

Universidad Pontificia Comillas
Facultad de Teología
Depto. de Sagrada Escritura
28049 Madrid

Universidad Pontificia de
Salamanca
Facultad de Filología Bíblica
Trilingüe
Departamento de Lengua &
Literatura Hebreas

Calle Compañía 1, Apdo. 541,
37008 Salamanca

Sweden

Göteborgs Universitet
Institutionen für
Religionsvetenskap
Mölndalsvägen 85,
41285 Göteborg

Lunds Universitet
Faculty of Theology & Faculty of
Humanities
Department of History of
Religions
Section for Jewish Studies
Allhelgona Kyrkogata 8,
22362 Lund

Institute of Middle Eastern
Languages
POB 652, 22007 Lund

Stockholms Universitet
Department of Comparative
Religions
10691 Stockholm

Uppsala Universitet
Faculty of History of Religions
St. Olofsgatan 10 b,
75105 Uppsala

Faculty of Theology
Slottsgraend 3, 75146 Uppsala

Switzerland

Baptist Theological Seminary
Dept. of General Studies

Dept. of Old Testament
Dept. of Practical Theology
Gheistrasse 31, 8803 Rüschlikon

Faculté de Theologie Protestante
Dorigny, 1015 Lausanne

Hochschule Luzern
Philosophisches Institut
Institut für Jüdisch-Christliche
    Forschung
Kasernenplatz 3, Postfach 7424,
6003 Luzern

Theologische Hochschule Chur
Bibelwissenschaften
Alte Schanfiggerstr. 7/9,
7000 Chur

Universität Basel
Theologische Fakultät
Altes Testament Theologisches
    Seminar
Nadelberg 10, 4051 Basel

Universität Bern
Evangelisch-Theologische Fakultät
Bibelwissenschaften
Christkatholisch-Theologische
    Fakultät
Bibelwissenschaften
Erlachstrasse 17, 3012 Bern

Universität Zürich
Faculty of Theology
Kirchgasse 9, 8001 Zürich

Université de Fribourg
Institut Biblique Miséricorde
Faculté de Philosophie
Faculté de Théologie
1700 Fribourg

Université de Genève
Faculté Autonome de Théologie
    Protestante
Centre d'Etude du Proche-Orient
    Ancien
3 Place de l'Université,
1211 Genève 4

Faculté de Lettres
Département de Philosophie
Département d'Histoire Générale
3 Rue de Candolle,
1211 Genève 4

Université de Lausanne
Faculté de Théologie
B.F.S.H. 2, 1015 Lausanne

Université de Neuchâtel
Faculté des Lettres
Ave. du 1er Mars 26,
2000 Neuchâtel

Faculté de Théologie
Faubourg de l'Hôpital 41,
2000 Neuchâtel

Ukraine

Donetsk State University
Department of Philology
Chair of Literature & Artistic
    Culture
Chair of General & Historical
    Linguistics
Department of World Literature
Universitetskaya 24,
340055 Donetsk

Dragomanov Institute of
    Education

Department of Philology
Pirogov 9, Kiev

Kiev University
Faculty of Philology
Vladimirskaya 54, 252601 Kiev

University of Chernivtsi
Department of Bible Studies
ul. Kotsyubinskogo 2,
274012 Chernivtsi

University of Kharkov
Department of History
Chair of History of Russia
Chair of Ancient World and
    Middle Ages
pl. Svobody 4, 310077 Kharkov

Uzhgorod State University
Institute of Karpatology
Universitetskaya 14,
294000 Uzhgorod

United Kingdom

England

Cambridge University
Cambridge University Library
Genizah Research Unit
West Road, Cambridge CB3 9DR

Dept. of Ancient History
King's College,
Cambridge CB2 1ST

Faculty of Divinity
St. John's St.,
Cambridge CB2 1TW

Faculty of Oriental Studies
Sidgwick Ave.,
Cambridge CB3 9DA

Centre for the Study of Judaism &
    Jewish/Christian Relations
Central House, Selly Oak
    Colleges, Bristol Road,
Birmingham B29 6LQ

Goldsmiths' College
Department of Historical &
    Cultural Studies
New Cross, London SE14 GNW

Leo Baeck College
Sternberg Center for Judaism
Manor House, 80 East End Rd.,
London N3 2SY

Oxford Centre for Postgraduate
    Hebrew Studies
45 St. Giles, Oxford OX1 3LP
Yarnton Manor, Yarnton,
Oxford OX5 1PY

Oxford University
The Oriental Institute
Dept. of Hebrew
Pusey Lane, Oxford OX1 2LE

Roehampton Institute
Dept. of Theology & Religious
    Studies
Roehampton Lane,
London SW15 5PH

Southlands College
Theology & Religious Studies
Wimbledon Parkside,
London SW19 5NN

University of Birmingham
School of History
School of Philosophy & Theology
Centre for Holocaust Studies
Birmingham B15 2TT

University of Bristol
Dept. of History
Senate House, Kindle Ave.,
Bristol BS8 1T

University of Durham
Dept. of Theology
Abbey House, Palace Green,
Durham DH1 3R

University of Exeter
Dept. of Theology
Queen's Building, The Queen's
   Drive, Exeter EX4 4QH

University of Hull
Dept. of Theology
Hull HU6 7RX

University of Keele
Dept. of History
Staffordshire ST5 5BG

University of Kent at Canterbury
Faculty of Social Sciences
Canterbury, Kent CT2 7NZ

University of Lancaster
Dept. of Religious Studies
Lancaster LA1 4YG

University of Leeds
Dept. of Theology & Religious
   Studies
Leeds LS2 9JT

University of Leicester
Dept. of History
University Road,
Leicester LE1 7RH

University of Liverpool
Dept. of Archaeology & Oriental
   Studies
Dept. of Geography
Faculty of Law
P.O. Box 147,
Liverpool L69 3BX

University of London
Heythrop College
Dept. of Biblical Studies
11-13 Cavendish Square,
London W1M 0AN

Jew's College
44a Albert Road,
London NW4 2SJ

King's College
School of Humanities
Dept. of Theology & Religious
   Studies
Strand, London WC2R 2LS

Queen Mary & Westfield College
Dept. of Political Studies
Mile End Road, London E1 4NS

Royal Holloway and Bedford
   New College
Egham Hill, Surrey TW2 0EX

School of Oriental & African
   Studies (S.O.A.S.)

Dept. of Near & Middle East Studies
Thornbaugh Street, Russell Square, London WC1H 0XG

University College London
Dept. of Hebrew & Jewish Studies
Gower Street, London WC1E 6BT

The Warburg Institute
Woburn Square,
London WC1H 0AB

University of Manchester
Dept. of Middle Eastern Studies
Dept. of Religions & Theology
Oxford Road,
Manchester M13 9PL

University of Newcastle-upon-Tyne
Dept. of Religious Studies
Newcastle-upon-Tyne, NE1 7RU

University of Nottingham
Dept. of Theology
University Park,
Nottingham NG7 2RD

University of Reading
Dept. of Classics
Dept. of French
Dept. of Sociology
Whiteknights, POB 218,
Reading RG6 2AA

University of Sheffield
Dept. of Biblical Studies
Dept. of History
Arts Tower, Western Bank,
Sheffield S10 2UJ

University of Southampton
Dept. of History
Parkes Lectureship in Jewish/Non-Jewish Relations
Highfield,
Southampton S09 5NH

University of Surrey
St. Mary's College
Dept. of Theology & Religious Studies
Aldegrave Rd., Strawberry Hill,
Twickenham TW1 4SX
(also validates degrees offered by Southlands College)

University of Sussex at Brighton
School of European Studies
Dept. of German-Jewish Studies
Arts Building, Falmer,
Brighton BN1 9QN

University of Warwick
Dept. of Sociology
Coventry CV4 7AL

Scotland

The Open University in Scotland
10 Drumsheugh Gardens,
Edinburgh EH3 7QJ

University of Aberdeen
Dept. of Divinity & Religious Studies
Hebrew & Semitic Languages
King's College, Old Aberdeen,
Aberdeen AB9 2UB

University of Edinburgh
Dept. of Hebrew & OT Studies
New College, Mound Pace,
Edinburgh EH1 2LX

University of St. Andrews
School of Divinity
St. Mary's College, St. Andrews,
  Fife KY16 9JU

University of Stirling
Religious Studies
Stirling, FK9 4LA

Northern Ireland

The Queen's University of Belfast
The School of Greek, Roman &
  Semitic Studies
Belfast BT7 1NN

Wales

St. David's University College
Lampeter, Dyfed SA48 TED

University College of North Wales
Dept. of Religious Studies
Bangor, Gwynedd LL57 2DG

Uzbekistan

Samarkand State University
Faculty of History
Chair of the History of the
  Peoples of Uzbekistan
Universitetskaya 15,
703004 Samarkand

Yugoslavia

University of Belgrade
Dept. of Judaics & Philology
Studentski trg. 1,
11001 Belgrade 6

AFRICA

Cameroon

Faculté de Théologie Protestante
BP 4011, Yaoundé

Grand Séminaire de Nkolbisson
BR 2030, Yaoundé

Cote D'Ivoire

Université Nationale de Côte
  d'Ivoire

Faculté des Lettres
01 BP V34, Abidjan 01

Egypt

Ain Shams University
Faculty of Arts
Faculty of Languages
Kasr-El-Zaafaran, Abbasiya,
  Cairo

Al-Azhar University
Faculty of Languages
Cairo

Assint University
Hebrew Language
Assint

Cairo University
Faculty of Arts
Orman, Giza, Cairo

Tanta University
Hebrew Language
Tanta Elgeishe St., Tanta

Kenya

Egerton University
Dept. of Religious Studies
POB 536, Njoro

Kenyatta University
Faculty of Arts
Dept. of Religious Studies
POB 43844, Nairobi

Moi University
Dept. of Religion
POB 3900, Eldoret

University of Nairobi
Dept. of Religious Studies
POB 30197, Nairobi

Morocco

(Hebrew Language Courses)

Université Cadi Ayyad
Ave. Prince My Abdellah, BP S
511, Marrakech

Université Hassan II
BP 9167, 19 rue Tariq Bnou
Ziyad, Casablanca

Université Ibnou Zohr
Faculté des Lettres et Sciences
Humaines
BP 3215, Agadir

Université Mohammed I
BP 524, Oujda

Université Mohammed V
Dept. of Oriental Languages
BP 554, 3 rue Michlifen,
Agdal, Rabat

Université Sidi Mohamed Ben
Abdellah
BP 2626, ave. des Almohades, Fès

Université Sidi Mohamed Ben
Abdellah
BP 4009, Meknès

Nigeria

Obafemi Awolowo University
Dept. of Religious Studies
Ile-Ife

University of Ibadan
Dept. of Religious Studies
Ibadan

University of Ife
Dept. of Religious Studies
Ile-Ife

University of Nigeria
Dept. of Religions
Nsukka, Anambra State

South Africa

Potchefstroom University for
Christian Higher Education

Faculty of Letters & Philosophy
Dept. of Classics & Semitics
Private Bag X 6001,
Potchefstroom 2520

Rand Afrikaans University
Dept. of Semitic Languages
POB 524, Auckland Park 2006

Rhodes University
Dept. of Divinity
POB 94, Grahamstown 6140

University of Cape Town
Dept. of Hebrew and Jewish
    Studies
Isidore & Theresa Cohen Chair of
    Hebrew Language & Literature
Mendel Kaplan Chair of Jewish
    Civilization
Private Bag, Rondebosch 7700

University of Durban-Westville
Faculty of Theology
Dept. of Old Testament, New
    Testament & Biblical Studies
Private Bag X54001,
Durban 4000, Natal

University of Fort Hare
Faculty of Theology
Dept. of Old Testament &
    Hebrew
Private Bag X1314,
Alice 5700, Ciskei

University of Natal
Faculty of Arts
Dept. of Europe Studies
King George V Ave.,
Durban 4001

School of Theology
Dept. of Religious Studies
POB 375, Pietermaritzburg 3200

University of the North (Qwaqwa
    Branch)
Faculty of Arts
Dept. of Semitic Languages
Private Bag X1106, Sovenga 0727

University of Port Elizabeth
Dept. of Semitics
POB 1600, Port Elizabeth 6000,
Cape Province

University of Pretoria
Faculty of Arts
Brooklyn, Pretoria 0002

University of South Africa
    (UNISA)
Dept. of Semitics
Program in Judaica
Program in Semitic Languages
Program in Modern Hebrew
Dept. of Old Testament
POB 392, Pretoria 0001

University of Stellenbosch
Dept. of Ancient Near Eastern
    Studies
Eric Samson Chair for Biblical
    Hebrew Grammar
Stellenbosch 7600, Cape Province

University of the Western Cape
Faculty of Arts
Private Bag X17, Belville 7530

University of the Witwatersrand,
Faculty of Arts & Sciences

Dept. of Hebrew & Jewish Studies
Private Bag 3, Wits 2050
Johannesburg

Swaziland

University of Swaziland
Dept. of Theology & Religious
  Studies
Private Bag 4, Kwaluseni
  Campus

ASIA

China

Chinese Institute for Peace and
  Development Studies
Center of Israel & Jewish Studies
1331 Fuxing Rd. No. 32,
Shanghai 20003

East China Normal University
Dept. of History
3663 North Zhongshan Road,
Shanghai

Fudan University
Dept. of History
220 Handan Road,
Shanghai 200433

Nanjing Union Theological
  Seminary
Nanjing

Nanjing University
School of Foreign Studies
Center for Jewish Culture Studies
China Judaic Studies Association
Dept. of English

Zaire

Protestant Faculties of Kinshasa
Faculty of Theology
Faculty of Humanities
Center for Jewish & Oriental
  Studies
POB 4745, Kinshasa II

22 Hankou Road N,
Jiamgsu 210008, Nanjing

Peking University
Dept. of Oriental Studies
Hebrew Language & Culture
Dept. of International Politics
Institute for Afro-Asian Studies
  (research only)
Haidian, Beijing 100871

Foreign Affairs College
Beijing Society for Comparative
  International Studies
Center for Jewish Studies
24 Zhan Lan Road,
Beijing 100037

Shanghai Academy of Social
  Sciences
Institute of Euroasian Studies
Center of Judaic Studies
Institute of Religions
622-7 Huai Hai Zhong Road,
  Shanghai 200020

Shanghai International Relations
Association
Judaic Studies Association of
Shanghai
7, Alley 622, Huaihai Zhong Lu,
Shanghai

Yunnan University
Southwest Asia Institute
52 Cuihu Beilu, Kunming 650091

Hong Kong

The Chinese University of Hong-
Kong
Dept. of Religion
Chung Chi College, Shatin,
New Territories

India

Banaras Hindu University
Varanasi 221005, UP

Dharmaram Vidya Kshetram
(Dharmaram College)
Faculty of Philosophy
Faculty of Theology
Center for Biblical Studies
Pontifical Athenaeum of
Philosophy & Theology
Center for the Study of World
Religions
Bangalore 560029

Jadavpur University
International Relations Dept.
PO Jadavpur University,
Calcutta 700032

Jawaharlal Nehru University
School of International Studies
New Delhi 110067

Marathwada University
University Campus,
Aurangabad 431004

VES College
Dept. of Sociology
Chembur, Bombay 400071

Japan

Akita University
School of Education
Tegata Gakuen 1-1, Akita-City

Chubu University
School of International Relations
Matsumoto 1200, Kasugai-City,
Aichi 487

Chuo University
School of Literature
Higashi Nakano, Hachioji-City,
Tokyo

Dokkyo University
Dept. of General Education
Dept. of Liberal Arts
Gakuen-cho 1-1, Soka-shi,
Saitama-ken 340

Doshisha University
School of Theology
Karasuma Imadegawa, Kyoto 602

Doshisha Women's University
Dept. of Literature

Imadegaya-dori, Kamigyo-ku,
Tokyo

Fukuoka University
Dept. of Humanities
School of Literature
Nanakuma Jonan-ku,
Fukuoka-City

Hiroshima Shudo University
Otsuka 1717, Numata-cho,
Hiroshima-City

Hiroshima University
Faculty of Integrated Arts &
 Sciences
Higashi-Senda-cho 1-1-89,
 Hiroshima-City,
Hiroshima 730

Hokusei Gakuin University
Dept. of Biblical Studies
Gyachi 828, Shiriaish-ku,
Sapporo-City

Hosei University
Dept. of Social Sciences
Dept. of Liberal Arts
School of Literature
Sagamihara 4342, Machida-City,
Tokyo

Hyogo University of Education
Dept. of Art Education
Shimokume 9-42-1, Yashuo-cho,
 Katoo-gun, Hyogo-ken 673-14

Ibaraki University
Dept. of Humanities
2–1–1 Bunkyo, Mito-shi,
Ibaraki 310

Japan Lutheran Theological
 College
Osawa 3-10-20, Mitaka-City,
Tokyo

Kanagawa University
School of Foreign Languages
Nishi-Kanagawa 1-7, Kanagawa-
 ku, Yokohama-City,
Kanagawa 221

Kansai University
Dept. of Literature
Yamate 3-3-35, Suita-City,
Osaka

Keio University
School of Literature
15-42, 2-chome, Mita, Minato-ku,
Tokyo 1

Kobe College
Dept. of Inter-Cultural Studies
School of Literature
4-1 Okadayama,
Nishinomiya City, Hyogo 662

Kumamoto University
Dept. of Literature
2-40-1 Kurokami,
Kumamoto-City

Kyoto City University of Arts
13–6 Kutsukake-cho, Ohe,
 Nishikyo-ku, Kyoto 610-11

Kyoto Junior College of Art
Uryuyama 2-116, Kita-Shirakawa,
 Sakyo-ku, Kyoto-City,
Kyoto 606

Kyoto University
Faculty of Integrated Human
Studies
Yoshida-honcho, Sakyo-ku,
Kyoto-Shi, Kyoto-fu 606-01

Meiji Gakuin University
Faculty of Law
Dept. of Politics
Christian Research Institute
1-2-37 Shirokanedai, Minato-ku,
Tokyo 108

Osaka City University
Law School
Sugimoto 3-3-138, Sumiyoshi-ku,
Osaka

Osaka International University
School of Political Science and
Economics
Sugi 3-50-1, Hirakata-City,
Osaka 573-01

Osaka University of Foreign
Studies
Dept. of Arabic Languages
Aomadani 2734, Minoo City,
Osaka 562

Rikkyo Jogakuin Tanki
Daigaku—St. Margaret's
Junior College
Dept. of General Education
4-29-23 Kuguyama, Suginami-ku,
Tokyo 168

Rikkyo University
School of Literature
3-34-1 Nishi Ikebukuro,
Toshima-ku, Tokyo

Seinan Gakuin University
Dept. of Theology
2-4-1 Hoshiyuma, Jonan-ku,
Fukuoka 814-01

Showa University
Dept. of Liberal Arts
1-5-8 Hatanodai, Shinagawa-ku,
Tokyo

Tenri University
Dept. of Liberal Arts
Somanouchi 1050, Tenri-City

Tohoku Gakuin University
Dept. of History
1-3-1 Dohi, Sendai-City

Tokyo Union Theological
Seminary
3-10-30 Osawa, Mitaka-City,
Tokyo

Tsukuba University
Institute of History &
Anthropology
Dept. of History
Dept. of Languages
1-11 Tennodai, Sakuramura,
Tsukuba-shi 305

University of Tokyo
Faculty of Letters
Dept. of Religious Studies
Dept. of Ethics
7-3-1 Hongo, Bunkyo-ku, Tokyo

Waseda University
School of Literature
1-6-1 Nishiwaseda, Shinjuku-ku,
Tokyo 169-50

Lebanon

Near East School of Theology
Hebrew Language
Old Testament
POB 13-5780, Beirut

Université de Balamand
Faculté de Théologie
Koura, Box 100, Tripoli

Université Saint-Esprit de Kaslik
Faculté Pontificale de Théologie
Jounieh

Université Saint Joseph
Faculté de Lettres et Sciences
 Humaines
R. de Damas, BP 293, Beirut

Philippines

Asia Pacific Theological Seminary
Bible Dept.
POB 377, 2600 Baguic City

Asian Theological Seminary
POB 461, Manila

Biblical Seminary of the
 Philippines
T. de León St., Karuhatan,
 Valenzuela, Metro Manila

Loyola School of Theology
Dept. of Theology
Loyola House of Studies, Loyola
 Heights, P.O.Box 4082,
Manila Q.C.

Maryhill School of Theology
POB 1323, Manila

The Philippines Women's
 University
Taft Ave., 1004 Manila

San Beda College
Dept. of Theology
Mendiola St., Manila

Union Theological Seminary
Dasmarinas, Cavite 4114

Singapore

Biblical Graduate School of
 Theology
19 Green Lane, Singapore 1953

Trinity Theological College
7 Mt. Sophia, Singapore 0922

South Korea

Asian Center for Theological
 Studies and Mission
187 Chuong Jeongro 3 ga, Seo
 Dae Moon Ku, Seoul 120-751

Catholic University
90-1 Hae Hwa Dong, Chong Ro
 Ku, Seoul

Christian Theological Seminary
981-7 Bang Bae 3 Dong, Seo Cho
 Ku, Seoul

Ewha Womans University
College of Liberal Arts

Dept. of Christian Studies
11-1 Daehyum-Don,
Seodaemun-Ku, Seoul 120-750

General Assembly Theological
　Seminary
193-180 Eungbong-Dong,
Sungdong-ku, Seoul

Kon-Kuk University
College of Human Sciences
Dept. of Jewish Studies
93-1 Mojin-Dong,
Songdong-ku, Seoul 133-701

Presbyterian College &
　Theological Seminary
Presbyterian College
Dept. of Liberal Arts
Theological Dept.
Theological Seminary
Dept. of Old Testament
Graduate School
Dept. of Old Testament
353 Kwangjang-Dong,
Sungdong-Ku, Seoul

Seoul Theological Seminary
Old Testament Studies
101 Sosa Dong,
Bucheon City 422-052

Song Sim College for Women
　(Institute for Religious
　Education)
43-1 Yeog Gog Dong, Bu-Cheon,
　Gyeong Gi Do

Suwon Catholic College
226 Wangrim-ri, Bongdam-myon,

Hwasong-gun,
Kyonggi-do 445-744

Yonsei University
College of Theology
134 Shinchon-dong,
Sudaemun-ku, Seoul 120-749

Sri Lanka

Lanka Bible College
Dept. of Old Testament
Dept. of Biblical Languages
POB 2, Christopher Road,
Peradeniya

University of Colombo
Dept. of History & Political
　Science
94 Kumaratunga Munidasa
Mawatha, Colombo 3

University of Jaffna
Dept. of Christian Civilization
Thirunelvely, Jaffna

University of Peradeniya
Faculty of Arts
Peradeniya

Thailand

Mahidol University
Faculty of Social Sciences &
　Humanities
Graduate Program in
　Comparative Religion
Dept. of Humanities
Salaya Campus, Nakornchaisri,
Nakornpathom Province 73170

OCEANIA

Australia

Australian National University
Dept. of Political Science
GPO Box 4, Canberra, ACT 2601

Bond University
School of History & Social Studies
Language Centre
Gold Coast, Queensland 4229

Deakin University
Faculty of Arts
Program of Jewish Studies
Toorak Campus, 336 Glenferrie
Rd., Malvern, Vic. 3144

Macquarie University
School of History, Philosophy &
Politics
Centre for Comparative Genocide
Studies
Dept. of Ancient History
Sydney, NSW 2109

Monash University
Faculty of Arts
Dept. of History
Dept. of Politics
Martha Jakobson Centre for
Jewish Civilization
Ada & Toni Murkies Chair in
Jewish Civilization
Dept. of Mathematics
Wellington Rd.,
Clayton, Vic. 3168

University of Melbourne
Dept. of Classical & Near Eastern
Studies & Dept. of History
Jewish Studies Programme
Israel Kipen Lectureship in
Hebrew Language & Literature
Parkville, Vic. 3052

University of New South Wales
Faculty of Arts
Dept. of History
Faculty of Law
POB 1, Kensington, NSW 2030

University of Queensland
Dept. of Studies in Religion
Brisbane, Queensland 4072

University of South Australia
Dept. of Education
Biblical Hebrew
GPO Box 2471,
Adelaide, SA 5001

University of Sydney
Dept. of Semitic Studies
Hebrew Language, Jewish Culture
& Bible Studies
Faculty of Education
Post Graduate Teaching Program
Sydney, NSW 2006

University of Western Australia
Dept. of Economics
Needlands, WA 6009

New Zealand

Auckland Consortium for
  Theological Education
*(affiliated to the University of
  Auckland, & the University of
  Melbourne College of Divinity,
  Australia)*
Biblical Languages
Hebrew Bible

Carey Baptist Theological College
473 Great South Rd., Penrose,
Auckland

The Catholic Institute of Theology
52a Temple St., Meadowbank,
Auckland 1005

Mount St Mary's College
76 Symonds St., POB 3440,
Auckland 1001

St. John's Theological College
202 St. John's Rd., Meadowbank,
Auckland 1005

Trinity Methodist Theological
  College

202 St. John's Rd., Meadowbank,
Auckland 1005

Lincoln University
Canterbury

Massey University
Palmerston North

University of Auckland
Private Bag 92019, Auckland

University of Canterbury
Dept. of American Studies
Dept. of Philosophy & Religious
  Studies
Christchurch 1

University of Otago
Dept. of Theology
POB 56, Dunedin

University of Waikato
Dept. of Religious Studies
Private Bag 3105, Hamilton

Victoria University at Wellington
Dept. of World Religions
POB 600, Wellington

IX

INTERNATIONAL CENTER FOR UNIVERSITY TEACHING OF JEWISH CIVILIZATION

34. ORGANIZATIONAL CHART

International Center for University Teaching of Jewish Civilization
Under the Auspices of the Israeli Presidency
Former Presidents: Ephraim Katzir; Yitzhak Navon; Chaim Herzog

Academic Chairman: Nehemia Levtzion

EXECUTIVE COMMITTEE

Chairman: Nehemia Levtzion

Yehuda Bauer
Yaacov Behar
Moshe Haskell
Simon Herman
Sara Japhet
Nissan Limor

GOVERNING COUNCIL

Chairman: Moshe Davis   Vice-Chairman: Yehuda Bauer

Haim Avni   Moshe Haskell, Treasurer
Moshe Bar Asher   Simon Herman
Yaacov Behar   Sara Japhet
Joseph Ciechanover   Nehemia Levtzion
Joseph R. Hacker   Nissan Limor

Shulamit Nardi, Secretary
Yitzhak Navon
Aviezer Ravitzky

Haim Roet
Haim Stoessel
Yisrael Yarkoni

Executive Director: Hagai Lev

Assistant to the Chairman: Shifra Shor

BOARD OF REGENTS

Chairman: Ralph I. Goldman
Founding Chairman:
Philip M. Klutznick
Honorary Chairman:
Richard J. Scheuer

Vice-Chairmen:
Jaime Constantiner, Mexico
Israel Finestein, Q. C., England
Herbert Neuman, USA
Nicole Goldmann, France

Regional Members

Australia

Israel Kipen; Isi J. Leibler; Louis Waller

Brazil

Leon Feffer

Belgium

Georges Schnek

Canada

Irwin Cotler; Sydney Eisen

England

Philip Alexander; Sir Isaiah Berlin; Sir Trevor Chinn; Lord Jakobovitz; Felix Posen; Chief Rabbi Jonathan Sacks; Fred S. Worms; Lord Young of Graffham

European Community

Izak Varsat-Warszawski

France

Rene Samuel Sirat; Adolphe Steg

Hungary

Jozef Schweitzer

Israel

S. Zalman Abramov; Zvi Arad; Yehuda Avner; Haim Ben Shahar; Avishay Braverman; Yoram Dinstein; Menachem Elon; Walter Eytan; Arthur Fried; Philip Goodman; Hanoch Gutfreund; David Harman; Chaim Herzog; Pnina Herzog; Joshua Jortner; Ephraim Katzir; Moshe Landau; Natan Lerner; Moshe Nissim; Emanuel Rackman; Elyakim Rubinstein; Aliza Shenhar; Moshe Yegar; Menahem E. Yaari; Haim Zohar

South Africa

Isaac Joffe; Mendel Kaplan

United States

Muriel Berman; Philip Berman; Irving Bernstein; Shoshana S. Cardin; Rosalie Cohen; Irwin Field; Miriam Freund-Rosenthal; Alfred Gottschalk; William Mazer; Daniel G. Ross

Memorial Foundation

Israel Miller; Gerhart M. Riegner

CONTRIBUTORS

PHILIP S. ALEXANDER is President, The Oxford Centre for Postgraduate Hebrew Studies, Yarnton Manor; Professor, Jewish Studies Department, Manchester University.

MORDECHAI ALTSHULER is Rabbi Edward Sandrow Professor of Soviet and East European Jewry, Avraham Harman Institute of Contemporary Jewry, The Hebrew University of Jerusalem.

ZIVA AMISHAI-MAISELS is Associate Professor of History of Art, The Hebrew University of Jerusalem; Director, Section on Jewish Art, ICUTJC.

YAAKOV ARIEL is Academic Coordinator, Section on Western Societies and the Holy Land, ICUTJC.

HAIM AVNI is Professor of Contemporary Jewry, The Hebrew University of Jerusalem; Director, Section on Jewish Civilization Studies in Latin America, Spain and Portugal, ICUTJC.

MOSHE BAR-ASHER is President of the Israel National Academy of the Hebrew Language; Professor of Hebrew Language and Aramaic, The Hebrew University of Jerusalem.

YEHOSHUA BEN-ARIEH is Rector of The Hebrew University of Jerusalem; Professor of Geography, The Hebrew University of Jerusalem.

PHILIP I. and MURIEL M. BERMAN are Members, Board of Regents, ICUTJC; Founders, Philip & Muriel Berman Center for Judaic Studies, Lehigh University, Bethlehem, Pennsylvania.

JUDIT BOKSER-LIWERANT is Professor, Faculty of Social and Political Sciences, Universidad Nacional Autónoma de México; Director, Judaic Studies Program, Universidad Iberoamericana, Mexico City.

MICHAEL BROWN is Professor of Humanities and Hebrew, York University, Toronto.

ROBERT CHAZAN is Skirball Professor of Hebrew and Judaic Studies, New York University.

GERSON D. COHEN was Chancellor Emeritus, The Jewish Theological Seminary of America.

JAIME CONSTANTINER is Regional Vice-Chairman, Board of Regents, ICUTJC.

JOSEPH DAN is Gershom Scholem Professor of Kabbalah, The Hebrew University of Jerusalem; Editor, BINAH Jewish Civilization University Series, ICUTJC.

MOSHE DAVIS is Chairman, Governing Council, ICUTJC; Founding Head, Institute of Contemporary Jewry, The Hebrew University of Jerusalem.

SERGIO DELLAPERGOLA is Professor of Contemporary Jewry, The Hebrew University of Jerusalem; Director, World Register of University Studies in Jewish Civilization, ICUTJC.

YORAM DINSTEIN is President, Tel Aviv University; Director, Section on Teaching Jewish Law in Schools of Law, ICUTJC.

DANIEL J. ELAZAR is President, Jerusalem Center for Public Affairs; Director, Section on Jewish Political Studies, ICUTJC.

DMITRI ELIASHEVITCH is Associate Professor, Institute of Culture, Jewish University of St. Petersburg.

EMIL L. FACKENHEIM is Distinguished Professor Emeritus of Philosophy, University of Toronto; Visiting Professor, Institute of Contemporary Jewry, The Hebrew University of Jerusalem.

YAEL S. FELDMAN is Professor of Hebrew and Judaic Studies, New York University.

ISRAEL FINESTEIN, Q.C. is Major Scholar, Trinity College, Cambridge; Regional Vice-Chairman, Board of Regents, ICUTJC.

BEN-ZION FISCHLER is Executive Vice-President, Council on the Teaching of Hebrew, Jerusalem; Consultant, Section on Hebrew Language and Literature, ICUTJC.

PRISCILLA FISHMAN is Associate Editor, BINAH Jewish Civilization University Series; Director of Publications, ICUTJC.

MATELLE GODFREY is Coordinator of Workshops, ICUTJC.

ROLAND GOETSCHEL is Professeur des Universités, Directeur du Centre d'Etudes Juives, Paris-Sorbonne.

FLORINDA GOLDBERG is Coordinator, World Register of University Studies in Jewish Civilization, ICUTJC; Lecturer in Spanish and Latin American Studies, The Hebrew University of Jerusalem.

RALPH I. GOLDMAN is Chairman, Board of Regents, ICUTJC; Honorary Executive Vice-President, American Jewish Joint Distribution Committee.

NICOLE GOLDMANN is Vice-Chairman, Board of Regents, ICUTJC; Vice-President, Conseil Representatif des Institutions Juifs de France.

BETSY HALPERN-AMARU is Professor, Department of Religion, Vassar College; Co-Director, Section on Teaching Jewish Civilization in Christian Academic Settings, ICUTJC.

CHAIM HERZOG is Sixth President of the State of Israel.

NICHOLAI IWANOW is Associate Professor, The Institute of Political Science, Wroclaw University, Poland.

RAPHAEL JOSPE is Senior Lecturer in Jewish Philosophy, The Open University of Israel; Academic Coordinator, Section on Jewish Philosophy, ICUTJC.

MENDEL KAPLAN is Chairman, Board of Governors, The Jewish Agency for Israel; Founding and Managing Member, The Center for Jewish Studies, University of Cape Town.

JEROME S. KATZIN is Member, Board of Regents, ICUTJC; Founder, Judaic Studies Endowment, University of California, San Diego.

EPHRAIM KATZIR is Fourth President of the State of Israel.

DAVID KLATZKER is Academic Liaison (U.S.A.) America–Holy Land Project, Avraham Harman Institute of Contemporary Jewry, The Hebrew University of Jerusalem.

PHILIP M. KLUTZNICK is Founding Chairman, Board of Regents, ICUTJC.

ERNEST KRAUSZ is Chairman, Committee for Overseas Students of the Planning and Budgeting Committee, Council for Higher Education; Professor of Sociology, Bar-Ilan University.

FREDA LEAVEY is Secretary to the Editor.

BARUCH A. LEVINE is Skirball Professor of Bible and Ancient Near Eastern Studies, New York University.

NEHEMIA LEVTZION is Academic Chairman, ICUTJC; Bamberger and Fuld Professor of History of the Muslim Peoples, The Hebrew University of Jerusalem.

REINIER MUNK is Lecturer in the Department of Philosophy, Vrije Universiteit, Amsterdam.

YITZHAK NAVON is Fifth President of the State of Israel.

HERBERT NEUMAN is Vice-Chairman, Board of Regents, ICUTJC.

RAPHAEL NIR is Professor of Education and Communications, The Hebrew University of Jerusalem; Director (1982–1991), Section on Hebrew Language and Literature, ICUTJC.

AVIEZER RAVITZKY is Professor of Jewish Thought, The Hebrew University of Jerusalem; Co-Director, Section on Jewish Philosophy, ICUTJC.

ILIA RODOV has an M.A., Art History, from St. Petersburg University; Doctoral Candidate, Art History, The Hebrew University of Jerusalem.

ALVIN H. ROSENFELD is Professor of English and Jewish Studies, Indiana University.

NATHAN ROTENSTREICH was Ahad Ha'Am Professor Emeritus of Philosophy, The Hebrew University of Jerusalem; Vice-President, The Israel Academy of Sciences and Humanities.

ANGEL SAENZ-BADILLOS is Professor of Hebrew Language and Literature, Universidad Complutense de Madrid; President, European Association of Jewish Studies.

JONATHAN SARNA is Joseph H. and Belle R. Braun Professor of American Jewish History; Chair, Department of Near Eastern and Judaic Studies, Brandeis University.

PETER SCHÄFER is Professor, Institute für Judaistik, Freie Universität Berlin.

RICHARD J. SCHEUER is Honorary Chairman, Board of Regents, ICUTJC.

LEONARDO SENKMAN is Lecturer, Department of Spanish and Latin American Studies, The Hebrew University of Jerusalem.

MILTON SHAIN is Senior Lecturer, Department of Hebrew and Jewish Studies, University of Cape Town.

GIDEON SHIMONI is Associate Professor of Contemporary Jewry, The Hebrew University of Jerusalem; Director, Section on Contemporary Jewish Civilization, ICUTJC.

DAVID SIDORSKY is Professor of Philosophy, Columbia University.

NAOMI B. SOKOLOFF is Associate Professor and Chair, Mideastern Languages and Civilizations, University of Washington, Seattle.

JOSEPH TEDGHI is in the Department of Hebrew Studies, Institut National des Langues et Civilisations Orientales, Sorbonne Nouvelle.

EPHRAIM E. URBACH was Professor Emeritus of Talmud, The Hebrew University of Jerusalem; President, World Union of Jewish Studies (1964–1984).

MERVIN F. VERBIT is Professor of Sociology, Brooklyn College–City University of New York; Director, Interuniversity Fellowship Program, ICUTJC.

LOUIS WALLER is Professor, Sir Leo Cussen Chair of Law, Monash University, Melbourne.

LEON I. YUDKIN is Lecturer, Department of Near East Studies, University of Manchester; Director, Section on Modern Hebrew Literature in English Translation, ICUTJC.